THE GRAND CHORUS OF COMPLAINT

The Grand Chorus of Complaint

AUTHORS AND THE BUSINESS ETHICS
OF AMERICAN PUBLISHING

Michael J. Everton

OXFORD
UNIVERSITY PRESS

OXFORD
UNIVERSITY PRESS

Oxford University Press, Inc., publishes works that further
Oxford University's objective of excellence
in research, scholarship, and education.

Oxford   New York
Auckland   Cape Town   Dar es Salaam   Hong Kong   Karachi
Kuala Lumpur   Madrid   Melbourne   Mexico City   Nairobi
New Delhi   Shanghai   Taipei   Toronto

With offices in
Argentina   Austria   Brazil   Chile   Czech Republic   France   Greece
Guatemala   Hungary   Italy   Japan   Poland   Portugal   Singapore
South Korea   Switzerland   Thailand   Turkey   Ukraine   Vietnam

Published by Oxford University Press, Inc.
198 Madison Avenue, New York, New York 10016

www.oup.com

Oxford is a registered trademark of Oxford University Press

Library of Congress Cataloging-in-Publication Data

Everton, Michael J.
The grand chorus of complaint : authors and the business ethics of American publishing / Michael J. Everton.
  p.   cm.
Includes index.
ISBN 978-0-19-975178-5 (acid-free paper)
1. Publishers and publishing—Moral and ethical aspects—United States—History. 2. Authors and publishers—United
States—History—19th century. 3. Authors and publishers—United States—History—18th century. 4. Book industries
and trade—United States—History—19th century. 5. Book industries and trade—United States—History—18th century.
6. Copyright—United States—History—19th century. 7. Business ethics—United States—History. I. Title.
Z473.E95 2011
174'.907050973—dc22   2010036772

1 3 5 7 9 8 6 4 2

Printed in the United States of America
on acid-free paper

For mom and dad.

Contents

Acknowledgments

I AM GRATEFUL to the staffs of the libraries and archives that made this project possible, as well as for permission to quote from their collections: Albert and Shirley Small Special Collections Library, University of Virginia; American Antiquarian Society; Baker Library, Houghton Library, Schlesinger Library, and Widener Library, Harvard University; Bennett Library and Belzberg Library, Simon Fraser University; Davis Library, North Carolina Collection, and Rare Book Collection, University of North Carolina at Chapel Hill; Firestone Library and Rare Books and Special Collections, Princeton University; Historical Society of Pennsylvania; Huntington Library; Koerner Library, University of British Columbia; Library Company of Philadelphia; Library of Congress; Library of Virginia; Manuscripts and Archives, Yale University; Manuscripts and Archives Division, New York Public Library; Massachusetts Historical Society; Morgan Library; New York Historical Society; Phillips Library, Peabody Essex Museum; Rare Book, Manuscript, and Special Collections Library, Duke University; Tampa Library and Poynter Library, University of South Florida; and Vancouver Public Library. My work at many of these institutions was facilitated by generous grants and fellowships from the American Antiquarian Society, the Bibliographical Society of America, the Graduate School of the University of North Carolina at Chapel Hill, the Huntington Library, and Simon Fraser University, which also provided funding for images via its University Publications Fund.

Special thanks to Simon Fraser University's interlibrary loan staff, whose resourceful-
ness and cheer made finding sources a much lighter task.

Early versions of Chapters 2, 3, and 5 appeared in *Early American Literature*, *Legacy*, and *ESQ*, respectively. Thanks to the editors and publishers of these journals for
permission to reproduce that material.

This book began as a seminar paper and then a dissertation at the University of
North Carolina-Chapel Hill, both under the direction of Philip F. Gura. In thanking Philip, I find myself in the back of a long line of former students shaped by his
now-legendary rigor and charity. In Chapel Hill I was also fortunate to be a part of
a vibrant group of Americanists, including Jennifer Connerley, David Faflik, Thomas Fahy, Tara Fee, Ian Finseth, Eric Goldman, Brent Kinser, Andrew Leiter, Emily
Rosenbaum, Jim Ryan, Mark Simpson-Vos, Bryan Sinche, Rob Spirko, and Elizabeth Stockton. In John Ware and Laura Mielke I had the best writing group one
could ask for. I wish I could have it again.

The generosity of the many other people who have had a hand in this project
leaves me almost dumbfounded. For guidance, assistance, criticism, and encourage-
ment thank you to Lisa Albury, William L. Andrews, Alma Bryant, Lara Campbell,
Dave Carlin, Joanne Chaison, Mary Chapman, Colette Colligan, Peter Cramer,
Nicole Discenza, Laurie Frankel, James N. Green, Robert A. Gross, Frank Harrison,
Leslie Howsam, Kate Ireland, Leon Jackson, Tina Jodrey, Joy S. Kasson, Thomas
Knoles, Robert Krut, Carolyn Lesjak, Erika Lindemann, Elizabetta Lofaro, Timo-
thy Marr, Susan Mooney, Meera Nair, Jim Owen, Leslie Paris, Chris Pavsek, Eliza
Richards, Mark Rose, Tom Ross, Laura Runge, Michael Silverman, Caroline Sloat,
Jon Smith, Reiner Smolinski, Pat Stogner, Jane Thrailkill, Mary Thurman, Thomas
A. Tweed, Mark Vaughn, Brad Vice, Dan Weiskopf, James L. W. West III, and Eric
Wredenhagen. Thanks as well to all my students, and especially Ryan Haczynski,
Michael Hingston, Laylan Saadaldin, and Peng Wei, for keeping me nimble. To my
mom, who volunteered her skills as a researcher in Chapel Hill and Worcester, I owe
a unique and happy debt, proud that few people can cite their mother's role in comb-
ing through manuscripts and microfilm. I cannot imagine a finer research assistant.
Finally, Melissa Homestead and Laura Mielke have been especially generous, prob-
ing, and even-tempered readers—readers who could have said any number of off-
color things about some of my gaffes but never did. It's hard for me to tell you how
much I appreciate your help and support.

Working with Brendan O'Neill, Rick Stinson, and Devi Dakshin at Oxford University Press has belied the many terrible things said by the writers in this book about
the wretchedness of publishers. And thanks to Oxford's anonymous readers, whose
criticism helped me tighten the manuscript immeasurably.

The Print Culture program at Simon Fraser University is a remarkable collection
of people whose expertise and curiosity have stimulated my work since I arrived in
2005. I am fortunate to be a part of this teaching and research community. I am
fortunate, too, to work in an English department so alive and amicable. Thanks to

my colleagues and to department administration and staff—especially Maureen Curtin, Carole Gerson, Tom Grieve, Betty Schellenberg, and Elaine Tkaczuk—for your faith in my work.

Vancouver is a long way from Richmond and Charleston and so from my family. To my mom and dad, Pam and Bob Everton; to my sister and brother-in-law, Susie Everton and Rob Williams; and to my brother and sister-in-law, Rob and Allison Everton: thank you for so often putting my interests ahead of your own. It is a fact that is not lost on me. And to my best friend and wife, Karen Ferguson, thank you for acting as a sounding board when my arguments became muddled, for propelling me when my energy flagged, and for critiquing the manuscript with a historian's terrifying precision. Thank you even more for our library lunch breaks, our escapades into the snow and sun, and our life together—not to mention for teaching me how to find the very best mountain blueberries.

THE GRAND CHORUS OF COMPLAINT

The moral law lies at the centre of nature and radiates to the circumference.

RALPH WALDO EMERSON, *Nature*

Introduction

BEGINNING A BOOK about the business of early American publishing with a quote from *Nature* (1836) is not as inappropriate as it might seem.[1] In *Nature*, Ralph Waldo Emerson famously located the moral in the material at a time when, as the United States moved gradually from a mercantile to an industrial capitalism, the material seemed anything but moral. Emerson's point, however, was that everything, even commerce, even publishing, was subject to moral law. He was far from alone in this belief. Long before the rise of what Henry James called "the new remorseless monopolies" of the late nineteenth century, and long before the inauguration of business ethics as a mode of inquiry in the late twentieth, trade morality was on the minds of Americans.[2] It was certainly on the minds of the nation's writers, many of whom believed that the business of print systematically broke what Emerson and others thought of as moral law. This book is about that belief.

In May 1865, a writer named William Giles Dix sent a manuscript to Boston's Ticknor and Fields. The modestly prolific Cambridge author had reason to hope that America's most respected literary publisher would welcome his work. W. D. Ticknor and Company, the predecessor to Ticknor and Fields, had issued four of Dix's books in the 1840s, and James T. Fields, the firm's convivial public face, was himself a poet and a champion of American authorship.[3] He was also a candidate for the most gentlemanly of Gentlemen Publishers, literary tradesmen whose self-styled belief in friendship over profit elevated them above competitors like New York's Harper and Brothers, men "governed," in the words of author James K. Paulding, exclusively "by their anticipations of profit or loss."[4]

3

For an era in which publishers were compared to vampires and parasites with some frequency, Fields was seen as the exception to the rule. For many, he was the exception that proved the rule. John Greenleaf Whittier immortalized him in a poem in which the publisher "judged an author's heart" "tenderly, gently, by his own."[5] Fields was graced, Whittier believed, with a supernal charge. This man "was Christ-like in kindness and sympathy and doing good."[6] Authors from Nathaniel Hawthorne to Grace Greenwood to Charles Dickens agreed there was something different about him. As Greenwood punned, he was the "most happy, most fortunate, most blest—in short, the very Elysian Fields."[7] Once when his minister gave Fields a knife as a present, he wrote in the accompanying note: "I give it to you with a certain *moral fearlessness*: for I know your friendly hand & kind heart never cut anybody else."[8] Fields's "gospel of cheerfulness" made Boston's Old Corner Bookstore the hub of American literary culture, and the small, curtained alcove in the back of the store, which served as Fields's office, was "the hub of the hub."[9] It was seen as well as the moral center of the American publishing trade, a place where publisher and author did right by one another. Now a distraught William Giles Dix appealed to this friend of authors. "I write to you from the depths of the greatest of all personal sorrows," Dix said in the letter accompanying his manuscript.[10] His mother was dead. He had written to the firm some months before, hoping to publish his book before she died, but now all he could do was honor her memory. He asked, or really expected, Fields to assist him.

The manuscript was returned—by express post—the same day. It was followed the next morning by a polite though frank rejection explaining that the author's circumstances were unfortunate but irrelevant. "We regret much the loss of which you speak to us," the note read, "but, that is not a consideration which we can allow to influence our judgment in favor of an enterprize which we have sufficient reasons for declining."[11] Authorial resolve and dead mothers notwithstanding, the poems would not appear under the venerable Ticknor and Fields imprint.

Dix was stupefied. With righteous outrage, he copied his letter and the firm's response and sent both to his neighbor Henry Wadsworth Longfellow, expecting him to share his indignation. "Mr Longfellow, do you believe that, considering the circumstances, a more cold, cruel and scornful letter than that has been sent by any publisher, for a hundred and fifty years, to an author striving for an honorable recognition of his rights! To write such a letter as that in answer to mine was to trample upon my mother's grave."[12] He told Longfellow that Ticknor and Fields was trying "to crush me, to trample upon me, to block up my way firmly, persistently and in the spirit of personal enmity." How else could he interpret the rejection? According to Dix, in reducing a moral issue to economic determinism ("an enterprize"), Ticknor and Fields had abdicated its moral duty.

However paranoid, Dix's belief that there was a moral component to publishing was far from idiosyncratic. Many authors subscribed to the idea that there was more to publishing than profit and loss. Many publishers did as well, and no publisher

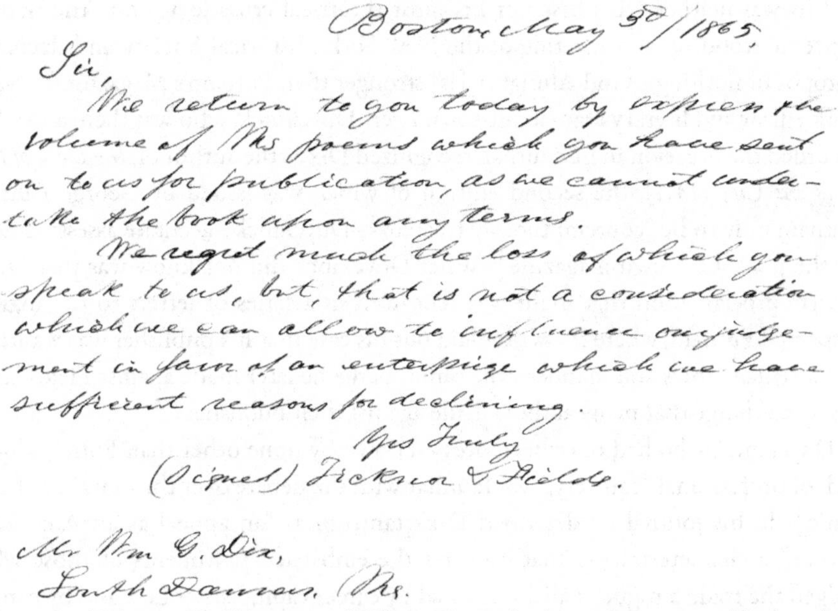

Boston May 30/1865,

Sir,

We return to you today by express the volume of Mrs poems which you have sent on to us for publication, as we cannot undertake the book upon any terms.

We regret much the loss of which you speak to us, but, that is not a consideration which we can allow to influence our judgement in favor of an enterprise which we have sufficient reasons for declining.

Yrs Truly

(Signed) Ticknor & Fields.

Mr Wm G. Dix,
South Danvers, Ms.

FIGURE I.1 Ticknor and Fields' rejection of William Giles Dix book manuscript, as copied by the author in a letter to Henry Wadsworth Longfellow, Courtesy Houghton Library, Harvard University.

more than Ticknor and Fields, which is perhaps one of the reasons Dix reacted the way he did. No American publishing house was more celebrated for downplaying what Emerson called "the dwarfish actual" in publishing: the quotidian realities of cost, sales, and profit that dictated the terms of the economic world in which literary businessmen moved.[13]

Longfellow likely read Dix's letter with ambivalence. Fields was his publisher, too, as well as a close friend. When Longfellow's wife burned to death in a horrifying accident in their Cambridge home, Fields was one of the people Longfellow relied on to break the news to acquaintances and help protect his privacy.[14] Thus when Longfellow did mention the matter to Fields, he probably did so without urgency and without the righteous presumption Dix expected of him. There was no evidence, after all, that Fields had actually done anything wrong.

Whatever was in fact said, nothing changed. Ticknor and Fields would not publish the book, and Dix was traumatized. A year later he remained convinced that Fields was out to get him. This publisher, who had "friendly feeling for me for years, revealed himself at last as a most hard and persistent enemy." "May God give him a thousand blessings for every one which he desires to see withheld from me," Dix wrote, just before asking Longfellow if he would defray half the cost of printing the book with Cambridge's Riverside Press, as though the intensely private Longfellow were looking for opportunities to meddle in other people's business at a cost of $300.[15]

This was neither Dix's first nor his most theatrical crusade against "the trade." Once he stood up at a meeting of the New York Historical Society and decreed, apropos of nothing, "God Almighty [is] stronger than Putnam's Magazine."[16] New York editor and literary man-about-town Evert Duyckinck, who was there and who recorded the occasion in his journal, recognized Dix as the author of *The Deck of the Crescent City* (1852), the second edition of which was issued by George Palmer Putnam only to be "contemptuously treated"—Duyckinck's accurate assessment— by the publisher's own magazine.[17] What Duyckinck did not know was that Dix's bizarre proclamation that night was rehearsed in a series of letters to the highly respected Putnam, where the writer laid out his case that his publisher was wanting in Christian ethics and manners, the same charge he later made against Fields, and the same charge that many authors made against their publishers.[18]

Duyckinck, who had once been dressed down by none other than Putnam for a lack of professional "courtesy," was familiar with the debate over the morality of the trade.[19] In his journal he described Dix's tantrum as "an appeal as an American author," a characterization that captures the embattled sentiments of those who judged the trade a rogue's gallery peopled by career capitalists at best and by career thieves at worst.[20] As Putnam's anger at Duyckinck suggests, it was not only authors who found the ethics of publishing wanting. Publishers, too, were surprised by what they saw from day to day in their business. "Publishing is very pleasant if one could carry it on in peace but it is in a sorry fraternity," one literary tradesman quipped to Duyckinck. "There is not among publishers the honesty that exists among thieves. The latter steal your purse, but the former filch your very brains, and insult you to boot."[21] Elizabeth Palmer Peabody, who ran the small publishing concern and Boston bookstore where Transcendentalist and editor Margaret Fuller held her "conversations," complained that running a bookstore and press was difficult enough; what made it disheartening was "finding rules of the trade so bad morally, and the whole concern so rotten."[22] She lamented finding only "here and there a man who cares more for his conscience than for money." Duyckinck's correspondent simplified the view. Publishers are, he suggested, "literary jackalls [*sic*]."[23]

Thus, while the bravado of Dix's various indictments was extreme, their moral terms were not exceptional. Critics believed that the business of books was rotten to the core. The husband of one supposedly jilted author complained to Boston publisher Sampson Phillips, "In any other than [a] mere business matter I should say that a nice sense of gentlemanly feeling would have led you to ask permission before infringing the terms of agreement as to authorship. But the natural eagerness of business men to save themselves from loss overrides nice distinctions & is, I presume, reckoned a good justification by 'the trade.'"[24] The irascible Captain Frederick Marryat, author of the popular novels *Peter Simple* (1834) and *Mr. Midshipman Easy* (1836), said much the same with less delicacy and a greater presumption of moral authority. "Tell [the publisher] that there is such a thing as right and wrong, and that character is of value, even in a bookseller. If he *repents*, which I'm afraid he will not, advise him to write to me, and I will point out to him the path of virtue."[25] Louisa May Alcott wondered aloud in a letter to her parents why it was that "Courtesy" did not play a bigger role in the trade's dealings with authors.[26]

In the summer of 1859 William Gilmore Simms of South Carolina wrote a grateful letter to the Virginia novelist John Esten Cooke, who had favorably reviewed one of Simms's books in the Richmond *Index*. Simms had had little to be thankful for during the previous year. Months before, he had buried two more of his sons; seven of his thirteen children were now dead. His professional life was as dismal. His Brooklyn publisher, J. S. Redfield, was in financial straits. Simms had to piece together the progress of his publisher's failure from afar, a situation he found intensely frustrating. Initially he thought Redfield must have been guilty of impropriety, but eventually he came to believe that his erstwhile publisher simply moved in a Mandevillian commercial world that had made a virtue of sin. "I really think that R. means to be honest if New York will let him," he wrote to his friend and agent James Lawson.[27] Simms may have been right: Redfield did seem too honest or too naïve for his profession. Earlier that year Simms had written to Duyckinck to unload his anger. "Briefly, the moral of the whole country of trade is especially base. We are a nation of mercenaries," he concluded.[28] Watching his publisher go down only further convinced him he was right. Publishers were not uniquely immoral, though. Those who know the history of the United States know, he sighed, that "it cannot be otherwise." Simms would have faulted Northern merchants. But they had their doubts as well. The *American Publishers' Circular and Literary Gazette*, the official mouthpiece of the New York Book-Publishers' Association put the matter best: "Mercantile competition often makes sad inroads into abstract morals. Such is the fact; we are not its apologists."[29]

Almost thirty years after its publication, Robert Darnton's "What Is the History of Books?" (1982) and its warning that theoretical models "have a way of freezing human beings out of history" remains an important, if now less urgent reminder of the social conditions of print culture.[30] That its urgency has moderated considerably is due in part to Darnton and D. F. McKenzie, who pushed scholars to complicate "techno-deterministic" accounts of print culture by attending to what McKenzie calls print's "full range of social realities."[31] A generation of scholars has done just that, so much so that now it seems as hard to avoid the personalities behind print in our scholarship as it is to ignore the personality of the printer behind a text like Benjamin Franklin's *Autobiography*. Franklin's example is especially relevant here. As Adrian Johns has illustrated, the social world that printers like Franklin inhabited was one of "conventions and customs," and if we are to understand print culture, then we need to understand the social proprieties—that is, the "civilities" and "courtesies"—that governed printers' conduct and thus the production of print.[32] "The sources of print culture," Johns argues, in a conclusion that resonates throughout the following chapters, must "be sought in civility as much as in technology."[33] My interest is in the ethical baggage of these terms and their historical meanings. Inherent in the very language of printing and later publishing are ideas of right and wrong, good and bad—morality. This should be no surprise. The *Autobiography*, after all, shows that in addition to the implicit rules that structured the behavior of literary tradesmen—the civilities and the courtesies—there were other kinds of ethics at work, the command of which Franklin famously styled the "Art of Virtue."

This book argues that ideas of moral propriety among authors and publishers provide an important framework for understanding American authorship from the Revolution to the Civil War. It argues that American print culture at large was a contested "social space," an occupational sphere of objective realities and subjective beliefs in which the behavior and values of subjects mattered a great deal more than we have acknowledged.[34] I am using the familiar language of Pierre Bourdieu, whose work makes this space more intelligible by providing a structural model—the "critical metaphor" of the field—for plotting the behaviors of social subjects, behaviors that cannot be wholly reduced to the profit motive.[35] Bourdieu calls the field a scene of "position-takings," and he suggests that if we are to understand authorship in a market society, we must situate authors in this volatile, situational space.[36] In doing so, we locate them at a permanent sociological crossroads, or at "the meeting of two histories": first, "the history of the positions they occupy," and second, "the history of their dispositions"—that is, their perceptions of and attitudes toward the field and its subjects.[37] My goal is to picture this crossroads and show how these positions and dispositions mattered to the conduct of the business of print and how, in turn, they were suffused by moral values.

In using the term "moral values," I draw on three ethical traditions: virtue ethics, deontological ethics, and utilitarian ethics. Virtue ethics locates the rightness of an action in the character of the doer. Deontological ethics locates the rightness of an action in its fulfillment of a moral rule or imperative. Both virtue ethics and deontological ethics may be contrasted with utilitarian ethics, which locates the rightness of an action in its consequences. What is important to understand about the first two ethical systems is that they locate virtue in the sources for an action, not in the consequences. For example, if we look at Fields's decision not to publish Dix's book according to these ethical systems, his options might break down as follows. According to virtue ethics, Fields ought to publish the book because it would be an honorable thing to do, and honor is a virtue. According to deontological ethics, Fields ought to publish the book because of the golden rule: do unto others as you would have them do unto you. Finally, according to utilitarian ethics, Fields ought to publish the book because it would (a) make Dix happy, (b) honor the memory of his mother, and/or (c) make a profit, making both Fields and Dix happy. Dix, incidentally, seems to have viewed the matter according to all three ethical systems, which was typical—and in a way typically hypocritical—of authors. Fields seems to have viewed it according to the last. Writers, most of whom interpreted utilitarianism to be nothing more than economic determinism, liked to think such utilitarian thinking was typical of publishers.[38] As I want to suggest, the ethical predicament was less lopsided than that.

It is true that utilitarianism abounded in eighteenth- and nineteenth-century print culture, and not only in publishers' reasoning that their profits were in the best interest of society at large. It is also evident in the figure of the gatekeeper-publisher whose self-proclaimed job was to stand between licentious literature and defenseless readers who might be corrupted by it. Early in his career, publisher James Derby received a letter from his mother admonishing him to remember this role. As Derby recalled the lesson, he and his partners could either "improve and exalt the moral faculties and unsubdued hearts of this intelligent but inconsistent people," or they could peddle "moral corruption."[39] Plainly, this utilitarian ethic was very real for publishers like Derby. But he also believed in the importance of a moral character that had nothing to do with its consequences, which means that there were alternative moral logics at work as well. One of this book's arguments is that while publishers rarely disavowed the part economic determinism or more complex versions of utilitarianism played in decision making, they also preached virtue and deontological ethics more than we might think. Even Harper and Brothers, at least early on, tried to privilege something other than the profit motive, supposedly asking itself before publishing any book, "Is this a proper book to do?"[40] Of course, as writers who had dealings with Harpers would have realized, "proper" could mean many things, most of which had to do with profit. If we momentarily bracket our (and authors') cynicism, though, what we get is a publishing house that at least claimed to be driven by moral, and more specifically religious, integrity. Harper and Brothers was far from alone in this belief that there was more to the trade than the bottom line. Or, more realistically, they were in good company when they *claimed* that other kinds of ethics mattered.

Outside of Franklin, printers and publishers did not sit around talking about deontological ethics or virtue ethics. The term "utilitarian" was thrown around quite a bit, but usually by authors who misused it to refer to any decision that seemed based on realizing profit as a consequence of action or that in some other way appeared teleological. Nor did the average publisher in Richmond or Boston think consciously of his decision making as a mode of ethical reasoning. In an effort to be faithful to the actual language and reasoning of those involved in the business of print, therefore, I do not load the following chapters with academic references to virtue, deontological, and utilitarian ethics, except where necessary to make a distinction. Often it is difficult to make a distinction at all. Even where it is clear that ethical reasoning was taking place, as in the Dix anecdote, the reasoning is a fuzzy amalgam of different ethics. This mishmash would give an analytical philosopher a headache, but it should bother the literary historian less. The principles and actions I analyze in this book did not occur in a vacuum. The tradesmen I write about did not stop to make sure that their conclusions followed from their premises. Nor did they always stop to ask if their use of the word "courtesy," for example—a word I will suggest had significant moral implications for the trade—was consistent with every other publisher's use of the word. As will be plain in the chapters that follow, writers and publishers alike often based their actions on starkly different ideas of what this language meant. Further, even if particular figures seemed to subscribe to a particular system, in practice they had trouble adhering to the theoretical bounds of that system. Instead, the figures I write about in this book would pick and choose principles from different systems depending on circumstances, in effect creating their own variable ethical practices. The reality of these mongrel moralities is another reason I generally avoid making distinctions between the different ethical systems as articulated by moral philosophy.

What is important is that these figures considered ethics, any ethics, as routinely as they did, and that these ethics could play an instrumental role in their ideas of themselves and in their decisions, as well as in their conception of their print culture at large. This widespread, composite belief is what I mean when I use terms like "trade morality" instead of the jargon of moral philosophy.[41] In his influential address "Self-Culture" (1838), William Ellery Channing suggested that while the ethic of selflessness went by different names—"sometimes reason, sometimes conscience, sometimes the moral sense or faculty"—such a disparate vocabulary did not belie the presence of "a real principle" compelling people of different beliefs to do "right."[42] Taking the historical accuracy of Channing's observation, I want to broaden and turn it to make my point clearer. The people I write about in this study used different words for similar ideas and held different beliefs about similar words, and some of these usages and beliefs contradicted one another, especially where keywords like "courtesy" were involved. This is not just because ethics are, as Alasdair MacIntrye points out, "time-bound," but because often the people using them were less interested in working through their logic than in wielding ethical discourse to express a conviction. My point is that despite their contradictions—contradictions I do my best to sort out—behind people's usages and beliefs there was "a real principle" based in one or more ethics, and this principle was a crucial part of their working lives.[43]

This book attempts to explore this moral instrumentality on its own terms. To the extent that it participates in the kind of ethical inquiry that has characterized much literary criticism over the past several decades and that in a broader sense has characterized cultural history going back at least to Karen Haltunen's superlative *Confidence Men and Painted Women* (1982), it does so by taking morality as a discursive ideal and as a historical fact.[44] The book is expressly not interested in literature's putative ethical value or in theorizing the ethics of alterity or selfhood, though both these concepts will be relevant. Rather, it looks at the ways in which specific kinds of moralities have been historically articulated and wielded in the business of print by those who came into contact with that business, and then at the ways in which these figures rendered judgments about that contact through their writings. In the following chapters, ethics is not a heuristic so much as it is an array of historical beliefs derived from personal and institutional notions of right and wrong.[45] The questions I ask, therefore, are largely historical. What principles were important according to authors and publishers? What did one author mean when he assumed he could rely on his publisher's "fairness & good feeling"?[46] What did publishers, editors, authors, and other commentators mean when they wrote about the "the laws of honor in force amongst book publishers"?[47] What did Philadelphia publisher Henry C. Carey mean when he cited in a business letter the "rules that govern gentleman," and what did Harper and Brothers mean when it cited the "ordinary civility" of the trade?[48] Why did writers like Louisa May Alcott call out their publishers for a perceived lack of courtesy? How did these ideas of character, laws, rules, and courtesy affect and even dictate relationships between and among authors and publishers, not to mention the texts authors produced? In all, how did morality matter to those who had a hand in producing American print culture?

While at times this morality was more performed than real—Harper and Brothers was accused repeatedly of moral opportunism, and for good reason—such performances demonstrate that morality mattered. Even if this morality was in many instances a discursive ideal, archival evidence suggests that it was never just a thought experiment. Quite the opposite. Ethics was a language, a tool, of critique. It had an unmistakable capital that belied any compelling "real" existence and informed the more conventional critical frameworks—economic, legal, gender, romantic— through which we historicize authorship. Part of this book's argument is that these conventional frames do not account for the debates in print and in manuscript over the moral structure of the field of publishing or the principles behind authors' and publishers' theories of their occupations. Prevailing ways of envisioning authorship generally do not recognize that American fiction and nonfiction may be read as sites of ethical struggle insofar as these texts explain, allegorize, critique, and in some cases reform, if hypothetically, the morality of the trade, cataloguing—rightly and wrongly, fairly and unfairly—the sins not only of American publishing but of national commerce at large.[49]

The clearest example of this moral framework is the nineteenth-century debate over international copyright. In the absence of an Anglo-American copyright agreement prior to 1891, American publishers could legally reprint British works without paying their authors. It was, as James J. Barnes observes, the equivalent of publishing in a "Hobbes-like State of Nature," as firms tried to out-maneuver one another in order to be the first to market.[50] Reprinting earned some firms, among them Harpers, handsome profits, but to an extent it undermined domestic authors who could not compete with names like Charles Dickens. Authors demonized the status quo. "Without an international copyright law," Edgar Allan Poe wrote, "American authors might as well cut their throats."[51] It was an exaggeration, but reprinting did affect the reputation of the trade. Much ink was spilled in the media and in business correspondence over the question of whether unauthorized reprinting was moral; indeed, it was this question that inspired the *Publishers' Circular* to concede the "sad inroads" business made into morals and prompted "reprinters," as these publishers were popularly known, to claim that morality was simply a function of the law. It was "a mere question of expediency," by which Philadelphia publisher Abraham Hart meant economic expediency.[52] To firms like Harper and Brothers it was also a no-brainer. Why should publishers apologize for "preferring the system of large sales and small prices to that of small sales and high prices," which they would suffer under copyright?[53] Their preference did not make them the "barbarians of the Western World," Harpers noted. It made them businessmen.

Critics of reprinting, on the other hand, argued that this practice was morally wrong. Informed by virtue ethics, or more specifically, by a residual sentimental morality—in Thomas Jefferson's well-known phrasing, the god-given "moral sense, or conscience" that was "as much a part of man as his leg or arm"—many critics argued that the legality of reprinting was irrelevant to the question of whether the practice was morally acceptable.[54] Thomas Carlyle summed up the complaint against reprinters in an 1844 letter to Emerson about American publishers. "It is strange that men should feel themselves so entirely at liberty to steal," he sighed, "simply because there is no gallows to hang them for doing it."[55] Simms wondered aloud about the character of a business that could, among other reputed moral transgressions, condone "piracy." Publishers "have had charges of burglary and arson insinuated against them, when the motive to these crimes consisted in no higher object than the attainment of a copy of a new work, which it was desirable to pirate," he wrote, referring to a suspicious fire at Harpers that was rumored to be the handiwork of a rival reprinter.[56] "True, this charge was only insinuated," he continued, "but, what must we think of the moral sense, where such things are even thought, much less insinuated?" Later Simms answered his own question, quoting Fitz-Greene Halleck's impression that publishers had "'long since survived all sense of shame.'"[57] For a Southerner like Simms, the trade lacked honor. For others, reprinting was, quite simply, a blatant violation of the golden rule and thus a violation of deontological ethics.

Debates over the conduct of the trade extended well beyond reprinting. Literary history abounds with authorial complaints that printers and, later, publishers were nothing more than liars who concealed their incivility beneath a carefully manicured, public façade of gentlemanly conduct, and who concealed their economic motives beneath a façade of principled morality. One writer stood outside Harper and Brothers, possibly the most reviled publishing house in American history, wearing a sandwich board:

ONE OF HARPER'S AUTHORS.
I AM STARVING.[58]

Most writers did not go so far as to actually don their anger, but they wrote about it at length. "While recognizing . . . the great power and prestige of a flourishing publishing house, and the great risk a writer runs in opposing it, I cannot bring myself to accept its invincibility, or its infallibility, or its indispensability," author Gail Hamilton would write in an 1870 account of her own feud with the estimable Ticknor and Fields. "Of course a good reputation is, or ought to be, the sign of a good character; but a thing which is wrong is wrong, whatever the reputation of him who does it."[59] In impugning the ethics of publishing, Hamilton joined what she called in her book the "chronic feud between authors and publishers."[60] In 1854, George Palmer Putnam assigned author and editor Parke Godwin the unenviable task of addressing this feud before a room of publishers and booksellers at a New York trade sale. Considering the circumstances, Godwin handled himself with aplomb. His comments were glossed by the trade journal *Norton's Literary Gazette*: "He thought it a very hard case that an Author should be called upon to address an association of Booksellers; because there was an old feud pending between these two classes. [Cries of No, No!] He would not, however, be so savage as those families in Italy which remain unsatisfied until every man on either side is destroyed; nor so implacable as CAMPBELL who was inclined to pardon NAPOLEAN of all his crimes because he once caused a bookseller to be shot. [Laughter.]"[61]

The debates also extended well beyond the print centers of New York, Boston, and Philadelphia. The well-known anecdote of Napoleon's favor to authors every-where—"Here's to Napoleon, he shot a bookseller," Lord Byron is rumored to have said—is a reminder of the European context (and prehistory) of the author-publisher feud in the United States.[62] An English correspondent spoke for countless writers in both countries when he grumbled to a New York newspaper, "Authors are the prey of booksellers, and have been, ever since the invention of types."[63] In a defense of William Makepeace Thackeray's knowing portrayal of the trade in his serial novel *Pendennis* (1848–50), a *North British Review* article widely reprinted in American magazines in 1850 abridged the "common complaint" without fully endorsing it: "publishers make large fortunes and leave the authors to starve [because] they are, in fact, a kind of moral vampire, sucking the best blood of genius, and destroying others to support themselves."[64] Carlyle, a Scotsman and another Harpers author, proposed that the world would be a better place without publishers in it.[65] For England's Captain Marryat, even this was not good enough. Best consign them straight to hell. "We all have our own ideas of Paradise," he wrote to one publisher, "and if other authors think like me, the more pleasurable portion of antici-pated bliss is that there will be no publishers there."[66]

The feud may have begun in the old world, but American print culture, with its exploding markets, provided it new and raucous life, as illustrated by a lithograph of an author's skull that Harper and Brothers allegedly exhibited in its offices. The import was clear. It was, Evert Duyckinck told his brother, "the last relic of a starved author. The brains have been picked out and the man dead long ago."[67] By and large, American authors sympathized with the victim. Early national playwright, poet, and novelist Royall Tyler called printers "the most impotent creature[s] living."[68] One of

Washington Irving's collaborators on *Salmagundi* (1807–8), James K. Paulding, complained to Philadelphia printer Mathew Carey in 1815 that he had never succeeded in making "a tolerable bargain with a Bookseller."[69] Three decades later the author was as skeptical, instructing a friend negotiating with New York publishers on his behalf, "Screw as much out of those rogues as you can."[70] By then Paulding had done business with some of the nation's most important literary publishers, all of whom were "Philistines."

The reputation of James T. Fields and George Palmer Putnam notwithstanding, tossing publishers into a bonfire, as in Hawthorne's "Earth's Holocaust" (1844), seemed to many authors a perfectly serviceable coping strategy. They applauded like-minded critics such as the *National Quarterly Review*, which observed the "remarkable fact, that no class of business men have made less progress, intellectually, morally or socially, within the last two centuries, than the book-publishers."[71] Famed Indian ethnographer Henry Rowe Schoolcraft considered himself lucky just to have survived his encounters with this savage class. "A man ought not, I suppose, now-a-days, to complain," he complained, "if booksellers do not swallow him whole, head first, as the anaconda does a stag."[72] Simms judged that he had been swallowed whole any number of times. "I have been wronged, robbed, cheated and abused by them in due degree with my good nature and simplicity," he said, probably overstating his naïveté and certainly his martyrdom but not his anger.[73] Simms and others envisioned American print culture as a morality play in which author-geniuses did noble battle with evil businessmen who lived fat and happy in an economic world into which they dragged authors, kicking and screaming. Responding to an 1852 article celebrating the profits of the trade, one writer suggested that the *Literary World* find out what "your city almshouse [is] built of," because it certainly was not the "free-stone" from which New York publishers' new "sumptuous quarters" were made. So "ridden by" their publishers, "authors *must be* asses."[74]

Not surprisingly, few tradesmen were sympathetic to such criticism. Authors' complaint that publishers were "mercenary wretches, coining the heart's blood of genius for their own selfish profits" was nothing more than a "historical prejudice," publisher Samuel Goodrich wrote.[75] New York *Tribune* founder and editor Horace Greeley proposed that the "hideous dissonance" plaguing American print culture was just the sound lousy writers made when prudent publishers rejected them. He laughed off the legends that circulated the trade, one of which had the four brothers who constituted Harpers sipping "rare wines out of the skulls of their plundered, starving authors."[76] Even Putnam, who was an indomitable champion of trade morality, tired of the "insinuations of sanguine authors." "Publishers have many sins to answer for," he wrote, "but not *all* the enormities which disappointed authors proverbially assess upon them."[77] In response to the "free-stone" editorial quoted above, Putnam suggested that even "the slightest reflection" would cause authors to realize that "most of these tirades about the wickedness and wealth of publishers is arrant nonsense."[78] In an 1863 memoir, Putnam looked back on a rough patch in his own business and recalled that competitors had abandoned their own counters to staff his bookstore during the Christmas season. He reminded Americans that there was a "bright side of the trading world," where "a magnanimous and large-minded spirit may and does prevail," and where an old publisher talking to young ones would leave off with this advice: go "about doing good!" (presumably, for good's sake).[79] Greeley could only nod. Like clockwork, he grumbled, "every year" the hum of the *genus irritabile* about the "niggardliness of publishers" erupted into a "grand chorus of complaint," a complaint that was all too often transubstantiated into fact.[80]

There were also authors who refused to join the chorus. "I have a great deal of dread of approaching even distantly to that irritable & jealous tribe of authors who are apt to imagine that there is a conspiracy on the part of the rest of mankind to keep in the background their transcendent abilities," Asa Mitchell wrote Putnam. "I have undying faith in the remark of [Richard] Bentley that 'a man is never written down except by himself.'"[81] Though Harriet Martineau, for one, put no stock in anything Bentley said, calling him "a vile personage" who was missing a sense of fairness, the famed British publisher had a point.[82] Authors impugned the character of the trade but most knew little about what publishers actually did. Obviously, they knew that publishing was a business, but they did not appreciate what that meant, as when they accused publishers of failing to share profits when in fact there were no profits to share. "Mortified pride and wounded self-love must seek consolation in the thought that many a higher flight of genius, than my own feeble effort, has met with scarcely a better reward," another writer confessed to Putnam after realizing he had presumed too much for his own book.[83] "Milton, if I mistake not, received but 5£s for his Paradise Lost." Even Fitz-James O'Brien, the supposedly starving author who donned a sandwich board and picketed Harper and Brothers when it refused him a loan, suggested that in America as nowhere else "the mysteries of the publisher's sanctum are open to all who wish to penetrate them."[84]

If anyone had cause to complain about hardship it was probably publishers, who in addition to struggling with a still-developing commercial infrastructure and severe periodic recessions had to put up with the incessant complaints of authors who seemed to expect their books to magically appear in every bookstore on the East Coast and then to sell hundreds of copies. The point has been made before, but it deserves to be made again at the outset of this study. Print was a business, and publishers were its merchants. As Bourdieu puts it, they are "'cultural bankers,'" involved by definition in the manufacture and maintenance of various forms of capital.[85] Like all merchants, the early American publishers' job was clear: in the words of one contemporary, "to supply men with what they want, but have not."[86] This was easier said than done. Even the arrival of the railroad, which opened vast new markets and made it easier to get the books there reliably, only exacerbated supply and demand problems. Then, beyond the problem of getting the books out, there was the problem of gauging taste. "There is no *spatula* with which you can hold the Public's tongue while you force things down their throat," James Russell Lowell said, with characteristic flourish.[87] In a letter to a man whose books actually did sell by the hundreds, Fields asked Bayard Taylor to explain to poet Richard H. Stoddard that Ticknor and Fields had to "look out for the breakers which are constantly rising around our bows and guard against the evils which lie in wait for mistakes in business." Yet another book of poetry, which was no more profitable a commodity then than it is today, was not in the firm's best interest. "Explain this to Stoddard," Fields asked, "& I will thank you."[88] Many of the books issued by large and small publishing houses failed to recoup costs, so it is no wonder that publishers could little hide what Emerson called their "terror" at untested authors and especially untested American authors.[89] Even William Giles Dix understood that no "mortal man" could "make an unsalable book saleable."[90]

This view, voiced by an author who was never slow to believe the worst of the trade, should make us pause when looking at writers such as Herman Melville, who decried Harper and Brothers for ignoring his pleas for advances when the firm had good cause to doubt *Moby-Dick's* (1851) market potential. Had Melville not become *Melville*, we might remember him as one of those authors who, in Greeley's words, "far from being victims of publishers, have victimized *them*, and will do it again whenever they shall induce one to bring out another of their dreary inanities. All the wine that will ever be made by publishers out of these plaintive gentlemen's productions might be drank out of *their own* skulls, while they are yet living, and leave abundant room therein for all the brains they have to fulfill their ordinary functions undisturbed and unstimulated."[91] James Fenimore Cooper had an even more inflated sense of his market value, as Henry Carey told him in no uncertain terms in 1827: "As regards the new book we will be perfectly candid with you, & we think you will admit that we are disposed to be liberal. By the [*Last of the*] *Mohicans* we have not made one dollar!—The first edit[ion] of 5000 when sold did not quite pay its expenses, & we have since printed 750 copies, not more than half of wh[ich] have yet sold. We wish to make money by business, as you may suppose, & we do not like to work for nothing, although in this case, we should be content with a moderate profit."[92] Cooper posed other challenges to publishers as well, not the least of which was a control complex in matters of production and, according to James Derby, "exacting requirements" for hotel rooms.[93]

So if authors felt they were ridden by publishers, publishers often felt they were ridden by authors, markets, and every other person and firm involved in the process of making and selling books. In 1829, publisher Samuel Gardner Drake of Boston explained to a friend that if he "were acquainted with the multiform manoevers [sic] of my business you would not wonder that I do not write often."[94] Those who were more acquainted with the trade knew its trials, and they knew that those trials made for good entertainment. "You may depend upon it that all your *outcomings* are known and noticed, your *shortcomings* are sharply looked after, and your *incomings* are at least guessed at," a friend joked with Putnam.[95] Putnam was well aware that he was being watched, not only by authors and publishers but also by mercantile agencies, which sprang up in large (and small) cities as the commercial sphere began to decentralize in the mid-nineteenth century. Ever-expanding railroad lines and canals meant that it was not as easy as it once was to evaluate the business skill, or for that matter the basic honesty, of potential trading partners. No longer was it simply a matter of asking around. Agencies specializing in commercial credit reporting stepped in to assist businesses deal with the loss of local networks. One was New York's R. G. Dun and Company, which had branches all over the United States, and which kept a close eye on publishers, including Putnam. The firm's reports fairly consistently noted that while he was broadly "respected for his honor & integrity," Putnam was not the best credit risk.[96] "He is an honest and respectable man, but has no means, & will probably never be able to pay his liabilities," another agent estimated, more or less accurately, a few years later.[97]

Putnam had said it himself in the *Literary World*: publishing could be a brutal occupation. Even very successful firms like Harper and Brothers and D. Appleton and Company experienced many more "failures" than "*hits*." On average, a bookselling businesses in the 1840s lasted about sixteen months, victims of what Robert Darnton styles the "mishaps" of the trade: delays, debts, and deficient capital.[98] "A large proportion of the publishing business is up-hill work," Putnam wrote, "and the greater part of all the books produced yield less profit on the investment than almost any article of merchandise in the market." Amid this uncertainty, publishers nevertheless tried, he said, to respect the needs and the "true rights of authors."[99] What he meant was that the character of publishing was a marriage of conscience and capitalism.

What follows is not a straightforward history of American publishing. It does not focus on what John Sutherland has called the "undramatic," noncontroversial activities of the day-to-day business of publishing, or on activities that did not earn the wrath of a Thomas Paine, a Herman Melville, or a Fanny Fern.[100] In other words, this book is not an index of the everyday practices of the thousands of people and hundreds of firms involved in the production of print in America.[101] Over the past few decades especially, this kind of spadework has been undertaken by scholars working in the many disciplines that intersect under the auspices of the history of the book. My focus is precisely on the controversial activities of literary tradesmen between, roughly, the Revolution and the Civil War, as well as on the writers who critiqued them. It is these moments of crisis, as Bourdieu suggests, that expose the field's "objective relations" and the "values" that shaped them.[102]

The scope of the book is, first of all, practical. A study of the long feud between and among writers and publishers, and of the ethics informing it, could go to the present moment to consider the impact of all things digital on the ethics of authorship, publishing, bookselling, and reading, or, for instance, the ethical questions raised by Yale University Press's recent decision not to reprint cartoons depicting Mohammed in a book *about* the controversy over a Danish newspaper's 2005 publication of cartoons depicting the prophet.[103] (Even more recently, the author of the *New York Times*'s "The Ethicist" jumped into the ethics of print culture, an indication of the role ethics plays in popular understandings of the trade and our relationship to it.)[104] On the other side, I might have extended the study back to consider the religious ethics of Increase Mather's purported involvement in the production of Mary Rowlandson's *Narrative of the Captivity and Restoration* (1682) or to parse the relationship between Franklin the printer and Franklin the author. Unable to cover more territory in detail, in short, I have limited my study to the years between the nation's founding and its near-collapse, though I move considerably outside that range from time to time in order to illustrate a point.

My reasons for concentrating on the years between 1776 and 1865 are also conceptual. When in the late 1980s a prominent editor for Harper and Row—now HarperCollins, and once the notorious Harper and Brothers—caused a sensation by referring to publishing as "the literary-industrial complex," he was simply putting a new spin on a century-old complaint.[105] Publishers in the late 1800s were already concerned with the effects of industrialization. So were authors. In 1870, Gail Hamilton accused James T. Fields of being the wiliest capitalist of them all. As her friend William French put it, no one should expect too much from publishers, because in the end they were nothing more than traders. In his words, "business is business, and, though a prophet spake unto [Ticknor and Fields] from above, a larger, louder profit speaks to them from below."[106] It is convenient, at least for my purposes, that the same year Hamilton issued her exposé, John D. Rockefeller incorporated Standard Oil, inaugurating an era of business popularly reckoned to be governed entirely by mammon. The story is incredibly familiar. The Gilded Age was the culmination of the "commercial enterprise" that, as one 1817 book proposed, discovered the continent and the "individual enterprise" that settled it.[107] After the Civil War, a person's actions performed in service of his work became divorced from the generally accepted rules of behavior governing his actions as an individual. "I have done many things as president" of a company, one railroad executive reportedly said, "that I would not do as a man."[108] The ethic of competition became the rule. In the process, as Thorstein Veblen observed in 1904, core ethics lost their "axiomatic force."[109] Corporations could calculate "profit and loss" without recourse to "sentimental considerations" like "human kindness" or "honesty." While the earlier period discussed in this book was never driven quite so self-consciously by "this terrible old brute doctrine of competition," derived from what George Haven Putnam called the "inexorable laws of supply and demand," neither was it the genteel world the publishers of this era envisioned.[110] The first century or so of American publishing presented its own ethical problems, as the people and institutions involved in the trade fought over how the business of print ought to be conducted. What I want to look at in this study is what these beliefs were and why they clashed so spectacularly with the expectations of writers in the preindustrial United States.

Chapter 1, "The Character of the Trade," surveys these beliefs generally, examining the two predominant views of the trade between the Revolution and the Civil War.

In the first view, the book business was a gentlemanly sphere where publishers' conduct was driven by principle. In the second, the trade was governed by a commercial ethos that privileged profit above all else. A single person, Evert Duyckinck, one of the most influential figures in American print culture, embodied both these views. Using Duyckinck's extant papers and published writings, as well as the archives and published commentary of tradesmen who came before and after him, I reconstruct the character of the trade: first, as it was; second, as publishers and authors thought it was; and, third, as they thought it ought to be.

Each of the remaining chapters focuses on a debate over this character, beginning with the controversy over the printing of *Common Sense* in 1776. Chapter 2 reads a selection of Thomas Paine's political writings—including *Common Sense, The American Crisis* (1776–83), *Letter to the Abbe Raynal* (1782), and *The Rights of Man* (1792)—as a commentary on moral agency in the print trade, including the agency of the printer who issued the first edition of Paine's pamphlet. Paine's belief that the putative deficiency of civility and character among printers would result in a debased and inconsequential American literature was not a unique argument, but its place within his larger critique of political tyranny helps us understand the cultural function of his attack on the business of print: that the trade ignored the "civil manners" that ideally should characterize American civil society.[III]

Chapter 3 explores how authors argued among themselves about these issues of "civil manners" and moral authority in the context of a much less known debate over the conduct of the trade. In 1804, the historian Hannah Adams became embroiled in a dispute with Jedidiah Morse, a minister and the author of a best-selling geography, over who had rights to the flourishing school textbook market. This quarrel is usually read as a battle over gender in authorship, which it was. It was also, though, a contest over authorial decorum in America's nascent print culture.

The next chapter moves from early national to antebellum America, and from a little-known feud to perhaps the century's most infamous one: the international copyright debate. For obvious reasons, this debate is usually framed as a battle over law and economics. Many of the antagonists saw the law and economics of intellectual property, however, as subsets of a larger ethical question. And reformers such as Cornelius Mathews, William Gilmore Simms, and Edgar Allan Poe relied on a moral rhetoric that tried to do for copyright what Hannah Adams had done in her debate with Jedidiah Morse: make ethics, rather than custom, law, or economics, the predominant factor in the conduct of American print culture. These reformers, I argue, consciously and unconsciously ignored the reality of literary property and fabricated a realm in which Emerson's "moral law" was paramount and principle trumped judicial and political imperatives.

One of the effects of the copyright debate was to drag the trade's name through the mud. "Publishers are the only class of business men whose sins, real or imaginary, come into literature," George Haven Putnam lamented in 1883, ignoring, it would seem, a growing body of literature in his own time about all manners of businessmen.

Still, he had a point.[112] Putnam asked readers to keep in mind the meaning of the term *genus irritabile* and to remember that authors' "perceptions of the facts and equities of business transactions must . . . be taken with much allowance." Some of them, he warned, "can hardly be trusted to tell straight stories of matters in which their own vanity or interests were involved." Generally speaking, book historians on one side and literary critics on the other have taken Putnam's warning to heart, casting a wary eye on work that draws conclusions about historical print culture from literature. Obviously, most writers' fictional accounts of their experiences are anything but "straight." But that does not mean that we should reduce them entirely to textual facts and artifacts. In a forcefully argued study of authorial perceptions of Enlightenment-era French publishing, Geoffrey Turnovsky suggests that we need to move past simplistic accounts of the trade as saintly or sinful. "Publishing was instead experienced, conceptualized, and ultimately represented by writers in ways that are less self-evident than these bi-polar accounts would suggest."[113] Bracketing imaginative reactions to publishing, relegating them to the ghetto of allegory, I would add, misses the whole point of representation and conceptualization and contributes to the oversimplification. Fictional accounts of book history should matter to book historians because they help us understand perceptions of that history, regardless of their "truth," and they can coexist with fact-based and archival accounts as part of a fuller picture of what book history *was* and what it has been *thought* to be. Therefore, in addition to drawing on a range of print and manuscript sources—letters, business and union records, association meeting minutes, diaries, memoirs, court cases, newspapers, magazines, subscription advertisements, speeches, sermons, and pamphlets—this study relies as well on literary interpretation in making arguments about the social realities of author-publisher relations.[114]

Chapter 5 and 6 bear out the points above. They look at two notorious members of the *genus irritable*, Herman Melville and Fanny Fern, both of whom told very different stories about the function of morality in the business of print. Chapter 5, on Melville, illuminates implicit and explicit correlations between trade morality and Christian ethics and particularly the penultimate sociocultural morality of the golden rule. This Christian-cum-economic morality was really a function of the broader evolution of labor relations as the market attempted to balance conscience and capitalism. Yet owing to their prominent roles in the burgeoning nationalism of American literary culture and national economy, publishers figured more prominently than most businessmen in debates over business ethics in the nineteenth century. This chapter argues that the golden rule provided a culturally valuable doctrine for early American publishers even as it did little to actually regulate the trade, a fact that Melville tried to represent in *Pierre; or, The Ambiguities* (1852) and "Bartleby, the Scrivener" (1853), both of which present authors debating the morality of a vocational sphere based on moral fraud.

"If there is any truth in the picture which represents the publisher as a sort of ogre, whose den is strewn with the bones of authors, and who quaffs his wine out of their skulls, this assumption is certainly natural enough, as between the eater and the eaten there can be little love lost," George Haven Putnam wrote, looking back upon the strife between authors and publishers in the time of his father, George Palmer Putnam.[115] Fern's novel *Ruth Hall*, about a popular female magazine writer trying to make a living from her pen and encountering various wretched literary tradesmen along the way, probably contributed to such stereotypes. The novel's publication in 1854 caused a scandal, not only because of its autobiographical elements but also because of the vitriol with which Fern attacked the trade. Much scholarship on this novel focuses on this attack and on the ways in which Ruth does and does not represent the condition of women in the mid-nineteenth century. However, little of this scholarship takes note of something Fern's narrator calls attention to: that as an author Ruth is a "business woman."[116] Chapter 6 asks what it meant to be a businesswoman in the mid-nineteenth century and what it meant to be a woman conducting literary business. Through Ruth, Fern arrives at a very different theory of trade morality than does Melville. *Ruth Hall* sees the potential for a moral capitalism based on the very ideal publishers themselves espoused. Fern, who is often characterized as one of the most despondent critics of American print culture, argued that there could be love between Putnam's eater and eaten, between trade and author, even if only in theory.

Somewhere between fact and fiction was Gail Hamilton's controversial account of her dispute with Ticknor and Fields, *A Battle of the Books* (1870). In an epilogue, I read this text in light of the ethical issues raised before the Civil War and against the backdrop of the changes publishing would go through after the war. Here, Hamilton returned the publisher to the cave where George Haven Putnam would find him camouflaged a decade later: lying "in wait, seeking what chance he may have to devour his author."[117] Despite her skepticism of trade morality, however, and unlike Captain Marryat, Hamilton did not relegate the publisher to hell. He was too much a part of the living world of the author, too essential to the business of authorship. Perhaps the author simply needed to be more like Fern's Ruth: capable of understanding the transactions of the counting room if she was to expect anything like fairness. "If I had been wiser," Hamilton said about her relationship with Fields, "he would have been juster."[118] But such a statement is deceptive. It implied that the trade never was, and likely never would be, capable of the kind of self-regulation it ballyhooed. And it implied that the ethics so hyped by publishers like Fields was, ultimately, a kind of discursive slight of hand. By setting her story in the eighteenth century, Hamilton suggested that this was the way the trade always had been. And the ending of her account suggested that this is the way it always would be—at least from the perspective of the writer.

On December 12, 1853, Harper and Brothers burned in a spectacular midday fire. Thousands of people crowded the streets and alleys of lower Manhattan to witness the conflagration. The New York *Daily Times* exaggerated the scene—if "it could be transferred to canvas, [it] would exceed anything ever painted"—while playing down speculation that the fire had been set deliberately.[119] The rumor was persistent and credible. Harper and Brothers' "'eye for an eye' principle of justice" earned the firm many enemies among tradesmen and authors alike.[120] About a week after the fire, George Palmer Putnam received a letter from his friend Erastus Ellsworth. "If one were to remark to you that 'Harper & Brothers' had at length been overtaken by a righteous retribution, would you not acquiesce in the sentiment as a striking and impressive one," Ellsworth asked with a wink and a nudge, "and would you not think of that providence as a discriminating providence which permitted that lighted match to drop into 'Harper & Brother's' [sic] camphene instead of your own? Would you not?—In confidence?—Ha?"[121] Ellsworth expressed the sentiments of many in the trade. They would not have said so in public, but most probably thought Harpers had it coming.

Putnam was in no mood to joke about the fire, however. Two days after its impressive and imposing Cliff Street complex burned to the ground, burying the firm's plates, including those of *Moby-Dick*, Putnam wrote Harper and Brothers an unusual letter. In recent years Putnam had had a number of very public run-ins with Harpers, which he acknowledged outright. "There has been an *appearance*, at least, of *ill*-will between your house & myself," he wrote, before saying he hoped that Harpers would not look skeptically on his motives for writing.[122] No one publicly accused Putnam of having anything to do with the fire—arson was not his style—but he was anxious that Harpers might not be so sure. "I only thought the opportunity a suitable [one] for me to say, that anything else than cordial good will and friendly relations between myself and all engaged in the trade & especially those at the head of the trade, is deeply repugnant to my feeling—and that however I may have considered myself aggrieved and however you may have thought I had done amiss, and however warm I have been in speaking of a supposed grievance as I honestly felt—this may be a time when all these things may be properly and easily buried and forgotten." The letter is awkward. Putnam was clearly nervous, but he just as clearly had something to say, and he practically trips over himself trying to say it. Chapter 1 is about what Putnam was trying (badly) to say about the role feeling, appearances, and goodwill played in American publishing.

1

The Character of the Trade

EVERT AUGUSTUS DUYCKINCK was the son of a New York printer best known for giving fledgling Harper and Brothers its first printing job in 1817. The job was *Seneca's Morals*, an irony that would not have been lost on the firm's competitors, most of whom judged Harpers (or "the Harpies") "the leviathans of the trade."[1] Evert Duyckinck had a markedly different reputation. The "friend of authors in distress," said author John Esten Cooke; the "President of the Republic of Letters," said poet D. A. Gallagher.[2] William Gilmore Simms and Richard Henry Dana, Sr., men not known for their effusion, likewise saw in Duyckinck something different: an honest man in a business in which, Simms judged, most were "guilty—or worthless."[3] Duyckinck earned his reputation by helping writers navigate the rapidly expanding New York publishing trade. He earned it as well by playing father confessor when they found that trade to be wanting in gentlemanly feeling. Part of him commiserated with the writers. The bottom line mattered more to publishers than Duyckinck felt comfortable admitting in public—"'sympathy' is a word unknown to the trade," he complained once—and in his letters he expressed embarrassment at everything from publishers' focus on profit to the ways they abused each other's trust to their opposition to international copyright, opposition he chalked up to a lack of character.[4] In an 1841 letter he put the matter baldly: "there should be more honor among publishers."[5]

These attitudes make an article Duyckinck later published on the ethics of the trade all the more curious. "The Morality of Publishers" was an angry defense of the "conscience of publishers" against charges that they had none. It was also a tongue-lashing of "apologists" who justified publishers' questionable behavior by suggesting

FIGURE 1.1 Evert Duyckinck, Courtesy General Research Division, New York Public Library, Astor, Lenox and Tilden Foundations.

that little more was to be expected of businessmen who were, the argument went, materialists by nature.[6] In response, Duyckinck conjured up the "true publisher," an ideal literary businessman whose behavior was regulated not by profit but by principle. "If Lot had been a bookseller in Sodom, though surrounded by a unanimous company of sinners, and Voltaire had existed and written a few thousand years earlier," Duyckinck proposed to illustrate his point, "Lot would certainly not have published his writings." His idealism was sincere, but so was his cynicism. After his death in 1878, one eulogist portrayed Duyckinck as a transitional figure caught between America's "old faith" and its "new materialism."[7] This transition occasioned a great deal of comment in Duyckinck's father's time, but as American markets expanded rapidly, it took on even greater moral urgency in his own. As Scott Sandage notes, "the market revolution begged the question of a market *reformation*: a dual realignment of economic relations and the moral and legal codes that gave them meaning."[8]

Historians like Sandage and Bruce H. Mann have written about this realignment in the context of credit, debt, and insolvency. This chapter considers it in the context of publishing. Amid what Sandage calls the "new ethics of capitalism," questions about the character of literary businessmen took on new meanings. When Cooke asked Duyckinck, for example, "What is the character of the publishing firm of Bruce & Huntington?" his question was not simply empirical—it was theoretical.[9] On one hand, it was a factual question about a publishing house's bottom line and its practical ability to maintain it. On the other, it was an inquiry into the publisher's moral disposition. Duyckinck fielded his share of these questions, and while he drifted back and forth between cynicism and idealism, he tended toward the latter. In this sense he was representative of the trade's quixotic self-conception.[10] He believed that more often than not literary tradesmen possessed what philosophers called the "moral sense," what influential business writer Freeman Hunt called the "inward principle," and what trade moralists generally called "character."[11] Most of the writers discussed in this book called it bunk.

This chapter articulates the character of the trade against which these writers reacted. Its point is not to air the trade's dirty laundry. Instead, it is to show that behind the position-takings that constituted the field of publishing were complex and often contradictory moral dispositions. These dispositions were usually idealized by the trade itself, and in the first three sections of the chapter I locate the analog for this romanticization in the broader redefinition of business that took place in the late eighteenth and early nineteenth centuries, using Duyckinck's writings and those of other literary tradesmen as measures of the sincerity and the pretensions of the trade's moral self-conception. As I couch it, these sections present the trade "in theory." The next section presents the trade "in fact." As might be expected, this is a more skeptical, even sardonic appraisal of the character of the trade. It is based in evidence that the virtue and deontological ethics so integral to the trade's self-conception were at best inconsistent and at worst chimerical. I conclude the chapter with one of the more notoriously extravagant visions of trade morality, an 1867 *Atlantic Monthly* article by James Parton that returns us to where the chapter began: with political economists like Adam Smith insisting on the fundamental morality of the free market and its traders. If the chapter's logic seems circular, that is because it is, insofar as it impersonates the moral logic of the trade. Parton's article was a rearguard maneuver to combat lingering criticism of publishing with a romantic portrayal of its conscience. His account of the true publisher was redolent of Duyckinck's, which itself was simply a trade-specific rendering of the moral merchant constructed by contemporary commentators like Freeman Hunt and Ralph Waldo Emerson, who, though aware of the dramatic failures of commercial morality in America, nonetheless romanticized the character of business and the businessman.

THE NATURAL MERCHANT

"Moral philosophy takes it for granted that there is in a human action a moral quality," Francis Wayland taught in *The Elements of Moral Science* (1835).[12] Wayland
defined his subject as the "science" of morality, and he began his textbook by directly
comparing moral law to Newton's laws of motion. The fact that two years later he
published the most influential political economy textbook in the country is a
reminder that political economy descended directly from moral philosophy.[13] Moral
philosophy sought to discover in nature the laws governing human conduct; political
economy sought to discover in nature the laws governing the acquisition of wealth.
Both disciplines detected in the natural world divine law applicable to everything
from gravity to whether sellers had the moral right to deceive buyers. "The Creator
has subjected the accumulation of the blessings of this life to some determinate laws,"
and political economy was their "systematic arrangement." It taught men not just
how to *be*—the traditional goal of moral philosophy—but how to be wealthy.

Wayland was not the most influential moral philosopher-cum-political economist. He wrote in the long shadow of Adam Smith, who in 1776 articulated what
many merchants had long believed: an individual's economic self-interest also works
in the best interest of the general good. "It is not from the benevolence of the
butcher, the brewer, or the baker, that we expect our dinner," Smith proposed frankly
and famously early in *An Inquiry into the Nature and Causes of the Wealth of Nations*,
"but from their regard to their own interest."[14] Of course, Smith was also the author
of the *Theory of Moral Sentiments*, arguing "that to feel much for others and little for
ourselves, that to restrain our selfish, and to indulge our benevolent affections, constitutes the perfection of human nature." The development of Smith's thought would
not have struck the tradesmen of Duyckinck's era as inconsistent any more than
Wayland's, though the yoking of self-interest to selflessness prompted some nineteenth-century German economists to dub this apparent contradiction the "Adam
Smith problem."[15]

Not everyone believed that morality and money were commensurate. To many
observers, Americans' often-unapologetic pursuit of commercial gain was both
uncivilized and immoral, whatever political economists like Wayland or Smith said.
Alexis de Tocqueville suggested that the only time Americans stopped chasing
money was when they were in church.[16] He could have added that while in church,
Americans might hear that their pursuit was divinely sanctioned, that wealth would
not "consign" them to "perdition," as Ishmael frets in *Moby-Dick*.[17] Nonsense, said
Charles Dickens. Disgusted by American reprinters who capitalized on his books
("men of very low attainments and of more than indifferent reputation"), Dickens
judged that the nation's habit of worshipping its merchants "enables many a knave to
hold his head up with the best, who well deserve a halter."[18] Many Americans agreed,
and they did so long before Dickens got up on his soapbox in the 1840s. Troubled
that early seventeenth-century New England was perceived as a kind of commercial

Sodom, Cotton Mather reminded Protestants that disobedience to the terms of a bargain was disobedience to god.[19] He compared his flock to the early Christians rebuked by the apostle Paul: "I hear there are deviations among you, and I partly believe it."[20] In 1809, Philadelphia's *Port-Folio* pointed out that in America, jeremiads on commercial sinfulness were the stuff of everyday life. "Judging from the invectives of the teachers of mankind, one would think that rank, office, and riches would be as sedulously avoided . . . as any other road to ruin," yet people went right on chasing money.[21] Really this was a version of Benjamin Franklin's "Way to Wealth" (1758), where Father Abraham's cautionary speech on consumerism is cheered and then promptly ignored as his audience turns around and goes on a shopping spree. By the time Duyckinck entered business, little had changed, according to critics like Henry Ward Beecher: "On Sunday, the exemplary merchant hears from the pulpit, 'Look not every man on his own things, but every man also on the things of others,' and he says amen to that. On Monday he hears the genius of Commerce say 'Every man for himself,' and he says amen to that."[22] Businessmen were practiced at casuistry, masters at making god serve mammon, so much so that for thousands of years what we today call business ethics was little more than the belief that there was no such thing.[23]

Others in this back-and-forth debate thought such criticism reductive. With its "many desires, various engines, some nobler and some meaner," America was complicated, Harriet Martineau said.[24] She spoke for many who believed that political economists like Wayland, Smith, and David Ricardo could be the source of both economic and moral wisdom. Indeed, two of the sources cited earlier may be read not as cautions but as sanctions of the acquisitive life. *Port-Folio* recommended that moralists reevaluate their blind hatred of the trading spirit given the potential moral ends to which "power and riches" could be put.[25] As for Benjamin Franklin, his Father Abraham advocates a moral materialism no less persuasively than Franklin himself did. ("If money matters, Franklin matters," one contemporary business ethicist observes.)[26] In 1853, Unitarian minister Henry Bellows stood on the very stage from which Emerson delivered "The American Scholar," challenging Harvard students to shake off suffocating European customs. Bellows had a different message. He challenged the students to move beyond backward-looking skepticism of business and businessmen. America was a new world, and here trade was not damning but redeeming. "Other lands cannot estimate the amount of thought, of self-respect and moral force, that accompanies the labor and trade of this country," Bellows proposed.[27] "Shopkeeping may be a . . . belittling business to those who deal *with* fools and *like* knaves" but in the United States "the character of the agents was new and different."[28] Yes, the merchant's "trial by gold" meant that he was in danger of bargaining away his soul, but it also meant that he had occasion for the most brilliant show of integrity possible.[29]

Bellows spoke for an influential faction of Protestant clergy for whom the writings of Adam Smith "had the ring of gospel truth about them."[30] These "clerical economists," to borrow historian Stewart Davenport's apt label, held that "the world of commerce was one big harmonious mechanism with the God of Providence and progress behind it, and should therefore be exalted as good, right, and natural rather than maligned by skeptics as something sordid, speculative, and immoral."[31] Their ranks included not just Bellows and Wayland but also Duyckinck's friend Francis Lieber, a legal scholar with whom Duyckinck debated everything from copyright to what it meant to be a gentleman. The influence of the clerical economists was extensive, in part because of their leadership roles in the religious, legal, and educational establishments. Among the most prominent was Wayland, whose *Elements of Political Economy* (1837) became the textbook of choice in college capstone courses intended to turn out principled and pragmatic—in sum, republican—citizens.

But few businessmen, or publishers, went to college. The counting room was their Yale and their Harvard, and their professors were men like Freeman Hunt, a rags-to-riches editor and former printer whose *Merchants' Magazine and Commercial Review* was the publication of record for mid-nineteenth-century American business and a mouthpiece for the gospel of commercial morality. In order to "elevate the commercial character," Hunt and his contributors redacted the lessons taught in more academic ways by Smith and Wayland. In its inaugural article, the *Merchants' Magazine* proclaimed, after Wayland, that the wedding of money and morality was "the beautiful order and arrangement of Providence," and that there was more real danger in denying this fact than in acting on it.[32] The moral future of the nation was thus tied to its economic vitality. Like all covenants, there were glories in acquiescing and consequences for defaulting. The message was timeless. It was what Bellows told Harvard students in 1853, what Mather told Protestant merchants in 1713, and what John Winthrop told his shipmates aboard the *Arbella* in 1630. Most famously, it was what Franklin told British colonials and Americans throughout his life.

Hunt's edition of the message took hold. When the body of drowned businessman and former New York mayor Stephen Allen was pulled from the Hudson River, he had in his pocket a clipping from the *Merchants' Magazine*: it was a copy of Hunt's Franklinesque "Maxims for Young Merchants."[33] In 1856 Hunt reached out to an even wider audience with the publication of *Worth and Wealth*, a collection of writings from the magazine. It was, in essence, a conduct book, a practical guide for young businessmen as they began their careers. For Hunt, practicality did not mean one had to be a utilitarian. He believed that moral principle was essential to success, but it was not valued for that alone. In *Worth and Wealth* he attacked what he called the "utilitarian scheme" for overstating success as a cause of behavior.[34] Drawing on *Essays on the Principles of Morality* (1829), a slim volume by a British linen draper-cum-moralist named Jonathan Dymond, Hunt proposed a virtue ethics for businessmen based on "principles of justice."[35] John Greenleaf Whittier, also familiar with this folk moral economist, construed Dymond's message as "practical righteousness," a blending of common sense with rigorous attention to principle. It was this matter-of-fact and matter-of-faith approach to commerce as well as the theory's antirelativism that attracted Hunt, who christened Dymond the "merchant moralist."[36] He treated Dymond's writings like scripture.

Hunt's applications of Dymond's theory helps explain his reading of one of the more influential conduct books of the time, Edwin Freedley's *A Practical Treatise on Business* (1852). Freedley's text was a fairly standard approach to political economy, but for Hunt it was nothing less than a modernization of Franklin's writings and a full-fledged "theory of business" based on the character of the merchant.[37] "Honor," Freedley wrote, "is the patron-saint of business."[38] "Let him who desires to test the strength of his principles, or improve his moral nature by wholesome discipline, embark in trade. Let him who considers himself a skillful arbitrator or adjudicator of nice questions in morals or metaphysics, place himself in a position where, every day of his life, he must adjust those in which he himself is an interested party." Freedley had fleshed out the work Franklin had begun and had proven, according to Hunt, that the master's teachings were anything but "mercenary," a charge Hunt seemed to take personally.[39] Most important, Freedley's belief that business was about "perfecting the moral nature" dovetailed with Hunt's maxim "Make *character* supreme."[40] Both, in turn, would dovetail with Evert Duyckinck's vision of the true publisher.

For all its importance as a bellwether of morality, character was and remains a slippery concept. In Joanne Freeman's useful formulation, character was "personality with a moral dimension."[41] Early Americans put a less technical spin on it. Wayland defined it as "the present intellectual, social, and moral condition of an individual."[42] Dymond spoke of the springs of "virtuous conduct," Hunt of an "inward principle," and Freedley of a "moral nature."[43] Recognizing both its ubiquity and its slipperiness, Ralph Waldo Emerson recommended a characteristically Emersonian solution. In his essay "Character" (1844), he suggested looking at the merchant as physical proof of an immaterial moral ideal:

> There are geniuses in trade, as well as in war, or the state, or letters; and the reason why this or that man is fortunate, is not to be told. It lies in the man: that is all anybody can tell you about it. See him, and you will know as easily why he succeeds, as, if you see Napoleon, you would comprehend his fortune. . . . Nature seems to authorize trade, as soon as you see the natural merchant, who appears not so much a private agent, as her factor and Minister of Commerce. His natural probity combines with his insight into the fabric of society, to put him above tricks, and he communicates to all his own faith, that contracts are of no private interpretation. The habit of his mind is a reference to standards of natural equity and public advantage; and he inspires respect, and the wish to deal with him, both for the quiet spirit of honor which attends him, and for the intellectual pastime which the spectacle of so much ability affords.[44]

Emerson's logic looks deceptively utilitarian insofar as the "natural merchant" conducted his business not just on principles of natural right but also on the outcome of social utility. However, Emerson did not advocate performing actions because they maximize the good. Like Hunt's, his was a convoluted virtue ethics. For Emerson, "public advantage" was inherent in the motives and actions of the natural merchant. It was prefigured by his moral disposition. The natural merchant acted a given way because it was right according to moral law—which operates as a kind of magnet for those disposed toward it—and not because his actions would produce certain benefits. In other words, the natural merchant acted virtuously because he was good; he tended toward goodness. That goodness then bettered society.[45] The natural merchant was moral principle made flesh.

In "The Morality of Publishers," Duyckinck would adapt this theory of commercial morality to the business of literature in an effort to recast the publisher as a natural merchant. In Duyckinck's hands, the publisher was a tradesman whose goodness was as innate to him as genius was to Milton, and whose effects on society were as morally estimable.

THE MORALITY OF PUBLISHERS

Evert Duyckinck was barely out of his twenties when in February 1847 he wrote "The Morality of Publishers" for the *Literary World*. He was already an established editor and a well-regarded trade pundit. In only two months he had made the *Literary World* the preeminent trade magazine in the United States, fulfilling his vision for it as "a centre of information for the booksellers of the whole country."[46] "I congratulate you on the appearance of your Literary World, which is the sturdiest bantling I have ever seen born," Richard Grant White told Duyckinck a week before "The Morality of Publishers" appeared. White echoed the view of literati who wanted a more public venue for debate about American print culture, one that did not cater to London or Boston. And they wanted an editor who would not pull punches. "I hope it will 'cry aloud & spare not,'" said White; "indeed I feel sure of this from the tone of the whole affair."[47]

The *Literary World* was not Duyckinck's first editorial undertaking. In the early 1840s he co-edited the short-lived but respected magazine *Arcturus* with his friends Cornelius Mathews and William Jones. Between then and the time he penned "The Morality of Publishers" he wrote for a number of major antebellum magazines and edited Wiley and Putnam's groundbreaking Library of American Books, the first American series to focus exclusively on domestic literature. It is most famous today for its inclusion of a young sailor's first novel, a rather lecherous account of a sabbatical in the Marquesas. The book was *Typee: A Peep at Polynesian Life* (1846), and its author, Herman Melville, would eventually become painfully aware of Duyckinck's habit of defending a commercial morality he lamented in private.

Duyckinck came of age at an auspicious time in American publishing. Improvements in transportation and technology combined with a robust reprint trade made possible the cheap publishing revolution of the 1830s and 1840s, during which houses produced books in hitherto unimagined numbers and formats. "Mammoth" weeklies like *Brother Jonathan* and the *New World*—so nicknamed because some editions were more than four feet tall—pioneered the distribution of novels in large-format newspaper editions, an innovation that in a span of a few years changed the ways publishers and before them printers had conducted business for centuries.[48] The speed at which books were now produced and the effect this had on modes of production and financing made the print trade in 1840 a completely different environment from what it had been only a decade earlier. "You must know that the cheap press has, within a few months, made a total change in our book markets," Emerson explained to Thomas Carlyle. "Every English book of any name or credit is instantly converted into a newspaper or coarse pamphlet, & hawked by a hundred boys in the streets of all our cities for 25, 18, or 12 cents."[49] Publishing houses opened outposts in London in order to expedite the movement of English titles to waiting East Coast presses. Publishers like George Palmer Putnam and James T. Fields cut their teeth in the London trade representing the interests of American firms whose fortunes were often dependent on clipper ships speeding west across the Atlantic. And though Putnam and Fields compensated British writers as much as they could, many authors were never paid a thing. As Emerson tried to impress upon Carlyle, despite what publishers said, authors' interests were not really part of the publishing equation. It is a fair question whether they ever had been.

Competition was intense. So many American presses fought over the same English novels that some houses sometimes transmitted sheets by multiple vessels simultaneously lest one be delayed—or lest a crate of loose sheets mysteriously disappear over the side of a moored ship. In 1834, during one especially acrimonious struggle over a new title by the popular English writer William Beckford, Harper and Brothers informed rival Henry Carey of Philadelphia that a package of sheets bound for his firm had "accidentally dropped between the ship and the wharf."[50] Strange, that. Even stranger was the fact that another Philadelphia firm, Key and Biddle, reprinted the book soon after.[51] The next year, after Harper and Brothers challenged Carey's brother's firm by reprinting a book to which the latter had rights, Carey struck back, reprinting a popular Harpers' author, Edward Bulwer-Lytton. Getting advance sheets the same day Harpers received its own, Carey farmed them out to twelve printers to try to beat his rival to market. James Derby recalled the rest of the story as he heard it from Carey's partner, Abraham Hart: "That afternoon 500 complete copies were forwarded to New York booksellers by the mail stage, the only conveyance by which they could reach New York by daylight the following morning, and this could only be accomplished by hiring all the passenger seats. Mr. Hart was the only passenger of the stage that morning, the remaining space being taken up with Bulwer-Lytton's 'Rienzi.' The volume was for sale in all the New York bookstores, one day earlier than Harpers' edition of the same work."[52] Carey spelled out the point of such actions later during another duel with Harpers. "You must think we are easily to be pushed aside judging from the tones of your letters," he wrote, with characteristic frankness. "We do assure you, however, that we will maintain our rights & if you choose to raise a storm we shall be greatly mistaken if we are not able to carry sail as large as you can. In the contest you have much more to lose than we have—[.]"[53] Harpers discovered this fact on its own during the battle over *Rienzi*, when it sabotaged Carey's edition by underselling it by so much that Harpers was guaranteed to lose money.[54] It was these kinds of duels that tried the patience of Duyckinck, who grew tired, he told his brother, of tradesmen "cutting each other up on points of veracity."[55]

Duyckinck's allusion to dueling was apropos given his and other literary trades-men's use of the charged term "honor" in their writings and correspondence. In 1785 the irascible Boston printer Benjamin Larkin advised his partner John Mycall to "pay more attention to your Word," or Larkin would show up "personally to demand Satisfaction."[56] Such a threat makes Larkin sound as though he were from Charleston, South Carolina, not Charlestown, Massachusetts. Edward L. Ayers notes that while to most Northerners "honor was just another word for lack of self-control"—a reference to its use as an excuse for violence—to white, South-ern males honor was the invisible hand that regulated conduct in everything from courtship to commerce.[57] In his classic study, *Southern Honor: Ethics and Behav-ior in the Old South* (1982), Bertram Wyatt-Brown defines honor as a morally amplified version of reputation situated "in the individual as his understanding of who he is and where he belongs in the ordered ranks of society."[58] Strictly speak-ing, most Northern printers, publishers, and editors did not subscribe to the social caste system that gave codes of honor their force in the South. Yet, as Larkin's language demonstrates, some did accept not just the idea that there was an ordered rank of commercial society—"a social order of deference," in Michael Warner's words—but that the rank of a printer or publisher depended on his character and reputation in trade.[59] In 1821 Henry Carey admonished a Boston publisher, Cummings and Hilliard, for underselling an atlas printed by his firm. "To this procedure, so vitally hostile to our interests, you had no temptation whatever," he wrote. "You could not have been undersold by any other Bookseller had you adhered to the regular price."[60] Such conduct was in bad taste. "The injury you have thus done us is of the most serious character & which from a house of your standing & respectability we could not have expected." Carey was direct. He expressed "Deep Regret and extreme surprize" that his competitor would so jeopardize "the Credit and Character of a useful Business" like publish-ing. (For its part, Cummings and Hilliard observed, reasonably, that M. Carey and Son's sources might be less than trustworthy.)[61] When Carey spoke of the "the Credit and Character of a useful Business," he was speaking not of Cummings and Hilliard or even his own firm but of the honor of the trade at large. Publish-ing "has so powerful a tendency to illuminate & reform mankind," he preached, but this ostensible tendency, and more importantly the reputation for it, was undermined by reckless competition. Honorable firms did not undersell one another. As Duyckinck had complained to James Russell Lowell, "there should be more honor among publishers."

"The Morality of Publishers" was an attack on a reprint trade that made such breakneck print runs, drowned packages, and questions of character more common occurrences than they otherwise might have been. The trade favored British titles, which legally could be had for free, over American titles for which they had to pay. This had a number of consequences. It kept American writers out of the exploding domestic book market and froze domestic literature in its embryonic stage, according to Duyckinck. Also, it encouraged publishers to sell books of "the worst licentiousness."[62] Duyckinck saw in the reprint trade "a moral pestilence" capable of undermining not only American literature but the nation itself. Duyckinck's friend and co-editor Cornelius Mathews suggested that even virtuous publishers could not help but participate in this "unnatural trade" in ill-gotten books if they wished to stay in business.[63] "You see the morality of the system," he complained to Duyckinck, "good & bad, confounded with a vengeance."[64] In this environment, it was impossible for the natural merchant to survive.

The "unnatural trade" offended Duyckinck too, but so did its critics. In early 1847, criticism of the trade reached one of its periodic crescendos. In January the *American Review* published a forty-six-page review of Philip James Bailey's controversial poem "Festus" (1839), which had already run through multiple editions since first being reprinted in Boston in 1845. These editions sold not because the poem was any good, the *American Review* charged, but because the publisher had paid off reviewers, a practice known as "puffing."[65] Mathews called puffing "the manufacture of authors": creating reputations for writers in order to maximize profits on reprints.[66] Editors and publishers could "turn out a flourishing author, ready made autograph and all, in a month, by a preliminary series of puffs preceding the magic publication."[67] It was also used to inflate the reputations of domestic writers, as Ticknor and Fields did to great effect with Nathaniel Hawthorne. Puffing was a tried and true advertising strategy, and it gave critics more reason to doubt the morality of the trade. That "'Festus' should *jump* into a reputation which Paradise Lost has even yet hardly *grown* into, is a truly a most significant phenomenon," the *American Review* noted.[68] It was direct in assigning blame. Not only did the author seem to believe in the divine dispensation "to complete the Revelation," but publishers seemed to believe that they acted out the will of god in duping readers for profit.[69] Pandering to authorial "vanity" and abusing readers' "gullibility" should be expected of publishers, the *American Review* suggested, before adding this zinger: "'tis their vocation."

Duyckinck's "The Morality of Publishers" was a response to this article. He did not dispute the culture of puffing that had grown up—indeed, he had attacked it himself in the pages of the *American Review* only months before—nor did he defend "Festus." Instead, he disputed the charge that practices such as puffing meant that the trade was inherently immoral. The trade's honor may have suffered, but its character was intact.

A great deal has been lately said in various ways of the conscience of publishers, of their unquestionable right to publish bad books, and like Falstaff, to sin "in their vocation," of a certain independence of the laws of morals supposed to govern the rest of the world, the argument for which is generally summed up in the one word, "tradesmen." . . . An elaborate article in the *American Review* tells us—"one can hardly help seeing . . . they probably would not be publishers, if they were ambitious of martyrdom in any cause but that of self interest. Far be it from us to blame publishers for the course they take. Doubtless they are as worthy a class of cormorants as any other . . . ." "This is not a question of ethics but of business," says another, an apologist. . . .

The charges are immorality, quackery, and puffery, the facts are admitted, and the defence is, "tradesmanship."[70]

Why were publishers held to a higher standard than other genteel professions? "If a divine turns fifth monarchist, millerite, Swedenborgian, or what not, he is whistled off handsomely, but churches remain, pulpits are filled, and the cloth respected. Even stockbrokers and tailors have something to be said for them, though, upon the whole, hopeless cases." Upstanding publishers were damned by the supposed immorality of their profession while reprobates were saved by the assumption that their professions were inherently moral? The answer, that publishers were by definition tradesmen and therefore suspect, however popular a view, was to Duyckinck a specious claim, "as if trade sanctioned the pursuit of gain by any means, at the expense of any interests, human or divine." Like all trades, Duyckinck proposed, publishing was shored up "by justice and honor." There were dishonest publishers, to be sure, but the upright publisher based his conduct not on what he could get away with but on "what is right." "On the trading principle, even as it exists, no dishonest publisher could stand." Good will out, in part because morality and the business of publishing went hand in hand.

"The Morality of Publishers" showcased the frustrating idealism characterizing Duyckinck's public views of the trade going back to his first major article in 1840, "Authorship," which presented the writer as a misunderstood genius so terrifically alone that his desk is his only friend.[71] "Literary Prospects of 1845" picked up where "Authorship" left off, with the genius author striving against all odds. Now, however, in addition to fighting to be fairly treated by the trade and by a society more focused on making money than nurturing domestic literary talent, the serious writer must compete with the "quack" author. It is unclear just who or what a quack author was, since all Duyckinck said of him in the article, apart from the fact that he "sends his noisy nostrums through the street with trumpet and placard at all hours," is that he was not a "true author," "the proud, humble man, who does not bray his affairs constantly before the world."[72] The true author was a figure of Duyckinck's imagination, a kind of virtuous, better angel that existed outside of the day-to-day jostling with the business of letters in which nearly all writers had to participate.

NEW YORK, SATURDAY, FEB. 13, 1847.

THE MORALITY OF PUBLISHERS.

A GREAT deal has been lately said in various ways of the conscience of publishers, of their unquestionable right to publish bad books, and like Falstaff, to sin "in their vocation," of a certain independence of the laws of morals supposed to govern the rest of the world, the argument for which is generally summed up in the one word, "tradesmen." Says one authority—"booksellers deal in literature as merchandise. They are merchants, and with them the value of a book depends altogether upon its sale. There is no other way in which booksellers can deal in literary commodities." An elaborate article in the *American Review* tells us—"one can hardly help seeing that the interest of publishers lies most in mediating between such as want nothing but puffs for their labor, and such as want nothing but shams for their money; and they probably would not be publishers, if they were ambitious of martyrdom in any cause but that of self interest. Far be it from us to blame publishers for the course they take. Doubtless they are as worthy a class of cormorants as any other; and are perfectly right in humbugging those who will consent to patronize them on no other conditions." "This is not a question of ethics but of business," says another, an apologist.

We cannot help remarking that there must be a great deal of impudence on one side, or of demerit on the other, to warrant the officious advice and intermeddling in this humiliating way with a body of men, the publishers, who it might be supposed were as entitled to respect as any other particular class of the community. The whole pack, "Tray, Blanche and Sweetheart," the monthly, the twopenny, the threepenny, are not let loose all at once upon the whole body, even of the lawyers, who certainly get their full share of newspaper exhortation. An occasional medical practitioner is picked off, and the public is satisfied with, say, a steam doctor now and then, and is willing to admire the skill of the profession generally. If a divine turns fifth monarchist, millerite, Swedenborgian, or what not, he is whistled off handsomely, but churches remain, pulpits are filled, and the cloth respected. Even stock-brokers and tailors have something to be said for them, though, upon the whole, hopeless cases. Of the publisher alone, "there is none so poor to do him reverence," for we take the apologies we have quoted as pepper and salt to the scourgings.

The charges are immorality, quackery, and puffery, the facts are admitted, and the defence is, "tradesmanship."

The learned newspaper counsellors seem to lose sight in this matter of one very simple consideration, that publishers, whatever may be their accidental position in time and place, are, after all, men, and as individual human beings, governed by the laws which regulate the responsibility of the rest of the world. Publishers are therefore not likely to be all corrupt: some will have higher aims, a more delicate sense of right and wrong than others; nay, they will, and must upon the whole, be governed by honorable considerations. They do not need to shelter themselves under the plea of tradesmanship, as if trade sanctioned the pursuit of gain by any means, at the expense of any interests, human or divine. Trade, as we take it, is sustained, like everything else in the long run, by justice and honor. The career of evil must be short. We see virtue and industry every day triumphing, and fraud inevitably

leading to failure. On the trading principle, even as it exists, no dishonest publisher could stand. But the customs of society may allow many things which the enlightened individual judgment must disapprove of. Is the publisher exempt from this restraint? surely not. He will weigh every case, determine every point, and ask not what is expedient, but what will bear without putting him in Coventry, but what is right.

It is no apology for the publication of a corrupt book, that purchasers will be found for it, that a jewel may be got by scratching for it in the dunghill. The publisher is not to impose his peculiar tastes upon the community exclusively, and set up, by combination or otherwise, a censorship of the press; he is not to fetter opinion; if he has doubts about the propriety of "cakes and ale," he is not to forbid them because he is over scrupulous in his virtue; he need not tell a gentleman to walk out of his store because he differs from him on a point of theology. He is to be governed in all these things by the suggestions of common sense, if he would not be laughed at; but on a question of good morals he is certainly called upon to exercise his judgment. There can be no hesitation in the matter. If Lot had been a bookseller in Sodom, though surrounded by a unanimous company of sinners, and Voltaire had existed and written a few thousand years earlier, Lot would certainly not have published his writings. As for the matter of puffery, we may have something more to say of its natural history hereafter. At present the simple remark is sufficient, that no honorable publisher either does or can seek to defraud the public in this way; and that if any publisher should make the attempt, he will in no long while find out his blunder. The greatest injury a publisher can do his permanent interests is, to sacrifice them to the temporary advantage of a particular book or author. Success worth having cannot be matured on fraud.

In the relation borne by the American republisher to the foreign author, we see one of those cases, where, from insufficient legislation, what is in itself wrong, is yet perfectly legal. In the absence of an international copyright law, the republication of books is beset with peculiar difficulties. As the passage of such a law would not be retroactive in its operation, it follows that until the law is enacted the right to reprint all books is as perfect as it will be after the law to reprint those which do not then come under its operation. To republish Dickens now, for instance, is similar to such a republication of Shakspeare, to whose writings the law would not apply. No republisher can with any propriety, therefore, be branded as a pirate, a book thief, &c., terms which have been courteously lavished on the trade. There is, however, an equity in the matter which many of the large republishing houses recognise. We may name Harper and Brothers, Carey and Hart, Wiley and Putnam, and others, who have in some cases gone beyond the necessity of competition and paid the foreign author with liberality. They have shown in this, that publishing may be something else than "tradesmanship," as it is called.

The relation, under these circumstances, of the publisher to the American author, is one of yet greater difficulty. In all cases of doubt the true publisher will turn the scale in favor of the American writer. We believe this to be getting to be as good policy as it is good patriotism or anything else. American books will be before long the staple of the trade.

Every year the interest in the productions of Europe diminishes as the growth of this great Continent advances. If this strike any of our publishing friends with surprise, let him glance at the map and see over what extent of soil, under what varieties of climate, with what unprecedented physical circumstances a great nation is growing up, and let him ask himself how long such a people is likely to import its literature !

Reviews.

"In the best weekly reviews the public do not expect elaborate criticism—the object of the reviewer is novelty, arrangement, amusement—he wishes to give faithful accounts (which he generally does by extracts) of new publications; and doubtless this, after all, is the proper and exact duty of weekly reviews. Elaborate criticism is seldom light reading : and though the public might once a quarter, they certainly would not once a week permit themselves to be seriously instructed. Yet altogether the reviews in the best weekly publications are considerably fairer and truer than those in the quarterlies ; and in nine times out of ten produce a greater influence on the sale of the book."—BULWER.

The Lives of the Lord Chancellors and Keepers of the Great Seal of England, from the Earliest Times till the reign of King George IV. By John Lord Campbell, A.M., F.R.S.E. First series, to the Revolution of 1688, from the 2d Lond. ed. Philadelphia : Lea & Blanchard. 1847. 3 vols., 8vo.

THE Lives of the Chancellors of England !— how much paltry ambition, petty intrigues, slavish obsequiousness, and far-spread and long-enduring tyranny and extortion, do these words imply. To us, the offspring of the English nation, her history—too often the mere recital of the lusts and the usurpations of some detestable tyrant—has a charm unequalled ; for it is from the manliness and the indomitable spirit of a race, uncrushed by centuries of oppression, that we, and the world at large, now begin to enjoy better political hopes.

The Chancellor—whose state is so drolly described by Mr. Solomon Pell to Mr. Weller, Senior—the Chancellor, whose tyrannical power and practice have consigned many a poor suitor, even till within a few years back, for life, to a prison—the shadow and name of whose office have been transplanted to America —may very easily awaken an interest as strong as any other name of office. The history of the Chancellors gives perhaps a more lively picture of the times in which they lived, and the manners and social condition of the people, than could ever be gathered from the more dull account of State affairs, battle, and intrigue, which form the staple of history. The Lives of the Chancellors, in addition to that which belongs especially to the biographical part, contains incidentally a history of the law, generally consisting of a notice of the laws passed during the time they presided in Parliament. No better plan could have been devised to give a sketch of the most remarkable English subjects from the Conquest down, than to take the Chancellors, who have been for the most part self-made men, as the men ; and whose rise and public life would naturally embrace, as far as possible, all the phases of English life.

The style of the lives is clear, distinct, and even familiar, and there is a certain vein of dry waggishness that puts the reader very much at his ease with Ex-Chancellor Campbell, and is a proper sort of introduction to those official personages who have much of that chilliness and sense of personal danger about them which may be supposed to await a visitor in the chambers of the Inquisition. In fact, Lord Campbell's lack of respect, and

FIGURE 1.2. [Evert Duyckinck], "The Morality of Publishers" from the *Literary World*, Courtesy Library of Congress.

In the figure of the true publisher Duyckinck created a trade corollary for the true author. Like his authorial counterpart, who hovered above the dirty fray of hacks, the true publisher quietly and honorably went about his work despite the "corruption" of the reprint trade.[73] While the "dishonest" publisher was all too ready to profit off immorality because of his utilitarian ethics, the true publisher was incapable of doing so, even in the face of overwhelming temptation. Like the true author, the true publisher would not (that is, could not) sell out, because he was governed by "good morals" and not by economic expediency. He was disposed to good. Duyckinck spelled out that disposition, writing that the true publisher "will weigh every point, and ask not what is expedient, what society will bear without putting him in Coventry, but what is right." Duyckinck's faith in a commercial "equity" that would ultimately punish publisher-sinners and reward publisher-saints was a function of his belief that the character of the merchant was essentially moral. He believed that right and wrong could compel behavior in the same way as economics or the law. As early as 1839, when in discussion with William Jones about beginning the magazine that would become *Arcturus*, he felt he and Jones could do things differently and disprove the "old proverb that two of a trade can never agree."[74] "I do not see why we should not live together very happily," he wrote of the planned partnership. Duyckinck believed that business was fundamentally a moral field, a social endeavor in which each individual depended not just on the self-interest but also on the goodwill of others. He called this goodwill "the general buoyancy of trade," the state in which the individual's "efforts are united with those of others upon whom he may lean."[75] For Duyckinck, the collective moral disposition of true publishers forged a social space characterized more by right than by profit.

Duyckinck never said what he meant by "right." Nor did he ever speak explicitly about what exactly constituted "good morals." It is unlikely that he ever thought systematically about his beliefs. In this he would be typical. His extant papers suggest he shared with most Americans—and many tradesmen and publishers—the belief that morality was intuitive. In 1863 he wrote to Francis Lieber to congratulate his friend on the impending republication of a lecture Lieber had given in 1847 under the title "The Character of the Gentleman."[76] The letter is one of the few instances in which Duyckinck stated his ethics directly, defining the gentleman as a "man of feeling who instinctively puts himself in the situation of another, on the instant, and acts on his educated impulses."[77] Duyckinck's debt to sentimental mortality is plain. His ideal figure was not defined by reason, or by pragmatism, or even by that great sin of commerce, expediency, but by feeling what is right, the same ethic adopted by Putnam when he wrote to Harpers about its 1853 fire. The gentleman acted virtuously as a "result of study, personal experience, knowledge of the world and the human heart baptized in genuine Christian charity." Yet, like Emerson's natural merchant, the gentleman did so unthinkingly, Duyckinck told Lieber, mildly rebuking his friend's ill-compounded reliance on both objectivism and subjectivism, which made him look like a utilitarian. "A cultivated sympathetic imagination is," Duyckinck told Lieber, "the one faculty for the gentleman." Duyckinck's published writings suggest a belief that the trade, as constituted by numerous examples of the true publisher, boasted a kind of collective "sympathetic imagination" that tended toward fellowship. "There is . . . an equity in the matter [of reprinting] which many of the large republishing houses recognize," he wrote in "The Morality of Publishers." "We may name Harper and Brothers, Carey and Hart, Wiley and Putnam, and others, who have in some cases gone beyond the necessity of competition and paid the foreign author with liberality. They have shown in this, that publishing may be something else than 'tradesmanship,' as it is called." In fact, the "liberality" of Harpers and Carey was not so extensive. If these publishers recognized "equity in the matter," they did so unevenly and not because of any moral obligation, as Duyckinck would have it. Yet Duyckinck, like Putnam, nonetheless continued to believe.

In his study of the antebellum Protestant encounter with economics, Stewart Davenport finds two groups in addition to the clerical economists described earlier. The second group he calls the "contrarians," thinkers like Orestes Brownson who saw in the developing market economy "only the work of the devil."[78] The third group Davenport names the "pastoral moralists." These Protestant writers—among them, Orville Dewey, whom I discuss in Chapter 5 and with whom Melville associated Duyckinck in his fiction—did not argue that the economy was an unabashed good, but neither did they condemn it outright. They sought a "middle ground."[79] They understood, according to Davenport, that Americans "found themselves living" in a new world in which the competitive marketplace was almost impossible to ignore. That new reality did not mean that individuals should "use the complexity that the economy had brought into their lives as an excuse for immoral behavior."[80] People ought not to allow the demands of the market to hurt themselves or others.[81] According to "The Morality of Publishers," the true publisher, the natural merchant of the book business, would never allow it.

Just after midnight on New Year's Day 1848, Duyckinck reflected somberly to his brother on the importance of "imperishable virtue." He was thinking about an uncomplimentary article about a friend he had pulled at the last minute from copy for an upcoming issue of the *Literary World*. The friend had died and Duyckinck was relieved he had not let the article go to press. "By that forbearance may I be thus dealt with. No man repents of an act of faith or charity," he wrote. "Better be now and then deceived than unjust, as the law lets the guilty escape rather than punish the innocent."[82] Duyckinck had not allowed business to eclipse principle. He believed that others in the trade did the same, at least more often than not. When they did allow principle to succumb to profit, the trade was not to blame so much as the errant individual. According to the kinds of stories the trade told about itself, those errant individuals were few and far between. Indeed, according to the stories, which would appear again and again in the pages of trade journals and more popular magazines, Benjamin Franklin had begotten a race of publishers in the United States unequaled in character.

THE TRIUMPH OF VIRTUE: THE TRADE IN THEORY

A few weeks before Duyckinck spoke to his brother of "imperishable virtue," his friend Thomas Delf wrote him to talk shop about the New York trade. "Of the nothingness of its present condition in the unhallowed hands which monopolize it I think," Delf presumed, "we are tolerably agreed."[83] It was a safe presumption.

Duyckinck had had a difficult year. He had been fired from his post as editor of the *Literary World* not long after writing "The Morality of Publishers" because of a disagreement with the magazine's publishers, William Appleton and John Wiley. Though he had returned to his post by December, he felt he had been used poorly. Still Duyckinck refused to condemn the trade outright. "You must not think because American publishers are not the cheeriest fellows in the world and since newspapers are quicksands and trade a rat trap that there's no living in America," he wrote to his brother, who was then in Europe. "There are cakes and ale even if Griswolds, Wileys, Appletons, &c are *not* virtuous."[84] He was quite aware that the conduct of some in the trade was wanting in gentlemanly feeling. But at the same time he badly wanted the trade to be good. The problem is that in his public writings Duyckinck worked backward from prescription to description. Most of the trade press did as well, confusing what ought to be with what was.

Gail Hamilton understood this confusion well. She barely exaggerated when she joked that "time and scissors would fail me to cull from the journals all the ingenious paragraphs which show" the selflessness of Ticknor and Fields.[85] She might have said that about any number of the firms that were praised in issue after issue of American magazines and newspapers and especially, as might be expected, in trade journals. Publisher Mark H. Newman, for example, was described as "an intelligent and liberal philanthropist."[86] The house of Carter and Brothers was "sagacious" and "honorable."[87] D. Appleton and Company was "honorably distinguished for the good taste and careful morality displayed in its selections for publication." Law book publisher Banks, Gould, and Company's prosperity was the result of "patient labor, united to habits of temperance and strict integrity." Harper and Brothers never published anything to offend anyone's morals.[88] Roberts Brothers was "as fairly distinguished for their courteous and honorable business habits as for [their] good taste and sound judgment."[89] The *Atlantic Monthly* summed it up: "There are no business men more honorable or more generous than the publishers of the United States."[90]

Nineteenth-century publishers liked to draw a direct line of descent from their moral ancestor "B. Franklin, Printer" to themselves. As one magazine asked, what other businessmen could trace their lineage to an uneducated man of "wondrous humanity" who gave to Philadelphia libraries, newspapers, colleges, and charity hospitals; gave to the nation liberty; and gave to the world electricity?[91] Franklin was proof positive that "the publishers were ahead of the scholars, and the authors, and the politicians."[92] He was the progenitor of all things material and immaterial, the Adam from whom sprang fully formed the moral character of the trade. In an 1852 history of American publishing, one tradesman mapped out the genealogy: Duyckinck's father "faithfully carried out the proverbs of Franklin, and the sayings of Noah Webster's *Prompter*," which counseled young men to do "as much good as possible."[93] The elder Duyckinck, in turn, "gave to the Harpers the first job of printing they executed."[94] Finally the little "acorn" of that once-insignificant firm grew up to become "the pride of the forest—the Cliff-street tree, whose roots and branches now ramify all the land." Who else but Franklin could inspire an army of young men to enter the trade? One was John Francis, the author of the family tree above, who first encountered Franklin's "wondrous character" at age ten.[95] Another was James Harper, who read Franklin around the same age and then left the family farm for New York. There he founded "the pride of the forest," Harper and Brothers, and published books by classical moralists like Seneca and by merchant moralists like Jonathan Dymond, whose *Essays on the Principles of Morality* the firm reprinted in the United States in 1834, inspiring Freeman Hunt's theory of commercial morality and thus helping to redefine the image of American business.[96]

Franklin loomed large in the trade's idea of itself. So did other figures. Isaiah Thomas snuck his presses out of Boston on the eve of the Revolution in order to aid the cause from afar. Then there was Mathew Carey, whose struggle against Catholic repression in his native Ireland landed him in America, where he continued his education as a printer under Franklin himself before returning to Ireland. He came back to the United States for good in 1784 and quickly became an influential member of the print trade, not to mention an upright citizen of Philadelphia. Carey was one of Freeman Hunt's model businessmen in his *Lives of American Merchants* (1857), where he was praised as a man of "unceasing industry, perseverance, and integrity," whose "rigid mercantile integrity" required him to conduct business "the right way."[97] (Hunt's description failed to note that Carey essentially disinherited his own children after nearly bankrupting his family, or that he tried to sabotage his son Henry's publishing career.)[98]

Compared with the death-defying charity and hair-raising political escapades of Carey's biography—he fled England disguised in a dress, nearly killed a man in a duel, remained in Philadelphia to help the sick during the city's yellow fever epidemic of 1793, and campaigned for social justice for the poor—the life of publisher James Brown, which was also featured in Hunt's *Lives of American Merchants*, was less romantic but no less instructive. Born into a rural Massachusetts farming family, Brown left home after the death of his father and made his way to Cambridge in search of work. He found it as a domestic in the home of a Harvard professor. *Lives of American Merchants* took pains to stress that Brown never spoke of this position as degrading, even after he amassed his fortune; for him, "like every other relation between man and man," the job was less important than the "spirit that animates it."[99] Brown so impressed the professor that he considered paying his servant's way to college. He would not need to, because the trade got him first. Out for a Sunday walk in 1818, Brown found himself face to face with Boston publisher William Hilliard, who had heard of the young man's "moral worth" and offered him a job on the spot.[100] Hilliard must have liked the boy's face, too. According to Brown's biographer, "An Arab in the desert would have trusted such a face with uncounted diamonds."[101] Judging by the number of times they appear in memoirs, honest faces were a stock-in-trade for publishers.

In this way James Brown, the intelligent but sickly domestic with the honest face, entered publishing. He slowly and steadily learned the business from Hilliard. His apprenticeship involved no plagues, no revolutions. Unlike William Gowans, he never piloted a raft on the Mississippi; unlike Isaiah Thomas, he never fled an invading army; unlike Mathew Carey, he never met, much less learned his craft, from Benjamin Franklin himself, or selflessly aided Franklin's beloved Philadelphians when they were dying of yellow fever.[102] Brown's trials were more mundane. They were the kinds of trials tradespeople faced every day of their working lives—the fiery furnace, as trade moralists would have it, that refined the merchant's character. "His progress was not very rapid, nor were his gains large. He was not of a scheming and speculating turn: the foundations of his success were laid slowly and deeply in industry, economy, sagacity, and a rigid adherence to plain and safe rules in the conduct of business."[103] Brown could afford to wait, his biographer explains, because his character guaranteed his eventual success, "as the oak is of the acorn."[104] By the time of his death almost forty years later, his own firm, Little, Brown and Company, would be one of the most successful in the United States, and Brown would be immortalized by Freeman Hunt as one of America's quintessential merchant moralists. It was as though he stepped from out of the pages of Freedley's *Practical Treatise on Business*—a not-so-larger-than-life example of what was possible when "the manners of a gentleman" were combined with "the habits of a man of business."[105] Here was a natural merchant whose morality was not compromised but deepened by his industry. Brown was one of Duyckinck's true publishers, a tradesman driven by "charity, sympathy, and love" rather than self-interest, expediency, and profit, and who was unafraid to show his "beautiful soul."[106]

This was all a little much, but then *Lives of American Merchants* was more hagiography than biography. That was the point. The American merchant was an exemplar. Duyckinck and others applied this reasoning to publishing, arguing, as Hunt and Freedley did for the merchant generally, that if the individual publisher were moral, then the character of the trade at large must be moral, and so on until one reached the character of the nation's commerce as a whole.

Late nineteenth- and early twentieth-century publishers tended to look back on the early trade, as Donald Sheehan has said, with "mist in the eyes."[107] Massachusetts publisher Theodore Bliss did not. "I must not idealize those times . . . beyond a fair estimate," Bliss wrote of his beginnings in the mid-nineteenth century. "It was not the 'golden age.' We rather enjoyed hearing the Ten Commandments read, and felt the need of their application to the lives of our neighbors. As a code of human conduct, with the thunders of divine sanction, we esteemed them highly, but we broke them every day."[108] While he noted that business excesses were not looked upon kindly in the days of Brown, Putnam, and Duyckinck, even recounting his own success at reforming the character of a wayward partner, Bliss insisted that publishers spent more time shining their halos than earning them.

THE FAILURE OF CIVILITY: THE TRADE IN FACT

Bliss's reference to Christian ethics is revealing. It attests to the reality that no one could possibly be as virtuous as the trade made itself out to be. In the absence of some governing, inherent virtue, rules were required. It also attests to the fact that, by and large, these rules, these deontological ethics, were ineffective. Publishers' archives confirm Bliss's view. They describe everything from delinquent bills to slip-shod tradesmanship to lying competitors. Efforts to resolve trade conflicts could be messy, and they suggest that the myths of the natural merchant and true publisher, while pervasive, were far from the mark. In 1795, New York printer James Rivington wondered how it was that a package of books he had long-since requested from Thomas Bradford was found in a postal warehouse, where, Rivington's servant was told, Bradford had never paid for the delivery. "I suggest," Rivington wrote in a post-script, "demanding receipts from the Stage owners on the delivering of every parcel."[109] In a subsequent letter, Rivington requested that Bradford enlist the aid of an "attentive attorney" to sue the stage owner.[110] Bradford, the son and business partner of the late William Bradford, one of the most respected printers of the eighteenth century, surely already knew this necessity—unpredictable and unreliable postal service was an everyday reality—and thus would not have appreciated Rivington's charge that he had behaved incompetently or, for that matter, the implication that he had acted less than honorably. In an 1834 exchange with a bookseller whose out-standing bills spanned nearly two years, Henry Carey's frustration with his fellow tradesman boiled over. "Under such circumstances what course could we pursue other than the one we have taken?" he asked the bookseller indignantly, assuring him that he made it a rule to be forgiving within reason. But the language of the bookseller's letters apparently left much to be desired. "That you have not given us that satisfaction can be readily shown by some of your late letters—The art of which has been almost equivalent to 'Do what you like, I do not care a dxxn for you.'"[111] Elizabeth Peabody was equally distressed by the obstructively self-interested behavior of her fellow tradespeople. Tethered to short credit leashes by large firms like Wiley and Putnam, she and other small-time dealers complained that the large houses cared only about profit.

Printing occasioned especially dramatic clashes. "Your printers have used us very ill indeed," Carey and Lea wrote James Fenimore Cooper in February 1826 as the firm attempted to get a handle on the publication of *The Last of the Mohicans*. The printers had not delivered the sheets as promised, and now Carey and Lea was trying to contain the damage. "We have rarely known," the firm wrote, "greater misconduct in a printer."[112] Printers' increased numbers and changing occupational identities—the transformation of some printers into publishers—contributed to the labor strife. But even before this shift, relations were rarely harmonious, as illustrated by a letter from Hugh Gaine to Isaiah Thomas in 1789 lamenting fellow printers' efficiency at underselling one another and doubting whether they could be controlled through regulation.[113] Gaine's comments were prescient. Imposing morals on the trade via regulation yielded mixed and sometimes violent results. Indeed, labor historians categorize printing as a "conflict trade" because it was prone to the kind of unrest that broke out in 1835 when rival groups of journeyman printers came to blows in the streets of Washington, D.C.[114] Though the causes were systemic, the unrefined character of these freelance printers was usually blamed. One master printer in upstate New York grumbled to Rufus Griswold that for every decent journeyman there were "nine clowns who ought to be tied to the plough and the flail, and who would, if possible, disgrace even those agricultural implements. Oh for the days of Faust, when there were not above two printers and a half in the world!—better [there] be but devilish few, if they must be so diabolically ignorant."[115]

Booksellers' unions illustrated the difficulty of regulating behavior via a deontological ethics.[116] The Boston Association of Booksellers was born in 1801 and died by "nearly unanimous" consent in 1820.[117] Its goals were typical: to address the "want of system" in the trade, that is, to rein in the capitalistic impulses of individual members via "proper regulations," as well as to establish "confidence in each other."[118] One of the few things members could agree on was that cooperation was impossible. They caught one another violating the principles of cooperation again and again— everything from absenteeism to undercutting prescriptions on discounts to making deals behind one another's backs. The actions of Cummings and Hilliard, which was found to exceed the allowable discount for libraries, exposed the union's fault lines. The firm acknowledged wrongdoing and was disciplined, but it never provided "sufficient excuse" for its behavior. It neither explained why it knowingly violated the rules nor apologized for doing so.[119] But the firm did suggest that the union's principles were a farce in the face of commercial pressures.

By 1817, complaints that some members interpreted association rules more liberally than others were frequent and loud.[120] Discipline problems multiplied. If members had to be told to stay at meetings past roll call, how could anyone expect them to follow price controls in their business dealings?[121] In 1820, the union disbanded after an ad hoc committee concluded that voluntary trade associations were a kind of anathema. "There seems to exist," the committee observed, "a necessity for each member to be at liberty to act for himself in transacting his Business, unshackled by existing Rules & Regulations."[122] The imagery is instructive. The association obstructed the freedom of businessmen to make money by chaining them to injunctions that unnaturally constrained such natural impulses. A trade catalog published by Cummings and Hilliard after the dissolution reiterated the lesson for the trade, presumably addressing questions from other cities about the fate of the association. "At length restraint became irksome, the bands were burst, and the shackles of by-laws thrown aside."[123] It was another revolution, albeit quieter than the one for which Boston was best known. More to the point, its logic flew in the face of the archetype of the true publisher, for whom economic gamesmanship was supposedly always checked by inward principle.

The language of the Boston Association of Booksellers records is especially interesting in light of the early nineteenth-century practice of blacklisting those who violated union rules. In 1809, the New York Typographical Society proposed to exchange with its Philadelphia counterpart their "rats," as these miscreants were known. It acknowledged the presence of businessmen who, having laid "aside those principles of honor and good faith which ought to govern their conduct," upset their "obligations" to the trade by seeking "mere gratification of private interest." Noting that "nothing . . . acts more powerfully on the human mind than shame," the New York society asked Philadelphia to disclose the names of journeyman printers who had left for New York under suspicion or because of outright violation of union bylaws. In essence, New York was asking for a heads-up on printers who were "wanting" in character.[124] The president of the Philadelphia union noted his opposition to the proposal but was voted down in favor of abiding the request.[125] Evidently there were just too many in the trade wanting in character.

Like trade associations and their guild mentality, trade sales encouraged good relations in order to control stock and prices.[126] It was Henry Carey who modernized the practice beginning in 1824. Brought up in the trade—it was said that his father Mathew Carey sent little Henry at the age of twelve to Baltimore to superintend his interests there, a feat that earned the boy the moniker, the "Miniature Bookseller"—Carey spent much of his publishing career looking for ways to minimize conflict and increase profit.[127] The trade sale was an effective scheme. Inherited from Europe, it brought together tradesmen under a set of rules intended to protect the interests of all and provided them a sense of vocational community.[128] For many publishers such connections could not happen often enough. Encouraging a sense of community among tradespeople helped prevent the kinds of disputes that, for good reason, gave the trade a reputation for artful dealing.

The first trade sale in the United States was held in New York City on June 4, 1802. Hugh Gaine opened the sale with a patriotic speech that in many ways prefigured the celebratory industrial independence that Americans trumpeted after the War of 1812. Noting the role domestic paper manufacturing played in making the trade more independent than most other manufacturing sectors, Gaine lauded printing as a vanguard of American industry. In veiled language he also spoke of the challenges facing it. One was the fact that unless American printers could produce large editions of works, any advantage they had over imported texts was erased. Hence the necessity of trade sales, at which booksellers could unload unsold copies. Seemingly incongruously, Gaine then embarked on a vision of the trade—one that had predominated since the Revolution and would continue to do so through the mid-nineteenth century—as the guardian "stand[ing] in the gap between our country and the torrent of impiety which rages to overwhelm her."[129] Gaine warned those in attendance against seeking unfair advantage, of forsaking trade and country, of "sink[ing] the patriot into the dealer." Booksellers must respect one another's editions for trade and thus the nation to thrive. In this way "security" would emerge: "a security founded on the strong basis of self-interest,—and which will prove to us all, by happy experience, that"—quoting Alexander Pope and prefiguring Hunt, Freedley, Emerson, and Duyckinck—"'true self-love and social, are the same.'"

The trade sale also put a good face on strained internal relations and questions about the character of those who represented the trade. *Norton's Literary Gazette* depicted an 1853 trade sale as the best of all possible worlds. At the New York offices of Bangs and Company, across from Central Park and adjacent to Astor Place, the auctioneer rose to introduce Harper and Brothers. James Harper was on hand and joined the auctioneer on the platform. The ruling hand behind one of the most powerful publishing houses in the world and a former mayor of New York City, Harper was something of a celebrity. He dutifully played the part of the affable businessman and trade emissary: "The Honorable James, neatly clad in sombre black, with spectacles on nose . . . rises with great solemnity, and bows three times very profoundly to all present, at which all present immediately burst into three violent roars of laughter and stomp prodigiously. This proceeding throws the honorable gentleman himself into a bland and appreciating smile, and he makes a brief speech expressive of the thanks of himself and 'brethren' for the 'kindness always evinced toward a humble house like theirs, which is endeavoring to get an honest living.'"[130] James Harper's behavior was as much a performance as the article itself. The "five or six hundred gentlemen" in attendance were quite aware that Harper and Brothers was anything but a "humble house," quite aware that the firm was honest only when honesty served its interests. Just as in the 1830s, the firm refused to formally join an association of publishers, though this did not stop Harpers from attempting to tweak the trade to better serve its interests. The New York Book-Publishers' Association told the firm that its ideas might receive a more enthusiastic reception if it would condescend to play consistently and, better yet, play fair.[131]

Trade sales did encourage "a certain freemasonry," Theodore Bliss recalled, but the spirit seldom survived longer than the sales themselves.[132] Once the individual businessmen returned to their counting rooms out of the public eye, all bets were off. That was the real character of the trade. What Bliss recognized was that the trade was governed neither by "inward principle" nor by civilities, or rules. Nevertheless, as the final section of this chapter suggests, both theories carried on, at least through the Civil War era.

TRADE COURTESY: A MOST EXQUISITELY ORGANIZED SYSTEM OF IMMORALITY

In 1867, James Parton opened a long article on international copyright with an anecdote about "an American lady living at Hartford, Connecticut." She had been taken for a ride by the government, which had "permitted her to be robbed of $200,000. Her name is Harriet Beecher Stowe. By no disloyal act has she or her family forfeited their right to the protection of the government of the United States. She pays her taxes, keeps the peace, and earns her livelihood by honest industry; she has reared children for the service of the Commonwealth; she was warm and active for her country when many around her were cold or hostile;—in a word, she is a good citizen."[133] Parton blamed the government, not publishers, for Stowe's misfortune at the hands of foreign reprinters. Publishers had long argued that international copyright was a moral necessity, he said. Even Harpers wanted it; Parton knew because one of the brothers had told him so. Harpers, he swore, "is not now, and has never been" against international copyright.[134]

Actually, Harper and Brothers was and had long been opposed to international copyright. The year after Parton published his article, the firm was invited to respond to copyright legislation pending in Congress. It submitted a detailed brief outlining its opposition. Harpers was surprised that "under the existing business and financial difficulties of the country" Congress would waste its time (again) on such an "abstract question."[135] In the letter accompanying its brief, Harpers said it was "more convinced than ever" that the law would be "disastrous."[136] Given the number of times Harper and Brothers was caught in a lie—Henry Carey was especially touchy about Harpers' habit of bending the truth—it is likely that Parton really was told by someone that the firm supported reform.[137] Even its congressional brief began disingenuously: "As far as we are concerned, personally, it will make little or no difference, whether there is or is not an International Copyright Law."[138]

At the time, Parton was the secretary for a group of writers and publishers pressing for international copyright. The minutes of the group's 1868 meetings suggest the extent to which advocates saw copyright as a character issue. It was, the group decided, "time that the moral sense of the Community rose to overthrow" reprinters like Harpers.[139] The fight would be difficult. The coffers of the antireform lobby were full. But on the side of reformers was something more valuable: "intelligence, virtue and righteousness." Because "honesty invariably triumphed over dishonesty," and because "dishonest men were an exception to the human rule," it was only a matter of time before a new copyright law was enacted.[140] It is noteworthy how little the rhetoric had changed since international copyright first became a public issue in the 1830s and 1840s, when reformers like Cornelius Mathews had proclaimed that the trade needed to "return to the contrary course of moral honesty."[141] Then, too, reformers had believed that it was only a matter of time before Congress realized its moral obligation.

Parton's progressivism fit well with such views. Despite the copyright situation, he did not doubt the fundamental morality of the trade any more than he doubted the morality of American commerce generally. In a speech a few years later titled "The Pilgrim Fathers as Men of Business," he noted that the theory that the moral self was indistinguishable from the economic self—in Max Weber's formulation, that the "devotion to the calling of making money" had become a virtue—was as old as English settlement in North America.[142] New England's Puritan forebears were moral "capitalists."[143] Publishers were no different, Parton said in the *Atlantic Monthly*. Engaged in the world's "most difficult" business, they were interested only in good because they were themselves good men.[144]

It was because of his belief in this inherent virtue that Parton disliked what was perhaps the most common attempt at trade regulation, "courtesy of the trade."[145] Trade courtesy was an imported European custom that gave printers and publishers the exclusive right to texts they were the first to declare an intention to reproduce. It had been around the United States for some time in different forms. In the early years of the nineteenth century the Booksellers Company of Philadelphia, presided over by Mathew Carey, stipulated that members must respect the "exclusive privi-lege" of other members who registered with the group's secretary their intention to publish a book.[146] But in the 1830s trade courtesy began to evolve. Four more criteria were eventually adopted in various forms: a publisher with an existing publishing relationship with a foreign writer had an exclusive right to reprint future works; a publisher who purchased advance sheets had the right to publish the book; a pub-lisher could buy and sell these rights in a kind of open market; and publishers had the right to retaliate if "printed upon," that is, if a competitor violated one of these rules.[147] Grudgingly, Parton admitted "a kind of justice in all these rules." They showed publishers "feeling their way to" an ethic in the "chaos of conflicting claims" that was the reprint trade.

Nevertheless, he blasted the cure that was trade courtesy nearly as hard as he blasted the disease that was unauthorized reprinting. Reprinting, for all its utilitari-anism, was immoral enough, but trade courtesy encouraged even greater immorality. For instance, how were publishers to regulate one another except through "venge-ance"? The records of Carey and Lea bear out this criticism. "We wish to avoid all interference with any one & hope that others will do the same by us," Carey wrote to a rival before reminding him that the so-called honorable practices of the trade were not without teeth. "If, however, we are interfered with we shall continue to do as we have usually done in such cases, that is, to return the favour."[148] And what was to prevent larger houses like Harper and Brothers from simply declaring an intent to publish every British novel it knew of, regardless of whether it actually intended to reprint any of them? "In the most exquisitely organized system of piracy," Parton wrote, "no man can rely upon the enjoyment of a right which he is not strong enough personally to defend." In sum, you cannot impose morality.

Most troublesome for Parton was the very notion of "rights" under trade courtesy, because these rights were not really rights at all. "No man knows what his rights are; nor whether he has any rights; nor whether there *are* any rights; nor, if he has rights, whether they will be respected."[149] Again, Carey and Lea's struggles in the 1830s evi-dence the logic of Parton's critique. After Harper and Brothers effectively prevented the firm from publishing titles it might have profited from and then tried to play the injured party, Carey rebuked Harpers for its morality of expedience. "There is not a single right or principle admitted among Booksellers, or asserted by yourselves," Carey pointed out, "that has not been contradicted by you in Practice when it suited you to do so, & *reasserted* afterwards when it was for your interest that they sh[ould] govern." For this reason, he would no longer "argue or discuss abstract rights or principles" with the New York firm, since it seemed that these rights somehow always favored Harpers.[150] Carey's mistake in pressing trade courtesy in the 1830s, according to Parton's logic, was that Carey assumed that trade morality could be imposed from without. It was a belief that informed Carey's second career as an economist and his influential theories of economic protectionism.

Parton did not believe in trade courtesy because he held that in matters of moral duty the individual should be self-regulating. That is, virtue ethics trumped deontological ethics; trade morality came from within the individual. To Parton, trade courtesy assumed that the natural state of publishing was one of unceasing war. It assumed that without international copyright or some kind of governing rule, publishers would spend their days fighting one another just to preserve their existence. Parton did not believe this. Like Duyckinck, he believed the opposite: that the natural state of the trade was one of collaboration and morality. Trade courtesy "scarcely mitigates the game [of reprinting] at all," he wrote, and "instead of the friendly feeling that would naturally exist among honorable men in the highest branch of business, we find feuds, heart-burnings, and a grievous sense of wrongs unredressed and unredressable." His article was "The Morality of Publishers" all over again. True publishers will out, if they only get the chance.

The Evert Duyckincks and James Partons of the world could say what they liked about the native virtue of the trade. There were plenty of observers who suggested that the character of the trade was no better than the codes of conduct reformers sought to impose upon it. And if these were ineffective, all the more reason to despair. Thomas Wentworth Higginson told a story about a "most eminent literary man" who as a farm boy was given a calf to sell.[151] Looking back, the man would recall the overwhelming desire to defraud potential buyers, or in Higginson's words, "the intense temptation to extort more than the animal was strictly worth, and to contrive little plots to conceal its defects and exaggerate its merits." While the experience taught the man to be "charitable" toward those trying to defraud him, it also schooled him in the fundamental "baseness of commerce." What was good for the soul, Higginson concluded, was not, by definition, what was good for trade. No matter how righteous the individual, commerce had a "tendency to accustom the soul to a lower standard of virtue."

For Higginson, ethics like trade courtesy were preconditions for a just commerce. But for a writer in the *Southern and Western Monthly Magazine*, "no courtesies of the trade could control parties who had so little scruple in the common spoliation of the author."[152] The next chapter considers the moral scruples of the Revolutionary era print trade, the supposed "spoliation" of one of its most famous authors, Thomas Paine, by one of its most infamous printers, Robert Bell, and what it all has to do with one of the most remarkable documents in American history.

2

Liberty in Business: The Printing of *Common Sense*

LECTURING BRITISH COLONIALS on the motives for revolution and registering the immediacy of insurgency, Thomas Paine's *Common Sense* focused on political change through the conventional lens of communal morality. "Society is produced by our wants," Paine preached, "and government by our wickedness."[1] *Common Sense* set out to parse that wickedness, and its effect was sensational. The pamphlet was one of the most successful publications in American history. It made revolution right and printers all but giddy with profit. But the circumstances of its production were sensational as well, or at least sensationalistic. The publication of *Common Sense* erupted into a spectacle in the early months of 1776. Paine had contracted with a Philadelphia printer named Robert Bell to print *Common Sense* but then, fearing he was being cheated out of profits and worried about the control his printer exercised over his production, demanded that Bell cease issuing the work after one edition. Bell refused. In response, Paine published complaints about the printer's behavior in the *Pennsylvania Evening Post*, which in turn became the venue for a tabloid war of words between author and printer. There, Paine argued that the trade, like government, was a function of our wickedness.

The contest and its language were timely. British colonialism made the business of print a messy and sometimes dangerous affair for authors and for printers. The latter had to navigate the legal ambiguities of colonial copyright as well as the shifting landscape of political allegiances, all the while trying to conduct their business profitably. The former, of course, navigated the same landscape and worked under the same ambiguous notions of literary property. However, at least under the umbrella ethos of republicanism, they were not supposed to care about fortune and fame, or even about having property in their productions. But some authors did care. And in caring they came in conflict with businessmen who had to care about these things for a living and whose reputation for protecting both profit and property often called their character into question. Young Benjamin Franklin was one such businessman, and as printer of the *Pennsylvania Gazette* he was fond of reciting trade slogans he overheard in the Philadelphia streets, slogans like "'tis a Pity Lying is a Sin, it is so useful in Trade."[2] Too often, as Franklin and others lamented, tradesmen deemed morality incompatible with business.

My broad interest in this chapter is how the conduct of authors and printers reflected competing attitudes toward morality in the late colonial and early national trade. Following historians such as John E. Crowley and Daniel Vickers, whose work investigates the contemporary beliefs and attitudes shaping social practice, as well as the work of Adrian Johns on the cultural and moral conventions of printing, I too wonder if "our knowledge of economic behavior and social structure in early America has far outdistanced our understanding of the values that infused them."[3] I want to argue that the debate over the publication of *Common Sense* was itself a debate over these values. I approach this argument in three parts, first discussing trade values in reference to more general understandings of morality in late eighteenth-century society. This section dovetails with Chapter 1 in its recital of the debate over commercial morality, but it also isolates the uniquely eighteenth-century aspects of that debate. Part two looks in detail at the controversy over *Common Sense*. The argument over the pamphlet's production illustrates not only the place of moral values in author-trade relations but also the small amount of control early writers had over their vocational lives, a fact we would do well to remember as we continue to underappreciate what has been called the "monstrous contingency" of authors in commercial societies.[4] Bell exposed what Bourdieu calls the "ideology of creation," which makes the author the first and last source of the value of his work and obscures the role played by the "cultural businessman" in creating such value.[5] Part three examines Paine's political discourse beyond *Common Sense*, reading it as a commentary on the tyranny of custom, a tyranny exercised by printers as much as kings. The morality informing revolution, Paine argued, should also inform the relationship of author and trade. The former was principled, defined by a virtue ethics; the latter pretended to be principled, defined by pragmatic customs. Michael Warner speaks of the "cliché" of eighteenth-century republicanism: its representation of "liberty as imperiled by rulers and requiring vigorous civic exertion against their ever-threatening encroachment."[6] Paine's political philosophy easily satisfies this cliché, of course, especially as set out in *Common Sense*. But Paine also recast the cliché by applying it to the business of print, where, in his view, authorial and national liberty was endangered by the immorality of printers.

VIRTUE AND CUSTOM IN THE LATE EIGHTEENTH-CENTURY TRADE

Despite historical models that posit a progressive shift toward individualism in the eighteenth century, colonials continued to subscribe to a community ethos based in virtue and morality, broadly defined.[7] The legal codes of the period, for example, reflected what historians call an "ethical sense of the community."[8] Even colonial criminal law existed to shore up a social moral cohesion rather than to "segregate and punish a distinct, identifiable, and downtrodden criminal class."[9] Property rights, too, were premised on the understanding that land (and, for that matter, books) was best used to benefit the community at large. Economics were, in other words, an ethical matter. "Views on the relationship between self and society were at the very core of considerations about men's livelihoods and appeared in almost every sort of economic discussion," Crowley writes. While we "might assume that such matters were susceptible to technical economic analysis, colonial spokesmen did not accept such situations as the unavoidable consequences of economic life itself and interpreted them instead with a view toward the morality of individuals' behavior."[10] Exercising choice among alternatives, individuals acted independently but in ways reflecting their ideas of the good. That is, they could act by principles, however vaguely defined, of right and wrong, and did so more than we tend to think. As Gordon S. Wood notes, "modern virtue flowed from the citizen's participation in society."[11] The orientation to moral virtue for the benefit of the community at large was as true for the cobbler as it was for the merchant.

This emphasis on moral virtue influenced the ways political theorists and pamphleteers envisioned eighteenth-century commercial life. In the popular conception of a moral economy, commerce was value-laden. Trade was as much a matter of a person's and a society's moral being as it was of formal, legal regulation. The volume and popularity of eighteenth-century ethical tracts subordinating commercial behavior to value judgments illustrate the resonance of communal moral economics. "Let your attendance in business be constant, your commodities good, the prices reasonable, and your deportment civil," one trade conduct manual counseled. Its author, William Dover, repeated an oft-heard suggestion, "Keep sacred thy Credit . . . by speaking and writing clearly and truly concerning thy self and all Men, as well as by acting sincerely respecting them."[12] The emphasis on good credit, as printers discovered in their domestic and transatlantic dealings, indicated the extent to which a tradesman understood his role in the wider economic community. And that economic community was part of an ethical universe larger than any professional sphere. A "tradesman ought no more tell a Lie in his Shop," Dover wrote, perhaps with intentional irony, "than a Parson in a Pulpit."[13]

The coupling of morality and trade was a principal dogma of eighteenth-century political economists and of prominent citizens such as Benjamin Rush, who put commerce "next to religion in humanizing mankind."[14] It likewise steered Thomas Paine's economic theories. Throughout his life he argued that too often government at best suppressed and at worst extinguished communal morality by constraining the individual's natural tendency toward moral commercial behavior.[15] "All the great laws of society," Paine proposed in *Rights of Man* (1791–92), "are laws of nature. Those of trade and commerce, whether with respect to the intercourse of individuals or of nations, are laws of mutual and reciprocal interest. They are followed and obeyed, because it is the interest of the parties to do so, and not on account of any formal laws their governments may impose or interpose."[16] Trade behavior was thus a function of human nature, a supposition that worked in tandem with the Enlightenment belief in the power of individual self-interest to regulate and perpetuate the resources of the state. Ingrained within the natural proclivity of the individual—in his character—trade morality was equivalent to good citizenship.[17]

In practice, colonial trade behavior was also a matter of custom. Inherited from England and other older colonial outposts such as Ireland, commercial customs passed down largely and most dramatically through immigrant artisans and merchants who brought to the new world old-world rituals of conduct.[18] The colonial economic and social landscape possessed, in the words of one historian, "the thick infrastructure of a settled social being."[19] Operating under codes of behavior defined by instinct and social custom rather than legal statute, eighteenth-century colonial commerce was a world where "right" and "wrong" were, as Paine himself theorized, tacit rather than categorical.[20] Few trades better demonstrate the role of custom than printing. Although colonial print culture was far from lawless, it nevertheless functioned largely outside legal frameworks taken for granted by later writers and publishers. It likewise functioned largely outside written codes of conduct that applied to the trade as a whole. Like the early modern printers, late eighteenth-century printers drew up terms of indenture for apprentices and contracts for journeymen, but these agreements reveal little about the implicit codes of conduct that structured the relations and behavior between and among printers and authors. Nor do they tell us much about the values underwriting these codes. For these implicit values it helps to turn to the writings and correspondence of the printers themselves.

Among the most pervasive and comprehensive of these values was honor. Prominent printers such as Franklin and his partner David Hall explicitly professed a concern for honor in the trade. In the *Autobiography*, Franklin paused a moment at the outset of the tale of his trade initiation. "Before I enter upon my public Appearance in Business, it may be well to let you know the then State of my Mind, with regard to my Principles and Morals."[21] Finding religious definitions of "Vice" and "Virtue" "empty," he settled on the creed that "Truth, Sincerity and Integrity in Dealings between Man and Man, were of the utmost Importance to the Felicity of Life."[22] For Franklin, as for most printers, and as for colonials at large, one proved these occupational pieties through one's actions. As printer James Holt wrote—ironically, in an attack on Franklin's own alleged hypocrisy and want of character—"a Man's Actions [are] the only sure Criterions of his Character."[23] Elsewhere, in a letter to infamous fellow printer James Rivington, Holt suggested that the "Nature of the Printing Business" is defined by honor and civility.[24] We find a more explicit testimony in Hall's letter to Franklin regarding their business partnership. "I flatter myself that my Conduct . . . is satisfactory to you," Hall wrote in 1759, "for I can, with great Truth, say I have never done anything, either with respect to public or private Business, but with a View to please all Parties."[25] Joanne Freeman has argued that in the

"maelstrom of discontent" that was early national political life there was nevertheless "a method to the madness." "Disagree as men might on the purpose, structure,
or tenor of national governance . . . clash as they must about the future of the
nation—they expected their opponents to behave like gentlemen."[26] As in politics,
so in printing. There was justice and virtue in reciprocity and success in honor.

By the late eighteenth century, commercial civilities became more structured,
and, in a sense, deontological, with the formation of trade societies, some of which
amounted to early unions. Although these kinds of organizations developed mostly
after the Revolution, historians have identified their effective presence much earlier.[27] Like the Stationers' Company, these organizations were predicated on the
good of the trade at large and in effect sought to regulate not only labor conditions
but also behavior. The Philadelphia Typographical Society, for example, attempted
to set uniform practices and prices in order to legislate that its members "act as men
toward men."[28] As discussed in Chapter 1, however, contemporaries often pointed to
the hypocrisy of these societies and to the questionable conduct of the trade at large.
Printer William McCulloch wrote to Isaiah Thomas, perhaps the most revered and
influential eighteenth-century American printer, of these "useless, if not pernicious"
societies. Citing the exuberant beginnings of one such association, he quipped that
though the new members "anticipated that there would be a new era of printing"
realized through shared duty, they immediately fell into old competitive behaviors,
as one member proved when he went straight to his shop after the first meeting and
undersold a fellow society member, the same behavior of which Theodore Bliss
would complain over a century later. McCulloch mocked the rhetoric of natural law
and enlightened social ethics that shows up in the records of these organizations,
pointing out that disinterestedness is not, according to his experience, a virtue characteristic of printers. While they boast "strong incentives to decorum"—he failed to
note what these "incentives" were—they prefer alcohol and money to moral goodness. "'Ah, sir,'" McCulloch lamented about the episode,

> There is no faith in man's obdurate heart.
> It does not feel for men. The nat'ral bond
> Of brotherhood is sever'd.[29]

McCulloch's nostalgic "nat'ral bond" resembles a commercial social contract in
which the consent of the individual printers constitutes the moral logic of the
trade. Because individual printers have little sympathy for their fellow tradespeople, they are incapable of a truly progressive occupational culture. Critiquing Isaiah
Thomas's landmark *History of Printing in America* (1810), McCulloch chided the
text's timidity in the face of questionable behavior. "If a man is a sinner," he spat,
"call him not a saint."[30] While it is distasteful to "record the progress of vice, or
depicture of debauchery . . . it is the part of the historian to narrate circumstances
as they really exist."

There was no shortage of questionable behavior. In 1770, Benjamin Towne issued an account of his misadventures with a fellow printer who tried to force him to join, as he described it, an "iniquitous design . . . directly subversive of the sacred laws of honour and justice."[31] Concerned that his reputation would suffer from what was essentially an interstate commerce scheme, Towne broadcast that his former partner was a criminal in search of a crime. Within the decade Towne himself would be the subject of a vitriolic satire, published by Robert Bell, flailing him for his politics during the early years of the Revolution. "In the first place then I desire it may be observed," the satirist claims, "that I never was, nor ever pretended to be a man of character, repute or dignity, for I was only a PRINTER."[32] His "conduct" resulted from an "attachment to my own interest and desire of gain in my profession; a principle, if I mistake not, pretty general and pretty powerful in the present day."[33] Printers' behavior was seen as individual rather than communal, profit-driven rather than character-driven—corrupt rather than moral. Printers were a case in point of the social dangers of unchecked capitalism, whatever kinds of ethics they espoused.[34]

In fact, eighteenth-century printers' behavior swung back and forth between malfeasance and righteousness. Their public roles opened them to attack from every unhappy author and reader. Even Franklin felt it necessary to confront these attacks publicly in his "Apology for Printers" in 1731. If "all Printers were determin'd not to print any thing till they were sure it would offend no body, there would be very little printed," he wrote.[35] Furthermore, what printers do print reflects not on their own natures, he suggested, but on that of writers and readers, "people so viciously and corruptly educated that good things are not encouraged." This latter comment illustrates printers' other, more utilitarian identity, that of the virtuous citizen arbitrating a society blinded by its own immoral tendencies.

In this latter role, printers wanted to be known as citizens and gentlemen, as merchants of culture and civility, and often they were. Since the time of Johannes Gutenberg and William Caxton, printers coveted a cultural authority beyond what others viewed as their "mercenary" mechanical trade.[36] London printers, for example, differentiated themselves from other tradesmen in their association of printing with culture. In 1643 the Stationers' Company declared "That the Mystery and Art of Printing is of publike and great Importance" to "all well-govern'd states."[37] Like other ostensibly mundane trade documents of early modern printing, this one grandiloquently posited a vital cultural role for printers.[38] Their vocation was more than a trade, the stationers affirmed. It was a "Profession . . . honoured with a habitation . . . in the suburbs of Literature itself."[39] Even the location of the Stationers' Company in London reflected this cultural status. Adjacent to St. Paul's Cathedral, it occupied a space that since the Middle Ages had been a seat of commercial, royal, and church authority, one "associated with the forms of manners and military training which themselves denoted high status."[40] And, later, despite new vulgar associations of printers with uneducated rogues, late eighteenth-century printers continued to press their roles as cultural arbiters. A biographer of Lord

Byron's publisher, the esteemed John Murray, writes tellingly that Murray's "career begins to explain the ways in which someone whose primary concern is making money contributes to culture."[41]

Colonial printers likewise sought a genteel reputation based on civic virtue, trade morality, and public service. Although subject to the vicissitudes of a colonial economy and the cutthroat nature of their trade, printers were preoccupied with morality. At the very least they were concerned with appearing moral to the society at large. Many succeeded. Isaiah Thomas was one of the most respected tradesmen of the late eighteenth and early nineteenth centuries. Franklin even more so. Other printers—some of whom may be thought of, like Bell, as early publishers—achieved fame for their ostensible moral ways as well. "Thank God!" one author wrote Mathew Carey, who, upon emigrating to the United States, purchased Bell's presses. "When I address you, I know I am speaking not to a mercenary mechanic, but to a man, who him self writes with elegance what he feels like a gentleman."[42] Like their English counterparts, colonial printers saw themselves as more than "meer mechanicks"; they were cultural agents responsible for the commercial and even moral welfare of the state. Thomas's opening to *The History of Printing in America*, "That art which is the preserver of all arts, is worthy of the attention of the learned and the curious," would not have sounded extravagant to most readers in early America.[43] Nor would printers' mongrel moralities necessarily have struck people as inconsistent, though they were fundamentally so.

Status was more easily obtained for colonial American printers than their English counterparts. Colonial print shops were town centers. As Lawrence Wroth notes, "the enterprising printer took advantage of the coming and going of his neighbors to conduct on the premises a shop for the retailing of stationary, small groceries, and notions."[44] He was ubiquitous in the community in ways the highly specialized society of English printing precluded; his "importance [was] based upon responsibility."[45] The provincial cast of colonial printing thus actually furnished the printer with a greater cultural standing. And while colonial discourse may have become disembodied via republicanism, the person of the printer remained an essential embodiment of the cultural, social, ethical, and even physical status quo, so much so that the colonial print shop might be thought of as the physical address for the public sphere.[46] The building functioned as a cultural highway, facilitating "contact with the outside intellectual world" in ways no other colonial institution could.[47] Where France had its salons and England its coffee houses, the colonies had their print shops. The printer presided over everything from lottery tickets to the newspaper, stationery to Milton, morality to iniquity. And it was this world into which Robert Bell emigrated in the 1760s.

COMMON SENSE, BY ROBERT BELL

Arguably the first best seller printed in North America, *Common Sense* sold 1,000 copies in a week. Almost immediately Paine announced plans for a German translation; within months presses throughout New York and New England issued editions. Soon after, significant excerpts graced and disgraced European newspapers and entire editions appeared in England, France, Germany, and Holland. Paine suggested that 120,000 copies had been sold in 1776 alone, and some historians estimate that as many as five times that number actually read the book (or heard it read)—one-fifth the adult colonial population.[48] Trish Loughran looks skeptically at such figures, suggesting that Paine's estimates should be discarded out of hand and that even the numbers provided by such noted Paine bibliographers as Richard Gimbel are the product of "an ideologically loaded generalization" not only about the importance of the pamphlet but about the way in which local and national print networks functioned and about the questionably representative status of those who actually read *Common Sense*.[49] Still, even with Loughran's substantial revision of how many copies could have sold—she estimates that the total number cannot have been more than 75,000, and was probably lower—the sales of Paine's pamphlet were remarkable.

The first edition of *Common Sense* was only forty-six pages, but its production was a considerable job at a time when supplies such as ink and particularly paper were expensive and becoming scarce. During the 1770s, even some well-to-do printers worried about their ability to feed their families. Bell had to salvage damaged paper stores just to meet the demands of some of his early editions.[50] The business risks in printing *Common Sense*, in other words, were very real. Robert Aitken, whose *Pennsylvania Magazine* Paine edited after emigrating to the colonies in 1774 with a note of introduction from Franklin, refused the job outright. Like other printers, he worried about offending his subscribers and strangling his own profits. It was Benjamin Rush who convinced Paine to contact Bell, who, Rush said, had a reputation for staunch republicanism. More important, as Rush surely knew, Bell was a cunning businessman well versed in the art of conducting a prosperous trade in a competitive, imperially regulated colonial economy.

Bell's story is the story of modern trade piracy. Until 1695 the Licensing Act restricted printing in England to London, York, Cambridge, and Oxford. Yet even after Parliament allowed the act to expire, provincial English printers remained economically and legally dependent on London. Cities such as Dublin, Glasgow, Philadelphia, Charleston, and Boston also maintained close trade ties with London, importing thousands of titles for an increasingly literate populace. However, colonial booksellers had another route open that the provincial English printer (legally) did not: reprinting. Although the copyrights to most English books were held by powerful conglomerates of London booksellers, prosecuting colonial copyright infringement was difficult at best. As a result, England's colonial empire did a brisk, predatory trade in pirated English texts.[51]

Among colonial (re)printers, few were more experienced or more outspoken than Bell. Scottish by birth, trained in Glasgow as a bookbinder and later in Dublin as an auctioneer, bookseller, and pirate, Bell knew the business of the colonial print trade better than most printers by the time he moved to Philadelphia in 1767. His proficiency in the different aspects of book production was not what set him apart, though. What did was his fastidious understanding of the colonial market. Bell published most of his books through subscription and as a result sold them "in every part of North America in a period when few books were sold beyond the province in which they were printed."[52] He was one of only a handful of colonial printers willing to risk his labor on large works—even most Bibles were imported until after the Revolution—printing a four-volume edition of Blackstone's *Commentaries* in 1772 and, in 1777, producing the first North American edition of *Paradise Lost*. Strictly speaking, none was authorized.[53]

Bell the auctioneer made Bell the printer even more successful. He was a boisterous and tenacious salesperson, noted for conducting book auctions with a beer in one hand and a book in the other. "There were few authors of whom he could not tell some anecdote, which would get the audience in a roar," McCulloch noted: "His buffoonery was diversified and without limit."[54] Bell worked customers into such a frenzy over politics, literature, or whatever else he happened to be selling that they would purchase from him as much for the entertainment as for the product itself. But Bell was no buffoon. He was an artful rhetorician and a cunning businessman. His advertisements were complex statements of American cultural nationalism and capitalistic bravado. He employed these social and economic ideologies to defend his position that unauthorized reprinting was within the legal framework of English law.[55] Piracy was liberty, an argument that sold well since economics were no small matter in revolutionary creeds. In a preface to his edition of William Robertson's *History of the Reign of Charles V*, Bell argued that the book represented "practical proof" of the vitality of American manufactures. He set "Men of Literary Taste, and Lovers of Country-born Manufacturers" against the "inimical incendiaries, exotics to the native rights of American Freedom" who argued that his work violates "the monopoly of literary property in Great-Britain." He then distilled Blackstone's argument—which he conveniently reprinted—that acts of Parliament, including copyright, did not extend to the colonies unless they were specifically named within the act itself. Thus, his books were "useful Manufactures" of and for "THE LAND WE LIVE IN."[56] Bell deftly created a space of authority within this process and did so by manipulating the traditionally self-conscious rhetoric of the printing trade. For Bell, the printer was an artist of liberty: the "artist's manual exercise at the PRINTING PRESS . . . shall durably support the honour of that glorious vehicle of KNOWLEDGE AND LIBERTY." As James N. Green argues, Bell's advertisements, prefaces, and books for "Americans" quickened the ideologies of an already frenetic Philadelphia revolutionary subculture. These texts were "vigorous, even defiant statements of American independence" at the same time that they were "declarations of independence from the London book trade."[57] From Blackstone to Hume, Ferguson to Milton, Bell's productions were publicized as "Food for the Mind," while he was the self-crowned "artist" of cultural and trade emancipation. Little matter then, or so Rush thought, that among printers Bell's "moral character did not stand fair."[58] Paine needed a salesman, and he got one.

Paine's suspicions about his printer's "moral character" emerged after Bell had published and sold the first edition. Bell agreed to print the work, but only if the author paid for any unsold copies. In the event the book sold, author and printer would split the profit. Whatever the actual numbers, *Common Sense* sold well indeed. Paine estimated his profit from the first edition at thirty pounds and sent two representatives to settle his account with Bell, who told them, apparently in no uncertain terms, that there were no profits. In fact, Bell calculated that he had performed "fifty pounds worth of work for the small price of twenty."[59] According to Paine, upon suspicion that Bell was withholding the profits, the representatives warned him that Paine would seek a new printer for the book. Bell was asked, moreover, to print no further editions of *Common Sense*, because the author now planned to add appendices. One can only imagine what Bell, whose dramatic demeanor reputedly made his book auctions "as good as a play," must have said in person.[60] He later denied that there ever were requests to cease printing the pamphlet, noting bitterly that even had there been "he would most certainly have treated them immediately with that contempt which such unreasonable, illegal, and tyrannic usurpations over his freedom and liberty in business deserved."[61] As Johns notes, immigrant printers like Bell brought with them the civilities—the vocational codes and customs—of the great pirate centers of Ireland and Scotland.[62] These customs were not open for debate, particularly not with authors.

In other words, Bell's posturing was typical of printers, who resented advice and especially dictates from authors about how to run their businesses. In 1774 the prolific Boston printer Samuel Hall wrote angrily to an author that he would only "be governed by my own judgment" in his prices. The author, he scolded, "has no Right to [be] the Director of my Business."[63] This was the same lesson Philadelphia's Carey and Lea tried to teach James Fenimore Cooper in the 1820s. Authors, the reasoning went, even if they knew something of printing, knew nothing about business and would only inhibit the sales of their texts by meddling with printing and dissemination. Bell's reaction to Paine's trespass on the printer's business was bombastic, like much of his prose, but it illustrates the customs of colonial and revolutionary era print culture. Samuel Hall's suggestion that the author has "no Right" to involvement in the production of his text or in the printer's "Business" was not high republicanism so much as it was a statement of custom. According to convention, authors were and should be disinterested in the processes of bookmaking and the material consequences of their efforts. Even were the colonial printing industry not mired in what amounted to a deep recession, Bell likely resisted Paine's right to a share of the profit because it was unconventional and, from his standpoint, unprofitable. It was a fair assessment.

Paine, however, famously disbelieved in the value of custom, and he thought writers possessed certain inalienable rights, whatever the supposed "civilities" of printers dictated. While Paine did famously equate some professional writers to prostitutes, it is a mistake to assume that he resisted the idea that authors could make money from their productions.[64] Paine wanted the money and believed in his moral right to it, as well as to his production. Indeed, according to James N. Green, *Common Sense* may have been the first North American publication for which the author was to have been paid in a currency other than books.[65] We know that Paine gave Bell the manuscript on "conditions": "that if any loss should arise I would pay it—and in order to make Bell industrious in circulating it, I gave him one-half the profits, if it should produce any."[66] While the shared-profit contract Bell agreed to with Paine had become common in England, it was not in the colonies. More to the point, it was rare for an author to issue "conditions" to a printer risking his own capital on a text, as Bell had done, an act that made Bell more a publisher than a printer. Although we do not know the exact terms, that Bell agreed to the job at all suggests that Paine bested him at his own game. Paine's language reflects this reading, particularly his suggestion that he "gave" the printer a right to half the profits. Before the text had even been published, Paine turned author-printer business relations upside down.

He continued to change the rules of the game after the book's publication, too. Paine's request that he be given full control over his text—that is, that Bell cease printing it entirely after one edition—flew in the face of trade customs. Specifically, it flew in the face of courtesy of the trade, one of the most important courtesies governing not only nineteenth-century print culture but the earlier trade as well. As in its later form, the ethic was based on prior right: the printer of the first edition of a text had an implicit right to subsequent editions. But whereas later incarnations of trade courtesy structured trade relations in the absence of international copyright, the colonial version structured relations in the absence of a well-defined domestic copyright, namely, the confusion over whether British copyright, in the form of the Statute of Anne, extended to the American colonies. Even if it did, as Bell knew, enforcement was practically impossible. There were colonial copyright laws, but they functioned essentially as legal analogs for courtesy of the trade, thereby protecting domestic printers, and certainly not authors, domestic or foreign. In 1672, for example, at the behest of the influential printer Samuel Green, the General Court of Massachusetts colony declared a kind of copyright bestowing limited terms for ownership of texts, but only for printers and booksellers. It did not grant colonial authors any power over their own productions and did not make authorship a legal category. The General Court of Massachusetts enacted a more explicit version of this "copyright" in 1673 that established terms of ownership lasting seven years for printers.[67] In reality, though, copyright in any form meant little in the colonies. It was essentially superfluous. Most printing was local, and the local trade was governed by customs like courtesy of the trade, at least until the federal government adopted its own copyright in 1790.[68] Thus it is not surprising that printers like Bell—well schooled in trade courtesy by their experiences in Ireland and Scotland and now residing in a world far removed even from the long arm of London booksellers—would adhere to courtesy of the trade. Insofar as it existed at all, literary property was a function of trade customs, not of law, and certainly it had nothing to do with fanciful notions of authors' rights. In sum, Thomas Paine had no right to tell his printer what to do, before or after publication.

It may be that Paine sensed that this particular courtesy among printers had little to do with the interests of authors. Like the 1673 Massachusetts copyright legislation, courtesy of the trade was an intratrade code. Its disregard of the ostensible natural rights of an author to his or her text would be the cornerstone of later state and federal copyright law. Paine no doubt recognized this indifference. Implicitly, he accused Bell of greed—the complaint lobbed at printers by authors since the invention of the printing press—by asserting a moral right to his creation. Again, though, Bell was simply defending the customs of his trade; hence his reference to Paine's demand as an "unreasonable" appropriation of his "freedom and liberty in business." Paine, on the other hand, suggested that these customs were inherently immoral, that the printer subjugated the author's abstract, natural right to his property with the flawed rules of a corrupt trade. And for Paine, that printers thought of these rules as ethics just made the tradesmen more immoral.

Bell resisted more than Paine's assumption that he had a right to profits in the first place and his contravention of accepted printing ethics. He refused the author's insurgence into the business of print—the presence of a competing agency in Revolutionary-era print culture. This is the connotation of his reference to Paine as a "Would-be-Author" and to himself as the "real Printer" in the *Pennsylvania Evening Post* in January 1776. Authorial agency is, Bell argued, conditional. Paine's identity, his text, his social value: all are entirely contingent. All are factors and manufactures of the printer, the bookseller, and the other faceless individuals and processes involved in the printing and selling of books. This is what Bell meant when he demanded that it was the printer who was "real." It was printers who enjoyed the practical skill and cultural reputation to truly affect society, and any claims authors made to a cultural agency were bogus and antithetical to customs of print culture. In America, the "mechanick" was a force greater than any author could ever hope to be.

Whatever the real or imagined impotence of the author in comparison to the literary tradesman, Paine followed through on his threat to try to make Bell obsolete, paying two other printers to produce 6,000 copies and then delivering these copies "fit for sale" to one of Bell's competitors, William Bradford of Philadelphia.[69] In the January 25 advertisement for his new edition, Paine attempted to disgrace Bell by warning the public that Bell had published a second edition of the original text against the author's wishes, as though Bell were pirating his own production.[70] Paine exploited the public's ignorance of trade customs by suggesting that the author had an innate right to his post-production text. Bell fired back angrily, accusing Paine of attempting to undermine the sale of his own book in order to increase his profits. Where Paine accused Bell of selfishness at the expense of the author, Bell accused Paine of selfishness at the expense of the public. His "brother booksellers," he wrote, wished that Paine would "find a more eligible mode of proving his attachment to generous principles than to lay the foundations of his generosity in the dishonest ebullitions of dishonest malevolence."[71] In the same issue Paine announced that he would sell the new edition at half the price of Bell's "in order to accommodate it to the abilities of every man."[72] Paine played the wretched author and populist. Bell played the businessman and republican.

Paine intensified his rhetoric. First, he threatened to sue Bell for his profits. Second, he noted that he had intended to use these profits to buy supplies for Benedict Arnold's troops, who had just been disastrously repulsed at Quebec. Bell, it seems, had deprived the defeated, freezing soldiers of new mittens.[73] Bell would have none of it. He began: "I suppose you took the field, without telling your anxious friends where you were going—weak man—they ought to forgive you. Feeble author— yourself did not know, that the humble Provedore to the Sentimentalists was able to follow.—Neither did you know, that the public could despisingly laugh at the folly of the foster-father author, who wantonly, and maliciously, dragged the real book-seller into the unwished for field of public altercation."[74] "Provedore to the Sentimentalists" was Bell's self-designated advertisement moniker, by which he suggested that he and he alone provided books for the reader capable of true sympathy.[75] He recast print culture as a battlefield and pitted himself, the enabler of feeling and the true "father" of *Common Sense*, against the naïve and "feeble" author. Translating the knotty issues for the *Post* readership, Bell implied that Paine did not understand the world he had so brazenly sought to dictate in attempting to exercise control over the printer, so much so that he made other authors anxious through his wrecking of trade customs.

In attempting to exercise his supposed rights, Paine confronted the customs, the "laws of functioning," that governed relations among literary tradesmen. Critiquing these customs by critiquing the actions of his printer, Paine disputed existing trade ethics, such as they were. In sum, he sought to change the rules by which writers and printers played the social game of printing. Bell's identification of Paine as a "foster-father author" is thus, I want to argue, less a critique of republican authorship— where the author essentially adopts and anonymously articulates the sentiments of the public at large—than a summary judgment on the author's lack of authority and moral recklessness. Paine's "folly" was his assumption that he, rather than his text, had a meaningful significance to the public, and that he tasked a printer who was "real." Bell pointed out that the only name to appear on the original "flaming production," after all, was the printer's, and that it was only through his "knowledge in business [that] the pamphlet was made respectable" in the first place.[76] Bell went on to reprove Paine for speculating with "public money" and for bragging about his authorship of *Common Sense* "in every beer-house" in Philadelphia. As Loughran suggests, Paine wanted it both ways. He wanted *Common Sense* to be part of what Warner calls the metadiscourse of republicanism, which negated the person of the author; at the same time, he aggrandized the person of the author, or as Loughran puts it, his "particular self."[77] "Whirligigged by imaginary importance," Paine became in Bell's hands a "self-conceited Englishman" attacking an "industrious

Bookseller, who never asked or received any thing from the public without giving an equivalent."[78] Through his practice of "catch-penny author-craft," Paine expected profit where there was none. The implication: Paine is no republican, no revolutionary, and certainly no businessman—everything Bell claimed to be as a printer. Instead, the author was an opportunist seeking to change the ethics governing printers to suit himself. In Bell's final attack in late February—by this point Paine had been silent for almost a month—Bell accused the writer of bursting into the public sphere "fully equipped" to assassinate the "reputation of authors."[79] Bell wanted the public and Paine to understand that authors should not make demands on their printers. If there were no liberty or principled behavior in authorship, he argued, there was in the conduct of business.[80]

Paine never responded directly to Bell's later accusations, but he did respond indirectly in his *Letter to the Abbe Raynal, on the Affairs of North America* (1782).[81] Paine's *Letter* was an answer to Raynal's best-selling study, *The Revolution of America* (1781). Here, Paine set out to correct Raynal, who had "misconceived and mis-stated the causes" of the war by crudely assigning it an economic motive. In contrast, Paine characterized the Revolution as a consequence of an enlightened free will informed, in part, by virtue. Colonists exercised their moral duty to rise from the "basest state of vassalage" the English crown had imposed upon them through dictates such as the Stamp Act and Townshend Duties.[82] For Paine, the Revolution was righteousness made tangible in the form of armed resistance. Economics were subsumed in the moral authority of the people. What is not remarked upon is the extent to which this thesis and parts of the *Letter* recapitulate Paine's argument with Bell over *Common Sense*. In the final section of the chapter, I want to suggest that Paine's political writing—including *Common Sense, The American Crisis, The Rights of Man*, and the *Letter to the Abbe Raynal*—is a meditation on trade morality and authorial agency. Paine viewed the author in much the same way he viewed British colonial America, which is another way of saying that when he looked at the nation he saw his authorial self. Both were moral constructs; both entities existed not so much as legal but moral subjects whose authority was vested in a communal sense of "right." In their relation to these constructs, economic, political, and vocational oppression were synonyms for a fraudulent code of conduct based illogically and dangerously in antiquated customs. Kings, printers, booksellers, and historians themselves confused what was customary for what was right.

POLITICAL ALLEGORIES OF INCIVILITY

Fittingly, the *Letter to the Abbe Raynal* opens with an attack on literary piracy. Observing the reprinting of Raynal's study by English and American printers even prior to its completion, Paine paralleled his own moral trials of authorship with Raynal's. Like Bell, the London pirate-printer of *The Revolution of America* characterized his action as patriotic, motivated by "an ardour that can be exceeded only by the nobler flame ... of the philanthropic author."[83] Paine mocked the "professions of patriotism" that "gloss over the embezzlement" of an author's manuscript, arguing that the printer and his pseudo-ethics trespass on the moral right of the author to his text.[84] Where the printer cast himself as a symbol of patriotic authority, Paine labeled him and his action counterfeit. "Illiberal and unpardonable," this illicit printing costumed immoral trade practices as patriotism: "This plausibility of setting off a dishonourable action, may pass for patriotism and sound principles with those who do not enter into its demerits and whose interest is not injured nor their happiness affected thereby. But it is more than probable, notwithstanding the declarations it contains, that the copy was obtained for the sake of profiting by the sale of a new author and popular work, and that the professions are but a garb to the fraud."[85] The typical reader, of course, more interested in buying the book at a good price than in the moral transgressions symbolized by its (re)production, likely had no reason to doubt the London printer's self-congratulatory preface to the pirated edition. Authors, however, might. Acquainted with the exclusionary trade ethics employed by printers, authors could see the printer's vindication for what it was: "fraud." Printers' claims of cultural proprietorship and agency were pretenses, Paine argued, a smoke screen assuring customers that they, like the printer, participate in the political project of the author. Paine punned on "profession," equating the printer's lie with his occupation: printers' "professions" were fraudulent, and so was the profession at large. Put another way, printers are professional frauds.

Thus, Paine's best-selling defense of the American Revolution in effect opens as an exposé on the immorality of printers who play patriot in order to sell books. Perhaps intentionally, it also echoes some of his writings in the wake of the Silas Deane affair. In his attack on Deane and Robert Morris, Paine suggested that monopolizing businessmen undermine the national community. "One monopolizer confederates with another, and defaulter with defaulter, till the cause becomes a common one," he said in "To the People of America" (1779); "yet still these men will talk of justice, and, while they profess abhorrence to the principles that govern them, they pathetically lament the evils they create."[86] Like Deane and Morris, whom Paine employed to illustrate the "shocking depravity of moral principle" common in American commerce, printers were charlatans who posed as moral stalwarts even as they monopolized the authority and profits of the international print trade.[87] Printers were the profiteers of the new literary merchant class. When Paine turned his attention explicitly to the author in the *Letter*, meanwhile, he argued that authorship is a moral category and that the wresting of control of a text from its author, as was the case with Raynal and with Paine, a moral offense. This is particularly true of societies without copyright. "The embezzlement from the Abbe Raynal, was . . . committed by one country upon another, and therefore shows no defect in the laws of either," he wrote. "But it is nevertheless a breach of civil manners and literary justice."[88] It was not the laws of nations that were to blame for the kinds of transgressions common in the business of print. It was the lack of principle in the men conducting that business.

Paine's earlier writings, such as *Common Sense*, likewise may be read as deliberations on the ethics of late eighteenth-century print culture. The pamphlet is, after all, a jeremiad against the way custom sedates the individual into apathy, against the hitherto unquestioned principle that monarchial rule was most effective for modern nations. "A long habit of not thinking a thing *wrong*," Paine wrote, "gives it a superficial appearance of being *right*, and raises at first a formidable outcry in defence of custom."[89] This is the moral thesis of *Common Sense*: definitions of right and wrong are less functions of reason than of political and social habit. Radicals become radical when awakened to the fraud of these definitions—that is, to the inadequacies of custom—and when made aware that custom is power. "A long and violent abuse of power," Paine wrote, "is generally the means of calling the right of it in question, (and in matters too which might never have been thought of, had not the sufferers been aggravated into the inquiry)." This claim resonated six years later in the *Letter*, where Paine accused book buyers of an unconscious immoral complacency in the face of commercial fraud.

Paine wanted his readers to comprehend the cultural, social, and vocational hegemony exercised by the customary authorities of the late eighteenth century. Politically, he railed against an unthinking dependence on England and on unspoken dissent in the colonies: "Ye that dare oppose not only the tyranny but the tyrant, stand forth!"[90] In an appendix to his third edition, he warned that "ceremony" is apathy.[91] Remarking that social order "depends greatly upon the *chastity* of what might properly be called NATIONAL MANNERS," he admitted to the virtue of the colonists' "prudent delicacy," that is, their restraint, in not speaking out against the crown at inopportune times. But he warned again that abiding abuse could create a custom out of that abuse. *Common Sense* was as much an attack on Paine's fellow colonists as on the monarchy, as much an attack on the idea of acquiescing to custom as on the custom itself. The "national manners," though effective in quelling passions, should nevertheless emanate from virtue and reason rather than habit and custom.

These "manners," this social abstraction of justice and civility, in other words, also informed Paine's thinking, as well as the thinking of many American writers, on the place of the author and his or her readers in transatlantic print culture. Paine feared a political landscape lorded over by English power brokers, a society ruled by unthinking adherence to custom, and a trade controlled by printers and booksellers such as Bell and the English pirate-printer of Raynal's *Revolution of America*. As he noted in *The American Crisis*, though the "Republic of Letters is more ancient than monarchy, and of far higher character in the world than the vassal court of Britain," it is subject to the same evils.[92] However, when he wrote in the same letter that "Universal empire is the prerogative of a writer. His concerns are with all mankind, and though he cannot command their obedience, he can assign them their duty," his idealism stands out in relief. Had the author this power, *The American Crisis* would be unnecessary in the first place. We can rewrite the sentence to more accurately reflect the reality of early American authorship: "Universal empire [ought to be] the prerogative of a writer" because it is the writer who recognizes and delegates moral obligation for citizens. Translated into the language of Paine's political and moral framework, it is the writer who understands what is "right" and "wrong" because it is the writer who works from reason and feeling, not, like Robert Bell, from an economically induced haze of counterfeit patriotism. As Paine defined the author in the *Letter*, he is that person who combines "the full expansion of the imagination with the natural and necessary gravity of judgment, so as to be rightly balanced within themselves, and to make a reader feel, fancy, and understand justly at the same time."[93] The writer is everything the printer is not: patriotic, sincere, civil, reasonable, and just. In a word, moral.

Yet the writer occupied a republic of letters subject to the same ills as the pseudo-republican government of England, and again we see in Paine the synergetic relationship of politics and vocation. For Paine, as Edward Larkin points out, "the republican public sphere was not so much real, as an ideal espoused by the elites, the Federalists, in order to limit access to public political debates and retain control of the political arena."[94] Paine feared the exclusion of "middling and lower sorts" from public debate.[95] He feared the instability of colonial society, an instability perpetuated by the wealthy, the English, and those with cultural power. And he saw within these factions of interests a cultural agency disingenuous to the moral principles espoused implicitly by colonial radicalism and explicitly by his own writings. "The present state of America is truly alarming to every man who is capable of reflection," he wrote. "Without law, without government, without any other mode of power than what is founded on, and granted by, courtesy. Held together by an unexampled concurrence of sentiment, which, is nevertheless subject to change, and which, every secret enemy is endeavouring to dissolve. Our present condition is, legislation without law; wisdom without a plan; a constitution without a name; and, what is strangely astonishing, perfect independence contending for dependence. . . . The property of no man is secure in the present unbraced system of things."[96] In Paine's voluminous political writings there is no clearer identification of a single principle to guide human behavior in the absence of law and governance: courtesy. But it is not printers' courtesy. Instead, it is a courtesy based in a moral sense, in common sense. Unlike printers' courtesy of the trade, Paine's courtesy is an intuitive morality derived from a perception of the needs and interests of others, an activity theorized, not incidentally, in the writings of prominent contemporary thinkers such as Francis Hutcheson and Adam Smith. For Paine, courtesy becomes a more authentic ethic than those used by commercial men like Bell—a sentimental code of conduct for a progressive society striving to shed its oppressive behavioral customs but yet to work out its own civil codes.[97]

But what may work for political economy many not work in the microeconomies of trade. Examples of the kind of courtesy Paine seemed to allegorize as an ideal trade morality are rare in the late colonial and early American historical record.

Whatever their moral capacity, without copyright, authors had no practical, legal identity in the public print sphere; they were, as Bell maintains, conditional. Thus, the customary ethics of printers could easily ignore the moral rights authors claimed for their texts, rights that informed Paine's notion of courtesy. In 1782, just one year before Connecticut passed the first state copyright law, Paine seemingly acknowledged the truth of Bell's claim in a footnote to his preface to the *Letter*: "The state of literature in America must one day become the subject of legislative consideration. Hitherto it hath been a disinterested volunteer in the service of the Revolution, and no man thought of profits [except maybe Paine]: but when peace shall give time and opportunity for study, the country will deprive itself of the honour and service of letters and the improvement of science, unless sufficient laws are made to prevent depredations on literary property."[98] His language forecast the language of early American copyright law. "It is perfectly agreeable to the principles of natural equity and justice," the preamble of the Connecticut copyright legislation states, "that every author should be secured in receiving the profits that may arise from sale of his works, and such security may encourage men of learning and genius to publish their writings; which may do honor to their country, and service to mankind."[99] Paine and the State of Connecticut were identical in their assumptions. First, republican authorship is a function of political crisis; peace engenders the desire for profit and private enterprise, although texts themselves will still exist to serve the nation. Second, the havoc played on authorship and "literary property" by "illiberal" printers will ultimately discourage authors from even trying to publish. The cultural nationalism and self-aggrandizement practiced by printers will be their own undoing, as well as the new nation's, if the trade continued to ignore the "civil manners"—for Paine, the natural courtesy—that should characterize American civil society. But what if, as Bell had argued, the problem lay with writers themselves? What if authorship were not by definition some ideal, moral category? Just a few years after Paine's contest with Bell the historian Hannah Adams began a long and controversial career that would beg that question.

3

Hannah Adams and the Courtesies of Authorship

IN 1814, A Boston lawyer and politico named John Lowell published an anonymous, critical review of a book by the accomplished Congregationalist minister Jedidiah Morse. Like Cotton Mather before him, Morse was as good a student of the gospels as he was of the literary market. His *Geography Made Easy* (1784) was one of the best-selling school texts of the era, and Morse understood keenly how to manage the market to keep it that way.[1] Lowell, though, was reviewing a very different kind of book. It was called *An Appeal to the Publick*, and it was a bitter account of Morse's encounter with another formidable writer, the colonial and religious historian Hannah Adams, who had challenged the very market Morse had dominated for so long. Despite his obvious sympathy for Adams and even more obvious disdain for Morse, Lowell was forced to concede that the question of who had rights to this market was complicated. The "right of authorship is," he wrote, "one of those ill-defined properties, which in all countries, leaves room for controversy."[2] What made it especially complicated was that the long, public debate between Morse and Adams over this right was not a legal battle but an ethical one. It was not an argument over proprietary rights but over propriety. This question of authorial propriety deserves more attention, especially with regard to women's authorship. Even with recent rich work on these women writers, more thought needs to be given to their interactions with the early trade and to the ways in which they steered its development and chafed under its customs, ethical and otherwise.[3]

This chapter argues that, like Thomas Paine before her and writers like Herman Melville after, Hannah Adams understood authorship as a moral construct and the trade as a moral space in which values were of primary rather than secondary importance. It argues as well that, like the careers of Fanny Fern and Gail Hamilton, the career of Hannah Adams indicates the ethical problems created by the confluence of the business of publishing and the rise of the woman writer as a legitimate occupational category. Focusing on what Charles Brockden Brown characterized as the "realm of national transactions," American print culture, this chapter examines the way Adams's name circulated, and was designed to circulate, within that culture.[4] Indeed, long before Fern, this "realm" made the successes and failures of women writers a public issue, a trend Adams recognized and lamented, so much so that her 1832 memoir, although perhaps one of the most revealing records of the early American authorial consciousness, is deficient in many details concerning her long authorial career. The *Ladies Magazine* observed as much: "She must have had much more to tell of the history of her mind, its struggles, and trials, and triumphs, and the effect of all these in forming her character—but her humble opinion of herself, induced her to attach less importance to trifling details than her readers would have done."[5] What little Adams did offer was carefully understated and oblique; at her most vituperative she is still vague, as when she wrote that her authorship exposed her "to the censure, or ridicule of those, whose ideas on the subject are derived from the varying modes of fashion, and not from the unchanging laws of moral rectitude."[6] Viewing Adams through these memoirs, as well as through the prefaces and public records that pertain to her work, yields an exquisite illustration of an author at once independent and dependent, intellectual and popular, gendered and ungendered, righteous and immoral, aggressive and reticent—an early writer struggling, I argue, with the ethical uncertainties of authorship, the trade, and the market.

At stake in this analysis is not just a glimpse of women's authorial practices in the early United States but, more broadly, an awareness of an early version of the authorial self and its relationship to the trade and market famously present in later writers. In the record of Adams's vocational life, we see the ancestor of Fern's "regular business woman," Ruth Hall, and, in another sense, an early incarnation of Emily Dickinson's lament that "Publication—is the Auction / Of the Mind of Man."[7] As one reviewer noted, Adams's career exposed before any other the "peculiar trial of a female presenting herself as the maker of bargains and the assertor [*sic*] of literary claims."[8] In my first two sections I explore this "peculiar trial" by dividing Adams into the two selves writers increasingly had to occupy: businessperson and writer. The former is practical and measured, dealing with the uncertain business of print. She is the "maker of bargains" in a trade that was economically and ethically "unbraced," to borrow Thomas Paine's language. The latter is aggressive, staking her rights to cultural capital and, in the process, compromising in surprising ways the conventions of republican impersonality. She is the "assertor of literary claims" in the public sphere. For Adams, gender ultimately defined both personae. Next, I apply this dualistic persona to Adams's dispute with Jedidiah Morse. Generally this debate is read as a battle over authorship and gender. Most commentators suggest that Adams sought to make gender the key issue, or that gender was in fact the central concern of both parties. I argue, however, that this was also a contest over trade morality, or, more specifically, authorial ethics. It highlighted yet unarticulated questions about authorial decorum in the marketplace of print. Adams addressed this decorum not so much through gender, as we might expect, but rather through the ideas of benevolence, sympathy, and courtesy. Although gender was a vital factor in the debate's verdict, Adams redefined the authorial persona by interpreting it morally, an interpretation that contrasted sharply with de facto market and legal formulations of authorship.

MAKER OF BARGAINS

"'She is an authoress!' has long been the sneering remark among ignorant witlings, of both sexes," the *Ladies Magazine* reported in 1829, looking back on the fate of the woman author in the opening decades of the nineteenth century.[9] How else could people "account for any seeming or supposed impropriety of behavior and inelegancy of taste, reported to characterize the woman, who has been so regardless of her sex's disqualification for thought, as actually to allow her own thoughts to appear in print?" Women's authorship was still the exception in the belletristic tradition of the gentleman writer, and certainly no American woman could dream of sustaining a living from her pen. The author was male. Further, the author was socialized to participate in the public sphere and educated toward that purpose. Many women were still neither. "The reason is plain—they are illiterate," an anonymous commentator in *The Gleaner* ascertained in 1809.[10] To "duly appreciate their talents, it will be necessary to give them the same advantages possessed by man." One anonymous "celebrated" writer, for example, remarked that while few women have the "talents to write" indeed they "all talk."[11] "We see things as they are," a man assures the father of a young girl with aspirations to write in Maria Edgeworth's *Letters for Literary Ladies* (1795), "but women must always see things through a veil, or cease to be women."[12] Occupation of the domestic sphere did not leave time to write, and women did so at the expense of their familial roles.

By 1829, however, the *Ladies Journal* could announce that "the scene has changed": "In our Republic . . . the lot of the weaker sex . . . is highly favored, and here, if ever in this world, appears to be preparing the theater where the abilities of woman are to be developed."[13] Some women authors had, "by the native energies of their minds, arisen to a degree of eminence that has excited the fears and alarmed the jealousies of great contemporary literary characters."[14] Women's authorship had created a "new kind of celebrity" that aroused simultaneously the curiosity, ire, resentment, and respect of the reading public.[15] Writers had begun to fracture the public and private policy of "rigorous exclusion" practiced by men against women in American belles lettres. Really, though, there is no progressive chronology for the opening of this "theater." From the 1780s on, the same argument is played out repeatedly in the

American press: men and women decry women's authorship; other men and women defend and promote it.

When remembered in Van Wyck Brooks's andocentric estimation of *The Flowering of New England, 1815–1865* (1936), Adams was the exception to this debate: "In the Athenaeum one might have seen . . . Hannah Adams . . . the lady of whom one heard so many stories, as that they were obliged to lock her in, because it was not polite to lock her out. Living, Miss Adams was the only female who ventured to claim her statutory right to browse in these, to her, celestial pastures."[16] Roughly a century after her death, Adams inspired reminiscences of a particular status in early nineteenth-century culture. Brooks, having heard "so many stories" about Hannah Adams, immediately uses her name to conjure a vision of celebrity and intellectual endeavor. He refers to her "statutory right" to the Boston Athenaeum, an understated way of validating Adams as an intellectual given that only "qualified scholars of respectable intent" could work in its remarkable collection. As "the only female" to benefit from this kind of attention, Adams represented something more to society than most writers, much less female writers, of her period.[17] For Brooks, Adams's cultural capital broke down the cultural chauvinism of the Athenaeum, one of the nation's most revered institutions. Even a century before, at a time when New England print markets and communications were circumscribed and fairly provincial, Adams's fame was national and even international. To one contemporary, her "labors . . . place her by the side of a Moore, an Edgeworth, and a Barbauld of her own, rather than among those writers of either sex, who have courted the heart, by a subservience to the fancy. Mrs. Adams has done much for the literary character of her sex. If she has not preceded them in the mother country, she has led the way in this."[18] Her work rested "on the shelves of the learned, rather than the toilet of the fashionable." In print, commentators explicitly heralded Adams's explosion of the accepted bounds of female public discourse.

Nina Baym has argued that women published far more than canonical literary history would have us believe, a claim substantiated by the historical record. Even so, Adams was exceptional. Contemporaries of both sexes viewed her status as transcending what was presumed typical for women authors.[19] While women were not "sealed off from public discourse," as Baym reminds us, they nevertheless generally had not garnered the kind of public esteem Adams had. Nor had any American woman writer been so consciously and publicly characterized as infiltrating a print culture overwhelmingly patriarchal. Thus when Adams was criticized it was not for her scholarship—critics then and now note its quality—but rather "her departure from the arbitrary laws of criticism," that is, her transgression of the social decorum that true authors were male.[20] Claiming that Adams had been censured "for the violation of rigid rules" in "the department of minor criticism," this writer praised Adams as an author by defending her scholarship. At the same time, though, he saw Adams in the context of "the good she has attempted for the cause of religion and her sex." In his remarks on Adams's *Summary History of New England* (1799),

Hannah Adams

FIGURE 3.1 Hannah Adams, Courtesy General Research Division, New York Public Library, Astor, Lenox and Tilden Foundations.

Charles Brockden Brown followed the same equation, spending nearly equal parts of his review praising Adams's scholarship and suggesting that it "is surely no small addition to the credit which belongs to the present writer, to observe that she is a woman."[21] Even Brown's enthusiasm for Adams and her potential as an author as well as his suggestion that the public accept Adams's literary vocation undermines his intimation that most women who wrote did so poorly (or with poor judgment). "We entertain sanguine hopes," he wrote, "that the public approbation will encourage Miss A. to persevere in this laudable and useful path."[22]

His diction here is crucial. As Brown well knew, prior to (and even after) Washington Irving and James Fenimore Cooper proved the viability of making money as a writer in the United States, doing so required perseverance at every stage, and the circumstances were far worse for women. Mary Kelley has shown that many nineteenth-century women writers, caught "between a private domestic existence and a public literary career," found "themselves in a world they did not know and that did not know them."[23] Short of the difficulties inherent even in placing their work in print, women authors such as Adams often struggled with the fundamentals of research and writing. Adams notes, for example, that it "was difficult to procure proper materials for the work in my sequestered abode."[24] Moreover, in addition to the vicissitudes incumbent in writing in the first place, authors of both sexes had to confront a disorganized and often provincially minded trade. Many of the costs of printing and much of the responsibility for distribution fell to writers themselves.

Early national writers, therefore, understood print culture as a business, an expensive one. The high price of production owed most to the scarcity and cost of paper. A late-colonial printer could exceed the combined cost of his other equipment with what he spent on only a year's supply of paper.[25] Considering that this other equipment was itself very costly—until 1796 the United States did not even boast a self-sustaining type foundry, so printers had to suffer the expensive importation of already costly European letters—the money spent for paper was immense.[26] These costs were often passed along to writers, who were asked to front the production costs. Adams herself lamented the difficulty of finding "any printer willing and able to print [a book] without money immediately paid."[27] As a result, writers were generally well-to-do: authorship prior to the 1830s was largely male because of custom but also because producing books took money and leisure time. According to Benjamin Rush, "Our authors and scholars are generally men of business and make their literary pursuits subservient to their interests."[28] This was not a matter of discrimination, at least not explicitly; Rush was simply stating fact. Jeremy Belknap complained bitterly that in the present system the author's economic insolvency was all but assured: "The several classes of tradesmen whom I employ in this work [of printing] do not run any risque at all. The paper-maker is paid by the ream; the printer by the sheet; the bookbinder by the volume; and the engraver at a stipulated price. I expect to be the bookseller myself, & I am the only person concerned whose expense is certain & whose profit is uncertain."[29] In addition to authors paying significant portions of the cost of production, it was also customary for them to realize profits only after others involved realized theirs. A more profitable arrangement, insofar as it practically guaranteed that at least the cost of the book would be covered, was subscription. In this imported European practice, individual buyers would promise to purchase a work advertised by a printer before he printed the book. This method was favored by authors and printers insofar as it helped to ensure profits and provided a bulwark against failure for less popular books.[30]

But in this arrangement writers were still at the mercy of the trade's infamous ethics. B. Edes and Sons, for example, had collected and kept all the subscription money for Adams's first book, *An Alphabetical Compendium of the Various Sects* (1784). Considering that some four hundred persons had subscribed, the profit to the printer would have been relatively good. Yet while Edes's actions were certainly questionable, the behavior of most printers, while not generous, was fair. As Rollo Silver reminds us, these printers were businessmen, and they had to answer to a market that had little sympathy for the profit-minded author, especially in an era of republican disinterestedness.[31] Thus the reasoning behind the "generally various, prolix, and ambiguous" written responses of printers to Adams's requests to reprint the *Alphabetical Compendium* was that printers had to watch their bottom line carefully.[32] Adams herself dealt with two printers who failed during or just after the production of her books, both at a loss to her.[33]

Given printers' economic distress and their suspicion of partners and competitors alike, it is not surprising that often their relations with writers could be difficult. While formal regulations such as copyright essentially protected the author, or at least made the author aware of her rights under the law, informal agreements and societies governing the early national book trade had little to do with authors' best interests, much as Paine had shown of Revolutionary-era tradesmen. These trade groups and their bylaws intended to benefit the profits garnered by trade piracy. Printers and other agents of the book trade were adept at promoting their ostensible morality in their dealings with writers, but little of their rhetoric was genuine: "THE LAW OF COPY-RIGHTS, by securing a reward to the labours of Genius, gilt the laurel that enwreathed his brow; and thus . . . the talents of Americans became the best support of their manufactures," Hugh Gaine proclaimed. "But it is not a consideration of private interest alone, which directs our views: as booksellers, as guardians of the press, we have a nobler aim! . . . Let us . . . spurn any whisper of private and pitiful advantage, which would draw us from our station, and sink the patriot into the dealer. Let us join as one man to raise the name of American litera-ture: and by uniting in support of each other's undertakings, give a strength to our social compact, which may ensure its prosperity."[34]

Understandably, these "guardians of the press" wanted to guard their profits. In fact, the purpose of this speech by Gaine was to open a meeting of booksellers and printers in New York so that they might reduce the kind of underselling about which Henry Carey would complain decades later. Gaine's "social compact," that is, was the implicit understanding that these trade representatives had an obligation not to interfere with one another—an idealistic mantra that would be sounded throughout the coming century—in order to assure that profits would remain high. In good laissez-faire fashion, these profits would eventually trickle down to the "Genius[es]." For her part, Adams understood everything she needed to about early American copyright. She was quick to act on the Massachusetts legislation, the first in the country, in 1783. Thus she was able to refuse Edes's request to print a second edition of *An Alphabetical Compendium* after she had lost money on the first owing to the printers' self-serving contract. Adams, a quick study in the political and legal issues surrounding authorship and publishing, returned, in her own words, a "laconic answer" to the scheming printer's request.[35]

Adams ultimately came to see the struggles with the business of printing to be nothing less than an ethical "trial."[36] Looking back on her introduction to the world of the book trade, she remarked, foreshadowing Fern and Hamilton decades later: "I was necessitated to exert myself in doing business out of the female line, which exposed me to public notice. And as I could not but be sensible that my manners were remarkably awkward, this consciousness, joined with my ignorance of the established rules of propriety, rendered me tremblingly apprehensive of exposing myself to ridicule. These unpleasant feelings, however, in time abated. In order to meet this trial, I considered, that what is right and necessary in the situation in which Providence has placed me, cannot be really improper."[37] In effect, Adams's "manners" contrasted with the status quo in the business of print. What is so intriguing about this passage, I would suggest, is not Adams's professed "ignorance" of how to act. Like most writers, she had little idea of the practical codes of conduct involved in the trade. Rather, what is intriguing is that not only did she quickly learn publishing "propriety," but she also attempted to redefine it according to principles that best served her own interests. Adams developed her own conception of trade morality, one based on an ethics of authorial priority and reciprocity.

The Memoir of Miss Hannah Adams is slight, but it is as good a record of a writer's interface with the business of the early national trade as any we have, and in this capacity it has been undervalued by literary historians. Adams goes into as much detail about her experiences with the trade as she does with any other aspect of her career. Her recollection of early American print culture reveals a world fraught with bankruptcies, trade piracy, and suspect ethics, perhaps the trade's most infamous badge of distinction. Almost fifty years later her animosity toward Benjamin Edes was still so strong that she understatedly attacked him in her memoir as one "whose name, out of respect to his descendents, I neglect to mention."[38] For the tactful Adams, this was a sharp rebuke. (Edes's reputation would survive intact: before Adams's run-in with him, the Boston Tea Partiers changed clothes in the back room of his Boston *Gazette* print shop.)[39]

Adams's early failures were typical, and she describes them in the terms Kelley alludes to above. "I felt that my ignorance of the world, and little acquaintance with business, would put me in the power of every printer to whom I might apply."[40] They did, at least initially. Indeed, when she had completed this first book, Adams knew nothing about these practices. Yet with the help of friends who "removed [her] perplexity by transacting" with printers, Adams quickly learned to navigate the business of books as well as any other writer of the first three decades of independence.[41] And while in the early years of the nineteenth century she found stability in the patronage of Federalists who, as Baym quips, "had no objection to publicizing a woman's intellectual work" when it accorded with their own beliefs, Adams nevertheless exhibited early in her career an ability to marshal the vocational and legal resources available to her.[42] In "meet[ing] this trial" of writing and publishing, whatever her successes and failures, Adams had become as much a businesswoman as an author.

ASSERTOR OF LITERARY CLAIMS

It is hard to exaggerate the pervasiveness of republican ideology in early American print culture. Even before the Revolution, printers such as Robert Bell could address frankly "Those Who Possess a Public Spirit" in a subscription advertisement, knowing that this spirit was the best way to people's purses. In an 1801 broadside, Mathew Carey based an appeal to printers and booksellers for the expansion of the print market on the prerequisite of print to a nation's growth. As "the grand means of disseminating improvements in the arts and sciences," printing was necessary for the continued "refinement of society." Without this expansion, the publishing "enterprize" would inevitably suffer along with "all that can render life of real value," that is, books.[43] Carey's rhetoric was not unique. His call-to-arms was primarily economic, of course, but its sentiments were underwritten by republicanism. Texts existed as didactic vehicles for individual and civic improvement. Again and again in the journals of the period the terms "use" and "usefulness" appear. As Michael T. Gilmore has observed, writers after the Revolution stressed that "literature was a public art and that, like the epic, it belonged and gave voice to the community."[44] As a literary occupation for women, meanwhile, history writing was the result of the popularity of republican discourse and Enlightenment educational policy. In the years following the Revolution, women were given a cardinal role in the making of a virtuous civic polity, an idea closely associated with references to women's "usefulness" to society outside their domestic duties in the new American home.[45] According to Baym, these "tenets guaranteed women intellectual parity with men and offered them the chance to serve their nation if they developed their minds."[46] Women writers began to look "to the past in order to substantiate their claims to intellectual equality in the present."[47]

One such writer was Mercy Otis Warren, whose *History of the Rise, Progress and Termination of the American Revolution* (1805) reveals the caution with which women used this ideology to legitimate their entrance into a male-dominated sphere. Appropriately titled "An Address to the Inhabitants of the United States of America," Warren's preface posits the dualism of the woman writer in the civic realm: "It is true that there are certain appropriate duties assigned to each sex; and doubtless it is the more peculiar province of masculine strength, not only to repel the bold invader of the rights of his country and of mankind, but . . . to describe the blood-stained field, and relate the story of slaughtered armies. Sensible of this, the trembling heart has recoiled at the magnitude of the undertaking, and the hand often shrunk back from the task; yet, recollecting every domestic enjoyment depends on the unimpaired possession of civil and religious liberty, that a concern for the welfare of society ought equally to glow in every human breast, the work was not relinquished."[48] Warren first articulates the weight of men's dual "provinces" as soldiers and chroniclers, reminding readers that she is "sensible" to the "duties" of her sex. But that she even mentions these duties acknowledges her awareness of the apparent contravention implicit in her authorship. Though she "tremble[d]" at her task, she nevertheless completed three volumes of Revolutionary history. Thus the impulse for her authorship was not that men have too large a responsibility to the republic but rather that she also had a dual function: to account for the war which protected her domestic role. "There is no country where the right direction of female influence is so necessary as in America," wrote a contributor to the *Ladies Magazine*, "because here the popular breath guides, as it were, the bark of state."[49] Republican discourse offered an arena for participation in the public sphere, albeit under a totalizing discourse of self-effacement—not the sort of activity likely to shatter gender boundaries.

Warren illustrates Mary Beth Norton's suggestion that successful women writers "managed to conceal their flouting of convention by subsuming their activities within the confines of an orthodox, if somewhat broadened, conception of woman-hood and its proper functions."[50] Adams and her supporters, however, embraced dissimilitude. This is not to say that the record of her career does not contain state-ments more typical of her contemporaries. After making a small return on the 1791 edition of her *Compendium* (retitled *A View of All Religions*), for example, Adams, sounding not a little like Paine, "formed the flattering idea, that I might not only help myself, but benefit the public."[51] Perhaps her best use of the republican persona was her preface to her *Abridgement of the History of New-England for the Use of Young Persons* (1805). "However this little work may be received," she wrote there, "the truths, that her desire to render herself useful, and her dependence upon her own exertions for a support, will be duly considered, and induce candid and gener-ous minds to acquit her of the charge of arrogance and presumption."[52]

But when we juxtapose the preface to Adams's first work with Warren's "Address to the Inhabitants of the United States of America," we find an example of authorial self-assertion unparalleled in early American women's authorship, even though it was composed for and not by her. As Adams and her supporters proved, republicanism, notwithstanding its universalizing discourse and ostensible disinterestedness, was a propitious sphere in which to establish the public self and, subsequently, to use that self to establish an authorial persona in the face of pervasive cultural chauvinism toward women intellectuals. This potential was also, of course, partially a result of a remarkably expanded print culture, which "introduced a world beyond the familiar that offered a host of alternatives."[53] Baym has argued that involvement with repub-lican ideology functioned as abstract female aggression toward emasculated republican histories—that the "act of writing history was itself, self-reflexively, the act of insert-ing a woman into history, as record keeper and referee if not major player."[54] I want to take her argument one step further. Just as Adams's dealings with printers immersed her in the business of print culture, her works inserted the woman writer into history. Where late in her life she would justify her trade "bargains" with a gesture toward providence (doing "what is right and necessary in the situation in which Providence has placed me"), the prefatory material to her histories justifies her claims.[55] The texts themselves become the "assertor[s] of literary claims." Adams and those writing on her behalf helped make the woman author a prominent feature among this "host of alternatives" because the print culture itself "served," in Kelley's terms, "as a catalyst in self-fashioning."[56] As with Paine, while in theory republican authorship purported to evacuate the authorial self from the text and its effects, in practice the authorial self could be vivid, especially when expressed as a moral ideal of right behavior in the face of political, cultural, or, more to the point, vocational constraint. In fact, the social practice of early American authorship could manifest a moral personality quite publicly and quite dynamically, in spite of pretenses to impersonality.[57]

Thomas Prentiss's preface to Adams's first book offers an excellent instance of this assertiveness.[58] Titled "To the Readers," it is a delicate rhetorical petition. Prentiss assured the reader that Adams did not venture "the vain ambition of appearing as an author" but nonetheless takes uncompromising positions on the potential for female learning and achievement.[59] On the surface the preface seems as conservative as Warren's, defensively justifying Adams's apparent intrusion into the public sphere as passive and the consequence of an "amusement" with the act of writing. We are told that the author has done nothing more than "impartially" collect information from "authors to whom she refers." The act of affixing her name to the title page of the text—a rare deed in the era of republicanism, especially for women—was done unwillingly; in fact, the very claim to authorship via her printed name did "violence to her own inclination" to remain anonymous. The final defensive posture was Prentiss's need to "sufficiently account" for Adams's use of Latin and Greek in her compendium by assuring the reader that her familiarity with these languages was the result of a childhood fondness for books.[60] This was a common method of introducing a woman-authored book. To preempt criticism regarding the indecorum of a woman's publishing, prefaces often alluded to the transgression of this decorum in a way that suggested that the respective author was aware of her infringement but felt she had sufficient cause—for example, Adams's learnedness or Warren's republican patriotism—to enter the public sphere. A writer often deferred censure of the "standards of propriety" by alluding directly to these standards and his or her faith in them.[61]

However, Prentiss's address was anything but conservative or paradigmatic, anything but complicit with the largely masculine decorum of the public sphere. At its most elementary, it is a political statement on the necessity of female education, which was a newsworthy issue of the period and thus a relatively safe polemic. Prentiss wrote that the "world has been absurdly accustomed to entertain but a moderate opinion of female abilities, and to ascribe their pretended productions [to] the craft and policy of designing men. . . . With equal advantages, it [is] far from being certain that the female mind would not admit a measure of improvement, that would at least equal, and perhaps in many cases eclipse, the boasted glory of the other sex."[62] What makes this an especially belligerent passage is its diction. "Boasted glory" indicates an element of male pomposity on the one hand and undeserved exaggeration on the other; "eclipse" is just as aggressive in its suggestion of one object casting another into shadow. His assurance that Adams does not harbor "the vain ambition of appearing as an author" served only to remind the reader, who was already in the act of reading a book by Adams, that Adams was *in fact* an author, whatever her gender. Writing for supposedly nothing more than the pleasure of scholarly endeavor, a woman—this woman—composed a work of history perhaps better than the works of men advantaged by formal education, leisure, and connections. Given the year, the republican climate, and Adams's talent, it is not unwarranted to suggest that Prentiss was announcing the arrival of the woman author into the public sphere and the potential consequences for male authors accustomed to writing works undeserving of the attention they received. This is precisely the issue that the Adams-Morse contest would foreground, laboriously.

Whether Adams agreed to the content of this paratextual introduction to her first book is of less importance than we might think, because public perceptions of an author have little to do with the reality of the author's life. This preface is an illustration of Baym's conviction that "the woman history-writer is necessarily engaging in a far more overt, directly political, and public literary practice than students of women's authorship have hitherto recognized."[63] Adams, in effect, began her career riding a bullet aimed at gender-exclusive conceptions of authorship in America. And she did not slow. Almost thirty years later the prefatory material to her books was significantly more assertive and even less apologetic. Whereas her first work in 1784 began with a justification of her labor, her *History of the Jews* (1812) opened on an aggressive note of scholarly maturity: "The history of the Jews since their dispersion has been but little investigated even by the literary part of the world."[64] Here Adams was plainly comfortable in her role as an intellectual, writer, and public figure. While at the conclusion of the preface she did thank her patrons, no longer did she attempt to justify her right to authorship and publication. More important, perhaps, in this 1812 preface she struck a note of scholarly originality. What effected the change? Adams's transition from "compiler" to respected and independent scholar-author was, I believe, the result of a very public argument with another very famous scholar-author, Jedidiah Morse, and the decision that she had a moral right not only to authorship but to agency in the business of print.

THE COURTESIES OF AUTHORSHIP

Literary historians have not recognized the importance of the Adams-Morse debate to the history authorship in America. At the very least, the debate is an illustration of the predication and maturation of Adams's authorial self along the murky ethical lines drawn by the trade. That is, it is an exemplary vision of the two versions of Adams I have presented thus far: a powerfully gender-conscious author and a versatile, even wily participant in the business of print. But it is also an illustration of Adams's effect on the moral status of the writer in the marketplace and in relation to her fellow professional writers, not to mention an indicator that author-author relations could be just as vexed as author-trade relations or relations among tradesmen themselves. If Adams's early career helped change assumptions about the de facto gender of authors, her later career revealed the problematic ethics of the newly expanded print culture she helped create.

In 1799, Adams turned to colonial history, publishing *A Summary History of New England*. Although she made a profit on *A View of Religions* in 1791, she was barely surviving financially, having published her *Summary History* at her own expense. Because at this time she could not afford to buy the texts necessary for her research and did not boast connections to individuals with personal libraries, she began researching in booksellers' shops, an image that ultimately became part of the myth of the celebrity scholar. Moreover, as with so many writers, her eyesight was failing intermittently and, as writing was essentially her sole means of procuring a living, she worried about her continuing ability to support herself. When her colonial history sold moderately well, she entertained the idea of abridging it for use as a school text, a market exploding in accord with the post-Revolutionary emphasis on education, and a market dominated by male writers like Morse.

In 1804 Adams approached Morse to ask if he were planning to abridge his history of New England for use in the schools. Morse assured her that she could proceed without worry. Destitute and placing her hopes for recompense in her abridgement, Adams soon received a letter from Morse suggesting that his co-author, Elijah Parish, had grave concerns about the concurrent publication of two histories of the same subject. Adams, after contacting Parish directly and receiving his word that he had said no such thing, completed her abridgement. Morse, it seems, had lied outright. When Adams went to Boston's Cushing and Appleton's bookstore to contract sales for her book, she discovered that the booksellers had already contracted to sell Morse and Parish's history and believed that there was no market for competing texts. It was at this point that wealthy Boston Federalists, specifically Stephen Higginson and William Shaw, both Unitarians, took an interest in Adams.[65] They helped her deal with Morse and, more important, handle the presentation of the dispute to a panel of referees. These judges passed down a vaguely worded but fairly obvious decision that impugned Morse and suggested (but did not mandate) pecuniary compensation for Adams's potential losses. For nine years, however, Morse evaded the judgment by claiming not to understand the terms of the verdict, though he did take from it that he owed Adams no remittance. In 1814, his reputation in shambles, Morse published *An Appeal to the Publick*, a hulking 190-page record of the events of the previous ten years. It only worsened his standing. The same year Adams published her own version of the

FIGURE 3.2 Jedidiah Morse, Courtesy Manuscripts and Archives, Yale University.

decade-long dispute, *A Narrative of the Controversy Between the Rev. Jedidiah Morse, D. D. and the Author.*[66]

Inarguably, gender is at issue in both accounts. Morse first attempted to paint Adams as "only" a woman, one used as the ideological device of men who purportedly exploit her sex and her reputation—a rather famous and sympathetic one, even as early as 1804—to advance their own causes. In his letters during the controversy and in his editorial comments in the *Appeal*, Morse portrayed Adams as an oblivious female "shield" and as a cultural bulwark for men intent on destroying his reputation.[67] In his version, Adams is a hostage to the polemics, invented by "ingenious adversaries," she does not and cannot understand.[68] Therefore, according to Morse, she had little right to "complain, if, in making my necessary defence against them, she should receive wounds." "Her character and sex are doubtless to be respected," he continued, "but if she would escape censure, she must have so much independence and self respect, as not to lend herself to my concealed assailants, to be used against me."[69] Morse could not recognize Adams as an author because he refused to recognize her intellectual or vocational independence. In the eyes of the referees, it was this incapacity to concede legitimate female authorship, a legitimacy based in part on a moral understanding of authorship, that ultimately undermined his case.

Morse employed the same logic in his letter to the referees in 1809. As Michael Vella notes, Morse masculinized the issue. "I am happy in submitting my cause to the decision of men . . . of men, who are accustomed to judge between man and man," he wrote, "and who can, therefore, with the more ease and precision, discern and define the prominent features and points in the controversy."[70] Morse again relegated Adams to a domestic sphere by defining her according to "her sex, her merits, her bodily infirmities, her poverty, [and] her aged parents."[71] He even called Adams's moral argument over authorial propriety and fair play in the print sphere—issues of colossal import in the growing print market, as he well knew—"complaints."[72] For Morse, this was a debate fit for men because only men understood the etiquette of the public sphere and the economics that shape authorship. If Adams erred by attacking a minister, a scholar, and an author, Morse condescendingly attributed the supposed affront to the "weakness in her, and in no degree to unworthy motives."

Morse recognized early, however, that Adams's reputation and, above all, her gender would put him at a disadvantage in the case. Notwithstanding the fact that he acted boorishly throughout most of the controversy, as one historian observes, Morse "found himself in an impossible position, for Hannah Adams was in all innocence using lethal arguments against which there was no defense."[73] As a result, he sought to expose the discrepancy in Adams's different versions of self. Publicly, observers and the referees repeatedly described Adams as a "lone" and "destitute" woman. In private, she was the opposite. Morse picked up on the fact that Adams and her benefactors employed two different discourses, which in turn produced two very different impressions of Adams during the years of the debate, and he sought to use this notion of a paradoxical and deceitful female self to his advantage. In the first discourse, Adams's correspondence with her advisors, she portrayed herself as a strong and willful agent; in the second, written largely by Higginson and Shaw, Adams's persona was weakened through an ostensible passivity.[74] To expose this duplicity, Morse juxtaposed two quotes that address the same idea in order to demonstrate these two personas and their origins. The first is Adams in a letter to Shaw (describing how Parish assured her that he had no concerns about the proposed abridgment); the second quote is from a statement made on Adams's behalf to the referees. I have reproduced both in the format Morse printed them in his *Appeal*:

STATEMENT TO MR. SHAW

"This interview, with Dr. PARISH, acquitted him in my opinion, and relieved my mind from a weight of anxiety which had injured my health, and retarded my publication."

STATEMENT TO THE REFEREES

"At an interview, afterward, this gentleman, (Dr. P.) overpowered her with professions of good will."[75]

In the later, public statement, Adams is the passive female victim, swayed by the kindness of gentlemen, an example of Adams's ability to consciously and rhetorically undervalue "her assertions of self."[76] Adams was adept at presenting, in Vella's words, "a false self-effacement, a posturing of a helpless female, something of a martyr." Also, though, Adams became the injured author, capable of holding an opinion and intimately familiar with anxiety over publication rights.

Why the difference? Higginson and Shaw probably believed that Adams had more of a chance to gain sympathy when perceived as a destitute woman than as a woman author. Adams's supporters employed the same paradigm of propriety that Morse did: they understood that women could hold copyright and negotiate "bargains," but implicitly questioned their rights to the print market and perhaps even the public sphere. Higginson and Shaw seemed unwilling to force the referees into a decision on authorship. They cared more about gender and saw it as Adams's best case. For Adams, on the other hand, authorial ethics overshadowed gender: it was a matter of market equity and justness. After all, she was pushed from the market in a competitive, opportunistic drive for sales. Morse biographer Richard J. Moss suggests that though we cannot know absolutely whether Morse did trick Adams, and if so whether he did so consciously, "one thing is clear: he acted with a keen sense of the market and his own self-interest."[77]

Thus, while critics such as Vella have explored the complex rhetorical use of gender, particularly by Adams and her supporters, I want to argue that the central issue in the debate was the author's moral right to the market. Though she rigorously vindicated her role as a woman author, Adams was more intent on coming to terms with her own intellectual capital and making gender serve her market parity in the early republic. In the *Narrative* she asked,

Had I no reason to complain, that such a man should enter on a literary ground preoccupied by me, helpless woman, dependent on the scanty products of my pen for subsistence? I do not question his legal right to publish a book on any subject that he pleased, nor his ability to write a far better book than I had done; but had I not a moral right to expect from my "patron and friend," that if he needed any addition to his splendid income, he would have devoted his talents to some other object, and have left to me the field chosen for my humble labours? Could I have expected, that he, who so well knew my situation, would come out to the world, with a book as copious as my original work, and nearly as cheap as I could be expected to be able to afford any abridgment of it?[78]

Initially the tone is chivalric: "such a man" takes advantage of a "helpless woman," conjuring the forsaken sentimental heroine. Clearly, Adams appealed to gender stereotypes to substantiate her argument that she had been wronged. Less clear was her appeal to trade morality. She suggested that Morse should have resigned the market to her because it was she who most needed the profits and because it was she who first voiced intent to publish. The latter claim is significant. It was the same logic that informed many of the informal ethics governing the trade, including, most notably, the ethic of prior right, on which legal and customary literary property formulas were based. In the jargon of the trade, she accused Morse of printing upon her. Where courtesy of the trade, for example, told printers what they could or could not print—that is, what rights existed and how they were to respect them—Adams proposed a kind of courtesy of authorship that bestowed on the author a prior right to a potentially profitable market, such as that of school texts. However, just as there was no legal basis for courtesy of the trade—indeed, as noted in Chapter 2, it was no longer applicable to domestic authorship—there was likewise no legal foundation for Adams's courtesy of authorship. Hence her admission that she had no "legal" complaint, only a "moral right" to authorship and the market.[79]

Recognizing the box into which Morse, Higginson, and Shaw relegated her and her authorship—a role she did not resist, necessarily—Adams went further than her defenders were willing to go. She attempted to redefine the social codes according to which writers interacted with one another in the market. Morse recognized this move. Perhaps anticipating the effect of Adams's courtesy of authorship, and the effect of an ethic yielding women market equity and cultural capital, he denied a woman author's ability to understand the system of social manners upon which the profession was based and which excluded, by and large, women writers. He denied the right of Adams to the market if she could not conceive of the implicit, "gentlemanly" rules governing authors' behavior. This is ironic, given that Adams showed that she understood quite well the social manners of their print culture. Morse had assumed that the de facto, belletristic culture of authorship predating Adams's career was sufficiently ordered and sufficiently male and that the referees would agree. Adams, on the other side, argued that this culture of authorship was insufficiently organized—it could not accommodate the changing market landscape—and that it was immoral.

This reading of the Adams-Morse conflict is less reductive, I would argue, with regard to Adams's own vocational identity. While it is tempting to apply exclusively reactionary readings to the contest, often the record will not sustain them. In her memoir, Adams essentially agreed with the principle of Morse's charge that she did not understand religious controversy:

> As I read controversy with a mind naturally wanting in firmness and decision, and without that pertinacity which blunts the force of arguments which are opposed to the tenets we have once imbibed, I suffered extremely from mental indecision, while perusing the various and contradictory arguments adduced by men of piety and learning. . . . Reading much religious controversy must be extremely trying to a female; whose mind, instead of being strengthened by those studies which exercise the judgment, and give stability to the character, is debilitated by reading romances and novels, which are addressed to the fancy and imagination, and are calculated to heighten the feelings.[80]

Her doubt of her own capacities implies that the presentation of Adams's authorial persona as privately aggressive but publicly timid was not necessarily duplicitous. Despite her stock attack on novel reading, Adams simply registers a complaint about women's education. It may be that she did not dispute Morse's attacks on her learning because she understood that her knowledge was not really at issue. Rather, at issue was the market, Morse's caustic public disavowal of Adams's rights as an author, and long-standing if implicit notions of trade civility. She appeared concerned primarily about the moral and legal formulations of the market and the author's place therein, not necessarily, or at least not as much, about attacks on her sex.

What is important about Adams's (re)construction of authorial ethics was its promotion of an authorial—and, in a sense, a vocational—ethic defined not by competition but by courtesy. In this sense it looked strikingly similar to Thomas Paine's vision of the proper relationship of author to trade. Whereas Morse conceived of authorial ethics according to issues of gender and social rank, envisioning authors as members of a kind of elite vocational club, Adams argued that the ethics of literary business should be based in principles of benevolence. In her rhetoric, gender was but one of multiple variables, albeit, in this case, a variable impossible for the judges to ignore. Rights were matters of an author's circumstances and honor. They proceeded, that is, according to a vocational ethic of benevolence. Gender was a point of strategic rhetoric both sides used to win the right to define codes of conduct among writers.[81]

At stake in this debate was the moral nature of authorship: whether authors had moral rights in the conduct of the business of print and how these rights could ultimately affect the market. "Does Miss Adams or do her friends," Morse asked, "claim the exclusive privilege of writing the History of New England?"[82] The question was extraordinarily pertinent. He recognized that Adams's salient complaint against him—that he lied about publishing a text that ultimately excluded hers from the market—was more ethical than legal (hence his ability to evade the referees' decision for so long). His subsequent questions implicated this changing definition of authorial ethics and the place of gender therein. "Will the laws allow" Adams to have exclusive right to this topic? Is her text more important, and hence should his be "suppressed," "merely because one was written by a worthy female, who is poor, and meritorious? Have we no rights?" The answer was easy: the laws did not create or recognize these kinds of rights. State and federal laws could not allow an author exclusive rights to any topic, because they did not recognize ownership prior to publication. Nevertheless, the referees decided that while Morse and Parish did "not violate any right, which any Judicatory, legal or equitable, is competent to enforce," these rights were trappings only.[83] The referees essentially adopted Adams's stated view of the case: that though she had no "legal" case, she had a "moral" one. Morse and Parish had brazenly injured her "moral right" by exhibiting an apparently wanton ignorance of the courtesy of authorship. "Miss Adams, by her pre-occupation of the subject, and her assiduous and useful labours in the management of it, was entitled to attention and respect from gentlemen contemplating a publication of like import, embracing the same period of time, and which, unless obviously defective, must necessarily exhibit strong features of resemblance to Miss Adams's work," the referees found. "The peculiar circumstances of that Lady, were also to be regarded, and would seem to require particular tenderness and attention, in any procedures which might tend to diminish the profits of her literary labours." The referees, swayed by Adams's self-effacement and her arguments proposing an ethic of benevolence, set a tenuous precedent for authorship and for literary property—a precedent that in effect superseded existing legal constructions of authorship and intellectual property. Where the 1790 copyright legislation had made the printed text into a legal right, Adams succeeded in locating this right in an author's "preoccupation of [a] subject."

Adams's argument and the referees' decision were clearly duplicitous. Bearing in mind that state and federal copyright laws came into being in the 1780s and 1790s and that the expanding markets forced authors to conduct themselves in ways that increasingly contravened republican conceptions of authorship, her assumption of an informal but governing ethical precedent was opportunistic. Adams had copyrighted her works as soon as she was able, after all, and she was a vocal advocate of the federal copyright law of 1790. In other words, Adams took very seriously the legal safeguarding of an author's intellectual property and the legal right of the author to participate in the market equitably, yet she attacked both in her complaint against Morse by basing her case on a moral premise. Adams wanted to subsidize the author's legal rights with a courtesy of authorship—a sympathetic vocational ethic that took into consideration an author's circumstances.

Had this ethic become custom in the business of publishing it would have had immense implications for the legal definitions of literary property. Meredith L. McGill has shown how, for example, the decision in the copyright case *Wheaton v. Peters* (1834) circumscribed an author's right to a text at the moment of publication.

The case established "the ideal American text as one that operates powerfully in the absence of an author" insofar as writers surrendered their natural rights to their productions when they went into print.[84] In the Adams-Morse debate, however, the referees took a very different view. Though noting the absence of legal relevance, in effect they located moral rights to a proposed text preternaturally in the author herself, before the text even existed. They radically privileged the author over the market—conception over production—an idea that would be negated legally by the majority decision in *Wheaton v. Peters* and, in fact, a decision at odds with most Western ideations of intellectual property. As Adams had wanted, the referees reduced the argument to an ethical question, isolating authorship from its legal definitions and making it a moral construct. Given the language of the decision, we may assume that had Morse's litigant been male, the issue would not have been so complicated. That is, the referees might not have gone so far as to define an author's moral right to a text as prefiguring the actual production of the text itself. Yet neither would it have forced this panel, or the public sphere, for that matter, to so specifically address the gender politics and ethics of authorship in the early nineteenth century.

Whether what privileged Adams's rights over Morse's was her sex or her "circumstances," the controversy revealed an ironic double standard attending early national authorship. Authors could publish what they wrote and could legally protect what they published, but some authors had more moral rights to the market than others. In this case, the woman had more rights, at least conditionally, than the man. Adams's application of varied personas and ethics, in effect, won the day. We should be careful not to claim this leverage for all women writers, however. As commentators have observed, had her cause not been taken as a "cause célèbre" by "some Boston ministers of the Unitarian faction who were already battling Morse," Adams likely would not have merited preferential treatment by the official sphere as represented by the referees or by the public sphere as represented by the periodicals.[85] Thus it is likely that the referees in the case would not have corroborated this courtesy of authorship or the consignment of intellectual property to the intellection of an idea. Adams was able to take authorship further than any woman before her because she was a respected scholar and a celebrity writer and because she had captured the imagination, pity, and respect of two important elements in society, the press and the Boston elite. But both contributed to the social and moral construction of Adams's authorship and, perhaps unconsciously, to the precarious courtesy of authorship on which she based her claims.

Both Adams and Morse lobbied for the first copyright legislation, enacted in 1790. A few years later, Morse was involved in the first case trying out the act, *Morse v. Reid* (1798). In it, Morse sued an American printer who reproduced an English geography text that had borrowed liberally from his *American Geography* (1789).[86] The case was a clear violation of domestic copyright as articulated by the law, and the court decided in Morse's favor, awarding him damages.[87] Had the offending book been printed only in England, however, Morse would have had no legal recourse, because there was no copyright treaty between England and the United States. Morse would have only had a moral right, a right based in the same logic of precedent espoused by Adams. The strange, sensational career of this moral right, about which so much ink was spilled after the deaths of Morse and Adams in 1826 and 1831, respectively, is the subject of the next chapter.

4

The Moral Vernacular of American Copyright Reform

IN 1847, A British expedition returned from the wilds of New York carrying an extraordinary cargo: American reprinters, or more specifically, "North-American Book-Men" from the "Brordweigh" tribe. The British were beside themselves. These "natives of Nooyorck" were "the first that, from their unprincipled and thievish habits, could ever be induced to visit a place of civilization." The primitive publishers would be studied carefully. There was even talk of mending their ways. The British trade, for one, was bent on "enlightening the minds of these North-American savages, and, if possible, [on] reclaiming them from their degrading and disgusting habits" of pirating English books. "We are happy to state that several worthy Christians in and about Paternoster Row . . . evince the greatest interest in the amelioration of the condition of these people; and will spare no pains to teach them the simple lesson of *meum* and *tuum*." Such lessons would likely be lost on the tribe's full-grown reprinters, however, whatever the optimism of some in the trade. The tribe's best hope, and the best hope for honest publishers and writers everywhere, lay in a child who had been born to the savages en route. While the infant reprinter was as healthy as could be expected—during the crossing he had been suckled by a pirated edition of Dickens's *Dombey and Son* "rolled into something like a sugar-stick"—his character hung in the balance. "MESSRS. LONGMAN have—with their characteristic benevolence and liberality—offered to take the poor baby Book-man, and bring him up, decently and honestly, in their own house. We trust they will be permitted to do this; otherwise, there is every fear that the child, on returning to Nooyorck, will join the pestilent tribe of *Amer-ic-anp-ubl-is-hers*; a race more brutal than the Cherokees, more ferocious than the Iroquois."[1]

NORTH-AMERICAN BOOK-MEN.

HIS will, doubtless, prove one of the most extraordinary exhibitions ever seen in Europe. The North-American Book-men are natives of Nooyorck; landed in Liverpool by the brig *Whole Hog,* Captain Go-a-head; and will be exhibited for the first time next week at the Royal Institution. They are two men, two women, and a baby—of the Book-men tribe from the Brordweigh; and are the first that, from their unprincipled and thievish habits, could ever be induced to visit a place of civilisation. This opportunity of gratifying the English author, and the student of English letters, has only been obtained by a party of gentlemen (connected with the LiteraryFund) who have brought the Book-men to England at an immense outlay of capital, with the Christian view of enlightening the minds of these North-American savages, and if possible, of reclaiming them from their degrading and disgusting habits. On the passage to Europe the baby was born at sea. Now, had the baby (it is a boy) been born in the Brordweigh, there is but little doubt that, bred to the customs of these forlorn Book-men —who do not know another man's property from their own—the poor child would have been as morally lost as its unhappy parents ; but there is now every hope that the child will be placed in Paternoster Row, and brought up in the respect of good men's good works.

These people are called Book-men, from their custom of living upon leaves of every kind. Indeed, they will gobble any substance upon which anything can be written or printed ; the leaves of the talipot, properly sauced with printer's ink—the bulrush, whereof was made the ancient papyrus, bark, parchment, anything soever that is printed upon—these Book-men will greedily devour. But there must be ink —printer's ink—English ink—enshrining the brains of English authors, their brains, and heart, and blood—to make it particularly palatable to these benighted Book-men, who are sometimes known under the compound name of *Amer-ic-amp-ubl-is-hers.* As an instance of the ravenousness of the tribe for this kind of nutriment, we may inform the reader that the baby of these Book-men lived upon a number of *Dombey and Son,* rolled into something like a sugar-stick, half the voyage.

The following is from a modern author's work on *The North-American Book-men* :—

"Miserable Bookman ! Thy hand has been against every one ! For generations past thou hast hunted the English author like the beaver or the civet-cat ; thou hast followed him like the wild ostrich, and not caring to meet his eye, hast robbed him of many a *Tale.* Depriving the British author of what Nature made his own—(but what the Congress of the freest nation upon airth opinionates he has a just right to be robbed of)—thou hast become cruel, fierce, insolent, and —in short, a nuisance."

(For particulars and habits of these Book-men see reprints of English books).

We are happy to state that several worthy Christians in and about Paternoster Row—with other good men at the West End—evince the greatest interest in the amelioration of the condition of these people ; and will spare no pains to teach them the simple lesson of *meum* and *tuum.*

We, moreover, understand that Messrs. LONGMAN have—with their characteristic benevolence and liberality—offered to take the poor baby Book-man, and bring him up, decently and honestly, in their own house. We trust they will be permitted to do this ; otherwise, there is every fear that the child, on returning to Nooyorck, will join the pestilent tribe of *Amer-ic-amp-ubl-is-hers ;* a race more brutal than the Cherokees, more ferocious than the Iroquois.

Dreadful Complaint.

THE prevalent complaint, in the City, is that the BANK is labouring under a severe tightness across its money-chest. If something is not speedily done to relieve the old lady, there is no knowing what the consequences will be. TRADE and COMMERCE (who are dependent for their daily support, and are generally fed by the BANK with a gold and silver spoon) are completely paralysed for the want of their usual food. Persons who know their cases the best, declare that TRADE and COMMERCE must certainly die of inanition if the BANK does not immediately give "a little bullion," or something nourishing, just to keep them alive.

THE BATTLE OF THE ARCADE.

THE traveller who has lately perforated the recesses of Exeter Arcade, must have remarked that the southern chain of that interesting pass is thoroughly depopulated. On making inquiry into the circumstances, we have found that the barbarian horde of a brutal bailiff has fallen upon the primitive inhabitants of that peaceful nook, which has been the scene of the most heart-rending and window-smashing struggles.

It is, perhaps, not generally known that the dwellers in this secluded fissure of the nook which divides the plains of Catherine and North Wellington, have hitherto led a life of rural indolence ; and, indeed, their Arcadian simplicity in taking shops in this Arcade must at once be recognised. The mild and patriarchal beadle had all along exercised a kind of parental despotism over the little family, and they might often be seen, at the close of day, drinking together the beer of urbanity from the pot of social intercourse. One afternoon lately, ere the simple Arcadians had retired to the fastnesses of their respective huts, a savage, armed with a writ, came to spread terror in their hearts, and furniture all over their pavement. The ruffian, aided by another of his unfeeling class, had got a *fi. fa.,* and, with a shout like that of—

> "FI FA O FEE fum,
> I smell the goods of an Englishman,"

he pounced upon the "little all" of an artificer of fancy slippers. Wild shrieks instantly rent the air of that little inclosure—the Vaucluse, or Val Chiuso of the British Metropolis. The good old beadle, startled from his post-matutinal dose, was instantly on his legs, and, grasping instinctively his official staff, approached the scene whence the cry of distress had arisen. There he found a table, evidently on its last legs, giving creaks of agony as it was being torn away from the spot ; while its affectionate owner, folding its flaps to his bosom—like the green leaves of hope—clung to its claws with passionate energy.

From the room above a cruel attempt was being made to let down a sort of sofa ; while a frantic voice screamed out, "Ye shall not lay low the ottoman !" The beadle had only time to mutter to himself— "Woman in distress !" before he was at the scene of confusion ; and, throwing himself into a majestic attitude, with upraised staff, before the shop-door, his sentiments formed themselves into blank verse without any effort :—

> "How now ! What's this ? Hallo there ! Who are you ?
> Come, come ! You 'll leave that chair alone, young man.
> A writ, pooh ! pooh ! so, so, if that's the dodge,
> You 'll please to look at this, and this, and this."

As he spoke the last line, he suited the action to the word, by producing three several distresses for three distinct quarters' rents which had never been enforced, and which he contended gave him a prior claim to the goods that were the subject of the struggle. The bailiff barbarian sneered in the face of the good old man, who suddenly, from a mere lamb, sprang up into a semblance of a lion. His eyes flashing with recent double X, his nostrils dilating with dignity, and his whiskers twinkling with electric fire, like that on the back of a cat, when its back is regularly up, he sprang upon the table, and taking an attitude of defiance, defied the bailiff to

> "touch it, with but a look."

The man of law was for a moment abashed ; but renewing the struggle, he had nearly succeeded in carrying off his prize, when the beadle, knowing the geography of the place, bounded off towards the western postern, which he secured by lock and key, his wife having already taken the hint, and barricaded the eastern frontier. The result was a parley, and it ended in the bailiff being obliged to march out with the honours—and raps on the knuckles—of war, leaving the beadle sole master of the field ; upon which, after the first excitement had passed, he "cried like a child," and buried his head in a small basket of toys, to conceal his emotion.

It is true victory crowned the efforts of the Arcadians ; but the *chaumière* had been desecrated ; and as the Eastern yellow-hammer never returns to the nest once looked upon by human eye, the debtor no longer finds repose in the dwelling that has fallen under the falcon glance of his creditor. In either case the twig must be for ever hopped ; and such has been the result of the scene we have been describing.

FIGURE 4.1 "North-American Book-Men," from *Punch*, Courtesy General Research Division, New York Public Library, Astor, Lenox and Tilden Foundations.

London's *Punch*, the source of this farce, was only slightly more tabloid than other media in its account of the international copyright debate in the mid-nineteenth century. The absence of an agreement between the United States and Great Britain meant that the unauthorized edition of Dickens that suckled the little savage was perfectly legal. To many, it was also morally reprehensible, since American publishers could reprint foreign books at will without paying their authors a shilling. Reformers, who argued that reprinting was an egregious illustration of an unprincipled trade running roughshod over the sacred rights of authors, petitioned Congress to change the law no fewer than 160 times before 1875.[2] The reprinter, the "pirate behind the counter," had subjugated these rights to an economic expediency protected and even encouraged by the state, or so the reform script went.[3] The debate, as carried out in newspapers, magazines, and books, on lyceum stages, in counting rooms, and in Congress, was complex and often angry. What was at stake? According to those against international copyright, the economy was up for grabs. An Anglo-American agreement would centralize publishing in London, and to London would go the considerable economic spoils. Book prices would skyrocket, because the few surviving domestic publishers would be forced to charge hardworking Americans for the privilege of reading Dickens, who supposedly already had more money than he could spend. The United States would again become a colonial dumping ground for London. Those in favor of international copyright, on the other hand, complained that under the present system London already dominated the domestic market, and thus the trade had no compelling economic reason to encourage domestic authors. Many of the books published in lieu of American titles were considered—almost never individually but en masse—corrupting. This literature corrupted American morals, and deserving American authors were made to suffer by publishers more interested in turning a profit than in promoting domestic genius. Worst of all, reformers said, the absence of international copyright was itself immoral—an embarrassing national failure that revealed the banal ideology of a country that had sold its soul for dollars.

Dreaming of a book trade governed by ethics rather than economics, reformers sought to revise American law to protect foreign writers. They targeted an antebellum audience that still regarded ethics as a fundamental component of economics and that believed in a law more compelling than that handed down by highly lobbied legislatures. Reformers performed for this audience with righteous rhetoric and sensationalist metaphors.[4] For example: "From the original wrong, lying in many cases close to the heart of society, there spreads a secret and invisible atmosphere of pestilence, in which all kindred rights moulder and decay, until their life at last goes out at a moment when no man had guessed at such a result."[5] This was Cornelius Mathews, a New York business lawyer and literary dilettante who rarely met a platitude he did not adore. Mathews, who really did believe that reprinting was a kind of cultural and political cancer, was the chief prognosticator in a prolific group of doomsayers whose apocalyptic rhetoric was more the rule than the exception in the media. Like other reformers, he used what Ezra Greenspan has called a "language of abstractions and ideals often far removed from the language of tough political realities" in an effort to convince Americans of the need for a new law that would recognize the absolute rights of authors to their texts regardless of national boundaries.[6]

This chapter is about the metadiscourse of international copyright in the mid-nineteenth century. More specifically, it is about the media debate over what George Palmer Putnam called, with ironic understatement, the "nice abstract question" of whether authors had natural rights in the first place and if so how far they extended.[7] While this debate has received impressive attention, the discourse of reform has not. Critics usually either confine themselves to noting its obtuseness, often euphemistically, as in the suggestion that reformers "expressed themselves energetically," or they demonize it, as in the observation that reformers "repeatedly suppressed the political issues concerning the act of public writing in favor of some tortured rationalizations about the corporeality of literature."[8] Rather than write off the discourse as a distraction, I argue that it was itself a central issue. These "tortured rationalizations" of reform were a strategy for foregrounding the ethics, as opposed to the economics or politics, of the question. Reformers used discourse to monopolize right and to cast authors as the persecuted moral authority in a nation ruled for the worse by the economic expediency of businessmen. The discourse of copyright reform, this unscripted but rather consistent moral vernacular, was the handiwork of an interpretive community that both consciously and unconsciously ignored the reality of literary property and created in its place a kind of unreal world in which natural law was paramount and morality trumped judicial and political decisions.[9] In this moral economy, reprinters had no place.[10]

While I begin with an account of Anglo-American copyright law, my subject in this chapter is not so much copyright as it actually existed but as reformers imagined it. Since no one imagined copyright more conspicuously or publicly than Cornelius Mathews, the chapter's second section focuses on his reform writings and his claims about the cancer of reprinting. Section three, in turn, tackles the primary weapon of Mathews and other reformers: metaphor. Reformers' metaphors, I argue, were neither haphazard nor illogical, as literary historians have charged. As if rising to Dickens's challenge in *American Notes*—that "it would be well" for Americans "if they loved the Real less, and the Ideal somewhat more"—reformers used metaphor to isolate reprinting from its legal reality and reframe it as a purely moral matter.[11] They wanted to make the ideal real. Following the lead of opponents of international copyright, the next section turns the reform argument upside down and asks how representative it and its discourse really were of authors' views of copyright. Archival evidence suggests that a few voices presumed to speak for all authors and that their rhetoric may have been the biggest stumbling block to actually passing an international copyright law. The chapter concludes with a brief consideration of the efficacy of the moral argument when divorced from the moral vernacular by commentators such as Edgar Allan Poe. Much copyright reform writing reads like a fretful Sunday school lecture on natural law and the business devils that would slit its tender throat. Poe's writings suggest, however, that the moral imperative behind reform did not have to be sensationalized to function as a sharp critique of the ethics of American publishing.

THE PUERILE TRASH OF COPYRIGHT LAW

When in 1829 the *American Jurist and Law Magazine* speculated about the future of copyright in the United States, it anticipated rich opportunities not for authors but for lawyers. The "darkness, difficulties, and uncertainty" of copyright law created a ripe litigation environment, the *Jurist* concluded.[12] Its ominous but accurate forecast grew from its own uneasiness with a law that left open the question of whether an author had a natural right to his productions, a right that preexisted law, or whether an author's right was created by law. Given Great Britain's long debate over just this question and the tenuous resolution of that debate in 1774, the indeterminacy of early American copyright law is hard to fathom. Why did it read as though it had been formulated in a historical vacuum?

The English copyright legislation known as the Statute of Anne ended the monopoly of the Stationers' Company, the London guild responsible for licensing and printing texts in England. The 1710 act created a copyright term of twenty-one years for works already published and a term of fourteen years for works yet to be published, with the possibility of a fourteen-year extension at the end of the initial term. Before 1695, when the Stationers' charter expired, copyright was perpetual, though printers owned the copyrights. Anne gave authors a legal right to their texts for the first time, but its framers carefully avoided bestowing a concomitant moral right by excising draft language suggesting that authors possessed "undoubted property" in their creations.[13] Nevertheless, Anne was sufficiently vague to leave open the question of who owned a text at the expiration of the statute's term. At term's end, did an author's rights revert to natural law, which was perpetual? Or did the statute take the place of natural law and so relegate the text in question to the public domain after it was no longer protected by the state?

The Statute of Anne was, as David Saunders reminds us, a practical solution to an economic problem: the Stationers' Company monopoly had become an economic liability to a rapidly expanding commerce. It was a "trade-regulation statute" and was thus not intended to invent a legal category of "author" complete with moral rights.[14] In fact, it was London booksellers and printers who superimposed on Anne a moral agenda, recognizing that with careful massaging the statute could be read as a state compendium to ratify and enforce the natural rights presumably retained at common law, an interpretation that would effectively reinstitute their monopoly and protect them from upstarts ready to capitalize on public domain titles like *Paradise Lost* (1667). The trade wanted rights to these titles in perpetuity. Governed by this strategy, the trade manufactured a case and then for thirty years agitated the courts in order to get Anne interpreted in its favor as an affirmation of perpetual copyright by virtue of its recognition of an author's unassailable natural right to his own creations. In 1769 these printers—or in the popular view, the forlorn authors they gallantly represented—seemed to win the long contest. In *Millar v. Taylor,* Lord Mansfield ruled that Anne coexisted with the common law rights of copyright holders; when the statutory right provided by Anne expired, an author's or assignee's right reverted to common law, which was based on natural law and was perpetual. The case was appealed, however, and in *Donaldson v. Beckett* (1774) the House of Lords overturned *Millar v. Taylor*, ruling that while there may once have existed a natural right to literary property at common law it was rescinded by Anne.[15] In the end, authors' rights to their productions were a function of the law and nothing more.

With *Donaldson v. Beckett* a popular mythology was born: an unjust state had stripped the author of his moral rights to his creations. In 1912, copyright historian R. R. Bowker complained that because of *Donaldson v. Beckett* literary property "lost the character of copy-*right*, and became the subject of copy-*privilege*."[16] In 1837, a Maine magazine put the matter more bluntly, lamenting that "the rights of authors were frittered away by judicial construction."[17] No matter that authors had never really had any rights before Anne or that after Anne such rights were but speechcraft in printers' frantic attempts to resuscitate their monopoly. No matter that Anne made no necessary equivalence between authorship and rights. *Donaldson v. Beckett* had the unintended effect of martyring authors' imagined natural rights and of making copyright a moral cause célèbre.

Two years after *Donaldson v. Beckett,* another moral cause was born out of a perceived transgression of natural law. In Philadelphia, the Declaration of Independence published "to a candid world" America's faith in "the Laws of Nature and of Nature's God." But was "Nature's God" present in the nation's early definitions of copyright? This was the question implied by the *American Jurist* in 1829. Such language was used explicitly in early state constitutions, but it was at best implicit in federal law.[18] Its presence in the Constitution and in the Copyright Act of 1790, for example, depended on how one interpreted the verb "secure." The Constitution "promote[s] the progress of science and useful arts, by securing, for limited times, to authors and inventors, the exclusive right to their respective writings and discoveries."[19] Opponents of international copyright would later argue that literary property rights were secured—that is, *bestowed*—not by nature but by the legal first mover, the Constitution. Reformers, on the other hand, argued that the Constitution secured—that is, *confirmed*—an a priori right. After all, how can one secure something that does not already exist? In 1834 the Supreme Court settled the question, dragging the United States into the *Donaldson v. Beckett* era. It ruled in *Wheaton v. Peters* that natural rights to literary property were, in effect, a myth. The Constitution did not ratify an existing right to literary property; instead, it "created it."[20] In addition, the court ruled, the state constitutions that explicitly recognized this right had no bearing on federal copyright law. The majority opinion claimed that "it has never been pretended, by any one, either in this country or in England, that an inventor has a perpetual right, at common law, to sell the thing invented." Though a dissenting opinion pointed out that *Millar v. Taylor* corroborated just such a right, it was too late. Authors' natural rights were already legal errata.[21]

Reformers reserved a special place in hell for anyone who denied the existence of these rights. The "bombastic, puerile trash" of British copyright law was a lesson in hypocrisy, judged the *North American Review*.[22] Worse, it said, the die was cast for Americans. "So deeply has the notion taken root" that the only right to a literary text is an artificial one, "that the framers of our constitution do not seem to have dreamed of [the author] having anything more than such temporary exclusive right."[23] "There was once such a thing as a law of nature and truth, such a thing as the light of reason, such a thing as the common sense of mankind, dictating what was base, what was honest, what ought to be done and what ought to be avoided," the *Southern Quarterly Review* protested, still fuming a decade later, "but all these are now abandoned as having been quite worn out in the service of our forefathers, and artificial speculation drawn from refined metaphysical reasonings, and Statutes and Constitutions and judicial decisions are established in their place."[24]

When antebellum reformers looked at the founders and their copyright laws, they saw what they wanted to see: concern for the absolute rights of authors to their texts across space and time. Further, they saw the restriction of such rights as an affront to the nation's founding principles and conventional morality. The *Messenger* went so far as to remind Americans of their philosophical heritage by rewriting the Declaration as a commentary on authors' natural rights: "when a long train of abuses and usurpations, pursuing invariably the same object, evinces a design to subject *our nation to the charge of injustice and oppression*, it is *our* right, *it is our* duty, to throw off such *practices*, and to provide new guards for the security *of the inviolable rights of genius and talent*."[25] Opposition to reform was not only immoral; it was un-American.

Early American copyright law was not designed, however, to endow authors with natural rights. Both the Constitution and the federal copyright act of 1790 were articulations of a utilitarian, economic vision of America's international role. As economist B. Zorina Khan notes, the country was "a net debtor" in the transatlantic culture trade, and so it made sense to encourage reprinting rather than restrict it.[26] Saunders's characterization of Anne as a "trade-regulation statute" is just as true of legal definitions of intellectual property in the post-Revolutionary United States as it is of early eighteenth-century England, and the most historically faithful definition of copyright in early America may be Khan's: "the economic bargain underlying the limited grant of a monopoly to authors and their assignees in exchange for the improvement of social welfare from the products of their efforts."[27] The particular form copyright law took was a reaction to and a reflection of the relatively unimportant place of the nation in Atlantic culture. It was not a reaction to or a reflection of the plight of genius in America. If anything, copyright divested genius of presumed natural rights.

Reformers might be forgiven for believing that the state had invested authors with statutory rights equivalent to the natural rights they claimed. The language of copyright is frustratingly open to interpretation. For the *American Jurist*, intellectual property was "subtle and perplexing," an imperfect marriage of positive law and abstract rights.[28] It forced authors and the trade into an uncomfortable proximity to what Supreme Court justice Joseph Story called "the metaphysics of the law."[29] But metaphysics makes for muddy legislation, as proved by English copyright cases of the late eighteenth century and Story's own muddled decisions.[30] Even in this, the age of William Blackstone, there was no shortage of skeptics who regarded natural rights as dangerously ambiguous. Edmund Burke saw their "abstract perfection" as their "practical defect."[31] One could not govern a country with abstractions, as the French had so horrifically proved. David Hume argued that what was right was bound up with civil society itself and was skeptical of instinctual notions of justice.[32] Jeremy Bentham denied natural rights altogether. Noting the shape shifting of such rights in Blackstone's writings, Bentham ridiculed this "phantom Law of Nature."[33] Like revelation, natural law was paradoxically "solid and conspicuous": solid for true believers, conspicuous for everyone else.[34] Outright denial of natural law on the order of Burke, Hume, and Bentham, though, was rare. More common was the belief in such rights but not in their application to an author's publications. People believed in authors' natural rights in theory but not in practice.[35]

It was relatively easy, therefore, for opponents to characterize reformers' argument for the natural rights of authors as speculative, unrealistic, and irresponsible. They saw no point in debating the metaphysics of copyright; the highest courts had already decided in favor of utility. Authorial right is "entirely the creature of legislation," one critic wrote, aping the matter-of-fact approach of most opponents.[36] This argument from legal fact was the favored strategy of the opposition. Harper and Brothers could justly stress, as the firm did in a congressional brief, that in opposing reform *"we do not inflict injustice or commit a wrong.* Copyright is not anywhere admitted to be a *natural* right, else it would be wrong to *limit* it, as all nations . . . do."[37] Opponents like Harper and Brothers argued, essentially, that whatever was legal was moral, a move familiar to modern business ethicists.[38]

Reformers, meanwhile, saw the law as a travesty, and they saw in the status quo an illustration of the immorality of the business of print. As the *Southern Literary Messenger* put it, the legality of reprinting "does not by any means make it innocent. . . . The principle is wrong; and it is beyond the power of man, by any method of association or combination, to make that which is radically wrong, right."[39] Reformers stressed the methodological function of natural law as a remedy for unjust positive law. This was not some sham argument. It is the same principle that informs Henry David Thoreau's "Civil Disobedience" (1848): "Can there not be a government in which the majorities do not virtually decide right and wrong, but conscience?"[40] Thoreau's reputation was not so different in his own time from that of Cornelius Mathews, really—a fringe figure whose rhetoric tended toward the transcendental and the preachy. George Ticknor Curtis stood considerably closer to the mainstream, though, and his reiteration of the role of natural law and morality in the American legal system better illustrates the logic of the reform argument. His

Treatise on the Law of Copyright (1847) reminded readers that natural law was germane when there existed a "defect of positive law," as in the case of "literary property."[41] Without natural law, all law is positive and created by the state. Natural law is thus a check on the state's power to define reality through the law, as the *Southern Quarterly Review* posited.[42] For most reformers, the international copyright debate was not about literature, or trade, or really even law. As Mathews framed it, the debate was about "the nature of things."[43]

CORNELIUS MATHEWS AND THE RHETORIC OF RIGHT

In 1843, Charles Dickens was happily home in England after a tour of the United States that left many Americans decidedly unhappy. During his visit, Dickens had had the gall the criticize the ways of American reprinters, an act that was seen as disingenuous because these reprints had helped make him the most popular writer in North America. The trouble started early in Dickens's tour, on the evening of February 18, 1842, in Boston, where the city's luminaries and guests, including Washington Irving and Cornelius Mathews, had gathered to welcome him. Aware of his very public feelings on the immorality of reprinting, his hosts asked Dickens to avoid the subject. Surprisingly, he complied.[44] Mathews did not. He stood and commenced an insistent speech on the evils of the status quo. Dickens, whose letters about the gala dinner suspiciously ignore Mathews, did not remain quiet on the subject afterward, and though his subsequent attacks on the American trade were infamously antagonistic, their acerbity fell well short of that of Mathews that night in Boston.[45]

Mathews was at his most belligerent and inventive, wielding metaphors like blunt objects. He mourned with persecuted grandeur the plight of authors, "victims of false systems," in an era whose other casualties, such as Native Americans and African slaves, were not figuratively but literally dying at the hands of expedient politics.[46] Mathews decried a world in which author-"orphans" were deprived of their property by an indifferent legislature and an unfeeling trade. Certainly his choice of analogy was in poor taste. Considering that the nation was just emerging from the Panic of 1837, a five-year economic downturn that nearly devastated the trade and crippled the American economy, most guests would not have said publicly that the lack of an international copyright law illustrated "that the conditions of human life are hard indeed." For Mathews, though, the status of literary property in America was a human rights issue.[47] Reflecting the tacit belief of many reformers, he looked forward to a time when opponents of international copyright would be made to answer for their sins.

For proof, one need only consider Harper and Brothers. In 1842, Harpers suffered one of the many devastating fires that plagued the house. Though fires were a frequent occurrence not just for Harpers but for all publishers and allied trades, there were loud whispers—just as in Harpers' 1853 fire—that the most despised publisher

FIGURE 4.2 Cornelius Mathews, Courtesy Library of Congress.

in the country was the target of industrial espionage: attempting to pilfer a reprinted novel Harpers was preparing to issue, some rival had inadvertently caused the blaze. Officially, the fire was declared an accident. For Mathews, it was divine judgment. "If the conjecture should not prove a fact," he preached, "it ought to be one, because this is just the period and the very order in which we might expect an incident of this kind to occur." "Piracy and burning are, perhaps, so nearly akin that, after all, they have wrought out the sequence more naturally than if it had been left to the friends of copyright to suggest to them in what order they should occur." Mathews employed deus ex machina to forcibly correct the moral wrongs of reprinting. It was "natural," even "logical" that Harpers should burn because of its commitment to reprinting and that it should do so at the hands of like-minded moral savages.[48] If Congress would not chasten these publishers, god would.

Mathews's lofty rhetoric is all over the best-known American reform treatise, *An Address to the People of the United States in Behalf of the American Copyright Club* (1843), where he, William Cullen Bryant, and Francis Hawks promised to eschew legal abstraction and speak plainly about the problem of reprinting. On behalf of the Copyright Club, a New York group formed to press for international copyright, they fashioned copyright advocacy into a nationalistic, moral crusade against the government and its passive encouragement of British cultural and economic imperialism. "The cause appeals to your generosity, your sense of justice, your self-respect, your patriotic attachment to your countrymen in their noblest pursuit," the Club's manifesto declared. Reform was the "duty" of all good Americans.[49] Maybe so, but to many the *Address*'s holier-than-thou language was more offensive than rousing. Even sympathizers were critical. One complained that its authors should not expect to win friends by damning the audience. "Expediency, liberality, good policy, good feeling & the present state of the literary world, all may be urged with propriety and possibly with effect," lawyer Joseph Ingersoll wrote to Francis Lieber. "But to urge upon a community of readers that they are all thieves, because they buy a novel of Mr Bulwer's . . . is a little extravagant."[50] Lowell wrote to Charles Briggs to praise an entirely different pro-copyright pamphlet, calling this latter one "the best writing upon that subject which I have ever seen." He suggested that the Copyright Club give it away in lieu of selling its *Address* because it "would do more good than 10000000 of their 'Addresses.'"[51] Like most of the Club's audience, Lowell apparently missed the point of the appeal. Briggs did not, though, writing that the Club's *Address* was an attempt "to induce the people to reflect on" copyright as an issue "which affects the morals and liberties of the country."[52] Briggs, at least, understood that the *Address* was meant to be sensationalistic.

The *Address* has been attributed to Bryant, but its hyperbole was more characteristic of Mathews.[53] Dickens may have boasted to anyone who would listen that he made copyright a public issue in the United States, but it had long been in the headlines, and Mathews's rhetorical efforts—Briggs called them "monkey shines"—kept it there, at least in the early 1840s when the debate was at its most heated.[54] Perry Miller rightly remarks that Mathews "excited among his contemporaries a frenzy of loathing beyond the limits of rationality."[55] There is no question that he was a divisive figure, and when he is remembered today, it is for the obsessive loyalty he inspired in friends like Evert Duyckinck. As Lowell put it, Mathews was a parasite who clung to Duyckinck and other well-placed friends who, in return, went "to work as systematically to make him a reputation as a joiner would to manufacture a box."[56] He was also known for rhetoric that tested, in the words of one magazine, "the limits of common sense" and drove even friends to distraction.[57] His writing smacked too much of Thomas Carlyle, whose name was synonymous with all that was dreaded and pompous in prose—in a word, "transcendental."[58]

Whatever his embattled personal and professional status, Mathews was a prescient critic who understood the commercial logic of reprinting, as demonstrated by his Boston speech. In it he envisioned Irving supplicant before American publishers. With a new work in hand, Irving travels to New York with a neighboring farmer, both with something to sell. The farmer sells his goods easily. Irving, the beloved author of *The Sketch Book* (1819), is not so fortunate. He calls first at Harper and Brothers and is told that his work must take a back seat to Bulwer-Lytton's new book. "'For heaven's sake, Mr. Irving,'" Mathews has Harpers say to America's most famous author, "'don't plague us just now,'" as the less-than-noble brothers focus their massive resources on getting the pirated Bulwer-Lytton novel on bookstore shelves before dawn. Irving moves on to Appleton only to meet with another rejection. "Behold," Mathews concluded, "the author of the Sketch Book . . . very much in the situation of the ostrich of the desert having an egg to lay, but no where to lay it; and, like it, I might add, greatly disposed to hide his head for very shame."[59] Opponents had a field day with the analogy, using it to attack Mathews's and by extension all reformers' credibility and tact. "If ever an individual established beyond controversion his claim to be written down, with honest Dogberry, 'an ass,'" the New York weekly *New World* said, "then did Mr. C. Mathews." It disputed that "any bookseller in the United States would not eagerly purchase" a new book by the beloved Irving.[60]

But Mathews was right about Irving, and he was right about the priorities of firms like Harper and Brothers. George Palmer Putnam's proposal to reissue the *Sketch Book* in the 1840s was a risky venture. Irving's Philadelphia publisher, Lea and Blanchard, had not done well by his books of late; three months after Mathews's speech, Irving's contract with the firm was not renewed. Later, Irving looked back on Putnam as a savior: "You had confidence in the continued vitality of my writings when my . . . Philadelphia publishers had suffered them to moulder. . . . You called them again into active existence and gave them a circulation that I believe has surprised even yourself."[61] Mathews's analogy was rude and goofy, but it was also exact and evocative. The trade's love of cheap foreign books allowed less room for the domestic author, even one as adored as Irving. And if Irving could find no quarter on Broadway, lesser American authors might as well give up. In sum, however preposterous he could be, Mathews was not quite the "ass" copyright opponents and even his friends thought he was, or that opponents needed him to be. There was substance to his bombast.

There was also design. "The weapons employed in the [copyright] controversy are, as might be expected from the antagonists, wholly intellectual," the *Southern Quarterly Review* said in 1843. "Words, and thoughts clothed in words—'thoughts that breathe and words that burn,' are the instruments of attack and victory."[62] The allusion to Thomas Gray's "Progress of Poesy" (1759) was a common one in the nineteenth century. The lines

> Bright-eyed Fancy hovering o'er
> Scatters from her pictur'd urn
> Thoughts that breath[e], and words, that burn

were shorthand for a belief in the power of poetic discourse.[63] The allusion appears as well in writings about mid-century reform movements as cultural shorthand for the belief in the power of reform discourse. The *Philanthropist*, for example, described the Convention of Anti-Slavery Women as an opportunity to experience in person the force of reform, "enjoy[ing] the satisfaction of seeing each other, face to face, and hearing from each other's lips, 'thoughts that breathe and words that burn.'"[64] The *Liberator* used the lines more than once to describe antislavery appeals and the rhetoric of abolitionists such as John Greenleaf Whittier.[65] For antislavery periodicals, Gray's lines were a way of articulating the "moral suasion" of early abolitionist writings: the rhetorical appeal to a morality independent of law without necessarily undermining the rule of law.[66] A similar rhetorical context informed copyright reformers' correspondence, as in Mathews's plea in an 1842 letter to "Agitate—agitate!" on behalf of international copyright. The same imperative appeared in the newspaper the *Colored American* the previous year: "let our motto be, Agitate, Agitate . . . until victory is obtained."[67]

Piggybacking on abolitionism was common among all manner of reformers, including copyright reformers. Not long before Charles Sumner was caned on the floor of the Senate for his antislavery views, Putnam asked him to lend his prestige to an elaborate festival scheduled to be held at New York's Crystal Palace by New York publishers to honor American authors. Sumner was Putnam's living symbol of "unflinching fearlessness" for "stand[ing] up in the front ranks of the battle for freedom & humanity."[68] The senator's proposed toast as well as a long speech on the history of printing and publishing that would open the event were, according to Putnam, "intended to hint in general terms, towards a suitable international copyright" and tie "a recognition of the rights of *authors*" to political duty.[69] Already designed to gloss the ill will between authors and the trade, the festival was further engineered to gloss the complex relationship among the state, the trade, and authors on the subject of literary property and so frame copyright as a nationalistic call to arms blessed by politicians, publishers, and authors alike. Putnam, like Mathews, wanted to send the message that higher powers smiled upon copyright reform. "The hour of Appeal passes rapidly away; the hour of Retribution swells darkly toward us," Mathews once warned, advising Americans to pray for "deliverance."[70]

When champions of the status quo found themselves facing the wrath of god, it is easy to see why John L. O'Sullivan, the influential editor of the *Democratic Review* and himself once a reform advocate, would half-jokingly fret his defection to the opposition.[71] He understood only too well how it would be perceived by reformers. With mock trepidation, he foresaw them "lift[ing] up their indignant hands in holy horror at our backsliding."[72] Reformers had long since assumed the moral high ground, so that anyone daring to disagree must be "damnably heretical."[73] O'Sullivan knew that the copyright debate had been stereotyped by authors like Mathews as "radical wrongs" versus "radical rights."[74] And the reformers were, naturally, radically right.

PIRACY AND OTHER OFFENSIVE METAPHORS

Despite the exaggerated clarity with which both sides of the debate saw them, the principles behind copyright were (and are) anything but clear. The *American Jurist* spoke for most observers when it complained that there were "no difficulties more subtle and perplexing than those which grow out of that species of incorporeal property which men have in the productions of their own inventions."[75] Justice Story called copyright "one of those intricate and embarrassing questions, arising in the administration of civil justice" that resists "satisfactory conclusion." Like patents, copyright depended on "distinctions" that could be "very subtle and refined, and, sometimes, almost evanescent."[76] Opponents were charged with a failure to understand this subtlety. Horace Greeley suggested that the "original sin" of opposition arguments lay in their separation of the metaphysical from the physical. Opponents of international copyright "attempt to draw a distinction where the laws of the Universe make none," he wrote, "between Property in the creations of the Brain and in those of the Hands."[77] But the difficulty of explaining the reality of the metaphysical—of making a novel's ideas as morally and legally real as the pages on which the ideas are printed—was a serious obstacle for the reform argument. In the act of reprinting, reprinters did not physically steal any books. How to prove, then, that there was a problem in the first place? How to prove that literature even constituted property? While some reformers balked at these questions—"It is not for [the author] to show that his property *is* property; but for such as doubt to show that it is *not*," Mathews spat—they nevertheless grasped for metaphors that would make arguments about illusory property ideas less illusory.[78]

No reformer's metaphors were more aggressive than Mathews's. As noted earlier, even reform sympathizers had trouble with them. It is "a very good argument, or rather a strong popular appeal . . . in which he considers the interests of the country as identical with its moral obligations," one sympathetic reviewer said of the Boston speech—a polite way of saying that Mathews's logic and style were wanting.[79] Another sympathizer could not suppress his bemusement over the more puzzling analogies: "Giants, elephants, 'tiger-mothers,' and curricles; angels, frigates, baronial castles, and fish-ponds, 'dance through his writings in all the mazes of metaphorical confusion.'"[80] Mathews was skilled at violating nearly every rule of metaphor taught by Hugh Blair's *Lectures on Rhetoric and Belles Lettres* (1783), the most popular rhetoric of the era. They could be "florid," inappropriate, inaccessible, and mixed.[81] He was not alone in running afoul of Blair's rules of the language, though. Reformers' metaphors often illustrated "more enthusiasm than depth of thought," as the *American Publishers' Circular* said about one particularly obnoxious example. Still, as bizarre and controversial as they could be, these metaphors usually served their purpose, which was to reduce the argument to its most basic principles—to compel Americans, as William Gilmore Simms put it, to "look behind the letter of the law."[82] This was a key strategy for reformers. "The law is not the code of our soul; the constable not the substitute for our conscience," Lieber told a Miami University audience in 1847.[83]

The most potent but also the most controversial metaphor was piracy. In 1842, *Arcturus* published a satirical letter from one "John Smith, a Convicted Felon." Writing from the Tombs, New York's most infamous prison, the author—likely Mathews—celebrated America's healthy kleptomania and advised Americans to resist enacting laws that would deny human nature: "let us all steal, and resolve society into its elements."[84] In the *Knickerbocker*, Briggs echoed this sarcastic call to arms. How could the United States live up to its "free and independent" ideals if "restrained, by self-imposed laws, from making free with the labors of rival nations?" Why not learn from the Algerines, Briggs asked?[85] Another reformer suggested that Americans had already learned all they needed, because here, in plain sight of god and country, walked "a number of reckless adventurers, who steal the property of foreign writers, and . . . make us a nation of literary Algerines."[86] All three authors used the presumed immorality of reprinting to suggest the moral corruption of the nation at large. The panic caused by Barbary pirates in the early years of the century, when the press whipped up hysteria over Algerian raids on shipping, was a recent memory for many Americans. Calling the United States a "nation of literary Algerines" associated it with the images of lawlessness and piracy that had dominated the press in the formative years of American foreign policy and domestic market development. Now, according to reformers, American reprinters, "fitted out and paid for by their countrymen," had been issued "Letters of Marque" [*sic*] and become the Algerines of the modern world."[87] The *Mirror's* allusion to the extralegal royal permissions granted to privateers by otherwise lawful nations was a refrain in reform writings. "It is only in the most barbarous and savage country, that the inhabitants rob and plunder, indiscriminately, all foreigners, who come upon their shores," the *North American Review* moralized. "By what rule of national or international law, then, are letters of marque [*sic*] and reprisal granted, against all foreign authors, in time of peace no less than in a time of war?"[88] Opponents of international copyright were too comfortable, it would seem, with the "moral obliquity" of theft.[89]

Because the unauthorized reproduction of foreign titles was not illegal, literary historians caution against the use of piracy in reference to reprinting.[90] Technically, the word *is* a misnomer, but it was meant to be. Reformers seldom used "piracy" literally. Moreover, they pointed out that such literalness missed the point. Piracy was a metaphor used to characterize reprinting as an illiberal appropriation of property. The word "sufficiently designates public sentiment, in its application to literary pilfering," the *North American Review* explained.[91] The connotation of criminality was just that—a connotation. By conspicuously ignoring the legality of reprinting and disentangling it from its complex economic reality, the metaphor reframed reprinting as a basic moral offense for a public that knew or cared little about the finer points of the law.[92] As Adrian Johns says of its European usage, "piracy" made reprinting a breach of civility.[93]

American reformers also used the metaphor to implicitly question the ethical climate of the law itself. "Piracy" was used to show, as Duyckinck put it, that "what is in itself wrong, is yet perfectly legal."[94] Its use was not a miscalculation of copyright law, therefore, but a discreet calculation and estimation of its perceived wrongs, a tactic, according to the *American Publishers' Circular*, for disclosing "all that injustice which, when committed in America, is pleasantly denominated piracy."[95] In 1888, publisher Henry Holt summarized the rhetorical appeal of "piracy" over the century. "As to definitions: the gentry who are accused of piracy indignantly repudiate the term, because their proceedings are within the law, that is, within the law of their own country," he wrote. But "In Algiers piracy was within the law too."[96] "Piracy" simultaneously presumed the impropriety of reprinting and protested against the law that made it permissible. Technically mistaking the law even as it determined public conceptions of the law's immorality, the metaphor advanced a moral reasoning that existed outside of the law in a cultural realm of popular notions of right and wrong. In sum, piracy as metaphor compelled people "fettered by technicalities" and suffering from what Simms called an incapacitating "literalness" to understand the principle at stake in the debate: that the status quo was immoral.[97]

Attention to the use of the metaphor of piracy helps explain why the oft-heard opposition argument—here voiced by tradesman Philip Nicklin—that morality was a function of the law, and as a result "English books are not *unjustly* reprinted," was met with almost violent impatience by reformers.[98] Reformers were not claiming that reprinting was illegal but that it was immoral. "The principle is wrong," the *Messenger* practically screamed at Nicklin, "and it is beyond the power of man, by any method of association or combination, to make that which is radically wrong, right."[99] For his part, Mathews took great delight in the fact that "republishers . . . groan under the aspersion of piracy and pillage laid at their door," that "they complain of the harshness of epithet which denounces them as Kyds and MacGregors," because it showed that efforts to reframe the debate via metaphor touched a nerve.[100]

If reprinters were uncomfortable being stereotyped as pirates, they were indignant at being marked slave traders, another favorite metaphor of reformers. The *Mirror* praised England for its willingness to embark on the "abolition of this intellectual slave-trade," this "most contemptible kind of 'man-stealing.'"[101] The *American Monthly Review* also tied the legally sanctioned tactics of American reprinters to the ways of slave traders. "There is no more justice in [reprinting] than there would be in the conduct of a strong man who should seize upon his neighbor and compel him to work for him, and when the work was done should pay him whatever he thought proper for his services."[102] The *American Monthly Magazine* suggested that the status quo endorsed "the oppression of one class of citizens for the benefit of another class"—a "principle . . . more obnoxious than any other to the spirit of republicanism."[103] Again, reformers wanted the fight for international copyright to be indistinguishable from the fight for the human rights of racial minorities, among them Africans and Native Americans. Indeed, without prior context it can be difficult to distinguish the natural law arguments against slavery or in favor of Native American land claims from copyright reform. William Ellery Channing opened his essay *Slavery* (1835) with the declaration that "The first question to be proposed by a rational being is, not what is profitable, but what is Right," a construction recalled in the *Messenger*'s criticism of opponents.[104]

Of course, there were severe incongruities in such analogies, most notably the fact that some Southern advocates of international copyright were also stridently pro-slavery, among them Simms, whose *Morals of Slavery* (1852) argued that Jefferson's assertion that "'all men are created equal'" was just "a finely sounding" rhetorical flourish typical of French "paradisiacal fancies." The "performance" that was the Declaration should not be "subject[ed]," Simms warned, "to a too critical scrutiny, in respect to its generalizations," one of which was the not-so-minor point that natural rights apply to all human beings. Simms believed that these rights instead depended on the execution of one's duties to nature, and clearly Africans and Native Americans had failed in their natural duties.[105] In short, Simms's calls for a universal respect for natural rights applied only to slaveholders, whites, and writers.

Surprisingly, opponents tended to overlook these incongruities and reacted with innocent outrage at the rhetoric itself.[106] One dressed down the London *Times* for "calculat[ing] to deepen the impression so prevalent in England, that the Americans are distinguished for a willingness to profit unjustly by the labors of others," whether by appropriating the intellectual labor of the British or the physical labor of Africans.[107] An indication of just how sensitive opponents were to similar insinuations is further provided by Nicklin, who bristled at the charge in an 1837 British Congressional petition that American reprinters not only immorally reproduced British texts but altered certain books in order to avoid offending Southern book buyers. This, Nicklin responded, is "a very grave charge."[108] He scoffed at the suggestion, noting that the petitioners failed to provide evidence for their accusation.[109] Worse, they implicitly equated Northern publishers with Southern slaveholders. "If the allusion be to slavery," he wrote, knowing perfectly well it was, "it was not respectful to make it to the Senate, in which *all* the states are represented in their corporate capacities." Given that most of the books published in the United States were produced in the North, "where British opinions on that grave topic are not in disrepute," publishers would not alter the texts. His logic was faulty, though; likely his facts were as well.[110]

Morality was not a priority for most publishers, the exact reality copyright reformers wanted to change.

American reprinters were not slave traders. Nor were they pirates. But reformers wanted and needed to create an equivalency between reprinters and pirates and slave traders to convey a sense of trespass. Reformers wanted and needed to encourage a prejudice against the status quo and create a belief that there was a better way to deal with literary property.[111] Their metaphors are best understood, accordingly, as rhetorical appeals to the ideal in the face of the real. As discussed in the next section, however, opponents of international copyright were adept at undercutting both the ideal and the presumed moral authority of reformers trying to actualize it.

THE TIRESOME RIGHTEOUSNESS OF REFORM

"War is waged in this country and England on the subject of International Copyright," the *Southern Quarterly Review* said in the summer of 1843, a year in which the debate was especially intense. "New-York, Philadelphia and Boston are the great battle-grounds, where are to be found, in secluded retreats, the garrets of the authors, and, in more frequented thoroughfares, the 'baronial castles'—as Mr. Mathews calls them—of the publishers."[112] That summer a small number of New Yorkers, including Briggs, Mathews, and Duyckinck, met at a New York hotel and formed the aforementioned American Copyright Club. In a gossipy letter to Putnam later that year, Duyckinck spoke of the group as though it were a gentleman's club. It "promises," he wrote, "to be a very agreeable affair."[113] (In the same letter, he noticed that ever since cheap publishing took off and Harper and Brothers stood to gain considerably by it, all because of the absence of international copyright, "Colonel" Harper had acquired quite a sense of humor: "He is as elastic and playful as India Rubber.") Putnam, meanwhile, spent part of the summer riding the East Coast in order to log what he, Duyckinck, and others believed to be true: that copyright was on the minds of all good Americans. Dickens and Carlyle thought so too, though they had considerably less faith in Americans' inherent goodness. *Brother Jonathan*, after quoting a letter from Carlyle to Dickens praising the latter's pluckiness during his 1842 tour, reported that conversations in its New York offices were not exactly drowned out by raucous mobs championing copyright reform. Let "the new school of Dickens and Carlyle" believe what it wanted; most Americans could not care less.[114] *Brother Jonathan*, a mammoth weekly that had made an art of mass-remediation, likely would have said the same even if there had been riots, but its observation that international copyright was not yet the public issue reformers believed it to be was accurate. While Putnam could boast that in one "quiet country town" he had witnessed a debate on international copyright conducted by Connecticut schoolboys, whose "arguments were really able and ingenious on both sides," for most Americans reform remained the hobby horse of a few spoiled authors and trade Pollyannas.[115]

Supporters of the status quo attacked reform on a number of fronts, though none so viciously as its self-righteousness. The most incisive critique was Augustin-Charles Renouard's *Traité des Droits d'Auteurs, dans la Litterature, les Sciences, et les Beaux-Arts*, better known under the title by which it was translated and reprinted by the *American Jurist* in 1839, "Theory of the Rights of Authors."[116] Like Henry Carey's antireform *Letters on International Copyright* (1853), Renouard's argument was not all that original, but it was straightforward and persuasive, and unlike Carey's book or Philip Nicklin's *Remarks on Literary Property* (1838), Renouard took on in a serious way the European philosophies girding natural law arguments for international copyright.[117] Denigrating reformers as idle "theorists" and their argument alternately as a "hypothesis" and a "theory," Renouard reasoned that international copyright advocacy was facile and based on emotion and impulsive conjecture.[118] Such righteous theories of literary property may have once been in force—Renouard admits laws once recognized copyright in perpetuity in England, France, and Holland—but now modernity "restrained" them, telling diction for a treatise that implied that both reformers and their case were trapped in conceptual adolescence. Mature nations and their citizenry recognized that "practice is the touchstone of theory" and that practice, in turn, is codified by law.[119] "I do not hesitate to say," Renouard patronized, "that the universal practice of enlightened nations" matters more "than the agreement of the theorists, even if they were unanimous."[120]

Renouard portrayed reformers as confidence men and the moral vernacular as propaganda. "The proper employment of words is not a matter of trifling importance," he reminded readers. "When they are confused or ill made, they introduce obscurity or disorder into the ideas of which they are the signs. I have no fear in saying, that the prejudices, which obscure the matter we are now considering, derive their principle strength from the right of citizenship, which the writers, an interested party in this controversy, have given to the expression, *literary property*, by the help of which they have habituated people's minds to their pretensions."[121] Renouard recognized reformers' presumption of moral authority through which they tried to make abstract rights seem real, all but saying: witness in the moral vernacular of copyright reform the caprice of a bunch of elitists who have forgotten what it means to live in a republic.

"Theory of the Rights of Authors" had a calculable impact on reform sympathizers. In 1840 Francis Lieber published an open letter to Senator William C. Preston that Preston in turn dutifully read to Congress.[122] But later, when Preston read Renouard's treatise, he admitted it "staggered" his advocacy, making him doubt that copyright had anything to do with "the moral law of property."[123] "Theory of the Rights of Authors" may have likewise shaken the senator's trust in the integrity of reformers who had, it charged, bamboozled the public into believing in the natural rights of authors. By uncoupling the issue from legal reality, reformers duped the public into sympathizing with the cause. Thus "literary property" was not simply a misconception, according to Renouard; it was a calculated ruse. Or as O'Sullivan put it, the moral vernacular of American copyright reform was "humbug."[124]

Like other opponents of international copyright, and like many who write on the antebellum debate today, Renouard assumed that there was a large critical mass of advocates for change. It is a fair question, though, how many authors actually worried about the "radical wrongs" of copyright. It was, to be sure, the "great *Literary* question of the day" for a number of editors, authors, and even publishers, as the *Southern Literary Messenger* called the debate, but not for everyone.[125] Letters about Kantian ethics or Lockean property theory do not overflow nineteenth-century publishers' archives.[126] Instead, these archives consist largely of correspondence from nervous authors asking practical questions concerning what they naturally cared about most: themselves, their manuscripts, and, if they were so lucky, their reputations. When authors did ask about copyright, their questions usually involved how much it would cost in dollars, not morals. When some authors were prompted outright to think about the morality of the status quo, they showed a lack of understanding of the kinds of theoretical issues and moral claims people like Mathews advanced. Such ignorance and disengagement are evident in responses to Mathews's appeals to acquaintances for help in the cause. The prolific Unitarian minister and author Orville Dewey responded, for example, that he "floated along upon tho'ts such as yours, which I supposed to be better than my own; but I really do not know much about the *pros* & *cons* of the matter." Dewey offered to lend his name to copyright reform but there is no evidence that he went much beyond that gesture. Like others, his concern stopped well short of activism.[127]

Most authors were happy simply to get into print. While Mathews and Dickens stressed the evils of reprinting, others stressed more mundane things. They asked for the return of declined manuscripts. They asked for puffs. William Giles Dix asked that his book be published before his "heroic" mother died.[128] Many authors, that is, cared less about the fate of natural law in the modern state than about getting into print and making sure others saw them there—or, alternately, making sure that others did not see them there. "I am a practicing attorney, just commencing the life of a business man, and some of my numerous scribblings in the Messenger & elsewhere have unavoidably been identified," John Esten Cooke wrote to Rufus Griswold in 1851, trying to explain why he wanted his name left off his sequel to Alexandre Dumas's *Le Bâtard de Mauléon* (1846–47). His plan was "to live down these trifling literary productions, and to gain a reputation for practical business talent. The reputation then of a writer of an extended work would be almost fatal to me—how much more so of a *French* work, a sequel to Mr. Dumas'!"[129] Two years later Putnam received a letter from Cooke begging a notice of his forthcoming *Leather Stocking and Silk* (1854) in *Putnam's New Monthly Magazine* and disingenuously cautioning the publisher against thinking he was asking for a puff.[130] Despite his apparent schooling in the art of advertising—he solicited another puff from Duyckinck a year later—his experience in producing three respectably selling novels (as he tells it), and not least of all his legal training, Cooke knew almost nothing about copyright. And when he asked Duyckinck about it, he gave no indication that he was apprehensive about any trampled natural rights. Instead, "a few practical points of information as to the Copyright usages of New York Publishers would be of very great service to me."[131]

Some authors did not understand even as much as Cooke did about these "practical points," a situation that could wreck a firm's already narrow profit margin on domestic publications. In 1849, Grace Greenwood, who knew the law enough to knowingly satirize it, nevertheless sought Fields's advice on it, feeling "as green as green can be" about the economic complexities of publishing her first novel, *Greenwood Leaves* (1850).[132] In 1865, Ticknor and Fields admonished its authors to be more careful in granting permission to use copyrighted material, warning of "serious results" if such "laxity" were "not checked."[133] When Louisa May Alcott failed to appear in Montreal on the London publication date of *An Old Fashioned Girl* (1870)—which would have been enough to secure English copyright for the novel—her English publisher, Sampson Low, could barely contain his displeasure. "Although we got the sheets and were enabled to publish the book here as soon as it was pub[lished] in Boston," he wrote, "the one essential element of residence on British Territory on the day of publication in Eng[land] was wanting to render the question of copyright indisputable." Now the book was out in the world without a legal guardian "and we shall have to fight with very weak and doubtful weapons should the pirates turn up as they undoubtedly will if the book proves a success and they can discover a flaw in the law."[134] This was the voice of experience. The "flaw in the law," euphemism for the total absence of law governing transatlantic publication, was common knowledge. As Low feared, a rival publisher quickly capitalized on Alcott's mistake. Low wrote to the reprinter asserting his dubious rights and was ignored, just as he had predicted.[135] Such warnings constituted the "weak and doubtful weapons" available to publishers in such cases. Had *An Old Fashioned Girl* proved the blockbuster *Little Women* was, Low would have had cause to post a less politic letter to Alcott. Alcott, incidentally, seemed not to have understood Low's lesson in copyright, given that she had to be reminded again later that year that her works had to be published in England first if they were to get British copyright—then reminded again the next.[136] Even Longfellow misunderstood his rights under copyright, earning him a sharp rebuke from Carey and Hart in 1845.[137]

Other authors understood copyright but were skeptical of the benefits of an international agreement. Author and editor Richard Grant White, a close friend and colleague of a number of reformers, fretted about the economic implications of a more expansive copyright law. "I am a free trader," he wrote, "not only by conviction & because free trade is a part of liberty, but because I need cheap clothes, cheap tools, and cheap books."[138] James K. Paulding worried that copyright would do anything but improve American literature, because for every one American author who secured British copyright, twenty British authors would do so in America, effectively monopolizing the transatlantic market. Plus, why would any British publisher pay American authors when the English laughed off their "republican sentiments"?[139] Paulding apologized to his correspondent for going against what seemed to be the popular opinion among authors, "but," he wrote sardonically, "you asked me for my opinion, and I have given it frankly."[140]

The average mid-nineteenth-century American, meanwhile, had no reason to care at all about copyright either way. Nor did the average congressman, much to the delight of opponents. As one British essayist put it, copyright reform smacked of elitism: it was a tax on "the very many who read for the benefit of the very few who write."[141] To most, the law was already fair. And it was already democratic. Congressional refusal to protect foreign authors, Meredith McGill reminds us, "was not inconsistent with but integral to many Americans' understanding of the nature and scope of domestic copyright protection."[142] Furthermore, American copyright law was consistent with the Constitution's economic rationale.[143] In the United States, readers outweighed authors. The positive social consequences of copyright were seen to be far greater than the negative consequence of morally disenfranchising a small group of elites, no matter how outspoken.

Self-serving reformers were nothing new in the antebellum United States, certainly, but at least it was obvious to most Americans how temperance or abolition could be motivated by selflessness. The push for international copyright was much less obviously so, if it was at all. Also, Americans were suspicious of massive internal-improvement projects, and copyright reform was an improvement project on a grand if abstract scale. As John Lauritz Larsen writes, "Schooled by experience to fear navigation acts, bounties, monopolies, tariffs, and restrictions—all designed in former times to benefit favorites or enrich the government—most Americans gravitated unconsciously toward . . . the liberal 'free trade' promise that the end of interference in the marketplace guaranteed equality for all."[144] Reformers came off as overzealous protectionists, or, more to the point, as selfish pedagogues. "There is an aristocracy in the literary, as well as political world. It would limit science to the few," the *Cincinnati Weekly Herald and Philanthropist* observed warily. "Cheap literature it abhors, as the social aristocrat does universal suffrage. With such, the clamor about an international copyright is most popular."[145] In an 1837 letter to the Philadelphia publishing firm McCarty and Davis, one bookseller worried that the concerns of the elite—worse, a foreign elite—might win out over the practical concerns of the book business: "Congress have had, as yet, but one side of the question presented to them. Unacquainted with the practical details of the book business, they are disposed to pass the Bill which is urged upon them, under the plea of 'justice to foreign Authors'; but which, it will be seen by those engaged in the business, is rather to be considered as a protective duty for foreign Booksellers."[146] Reformers' protectionism jeopardized the trade and the very foundation of republicanism as well: an informed electorate. Thus the logic of Harper and Brothers' view on copyright reform as expressed in the congressional brief alluded to earlier: that such reform was a threat to "popular enlightenment and prosperity."[147]

Who were authors to dictate what Americans should think, anyway? If they constituted "a persecuted class," as *Putnam's Monthly* said they did, maybe they were not ready for a modern economy.[148] *Brother Jonathan* cautioned that elevating the concerns of authors above others would engender a "race of pigmies unfit to aid in the development of the resources of the new world."[149] Even advocates perpetuated such characterizations of authors "wholly destitute of what we call 'a practical turn of mind,' and . . . of no use to themselves or to society except when busy with their quills."[150] Edgar Allan Poe and Charles Brockden Brown may have been gifted authors, but "they would have been unequal to the duties of ordinary clerks," one critic predicted. As McGill points out, the very "pretext for legislation that would discipline the reprint trade through the figure of the author-as-proprietor" was, ironically, that authors were incapable of making it on their own.[151] In addition, opponents suggested, and not without reason, that reformers' objectives were not selfless. They had mouths to feed—and egos. Authors "have had always," Carey wrote, "a high degree of belief in their own deserts."[152] That he echoed Robert Bell's view of Thomas Paine should not come as a surprise.

I want to be clear about my argument here. I am not suggesting that authors did not care at all about the morality of the reprint trade or that everyone worked in ignorance of its realities. Rather, I am suggesting that a handful of vocal authors cared a great deal and that these authors waged a war of words on the government and offending members of the trade on behalf of what they genuinely believed was the general good. What many authors did know of their rights they learned in bits and pieces from these reformers and their rhetoric. For this reason, I am uncomfortable with Grantland Rice's assumption that outside of slavery "there was perhaps no debate more insistent for writers in antebellum America than the issue of 'literary property.'"[153] Our idea of that debate comes from those for whom it *was* the most important debate, slavery included. When we presume to know what these authors cared about most we recite what figures such as Mathews, Simms, and Dickens wanted us to believe. As Arnold Plant warns, echoing Carey, Nicklin, and other nineteenth-century skeptics, "Bias, and fear of bias, makes an author's judgment on copyright a little unreliable."[154] I am equally uncomfortable with McGill's contention that "literary critics' ability to understand what was at stake in American opposition to an international copyright law has been obscured by the outsized figure of the aggrieved and indignant author; it is only by recognizing and circumventing this figure that we can begin to account for American resistance."[155] But in bypassing the reform personality and his rhetoric, we lose sight of the sine qua non of reform: the way the obfuscation of literary property makes plain how authors idealized not only copyright but, in the process, the moral and social authority of the author.[156] The relatively sober tone of Edgar Allan Poe's writings on copyright suggest, by contrast, just how far afield reformers' language had gone.

WHAT POE SAID

In 1857, the New York Book-Publishers' Association convened to formally address the international copyright question. While the Association ended up supporting copyright reform, multiple publishers worried both about the reform argument and the way in which it had been represented. Reformers had long blamed a powerful publishers' lobby in Congress for the stillbirth of international copyright, but, as publisher William Appleton saw it, the blame rested with reformers themselves. In a letter read at the meeting, Appleton laid out his view:

> "It seems to me that we must abandon the view of the question, based upon natural rights, and content ourselves with the fact that all civilized countries have not so regarded it, but have, on the contrary, limited the right by Legislative enactment; and that, but for legislation, all literary property would be unprotected. If this is the case in the country where the author resides, that even *there* he finds no *natural* right, it becomes a question of policy, whether another country shall create laws for his pecuniary advantage. It is not, therefore, a matter of right, but of expediency."[157]

This understanding of the issue—as a "question of policy"—directly opposed that of reformers like Mathews, Simms, and Dickens, not to mention Putnam, for whom copyright came down entirely to natural rights. (Putnam was at the meeting but seems to have disagreed with Appleton's view.) A week after printing an account of the meeting, the *American Publishers' Circular* agreed in principle with Appleton. "To discuss the natural right of the author is now surely supererogatory," the journal said. "It is one of those vexed questions against which the sea of words has beat unavailingly for years."[158] In the end, publishing was a business, and matters of "justice and injustice" should be worked out not among literary tradesmen but "between the public and the writer."[159] International copyright was the right thing for the country and for its print trade, but the argument on behalf of reform must not confuse what is morally right for authors with what is economically right for commerce. Both the Book-Publishers' Association and the *American Publishers' Circular* also expressed discomfort with the rhetoric reformers used, not only because it did not agree with the logic of expediency but because it was too abstract. Apart from Putnam, most publishers were unwilling to participate in the debate when its terms of reference were so murky. They eschewed the moral vernacular and the "epistemological panic"—McGill's apt phrase—reformers tried to engender and on which they hoped to capitalize.[160]

As suggested earlier, some reformers had expressed frustration with the moral vernacular years before. In the early 1840s, the editor of the *Boston Miscellany* predicted in a letter to Duyckinck that the omnipresence of the issue in the press would backfire and make "that much abused beast 'the public' callous . . . instead of 'establishing a law.'"[161] Another sympathizer wrote to Duyckinck from Washington, D.C., to warn that no matter how loud his comrade Mathews yelled in print, "there are many men in high places, I assure you, who can understand no appeal" that failed to satisfy their self-interest.[162] For his part, Poe sympathized with the goal of reform, but he also understood the logic of these critiques. First, he worried that the debate was "overloaded with words."[163] Second, he worried that the moral argument as presented by writers like Mathews failed to address the economic interests of those whom it had to convince.

Though skeptical of moralistic discourse, Poe nevertheless appreciated the moral issues at stake, even praising, albeit quietly, the occult moral imperative compelling magazine editors to pay authors while book publishers "unblushingly" went about "pick[ing] the pocket of all Europe."[164] In "Some Secrets of the Magazine Prison-House" (1845), he wondered about the efficacy of a "demagogue-ridden public" that could "suffer their anointed delegates . . . to insult" its "common sense . . . by making orations in our national halls on the beauty and conveniency [*sic*] of robbing the Literary Europe on the highway."[165] It is a "gross absurdity" that Americans believed that an author lacks "right and title either to his own brains or to the flimsy material that he chooses to spin out of them." The author, Poe concluded, "stands in need of protection."[166] Despite this angry metaphor, Poe's few writings on copyright largely avoided the kind of moralizing typical of the conventional reform argument, and they exhibited an insider's appreciation of the economic argument floated by reform opponents, a knack for unpacking its moral assumptions, and a desire to put the argument to bed, something most reformers could not do effectively. In "Marginalia," published in *Godey's Lady's Book* in 1845, for example, Poe viewed the issue from a trade rather than an authorial standpoint. This was shrewd. Typically, if they ever deigned to descend from their moral perch, reformers—and especially authors—trotted out a simplistic economic formula couched in a popular metaphor: vampire publishers grow fat off the blood of authors. This allegation was easy for tradesmen to ignore, largely because it was not necessarily true. The economics of publishing were never so simple; in fact, there was not much of an economic case *for* international copyright in mid-nineteenth-century America. Poe admitted this outright: reprinting kept the price of books low. Argument granted.

The economic facts of reprinting did not seem to concern Poe so much as apologists' politicking of these facts. Opponents of reform allowed that while reprinting may not be strictly moral, it was economically prudent (read: expedient) for a nation with largely unproven literary talent and a growing, hungry reading public. Economics trumped right and wrong, though really in this argument these values were not just irrelevant—they did not exist. The principle of expediency, especially in the eighteenth and nineteenth centuries, connoted a divergence of self-interest and morality. Citing it was an artful way of affirming the importance of economic motives without nay-saying the ethics sacrificed to these motives. It was wordplay and therefore an easy target for Poe. His response to this argument is reminiscent of the words of

Thoreau and William Lloyd Garrison: "Expediency is only to be discussed where no rights interfere. It would no doubt be very expedient in any poor man to pick the pocket of his wealthy neighbor (and as the poor are the majority, the case is precisely parallel to the copyright case;) but what would the rich think if expediency were permitted to overrule the right?" Poe's point is that economic expediency is a poor justification for neglecting all rights other than statutory. Foregrounding the compromised "justice" of economic expediency, he observed that such a philosophy subjugates basic communal ethics to an even more basic greed.[167] He would have agreed with contemporary business ethicists who sometimes call the principle of expediency "Machiavellianism."[168] Poe was aware that while reformers could not disprove the economic argument—aware, perhaps, that this was the Achilles' heel of reform—they could underscore the moral assumptions embedded in that argument, assumptions that had implications far beyond the issue of authors' rights.

After Poe's death, his critique found ironic new life in publishers' adoption in the late 1850s of the reform platform noted earlier, which was based on the policy of economic expediency. Via statute, American publishers could make it more economically prudent for British authors to publish in the United States with copyright than without. If there were no hope "of government ever assenting to [the] principle" of an author's natural right, publishers decided, then the next best option was to change tactics: abandon the moral high ground and shift the battle to the dirty but familiar arena of the market.[169] It was, apparently, a "reasonable" strategy. This is exactly what Poe had argued against: the abandonment or the ostensibly justified shirking of an individual's natural and moral rights in the name of economic pragmatism and reason. If morality were not the first priority and the sole motive of reform, the economics of reform would be unjust. Publishers need not be beneficent, but they must be just. For Poe too, the want of justice proved a slippery slope. Like Mathews, only more clearly, he was quick to point out the broader, national implications of the status quo and of proposed economic solutions such as those of the New York publishers. The trade, much less democracy, cannot suffer a wrong, an abuse of virtue, committed in its name simply because to do so is expedient. The world cannot distinguish between a nation's trade and the nation, Poe suggested; it cannot tell the difference "between the temporary perpetrators of the wrong and that democracy in general which permits its perpetration."[170] It was up to reformers to enlighten businessmen who, as the *Southern Quarterly Review* hoped, "are anxious to do what is right, if they can only understand what right is."[171]

Poe's words were more measured than those of Mathews or Simms, but his point was identical. It was best expressed by James Russell Lowell's scandalous 1848 portrait of American print culture, *A Fable for Critics*. There Lowell reminded his fellow writers and tradesmen, "Man is a moral, accountable being."[172] The final chapters of this book look at the ways in which two writers, Melville and Fern, applied this thesis to the business of American publishing as it finally came into maturity, a maturity seemingly defined by economics more than principle.

5

Melville in the Antebellum Publishing Maelstrom

LIKE BARTLEBY'S "'I would prefer not to'" and Pierre's "'I write precisely as I please,'" Herman Melville's epistolary bellow "Dollars damn me" has become a sort of benchmark appraisal of the conditions of American authorship.[1] "What I feel most moved to write, that is banned,—it will not pay," he continued. "Yet, altogether, write the other way I cannot" (*WHM*, 14:191). Banned? Did the commercial failure of *Mardi* (1849) amount to a deliberate censure of Melville's wish to publish a philosophical "venture" (14:134)? Melville openly blamed the market, among other things, for rebuffing what he called elsewhere that "certain something unmanageable" (14:132) in him—his mania for writing "wicked book[s]" (14:212) like *Moby-Dick*. Though dramatic, his was not a peculiar indictment. To contemporary observers, the antebellum trade seemed to have thrown off the gentlemanly deportment that had once prevailed in a better business world that itself was largely a nostalgic myth. In the words of fellow New Yorker Cornelius Mathews, the trade needed to "return to the contrary course of moral honesty."[2] Modern publishers were the executors of million-dollar industries, the logic went, and answered to a Jacksonian market that, as Charles Sellers describes it, took "the competitive ego for human nature."[3] Melville inhabited a print culture manically alert to reform-minded criticism.

This chapter is about the mechanics of Melville's fictional reaction to the ethics of the antebellum trade. In recovering this reaction it is a mistake to overlook a fact recognized by his contemporaries: in his early career, Melville was a willing if ornery student of the business of literary publishing. In 1849, the elder Richard Henry Dana praised Melville's good sense in initially publishing *Typee* (1846) overseas, circumventing British reprinters by securing English copyright.[4] Then there was Melville's capitulation to John Wiley in sanitizing the second American edition of the novel. And despite a defensive claim printed in the *Literary World* that "Mr. Melville is not the man to 'hawk' his wares in any market"—a response to a report that Melville had tried to hand sell his manuscript for *White-Jacket* (1850) to London firms—he did know how to sell himself abroad.[5] Still, without a personal fortune and without a substantial reputation beyond that of a genre specialist, Melville had little leverage. For one who believed that serious writers should enjoy immunity from the presumed ignorance of typical book buyers and their influence on publishing, Melville was in a bad spot. ("Authors ought certainly to be as sensible as shopkeepers," said James Russell Lowell, "and to know that if the public does not want their wares, it will not buy them the sooner for being called fool and blockhead.")[6] Melville had little clout with publishers who of some necessity favored what was profitable over what was "right," a distinction highlighted more than ever by the mid-nineteenth century. He had little patience with publishers' adjustment of their ethics to the requirements of profit, particularly because publishers' ethics mirrored the negotiated Christianity suffusing reform-conscious New York. Critics have argued compellingly that "Bartleby, the Scrivener: A Story of Wall-Street" (1853), in describing just this world, attacks the pious hypocrisy of antebellum capitalism. Melville reveals how contemporary business culture espoused Christian ethics even as it compromised them in its market and managerial practices.[7] But in "Bartleby" and *Pierre; or, The Ambiguities*, I argue, he goes further, reenacting and mocking the business of publishing.

Vocationalism and its correlation to contemporary definitions of authorship and to antebellum literary markets constitute the backdrop for much Melville scholarship over the past few decades. Combined with recent studies of material print culture and economics, these readings help contextualize and distinguish the approach adopted here, which is to stress the relationship between the immaterial social conditions of production and textual meaning in Melville's work.[8] This chapter situates Melville in the debates over the ethics of literary production, and one of its implicit conclusions is that what has been called "the dull arena of publishing politics" yields an essential framework for antebellum authorship.[9] It is squarely in this arena that I wish to place Melville, whose two most bitter injunctions against the ethics of authorship and publishing, *Pierre* and "Bartleby," grew from and fictionalized his disgust with the politics of his print culture. They reveal a writer dogged not by an abstract market, I argue, but by the agents and ethics that constituted that market.

MELVILLE'S SECOND GIGANTIC HUMBUG

In 1850, George Ripley praised the toughness with which Melville criticized naval abuses in *White-Jacket*, warning that a "man of Melville's brain and pen is a dangerous character in the presence of a gigantic humbug; and those who are interested in the preservation of rotten abuses had better stop that 'chiel from taking notes.'"[10]

Melville's first "humbug" arose from his life as a sailor; his second came from his life as a writer and his experiences with antebellum publishing houses. "I shall write such things as the Great Publisher of Mankind ordained ages before he published 'The World'—this planet, I mean—not the Literary Globe," he confided idealistically to Evert Duyckinck in 1849. But between the market and the author stood the publisher, a fact reflected in the famous 1851 letter to Hawthorne in which Melville reported "the malicious Devil is forever grinning in upon me, holding the door ajar" (*WHM*, 14:149, 191). This was the printer's devil, or errand boy, who came each day to fetch the pages of *Moby-Dick* as the author saw it through its printing in June 1851 in an attempt to make a higher profit by fronting printing costs. For Melville, the image of the press's apprentice assaulting his door, waiting for copy, was smothering. Certainly he felt damned by his debts, readers, and reviewers, but also by publishers, who personified for Melville the impersonal market.

Antebellum publishers were well aware of this embodiment. In September 1855, the New York Book-Publishers' Association threw an elaborate party at New York's Crystal Palace, the Complimentary Fruit and Flower Festival. It was an ironically iconographic affair. Intended to honor authors, in fact it extolled the status of the American book trade. As spectators looked on from balconies, honored writers sat at elevated tables in the shape of a parallelogram. In the center of the figure, at a lower level than the authors, sat the publishers, "perhaps," according to one account, "in virtue of compunctions which compelled them to some atonement." Association president William Appleton rationalized the seating arrangement as a symbol not of penance but of service. He christened the festival a long overdue meeting of "kindred spirits," "where genius, sitting in its appropriate high place at the banquet, looks down with kind regard on the ministers of its power."[11] Appleton's intimation that the cultural agency of the trade resided with authors alone, however, could not disguise a certain desperation in the festival's public relations mission.

That same year, the *American Publishers' Circular* celebrated the swift maturation of the business of American publishing. "So rapid, and so great, has been the demand for books in the United States," it gushed, "that some of the leading publishing houses in this city . . . commenced business, certainly not much more than thirty years ago."[12] By the 1850s, American publishing had changed dramatically from those early days and even from the turbulent early 1840s. Rather suddenly American books were becoming big business, but American authors had relinquished much of their former control over the actual process of publishing to the houses themselves. Publishing was moving closer to becoming an industry proper, expanding and innovating its production and management strategies. As important with regard to business innovation as the railroad and textile industries, publishing and its corollary trades continued to move away from the artisanship that defined their early years in favor of mechanization and consolidation of technological and human resources.[13] Yet publishers tried to preserve the artisanal character of their profession and, more importantly, of their own public image. Thus even as publishing houses became regional, national, and international commercial powers, and as they adopted new methods to compete in a changing economy, they tried to do so under the guise of cultural refinement and business civility—presenting the illusion that they had settled internal conflicts with one another and external conflicts with authors.

The Fruit and Flower Festival was one such collective mirage, its object being to repair the damage done by years of such well-publicized controversies as those carried on by the powerful firms overseen by the Harper and Carey families. It symbolized, according to one invited guest, the "concord, which is growing among men in all the relations of life."[14] As orchestrated by Putnam, this gala did its best to exhibit the nationalism, the feats, and the good conduct of publishers. Yet the absence of so major a firm as Harper and Brothers exposed the consensual fantasy. The festival was little more than an opportunity for public self-fashioning and for personifying the imagined balance of power among publishers and between publishers and authors. As one naysayer wrote, the whole idea of the festival was "wildly and absurdly imaginative."[15] At its most innocent, the 1855 gala was a fine time for authors and, at its most suspect, an elaborate exercise in trade relations. How could the evening have been anything but friendly, Putnam's friend Erastus Ellsworth jibed, when all the attendees had to argue over were grapes and plums?

The debates over whether publishers were calculating businesspeople or literary gentlemen had become central to Herman Melville's professional life years before. In the course of his brief career he had worked with some of the most reputable and most infamous publishers of the transatlantic trade. He had smooth relations, relatively speaking, with none, including the esteemed British publisher John Murray, who was the living embodiment of the genteel myth of English publishing's golden age a century before, a myth American tradesmen revered. In 1847, Melville accused Murray of profiting disproportionately from *Typee* and *Omoo* (1847).[16] Before that, he had accused the distinguished publisher, in effect, of dishonesty. Melville wondered sarcastically why Murray was incapable of taking his word that *Typee* was based in fact and, more antagonistically, wondered why Murray did not defend him publicly against the "parcel of blockheads" who accused Melville of lying: "Not (let me hurry to tell you) that Mr John Murray comes under that category—Oh no— Mr Murray I am ready to swear stands fast by his faith, beleiving [*sic*] 'Typee' from Preface to Sequel—He only wants something to stop the mouths of the senseless sceptics." A few years later, in 1848, Melville was more direct in response to Murray's requests for proof of the novel's authenticity: "Bless my soul, Sir, will you Britons not credit that an American can be a gentleman. . . . You make miracles of what are commonplaces to us.—I will give no evidence" (*WHM*, 14:65, 107). However confident in Murray's abilities as a businessperson, Melville was skeptical of his treatment by the prestigious publishing house. It was not the publisher's authority or ability he questioned—only his integrity.

Melville directed less abuse at Richard Bentley. Although continuously overestimating the profit generated by his novels, Melville never accused Bentley of cheating him.

Nevertheless, as in his letters to Murray, he treated Bentley as a "distant authority"—assuming that the publisher's expertise was in trade, not literature, and that he therefore did not comprehend the plight of authorship.[17] Melville made this clear to Bentley in June 1849 after *Mardi* failed to sell in either America or England: "You may think . . . that a man is unwise,—indiscreet, to write a work of that kind, when he might have written one . . . calculated merely to please the general reader. . . . But some of us scribblers, My Dear Sir, always have a certain something unmanageable in us, that bids us do this or that, and be done it must—hit or miss" (*WHM*, 14:132). Melville felt it imperative to exonerate his behavior in the eyes of his publisher, who had lost money on the author's sacred right to act as he pleased. It was precisely the "unmanageable" in Melville that worried Bentley, whose acquisition of Melville was, at least initially, an attempt to capitalize on his popularity as a sea novelist.

The "unmanageable" in Melville worried no one more than Harper and Brothers, the American publisher of most of his novels, including *Pierre*. If the early American reviews were any indication to Harpers, *Moby-Dick* was Melville's most "unmanageable" book yet, and no book since *Typee* had been a true market success. Even before *Moby-Dick* appeared in November 1851, Harpers had refused Melville's request for an advance on his next work, citing two reasons. First, Melville already owed the firm almost $700. Second, as the publisher wrote in April: "The requirements of our business have compelled us to make an extensive and expensive addition to our establishment" (*WHM*, 14:613). Tales of Harpers' riches were popular in the American press, and Melville likely understood that these "requirements" were not in fact required: Harper and Brothers was expanding to increase production. It was a politic word choice for a letter to a writer in financial straits. In the firm's January 1852 contract for *Pierre*, Harpers continued to illustrate that literary publishing was a business. As Hershel Parker has judged, it offered Melville a contract for *Pierre* that was meant to be refused. In addition to a lower per-copy profit, Harpers charged him for review copies. In Parker's words, this was a "warning" to Melville, who would have to pay, in effect, "to publicize himself despite his revulsion at competing for Fame."[18] Harpers, already the largest publishing house in the United States and soon to be the largest in the world, had the financial resources to absorb a loss on Melville's novel; it could well afford the cost of review copies to attempt to sway literary reviewers, and in turn the reading public. Undoubtedly Harpers had made an expedient deal, but for figures such as Duyckinck and Melville, literary publishing was not, or should not be, about expedience. Melville may have remembered the *North British Review* article—reprinted in both *Harper's* and the *Literary World* in 1850 and 1851, respectively, and thus most likely read by Melville—implying the need for clemency for publishers: "Instead of protesting against the overcaution of publishers, literary men . . . would protest against their want of caution. Authors have a direct interest in the prosperity of publishers. The misfortune of authorship is not that publishers make so much money, but that they make so little."[19] The problem was that Harpers did not make "little" money. This would have been an ironic commentary on the

FIGURE 5.1 Harper and Brothers, Courtesy Library of Congress.

firm's behavior toward Melville, who believed more than ever in the privileges due to genius. Whatever the case, if we follow Parker's reconstruction of events, it was at this point that Melville revised his manuscript, adding the sections on Pierre's experiences as a writer among publishers.[20]

Initially Melville pursued Harper and Brothers in the 1840s to capitalize on the firm's prowess, begging the question of what behavior he expected from the house. His letters suggest his need for a literary sensibility but his actions indicate his appreciation for the business, the compulsory prudence of production. He required of publishers both sympathy for the literary imagination and a cutthroat under-standing of modern trade practices. By 1852, Melville seems to have reconciled him-self to the business of publishing. He ended an April letter offering *Pierre* to Bentley in the voice of a speculator striking a deal: "I trust that . . . on the new field of produc-tions, upon which I embark in the present work, you and I shall hereafter participate in many not unprofitable business adventures" (*WHM*, 14:227). Melville ironically anticipated *Pierre*'s entrance on the market with a mixture of chivalry and capitalism, while the novel decries the very "business adventure" to which he looks for success. Melville's tone was nearly as bitter as the novel he was selling. His appeal to Bentley's material interests masked his fictional assault on the publisher's profession, or, more specifically, on the immorality of that profession.

A VAST SCENE OF MORAL ACTION[21]

As New York's commerce swelled, so too did anxieties over moral corruption. Commerce "has never employed half the advantages that should belong to her," one observer suggested. "She has seemed to act alone for selfish, if not at present, purposes—for profits—profits—profits—not with an eye also to great moral and social consequences."[22] The age of reform had its sights set on what Henry W. Bellows called "the commercial spirit."[23] Beginning in the 1830s, Orville Dewey, minister to New York's most influential Unitarian congregation—and secular and spiritual presence to the Melville and Putnam families—spoke out on the problematic rela-tion between Christianity and capitalism, charging the church with ignoring the moral realities of parishioners' working lives. "Are not men daily making shipwrecks of their consciences in trade and politics?" He urged his congregation and the church at large to recognize trade as one of many "spheres of duty" potentially sub-ject to the prescriptions of ethical behavior.[24]

Dewey recommended a characteristically liberal Christian negotiation of conduct and capitalism. Businesspeople needed a moral salve for their everyday actions in trade. Horace Greeley, for one, agreed. The "Problem of our Age," he said, was the lack of a "social condition founded on and penetrated by the vital truths of Christi-anity," namely, "the great Law of Love," the golden rule.[25] "Above all other regula-tions and sanctions is needed Christ's Law of Love," proclaimed Universalist minister Edwin Chapin.[26] For a culture that had already witnessed the pulpit's dramatic turn toward Christ as a moral barometer, recourse to the golden rule in order to address commercial injustices was a commonplace rhetorical strategy. For decades the moral perils of business had been a fashionable theme on the American lecture circuit, as spiritual, social, and business leaders sought to accommodate Christian ethics to capitalism pragmatically—and, as Melville felt, imperfectly—via the golden rule. Speakers taught tradesmen to base their actions on scripture or warned them of the consequences of not doing so.[27] Juvenile fiction taught young men how easy it was to do right by others. (In one novel, even an abused dog experienced in turning the other cheek is an object lesson for the young protagonist, who is, in turn, "not ashamed to exercise toward a brute, the golden rule he had resolved should govern his conduct towards his fellow men."[28] The dog, of course, later saves his life, illustrating the practical, if unintended implications of moral behavior.) In the 1800s, lectures before mercantile societies and libraries, as well as business handbooks, warned of the moral pitfalls of a life in trade.[29] Dewey, for his part, compensated for the ethical negotiations of capitalism with "Commercial Morality," a textbook application of golden-rule ethics to business culture. Dewey accommodated Christian moral teachings to capitalism by softening them. Because there can be no perfect equity in trade, he taught, "perfect justice" is impractical. Businessmen should employ a "beneficent tendency," for while perfect accordance with the golden rule is impossible, a "tendency" toward it in trade is acceptable, even advisable. New York commerce must Christianize, but not at the expense of practical business sense.[30]

Discussions of trade conduct among social leaders reveal a great deal about the importance of ethics in the burgeoning antebellum markets, and, I want to suggest, about the behavior of Melville's own characters. As Paul E. Johnson notes, this reform "was not the idea of a few visionaries and cranks and political opportunists. It was the moral imperative around which the northern middle class became a class."[31] For Dewey, the golden rule resolved the daily moral compromises of capitalism in the same way as Adam Smith's invisible hand made what was right for the self right for society. Its attention to the ways in which individual self-interest drives social systems and economies provided a vague but venerable corporate ethics for a business sphere that had to justify itself to a still very Protestant public culture.[32] Commercial morality deemed moral those actions that were driven by self-interest so long as they accorded with accepted ideas of right behavior and so long as they produced a profit. Or, in the mouth of the "Bartleby" narrator, "mere self-interest . . . if no better motive can be enlisted, should . . . prompt all beings to charity and philanthropy" (WHM, 9:36). The lawyer exemplifies precisely the kinds of adaptations of trade to Christian ethics Melville found so repugnant in Dewey's theology and in that of the pastoral moralists generally.[33] Melville reveals the same behavioral ethic in Pierre's Plotinus Plinlimmon, whose "virtuous expediency" (WHM, 7:214) is a philosophic doppelganger for Dewey's "wise philanthropy."[34] Under the guise of Christian benevolence, Dewey and other leaders proposed—and Melville's characters attempt to practice—the wedding of a Christian life to modern capitalism. So too did many of the major figures in the trade. The failure of such reforms was for Melville a gauge of reformers' naiveté or, in some cases, insincerity.

As discussed in Chapter 1, Evert Duyckinck, tired of publishers and critics justifying their dissolute business dealings with the term "trade," lashed out at his profession in the pages of the Literary World. He lamented the excuse that publishers' "immorality" was an inevitable byproduct of business. Publishers, he fantasized, "will, and must upon the whole, be governed by honorable considerations. They do not need to shelter themselves under the plea of tradesmanship, as if trade sanctioned the pursuit of gain by any means, at the expense of any interests, human or divine." Like Dewey, Duyckinck saw no intrinsic conflict between trade and ethics. He ignored the elaborate relationship of commerce and ethics by oversimplifying trade behavior as a conflict of right versus wrong.[35] And like Putnam, he felt that the moral uprightness of most publishers was evidence of the industry's potential for self-reform.

Few tradespeople enjoyed a better reputation than George Palmer Putnam. Derby put him in "the front rank of our distinguished book-publishers," a sentiment endorsed in different ways by Washington Irving and Ralph Waldo Emerson.[36] Indeed, during the Panic of 1857, a time of "terrible derangement of business," in the words of John Pendleton Kennedy, Putnam's bankruptcy seemed to affect the very soul of the trade.[37] Because of what one congressman called his "well-known

FIGURE 5.2 George Palmer Putnam, Courtesy Library of Congress.

courtesy," Putnam set the standard for gentlemanly conduct.[38] And when his business failed in 1857, forcing him, among other things, to sell off his plates, his fellow publishers did their best to alleviate Putnam's troubles. One of them was Lowell Mason. "Mr. Mason was a neighbor and an old friend of my father's," George Haven Putnam remembered, "and he took hold of this troublesome and thankless piece of business [receivership] with a keen personal interest and undoubtedly did all that any man could do under the very difficult circumstances to realize from the assets, not only enough to secure a quittance from the creditors, but something over with which his friend Putnam might again resume business."[39] Putnam's reputation in the trade was in part the consequence of a career spent building the groundwork for a fair book trade between Britain and the United States and lobbying for international copyright. Whether or not such an agreement would in fact have benefited American writers, the perception among them and among publishers was that Putnam had both parties' best interests at heart. He was also committed to getting American writers into print regardless of the cheap availability of competing foreign texts. He announced as much when he went into business for himself in the 1840s, publicizing his intention to champion domestic authors and building a bookstore that was a symbol of that devotion. "Putnam has opened his store and it is the simplest and best in arrangement of any on Broadway—well-lighted, airy & clean as the deck of the Washington," Duyckinck gossiped to his brother. "You walk along black walnut looking cases of the poets &c on a footing of thick matting and drop into inviting arm chairs."[40] From Cincinnati to Constantinople, Putnam's reputation preceded him.[41] Writers practically worshipped him. Novelist and *American Monthly Magazine* founder Henry William Herbert told Putnam that he would deal with no one else in all of New York—and certainly not with Harper and Brothers.[42] Dana bent the steps of a Hungarian writer away from the wretched Harpers toward the morally upright Putnam, who, the writer was told, was "the generosest [*sic*] man among all your colleagues and a very good friend of the Hungarians."[43] "The man who does not value you," the prolific author Samuel Austin Allibone wrote to Putnam, "need expect no quarter from me: save quarters in the Lunatic Asylum." Allibone was so convinced of Putnam's special virtue that an 1857 letter of agreement with him spelled out the writer's absolute confidence in the publisher and absolute suspicion of his peers.[44] Putnam is best understood as one of the new breed of publishers who played liaison between, as the *Literary World* put it, "the public and authors, whose interests, next to their own, it is their province to foster and defend." As Putnam himself would suggest, he was a "New World" John Murray, a "prototype" of the genteel British publisher responsible, in large part, for the nineteenth century's collective nostalgia for a more civil age of publishing.[45] Putnam was the self-proclaimed moralist of American print culture and, for authors like Bayard Taylor, the "prince of publishers."[46]

The fact that Henry Carey also effectively wed publishing and ethics illustrates the difficulty in distinguishing between right and wrong trade behavior. In his influential study *Principles of Political Economy* (1837–40), Carey vilified economists who believed that capitalism affords laws applicable only to the pursuit of material wealth, an argument similar to that of the publisher-apologists against whom Duyckinck and Putnam argued. When properly framed, Carey suggested, the root laws of political economy parallel the tenets of ethical behavior. These "laws" yield "enlightened self-interest" and "diminish selfishness, by showing that our interests are so interwoven with those of our fellow men." For Carey, the "whole science of Political Economy may be reduced to a single line—DO UNTO OTHERS AS YE WOULD THAT OTHERS SHOULD DO UNTO YOU." Although short of prescribing a rigorous charity, an issue Melville would dramatize in "Bartleby," Carey advocated the need for a benevolent ethic in trade, reflecting a desire to regulate behavior by making tradesmen accountable as Christians.[47] Again, it was not a radical pronouncement. The golden rule was arguably the most influential nonlegal business ethic of the eighteenth and nineteenth centuries, appearing in many of the business handbooks of the era, from Joshua Bates's *A Discourse, on Honesty in Dealing* (1813) to Henry Bellows's *The Christian Merchant* (1848) to Freeman Hunt's *Worth and Wealth*.[48] Carey simply, or not so simply, made the golden rule serve the interests of all-powerful capital by using it to stress the importance of harmony of interests.

Carey's career as a political economist followed on the heels of his retirement from running one of early America's most dominant and bullying publishing firms. Indeed, it is likely that he arrived at his appeal to the golden rule in part out of his own long-term frustrations with the near anarchy of early antebellum publishing. As Algernon Tassin judged, looking back from the perspective of the early twentieth century, it was a world in which publishers expertly carried out the "systematic business of cutting each other's throats."[49] The trial for control of this market was in many ways a struggle between the houses of the Careys and the Harpers. Using the machinery of fast transatlantic shipping, horse-powered and later steam presses, all-night printing runs, and unremitting intimidation, the firms warred over the lucrative foreign reprint trade. The contest had lasting effects on the trade's reputation. As Duyckinck wrote a decade after Carey's *Principles* began to appear, "were a new race of publishers now disposed to do their worst, it is scarcely possible that they could regain their old ascendancy for mischief-making with the press and the public."[50] That the same publisher who had threatened not a few of his competitors could turn around and preach Christian trade probably would not have surprised Melville or his contemporaries. What we tend to think of in monolithic terms as "the trade" or "the market" was to Melville and others Janus-faced—gentleman and aggressor.

In part because they obstructed his own business, Carey organized the American Book Trade Sale in 1824 to rein in obstructive trade practices. Harpers, initiating the maverick tradition it would continue for decades, declined participation. Carey's attempts to solicit the house's attendance a decade later had the unintended effect of formalizing courtesy of the trade, the convention that stipulated, among other things, that the house first to advertise an intention to reprint a foreign title possessed the sole right thereto. In principle, as it was further theorized in the 1830s, trade courtesy was based on moral and economic equity; but it was also a version of the capitalist Christian ethics Dewey preached to New York business-men. It was a perfect ethic for antebellum publishers, allowing them to celebrate their rights one moment and invade the rights of others the next. If trade courtesy seemed to adapt the golden rule to publishing, it did so in theory more than in practice. Whatever the implied ethics of the industry, observers understood that the idealistic codes and pronouncements had little real effect on the business of publishing. Or, as James Parton quipped, courtesy of the trade was nothing more than a "pleasant and delusive name."[51] In 1851, Putnam and Harper and Brothers became embroiled in a controversy that exposed this illusion. It involved the domestic republication of the works of Swedish novelist Fredrika Bremer. Harpers had reprinted her novels in the 1840s, but Putnam arranged directly with the author for an authorized reissue of two of these books. In an effort to increase her profit as much as possible, Putnam and Bremer asked Harper and Brothers to scrap its already announced reprint of Bremer's works. Harpers flatly refused on grounds that Putnam had in an unrelated case violated the second principle of trade cour-tesy by stealing from Harpers George Borrow's autobiographical novel *Lavengro* (1851). In launching reprisals for a purported violation of their own trade interests, Harpers executed what house biographer Eugene Exman calls "the Harper 'eye for an eye' principle of justice."[52]

Harpers' actions afforded Putnam an opportunity to expose the firm's unethical dealings. In sum, Putnam accused Harper and Brothers of violating the trade's tacit golden-rule trade ethic and so intimated that there existed a conclusive trade morality in the first place. Putnam submitted the correspondence from the debate to the *Literary World*. In the now-public exchange, Harper and Brothers accused Putnam of a long familiarity with the firm's complaints about his own improprieties. He was also aware, Harpers noted, of "our intentions to defend our invaded rights." For his part, Putnam struggled to understand why Harpers claimed infringement when Putnam's authorized editions cost more than its own reprints and so cost the rival house almost nothing: "That this was an infringement in the slightest degree of your rights, either legal or according to usage, I never for one minute supposed." The irony of Putnam's charge was heavy: "Now I may take a wrong view of the subject; but it appears to me that so long as the fact remains that I pay for an early copy of the book, and for the express authority to reprint it; the particular mode or amount of the payment can be of no concern to anybody else."[53] His language was well calculated. For authors, this was anything but the "wrong view" of the trade: Putnam had as much as advertised his attention to fair dealing. And this moral uprightness was the image of the trade that most publishers wanted publicized. They were not supposed to be pirates. And, if they were, they were not supposed to act the part in public.

While Putnam had taken the moral high ground, his logic was dubious. His letters ignore the reality of the trade, a tendency biographer Ezra Greenspan finds throughout his career and which we might as easily apply to Duyckinck as well. His reference to legal rights implies that there were international laws to which one could appeal. There were not. His claim that he had not violated Harper and Brothers' "rights . . . according to usage" is more complicated. Here Putnam suggested that he had treated the trade fairly: literally, that he has "used" the trade to his own advantage and to no other firm's disadvantage. He insinuated the existence of a kind of chivalric code of capitalism, one that Melville reiterated in his own letters when discussing authorship—a golden-rule morality that required of publishers and editors fair treatment of authors and others in the trade. Putnam wanted to treat authors "right." However quixotically, he followed a golden-rule ethic in which his own charitable actions were to be the trade norm. When he confronted the rival house in person regarding the dispute, he was told by Fletcher Harper that "courtesy was courtesy and business was business," a funny statement for a firm priding itself on its religious publishing and schoolbooks and for a family that practically evangelized Methodism in New York City. It was, though, a characteristic statement for Harpers. This episode, according to Greenspan, "neatly captured a fundamental difference between the two sides in publishing philosophy."[54] Similarly, it captured both the idealism and the hypocrisy of the trade.

Whatever Putnam's animosity toward Harper and Brothers, writers such as Melville were attracted to the company's resources and market sway. The house had quickly grown into the largest publisher in the United States. In 1860, the typical manufacturer employed ten people; Harpers had employed 200 more than twenty years earlier. Even the *American Publishers' Circular*, which was not afraid to advertise its disapproval of the firm's trade practices, gushed that to write the history of this house "would be to write a volume of no ordinary dimensions."[55] In 1833, the *Knickerbocker* bragged with characteristically nationalistic fervor that this American publishing house had seventeen horse-driven presses and expended $200 a day on paper alone.[56] By 1853, the firm had seven interconnecting buildings with forty-one presses capable of producing thousands of volumes a week, more than any other publisher in the world.[57] That same year, when its buildings burned in the fifth serious fire to plague the house—the fire that compelled Putnam to write to Harpers of the importance of "good will and friendly relations"—Harper and Brothers constructed two massive fireproof buildings within six months, a feat extolled in the city's press. It was at this point that the firm on Cliff Street became a stop for New York City sightseers.

The company itself played no trivial part in the creation of its legend. In his memoirs, J. Henry Harper remembered the pamphlet the company offered visitors in the 1870s, "a brochure descriptive of [the visitor's] breath-taking experience, a diploma of romantic adventure to be carried back in triumph to Yaphank or Lonelyville for exhibition to envious stay-at-homes."[58] The romanticization was no less sweeping in the 1850s, when Melville was a regular caller. Published in 1855, Jacob Abbott's *The Harper Establishment* is a vivid illustration of how the firm saw itself and its role in the American book trade. Intended as a children's book—which it definitely was not—*The Harper Establishment* is an imperial testimony to the company's self-conception as a ubiquitous cultural enterprise.[59] Indeed, what made the period's publishing environment as tempestuous as it was had as much to do with Harpers' image of itself and its trade practices as with its physical scale. As James Kirke Paulding remarked to Carey and Hart, Harpers was "the more difficult to deal with, the richer they become."[60] The firm towered over the trade. Literary periodicals consistently if sometimes circumspectly complained about the firm's trade practices. In 1850, the *Literary World* noted that while the Harpers imprint was everywhere, the house invested little in the writers it published, British or American. Compared with "Longmans, who embark[ed] an immense amount of capital in authorship," Harpers went to great lengths to avoid such investment. The *American Publishers' Circular* declared that Harpers drew fuzzy conclusions about the state of the trade.[61]

Such internal bickering affected the relations of authors with publishers and further damaged perceptions of the role of publishers in American literary culture. Distressed, such industry insiders as Duyckinck idealistically asked publishers to consider what was right in their practices, not what they could get away with. And he embraced a progressive vision of American business ethics: "We see virtue and industry every day triumphing, and fraud inevitably leading to failure."[62] Observers must have been skeptical. Harper and Brothers had historically been able to ride out economic downturns because of its immense capital, in part the result of its mastery of the reprint trade. Profit seemed to matter most, and this actuality was not lost on writers such as Melville. "In all reasonable probability no International Copyright will ever be obtained—in our time, at least—if you Englishmen wait at all for the first step to be taken in this country," he wrote Bentley in 1851. "Who have any motive in this country to bestir themselves in this thing? Only the authors.—Who are the authors?—A handful. And what influence have they to bring to bear upon any question whose settlement must necessarily assume a political form?—They can bring scarcely any influence whatever. This country and nearly all its affairs are governed by sturdy backwoodsmen . . . who care not a fig for any authors except those who write those most saleable of all books" (*WHM*, 14:197–98). Representatives of American publishers argued that the British themselves were to blame, that America was simply following suit and, if anything, domestic publishers were in the habit of treating its authors better than the English. Commenting on the copyright legislation facing Congress in 1837 and initiated by English writers, Philip Nicklin, a former associate of Carey in the 1820s, charged, "British authors are now asking relief at the hands of our government for the injustice inflicted by their own." In 1853, when another round of legislation made its way to Washington, Carey aggressively challenged it: "If this country is properly termed 'the paradise of women,' may it not be as correctly denominated the paradise of authors, and should they not be content to dwell in it as their predecessors have done?"[63] Despite Carey's implicit and Putnam's explicit assurances that the trade had the best interests of writers at heart, the warring among antebellum publishers inspired little confidence that civil or equitable behavior mattered as much as profit. It was this predicament to which Melville reacted in his fiction.

PIERRE AND THE CHAOS OF AUTHORSHIP

The disagreements among publishers should remind us that "the trade" was short-hand for an array of vocational personalities and behaviors. Like most of his con-temporaries, and especially disgruntled authors, Melville could collapse these personalities and behaviors into serviceable generalizations. In his fiction, however, he provided a more detailed view of this world. While it usually did not acknowl-edge fairly the spectrum of ethical positions among these personalities—his fictional trade figures are almost uniformly immoral, unlike those of Fanny Fern—Melville's fiction does explore with some nuance the typical behaviors that, in his eyes, charac-terized these personalities. *Pierre*, for one, registers the writer's confrontation with the personalities and behaviors of this world. Melville's narrator forecasts a night-mare future—made inevitable by the state of the literary trade and its "ever multiply-ing freshets of new books"—in which earnest authors are antique myths and where "the printing-press [will] be reckoned a small invention" (*WHM*, 7:264). This disas-sociation of authorship from sincerity captures Melville's fear that the business of publishing had made a business of authorship; even the cultural revolution that was the invention of the printing press becomes insubstantial when it lacks "true" authors to print. Compromised publications like the *Gazelle Magazine* and the works of hack writers like Charlie Millthorpe fill the city's bookstores. All is commercialized: literature, philosophy, even religion. Residing in a church-turned-trade-space and with artist-philosophers who spend their time begging and digesting Kantian ration-alizations of Christian ethics, Pierre inhabits a world in which the "fools and pre-tenders of humanity" win out over the "glorious paupers" (7:267–68, 267). The Church of the Apostles stands down the street from "immense lofty warehouses of foreign importers"—Harper and Brothers and other reprinters—"and not far from the corner where the lane intersect[s] with a very considerable but contracted thor-oughfare for merchants and their clerks": lower Broadway, the heart of old New York's publishing district (7:265).[64]

The publishers of Pierre's world emerge from a hodgepodge of prior vocational identities, among them trash collector, tailor, and pirate. Melville is at his most skep-tical, and most self-critical, in his analogy of literary publishing and trash collection. For the "mature" author, publication means the removal of literary value and autho-rial intention; publications are but the waste products of "genius." The mature author is "like the occupant of a dwelling, whose refuse can not be clapped into his own cellar, but must be deposited in the street before his own door, for the public functionaries to take care of." These "public functionaries," the publishers, gather the litter of the writer's imagination, leaving him with the longing to offer "Truth to the world" but without a means to deliver it (*WHM*, 7:258, 283). What is an author without a publisher? It is a question that may have been on Melville's mind in January 1852, when Harper and Brothers offered its contract for *Pierre*.

Less personal and less astringent is Melville's characterization of the publisher as tailor. Two tailors-turned-publishers contact Pierre early in his career, most likely having switched careers "with [the] economical view of working up in books, the linen and cotton shreds of the cutter's counter, after having been subjected to the action of the paper-mill" (*WHM*, 7:246). Unable to leave behind the trade-specific discourse of tailoring, these neophyte publishers seek to adapt their skills to an occupation substantially more esoteric than that for which their formal training prepared them. Eager for the chance to make an easy profit from Pierre's popular early work by reissuing it in the "library form" Duyckinck, Putnam, and Melville introduced in the 1840s, the tailors represent, in another sense, the economic opportunism pervading Melville's publishing world (7:247). Labor sympathizers noted that tailors endured the "worst working conditions in New York." Their plight was exacerbated in 1850 when a tailors' strike became violent, "shock[ing] even the most militant journeymen." Labor conditions for printers were significantly better inasmuch as printing offered relatively high wages.[65] Melville's portrait of tailors moonlighting as publishers is, on the one hand, a critique of the dubious motives and abilities of publishers and, on the other, an annotation of the wretched state of antebellum labor relations. His allusion to the raw materials of the industry, "the action of the paper-mill" (*WHM*, 7:246), also forecasts his later equation of the publishing industry with exploited labor in "The Paradise of Bachelors and the Tartarus of Maids," first printed in *Harper's New Monthly Magazine* in 1855 and composed around the time of "Bartleby." There, it is the labor of young girls that ultimately feeds the "inflexible iron animal," the "great [paper-making] machine" (9:333, 331). The young narrator is shocked to see in the paper the "pallid faces of all the pallid girls" who constitute the trade along with publishers, albeit at a much lower station (9:334).

Most notoriously, Melville parodies reprinters. In the novel, Duyckinck himself becomes the editor of the pirate journal the *Captain Kidd Monthly*. In his view, anything that may be had—Pierre's daguerreotype, for example—must be published and therefore profited by. This is one meaning of "public property," likely a play on the embattled definition of literary property in publishing circles. While Melville's attack on Duyckinck is ruthless in that he draws on actual correspondence for his satire, more severe is his yoking of Duyckinck to Harper and Brothers, whose trade practices Duyckinck abhorred. The *Captain Kidd Monthly* is not just a reference to *Holden's Dollar Magazine*, a purely commercial endeavor for which Duyckinck had assumed editorial duties in 1851 and for which he had requested Melville's portrait, a request Melville refused emphatically.[66] It is also a fictional *Harper's New Monthly Magazine*. In a pervasive, ironically expansive condemnation of Duyckinck and Harpers, Melville outfits his fictional Captain Kidd editor with "personal profaneness," combining dogmatic insensitivity to the interests of the author with an energetic pursuit of profit (*WHM*, 7:254). Melville criticizes what he sees as the dualistic nature of publishers and their agents, figures who publicly claimed ethical standards even while behaving unethically within their field.

These are the personalities controlling the trade in Pierre and, importantly, these are the behaviors that typify them. This is the professional setting, the "lot," of authorship: a world all but absolutely controlled by idealists and liars who prefer a "shallow nothing of a novel" to a "deep book" (*WHM*, 7:303, 305). The culture of publishing, Pierre discovers, is a cult of trade immorality the author is helpless to affect. Melville compares his "sky-assaulting" protagonist to the "moss-turbaned, armless giant" Enceladus, who, lacking other means of offense, simply throws himself against the earth like a "battering-ram" (7:347, 346). Lacking the weapons employed by writers willing to follow publishing custom, Pierre throws himself in the form of his book against his publishers, and their response is the pronouncement of the antebellum literary industry on him and on Melville: "You are a swindler" (7:356). Pierre's novel is a "blasphemous rhapsody," perhaps because through it he blasphemes the publishers themselves. Rather than publish it, they bring legal action against him in order to recover the firm's advances. Melville's exemplary novelist becomes little more than an economic and legal nuisance to his publishers—and he becomes so by following the formula prescribed by Duyckinck and Young America in the mid-1840s: "let the author be true to himself."[67]

Pierre has been called "a drama of ethical knowledge" in which moral absolutes do not apply to social reality.[68] This is Plotinus Plinlimmon's philosophy, which warns that "in things terrestrial (horological) a man must not be governed by ideas celestial (chronometrical)." Plinlimmon assumes "that human life on this earth is but a state of probation; which among other things implies, that here below, we mortals have only to do with things provisional." "Accordingly," he declares, "I hold that all our so-called wisdom is likewise but provisional" (*WHM*, 7:214, 211). Like the compromise theology Melville so despised, "Chronometricals and Horologicals" advocates a responsiveness to circumstances in decisions of ethical action, where action is less a matter of what is "right" than of what is conditionally acceptable. It may be read, in turn, as a bitter deconstruction of antebellum publishing's ethical superstructure. Plinlimmon resembles Orville Dewey in his privileging of the self in matters of charity. He also resembles such figures as Carey, Duyckinck, and even Putnam, who argued that trade and ethics could coexist in the framework of modern publishing. Plinlimmon is a rough caricature, that is to say, of the antebellum publisher as seen through the eyes of a radically disillusioned writer for whom horological conduct is a regrettably compulsory component of success in literature. Plinlimmon's refutation of strict interpretations of the golden rule reads like a theological rationalization of Harper and Brothers' trade philosophy:

> If any man say, that such a doctrine as this I lay down is false, is impious; I would charitably refer that man to the history of Christendom for the last 1800 years; and ask him, whether, in spite of all the maxims of Christ, that history is not just as full of blood, violence, wrong, and iniquity of every kind, as any previous portion of the world's story? Therefore, it follows, that so far as practical results are concerned . . . the only great original moral doctrine of Christianity . . . has been found (horologically) a false one; because after 1800 years' inculcation from tens of thousands of pulpits, it has proved entirely impracticable. (7:215)

Brian Higgins detects a "sleaziness" in Plinlimmon's Christianity.[69] It is the same moral sleaziness critics and writers observed in antebellum literary publishing, a sordidness identical to that which we see in the narrator of "Bartleby" insofar as he practices a "common-sense incentive to whatever of virtue be practicable and desirable" (*WHM*, 7:215). Plinlimmon is an apologist, a figurative spokesperson for an industry convinced, in Melville's view, of the moral suitability of its actions— echoing Duyckinck's idealistic belief that because "fraud inevitably lead[s] to failure" virtue must be the mainspring of success and that in trade, "even as it exists, no dishonest publisher could stand."[70] Melville recasts Duyckinck's idealism five years later in the form of Plinlimmon's assurance that "sooner or later, in all cases, downright vice is downright woe" (*WHM*, 7:215). If there were a philosophical apology for antebellum publishing, "Chronometricals and Horologicals" would be it.

Pierre comes to understand the false ethics of his vocational world only too well but nonetheless obstinately strives against them. He commits "a sort of suicide as to the practical things of this world," asserting an idealistically expressive, self-determining authorship to make irrelevant the advice of editors, the economics of publishing, and the needs of booksellers (*WHM*, 7:213).[71] In the terms of Pierre's relationship to Melville's "field of productions," the provisional ethics that accommodate the desire for profit and the necessity of self-interest are antagonistic to the writer. Publishing, Pierre finds, is less about "Truth"—for truth is chronometrical and therefore unprofitable—than about the market, as Millthorpe knows. This is the vocational ethic hidden behind the mask of cultural intermediacy worn by publishers. Hence the irony of his publisher's accusation that Pierre is a "swindler" passing off a "blasphemous rhapsody" as a "popular novel," for it is the publishers who swindle in this novel (*WHM*, 7:356). Pierre's blasphemy is his unwillingness to abide the ostensibly ethical behavior of a trade that, according to Melville, sees its conditional duty—its self-interested duty—in providing books that sell.

Pierre's final authorial act is to nail his book to his writing table, fixing it to the place of its composition rather than to the market. Melville wrote into the novel the second doubloon of his career. "What the book means," the *Boston Post* reviewer of *Pierre* confessed, "we know not." Evert Duyckinck did. He saw in the novel the "chaotic state of authorship." "The most immoral moral of the story, if it has any moral at all," he wrote, "seems to be the impracticability of virtue."[72] Whatever else the unpublished manuscript nailed to the writer's desk would come to mean to readers, to Melville it likely suggested the absurdity of an authentic trade morality. It was also an attack on the ethical failures of writers, including himself, who resignedly conform to the trade's demands. In this sense, *Pierre* reads like a preface to "Bartleby."

"BARTLEBY": PUBLISHING'S ETHICAL INJUNCTION

In "Bartleby, the Scrivener," Melville recreates this vocational doomsday vision through an analysis of employer-employee/publisher-author social relations. Whereas in *Pierre* we get caricatures of publishers, in "Bartleby" Melville adopts the perspective of the representative publisher himself. What is absent in *Pierre* is painstakingly fictionalized in "Bartleby": the voice and ideology of the publisher in the first person. Here we reside briefly in the symbolic office of the antebellum literary tradesman.

"Bartleby" is in part a story of managerial ethics. How does an employer treat a passively obstinate employee? Henry A. Murray's "Bartleby and I" (1966) remains a good place to start in answering that question. In this account, the lawyer is capable of sympathy, but Melville chains the trait to a "calculating prudential philosophy" and tests it "with an insoluble problem": how to influence an individual who refuses to participate in the social, economic, and vocational status quo. How can the lawyer help, much less save, the scrivener? What is especially valuable about Murray's treatment of "Bartleby" is the narrator's meta-critical recognition that Melville bestowed on him an impossible dilemma: "For a hundred years, no critic . . . has come out with a definite statement as to what I should have done or what he himself would have done in my place."[73] Just as the presence of the scrivener inflicts "a limitless test on the lawyer,"[74] the antebellum writer committed to aesthetic independence represented a test for the publisher. There was no answer to a literary-vocational rendering of this conflict. What is the right way for publishers to treat authors? What does a publisher do with a writer who will not act on "common sense"? More to the point, what does a publisher do with a writer whose last major protagonist declared, "I write precisely as I please" (*WHM*, 7:244)—with a writer who has become anathema to the institution? We err if we assume that this was a conflict about which only authors worried. Antebellum publishers worried that the relationship between writer and publisher was one of such tremendous strife. This is the context for Melville's parable of the writer's struggle seen through the eyes of the publisher, a figure who believes, at least momentarily, that "all Broadway . . . were debating the same question with me" (9:34).

Manhattan was doing just that. At *Pierre*'s advent, one headline had pronounced "Herman Melville Crazy."[75] The novel embarrassed Harpers, which went so far as to seed gossip among other New York publishers that Melville had succumbed to madness—a stunning about-face for the firm that published the book in the first place. Then in the summer of 1853, about the same time Melville most likely wrote "Bartleby," the firm declined to publish his next manuscript.[76] Still, Melville had no intention of quitting authorship. In "Bartleby" he tried to clarify his understanding of the vocational relations inherent in the "field of productions," offering up a publisher who cannot understand the motives and conduct of a writer, much as Melville himself seemed confused by the motives and conduct of publishers.

After confiding Bartleby's singularity among a "singular set of men," the narrator begins the story with a sketch of his business. "Some such description," he notes, "is indispensable to an adequate understanding of the chief character about to be presented" (*WHM*, 9:13); to comprehend the author, in other words, we must comprehend his vocational milieu. Characteristically, the narrator begins with himself, the "unambitious" lawyer who prefers safely handling money to actively trying cases (9:14). We learn that the narrator is, or was, a political hack; that he is, as Brook Thomas points out, an equity lawyer who now "serves Wall Street"; that his office is essentially a sequence of walls within walls within Wall Street; that his other employees are copying machines with names, that they are Dickensian shells of people; and that his "general surroundings" are the "bright silks and sparkling faces" of "the Mississippi of Broadway" (9:13, 28).[77] The office is on the river of New York commerce, and this is the world Bartleby enters, the world in which publishing had quickly taken up residence over the previous few decades, and the same world Pierre inhabits. The narrator boasts of a career spanning thirty years—about the age of Harper and Brothers—and of his acquaintance with many scriveners. We find in Bartleby's "general surroundings" the copying ethos of Harpers and the dumb acquiescence of writers doing what they are told: "'With submission, sir,'" is Turkey's favorite response to his boss (*WHM*, 9:16). We find a lawyer, in one of the most stable vocations in the city, driven more by economics than by the law. The narrator even defines himself not against other lawyers but against New York's superstar capitalist, John Jacob Astor. The figure the narrator cuts is one reason critics of "Bartleby, the Scrivener" remain no closer to agreement on the story's meaning.[78] In career, person, words, and actions he stands as a confusing mixture of biblical metaphors, philosophical doctrines, and historical allusions. Yet despite all his inconsistencies, the lawyer may consistently be read as a moral barometer for antebellum capitalism—a transitional symbol of nineteenth-century economic and business life who represents the "old order of face-to-face contacts and mutual obligations ... giving way to the impersonal calculus of the market."[79] Or, as Allan Silver puts it in his elegant treatment of "Bartleby," "the lawyer ventures unknowingly towards our own time. For the story does more than strain and shatter an early business morality. It also says something about the character of helping bonds in the whole modern culture."[80]

There is no definitive means of citing a one-to-one correspondence between Melville's characterization of the narrator and actual publishers and editors. This is likely one reason that in the many readings of this work's authorial contexts there is little sense that the story of Melville's Manhattan lawyer is cynically allusive to Melville's Manhattan publishers, who to varying degrees share the narrator's contentment in false charity and commercial morality, his belief that writing is, above all else, utilitarian. In the narrator we find Melville's exemplary publisher charged with the task of deciphering a writer who will no longer write in an office full of walls, businessmen, and money. Read in light of the world of antebellum publishing, "Bartleby" is a sharply perplexing parable of Melville's vocational world: a lawyer who relishes money more than the law hires a writer who prefers "dead-wall reveries" to writing (*WHM*, 9:29). The story is a whirlwind of vocation, idealism, and hypocrisy— all confined to a city in which one of the dominant churches tried its best to accommodate business to its traditional ethics and in which business feigned, for the most part, the trappings of these ethics. And amid it all, standing on Broadway and its side streets, were the publishers, their offices, and the literary salons in which Melville had once been a celebrity.

The narrator tries to understand Bartleby's condition in hopes of understanding the writer's motives. He fancies that he is in such sympathy with the copyist that the "bond of a common humanity now drew [him] irresistibly to gloom." His mood is the result of horror at Bartleby's loneliness, his being "absolutely alone in the universe." How can one live in New York, he wonders, among streets that overflow during the week but are as "deserted as Petra" on Sunday (*WHM*, 9:28, 32, 27)? Unlike the narrator, Bartleby no longer knows any other world. Wyn Kelley suggests that "Bartleby and the lawyer seem to confront each other across a great divide— Bartleby as dispossessed, poor, laboring employee and the lawyer as sinecured, affluent, privileged employer."[81] Kelley argues that the conflict involves the right to the space of the office itself, that it is a struggle over occupancy. But the contest is over vocational authority as well, though in this reading there is less a struggle than a staid acquiescence. Like Pierre, Bartleby is physically and vocationally walled in by trade and by the circumstances of his occupation. Yet while Pierre lashes out at vocational improprieties from his own writing desk, Bartleby can only occupy the office of the publisher and passively refuse pleas to do his job dutifully.

Bartleby's occupation of the narrator's office prevents the narrator from seeing him as anything but a willful employee and forces him anxiously to acknowledge the potential danger of this vocational dilemma. He attempts to grasp his own tenuous situation by comparing it to that of Samuel Adams, a New York City printer bludgeoned to death by an author, John Colt, in 1841. In "a state of nervous resentment," the narrator recalls "the tragedy of the unfortunate Adams and the still more unfortunate Colt in the office of the latter." The murder is a matter of occupational proximity for the narrator: "It was," he decides, "the circumstance of being alone in a solitary office" (*WHM*, 9:36). Why should the narrator associate his present dilemma with the notorious murder of a New York printer by an author? It is a nightmare scenario, one that hinges on circumstances affecting professional behavior and the relationship of occupational resentment to physical violence. Colt, the narrator remembers, "dreadfully incensed by Adams, and imprudently permitting himself to get wildly excited, was at unawares hurried into his fatal act—an act which certainly no man could possibly deplore more than the actor himself" (9:36). What did Adams do that so "dreadfully" provoked the writer? At trial Colt argued that he had acted in self-defense, but the ambiguous circumstances allowed New Yorkers to take sides in debating the killer's motive.[82] The narrator's own language suggests sympathy with both figures—"the unfortunate Adams and the still more unfortunate Colt"—but rather more with Colt. Perhaps, the narrator wonders, it was the effect of something Adams did within the office itself? Despite the physical proximity of the two men in the room, the building was "unhallowed by humanizing domestic associations—an uncarpeted office, doubtless, of a dusty, haggard sort of appearance;—this it must have been, which greatly helped to enhance the irritable desperation of the hapless Colt" (WHM, 9:36). The office and the very relationship of the two men, in other words, triggered the murder. As T. H. Giddings has noted, Melville changes key elements of the case. Colt's building was in fact one of the busiest in Manhattan; a prosecutor went so far as to suggest "no one would suspect or believe that such an act had been perpetrated there."[83] Melville amends the scene to isolate the writer and printer from the bustling life of the city; Colt and Adams thus find themselves on the busiest street in Manhattan but in a building devoid of affability, love, or society. All that remains for them in the "haggard" office is business. And it is this business of print that kills them.

Giddings pairs the narrator with Colt because the narrator fears the consequences of his anger. But why not pair the narrator with Adams? This reading makes Melville's historical allusion less "carelessly applied," as Giddings evaluates it, and more appropriate to the story's vocational subtext. Both men are in positions of power over their charges, professionally and economically. Both represent the larger publishing trade of New York, Adams explicitly and the narrator implicitly. More important, both are embroiled in a tenuous vocational dilemma, the narrator knowingly and Adams unknowingly. The narrator has learned from Adams the peril inherent in the economics of authorship and its requisite behaviors. Violence becomes an unfortunate "circumstance" of the professional relationship, of writer and publisher being alone together in a room that reflects Bartleby's (and, not coincidentally, Pierre's) own loneliness in the midst of the thriving city. Through this allusion, Melville isolates the two most visible agents of the literary field, author and publisher, to explore the potential for catastrophe. In Giddings's view, Colt succumbs to "a sort of environmental determinism."[84] However, in the context of Melville's disgust with the trade morality he confronted, it seems that Colt, the author, the counterpart of Bartleby, succumbs to vocational determinism.

This recourse to the memory of a printer's death at the hands of an author is not a new sensation for the narrator. It is a story that occurs to him often and, apparently, more than in passing. The circumstances that lead to violence in the world of New York commerce preoccupy him. When might a copyist turn against an employer for no reason other than his "common usage" of that employee, for the simple give-and-take of professional relationships? What behavior is prudent for those in authority in this sphere? In a story so deeply historicized and so indicative of the author's vocational condition, the narrator's thought process—his consideration of right and wrong actions to take, of the potential for violent disagreement, and of the prudence required of those in power—reflects the ethical sphere of publishing: how a publisher ought to act toward the writer. As it turns out, the ethics employed by the narrator, and by the publishers in *Pierre* as well, are indistinguishable from the trade morality, or, in Dewey's terms, the commercial morality, that Melville saw employed by the publishers of his own time.

This morality haunts "Bartleby" and its characters. Stopped dead in a daydream of murdered printers and lonely writers, despairing of an answer to the question of what to do with a writer who will neither write nor leave the professional sphere, and aware of the need to understand Bartleby's own situation, the narrator falls back on "the divine injunction: 'A new commandment give I unto you, that ye love one another.'" "Yes," he intones, "this it was that saved me. Aside from higher considerations, charity often operates as a vastly wise and prudent principle—a great safeguard to its possessor. . . . Mere self-interest . . . if no better motive can be enlisted, should, especially with high-tempered men, prompt all beings to charity and philanthropy" (*WHM*, 9:36). The narrator subscribes to a cultural dogma in order to redress the situation that killed Adams and Colt: their meeting, as professionals, in a building characterized by commerce rather than domesticity. Putting himself in Adams's place, the narrator mouths an empty oath by "simply" deciding to love his neighbor, as it were.

Despite his obvious efforts to help Bartleby, the narrator's emphasis on preserving himself, economically and ethically, almost invariably disappoints. We want to remind the narrator that charity is nothing like a "prudent principle." It is just the opposite. He quickly compromises the golden rule by subscribing to a commercial morality. Melville highlights the narrator's hypocrisy, first by comparing him to the New Testament's good Samaritan and then by having him fail "to truly realize the Samaritan's ideal ethic": compassion.[85] As Thomas Wentworth Higginson suggested, the golden rule could not be used to justify selfishness. Those who argued that it could "explain how it is that it is arranged so, but you do not prove that this habit of looking to your own self-interest and leaving your neighbor to look to his, however well it worked in practice, did not prove in the end to warp and wither mind and conscience, as the one-sidedness of lawyers has always been admitted to do!"[86] Melville's lawyer participates in the ethics of compromise Melville saw practiced around him in the 1840s and 1850s, from ministers to publishers.

For all of these figures, the desire to act benevolently toward others—to whatever degree sincere, and however aggrandized at celebrations such as the Fruit and Flower Festival or in the confessional statements of magazine editorials—was fettered by an unenlightened self-interest. Yet the narrator seems to have little choice in the matter. When he decides simply to let Bartleby be, his legal peers remark on the scrivener's neglect of his duty. The "constant friction of illiberal minds wears out at last the best resolves of the more generous," the lawyer moans (*WHM*, 9:37). He comes to believe, as Adams may have done during his ill-fated interview with Colt, that an imperfectly defined moral equity does not and cannot structure the relations between author and publisher because the relationship is founded on neither charity nor on compassion— nor, in contemporary publishing terms, on cultural proprietorship—but on profit. In his dramatization of the story, Murray has the narrator complain, "Melville was out to flog me with the Sermon on the Mount."[87] Melville throws the trade's own ethics back in its face, and does so, ironically, in none other than George Palmer Putnam's own magazine. Putnam, the self-styled moralist of the antebellum print market, in fact treated his contributor handsomely. But not only did Melville use *Putnam's Monthly* as a platform from which to attack his vocational culture—an attack with which Putnam would have sympathized had he read the story as such— he did so with a vitriol Putnam likely would have found troubling.[88] Michael Gilmore reads "Bartleby" as a dirge on expressive authorship in the antebellum market, where it is "futility" to attempt to "free literature from its alliance with social and economic power." He suspects that Bartleby's startling jailhouse rebuke of the narrator—"'I know you . . . and I want nothing to say to you—'" is a warning to readers about the production of the literature they are reading (*WHM*, 9:43).[89] Bartleby's final sentence, however, may be less a warning to readers than a wholesale dismissal of the trade. And we should remember that the narrator's response to Bartleby's dismissal— "'It was not I that brought you here, Bartleby'" (*WHM*, 9:43)—has some justification. Once morally disenfranchised, the author, Melville suggests, withdraws from his or her industry. In this sense, "Bartleby" reads like a weary dramatization of Duyckinck's 1840 *Arcturus* essay, "Authorship":

> An Author now seldom ventures to state his case with the public. He either retires with the stricken deer to weep alone, or, by a strong effort of the will, abandons his books, leaves his seclusion, and comes forward to fall or rise in active life, as it may happen. . . . A certain latitude of conduct seems to have been allowed to authors formerly; they were privileged in eccentricity. . . . Now, none is so hardy as ever to claim the benefit of this indulgence. . . . [Society] has no sympathy with sorrow or melancholy: all its cry is action, action; let every thing be onward and successful.[90]

The parallels between Duyckinck's exposé and Bartleby's circumstances are striking. Bartleby falls in "active life" but maintains his silence with regard to his own "case."

Amid the "illiberal minds" who conduct the business of publishing and who cannot afford to indulge eccentricities or genius, Bartleby simply cannot succeed. As *Harper's New Monthly Magazine* reminded Americans, when publishers lose money "an injury is inflicted upon the literary profession" as a whole.[91] Whatever the cause of Bartleby's eccentricity, the narrator is powerless to help him. The narrator comes to appreciate, in other words, what Melville saw, rightly or wrongly, as the awful reality of literary publishing. "Conceive a man by nature and misfortune prone to a pallid hopelessness," the narrator realizes: "can any business seem more fitted to heighten it than that of continually handling these dead letters, and assorting them for the flames?" (*WHM*, 9:45). The compromise ethics of publishers reduces Bartleby's authorship to a business, a business at which earnest authors fail so perfectly and so predictably—as Bentley and Duyckinck tried to warn Melville—that publication becomes an act of sorting books "for the flames."

Though in "Bartleby" we inhabit a metaphor of the antebellum publisher, we still see the vocational world he represents through Melville's eyes.[92] We do not get and should not expect, therefore, a story that absolves the trade's sins, real or imagined. We do get, however, a story that, like *Pierre*, reveals a surprisingly extensive blueprint of the trade's ethical architecture, not only as one author saw it but, in fact, as some publishers and editors saw it. Like Fanny Fern's *Ruth Hall*, the subject of the next chapter, Melville's fictionalization of his print culture, while plainly exaggerated and indignant, is useful for what it discerns in the monolith of the trade.

6

The Tact of Ruthless Hall

AS COVER LETTERS go, Emily Dickinson's to Thomas Wentworth Higginson was more than a little unorthodox. Responding to Higginson's 1862 *Atlantic Monthly* article "Letter to a Young Contributor," Dickinson began by asking, "Are you too deeply occupied to say if my Verse is alive?" From there things only got more baffling:

> The Mind is so near itself—it cannot see, distinctly—and I have none to ask—
>   Should you think it breathed—and had you the leisure to tell me, I should feel quick gratitude—
>   If I make the mistake—that you dared to tell me—would give me sincerer honor—toward you—
>   I enclose my name—asking you, if you please—Sir—to tell me what is true?
>   That you will not betray me—it is needless to ask—since Honor is it's own pawn—[1]

Such letters were seldom so abstract. Dickinson, though, knew she was not addressing a magazine editor but instead an author more (or maybe less) like herself. Higginson had the luxury of celebrating the "mystery of words" without having to deal with the practical issue of getting them into print.[2] While Dickinson's letter bewitches students of American literature today—it looks like what we think these letters should look like—it would have annoyed the average editor or publisher.

There was no shortage of advice for would-be authors. Some of it was polite and encouraging, like "Letter to a Young Contributor," but much of it was not. Editors complained in print about everything from contributors' impenetrable handwriting to their unrealistic expectations of the trade to their rambling sentences. Even how-to books could be discouraging. *Haney's Guide to Authorship* (1867) was one in a series of self-help books published by the New York firm Jesse Haney and Company that enthusiastically taught readers how, among other things, to throw their voices, play dominoes, improve their memory, shoe horses, and get rich. About authorship, the series was less enthusiastic. Protesting that there were already too many bad books, the *Guide* went out of its way to dishearten new authors, opining that if it were successful in achieving its aims "we shall have fewer authors of all kinds."[3] After cataloguing reasons to avoid authorship universally—low pay, debauchery, novices' hopeless ignorance of the "rules of authorship"—the *Guide* turned its attention to discouraging a specific demographic: women authors. "The female writers have not generally made as much money as the others, less because of the unpopularity of their themes," the *Guide* observed, "than from their absence of business tact."[4]

The *Guide* did not need to explain this observation. Everyone knew women understood neither the economics nor the etiquette of business, and that the few versed in the kinds of discriminating social maneuvering demanded of businessmen compromised their femininity. "As a general thing," Fanny Fern remarked, "there are but few people who speak approbatively of a woman who has a smart business talent or capability."[5] While the belief may have been "Victorian nonsense," as Warren S. Tryon notes, it was powerful and pervasive nonsense nonetheless.[6] Young men could join one of the mercantile societies that were springing up from Baltimore to San Francisco to hear eminent businessmen talk about their worlds; the closest most women could get was serving the drinks. Books were not much help, either. There was no chapter on business tact in Catherine Beecher's *Treatise on Domestic Economy* (1841) or in other popular conduct manuals for women in the mid-nineteenth century, which meant that young writers like E.D.E.N. Southworth found themselves at a loss when they came to face to face with the business of literature for the first time, and why many found themselves thanking obliging editors or publishers so effusively. "The first day that you entered my little cottage, was a day, blessed beyond all the other days of my life," Southworth wrote to editor Robert Bonner long after she had made her mark on American literature. "I had some genius in popular writing; but not one bit of business tact and my pen was the prey of whoever chose to seize it."[7] Writers could learn the business quickly, but the curve was steep.

This all makes Fern's *Ruth Hall* a most interesting rendering of a culture in which being a woman writer was enough of an anathema without the added pressure of conducting business in the largely male world of print. No author, male or female, had ever so bluntly attacked this business as Fern did in *Ruth Hall*. Herman Melville couched his critiques in dense analogies, and even when his allusions are more transparent, as in his parody of Evert Duyckinck as Captain Kidd, he abstracted the people and processes of the trade and folded them into the tragedy of his protagonists. Other works depicting the trade were less abstract but also less acute. Ella Rodman's "An Author's Vicissitudes" (1851), published in *Graham's Magazine*, and J. T. Trowbridge's *Martin Merrivale: His X Mark* (1854) portray naïve young authors' encounters with the trade with a gentle sarcasm, and neither text explores the trade's inner workings or critiques its problematic ethics at much depth, despite the fact that in both stories literary tradesmen (and, for that matter, tradeswomen) behave questionably.[8] *Ruth Hall*'s sarcasm, on the other hand, was anything but gentle, and its critiques were pointed.

In her study of women and the textile trades, Wendy Gamber reminds us that literature bequeaths a "very different world" from that of history.[9] Fictional accounts of women at work "contained elements of truth but masked a more complicated reality," she writes. "They are best read not as accurate depictions of life and labor but as an index to anxieties concerning women's place." It is with this exhortation in mind that I want to look at *Ruth Hall*. In moving away from reading the novel as a one-to-one representation of Fern's life, we have replaced one false analogy with another: Ruth's experience as an author is too often read as a one-to-one depiction of the historical features of women's authorship, so much so that Ruth's well-known declaration "'no happy woman ever writes'" has become, as Susan S. Williams observes, "one of the most frequently cited critical shorthands for the plight of women writers in the United States," and, in turn, *Ruth Hall* has become the consummate example of the authorial female complaint.[10]

The chapter that concludes with "'no happy woman ever writes'" opens with another important, albeit less-famous declaration: "And now our heroine had become a regular business woman."[11] I want to ask what it meant to be a "regular business woman" in the mid-nineteenth century in order to understand how *Ruth Hall* represents the experience of conducting the business of print as a woman. Borrowing the language of historian Joan Scott, I want to think of Ruth's fictional experience as "already an interpretation *and* something to be interpreted."[12] Karen Weyler has argued that *Ruth Hall* is an "economic fantasy" in which Fern imagines a society based not on gender hierarchy but on parity, a society in which "the labor of all women [would] be valued at a living wage."[13] This chapter also sees the novel as an "economic fantasy," though of a different cast. The novel is a fantasy of an economic morality that works in accordance with the principles of liberal capitalism rather than against them. Fern wields these principles against the very literary tradesmen who claim to live by them. In so doing, she illustrates the intended presence of morality in an economic system assumed to be, according to the book's representative tradesmen, amoral. This claim does not mean that *Ruth Hall* endorses the very system responsible for the gender inequities that made Fern's authorship and that of other women a severe trial, as critics like Weyler, Kristie Hamilton, and Melissa Homestead have rightly shown.[14] Nor does it mean that Ruth is a good soldier of capitalism, as Gillian Brown has insisted.[15] Ruth is a capable businesswoman, but her ambition is a moral one, and her desire to see that ambition reciprocated makes the novel a call for justice within the economic status quo—a call for businessmen to look at the world with something other than what Fern called "a business eye."[16] Thus Ruth's is not "an anti-market individualism," I argue, so much as it is a moral individualism predicated on the ethics of capitalism itself.[17]

THE BOOK CANNOT ALL BE TRUE, CAN IT?

The New York house of Mason Brothers published *Ruth Hall* in December 1854, amid an advertising campaign of remarkable scope. Fern's story of a widow who turns to authorship to support herself and her two young children, who must teach herself how to deal with tradesmen whose sense of fairness is less developed than their sense of fashion, and whose success earns her a comfortable living, outsold many of the novels published in the 1850s, a decade of blockbuster books by women. Mason Brothers' contract with Fern all but promised record sales. In exchange for a "novel or tale to be comprised in a duodecimo volume of about four hundred pages," the firm pledged "extraordinary exertions to promote the sale thereof, so as, if possible, to make it exceed the sale of any previous work, & will, moreover, use every means in their power to attain that end."[18] This assured claim, made more arresting by the fact that most firms could barely compete against British reprints much less promise record sales for domestic titles, indicated Mason Brothers' confidence in its ability to convert Fern's celebrity into profit.[19]

Fern could only have delighted in the contract's terms and in its consequences. *Ruth Hall* was "placarded, in the daily papers, as the miracle of the age, as, indeed, it is, and distributed by a thousand carriers, wherever Yankee ingenuity or Yankee tact could penetrate," one reviewer surveyed. "The gigantic porters keeping watch and ward at the castle gates against all comers of ordinary size, found this little fliberty-gibbet skipping in between their colossal legs. Fanny Fern became famous in a day."[20]

Not quite a day. Fanny Fern was already famous for her newspaper writings. If anything, the book made her infamous. As Nina Baym has shown, there was a "special role for women authors" in antebellum America.[21] Criticizing one's family, acquaintances, and society was not it. Nor was criticizing the editors and publishers who alternately facilitated and obstructed women's authorship. In a letter to publisher Sampson Phillips, writer Ellen Louise Chandler asked excitedly if the rumors about Fern's sales were "*at all* true."[22] She was jealous, but she was also offended. A few months before the publication of *Ruth Hall*, Chandler wrote to Phillips predicting that Fern's immorality would be the end of her: "Fanny Fern—poor Fanny! It is to be feared her day is done! I hear no more about her successes. A lady friend who is a splendid critic, remarked to me recently, that she commenced the second series [*Fern Leaves, Second Series* (1854)], and found it so full of slang that she gave it up, with a pain at the heart, that any lady should so far forget herself."[23] Now, by 1856, Fern had sold thousands of books, and Chandler, though modestly successful, could only look on. Just before mentioning an enclosed "advertisement of Fanny Fern's

FIGURE 6.1 Fanny Fern [Sara Payson Willis], Courtesy Library of Congress.

book which I cut from a country paper," Chandler suggested that Phillips was just the man to remind authors of their moral duty. "I would like to hear your 'Sermon to Authors,' which I *know* you *could*, and I *hope* you *will* write some day," Chandler said. "I fear very few regard aright the responsibility of addressing so many thousand human souls as [must] be made worse or better by the contents of every successful book." For her part, she noted, she tried "not to write anything which *can* injure anyone."[24] It is a shame, she implied, that writers like Fern neglected their moral obligations. This is an ironic charge in light of *Ruth Hall*'s deeply moral look at a world that is deeply immoral.

Still, a battalion of critics damned Fern and her book for the same reason as Chandler: Fern had motives that were less than altruistic. More to the point, she had dared to openly criticize people from her life. Many of her characters, from her wretched family to her wretched in-laws to her wretched editors, are fairly obvious caricatures of Fern's personal and professional acquaintances. The most famous caricature was that of Hyacinth Ellet, a depiction of the prominent author and editor Nathaniel Parker Willis. Fern had lampooned him once already in an 1853 newspaper column, but that was before the world knew that Willis was her brother, a relationship that became unambiguous when one of Fern's former editors, the *True Flag*'s William Moulton—the future husband of Ellen Louise Chandler and the model for John Tibbetts in *Ruth Hall*—took revenge upon Fern by revealing her identity (Sara Payson Willis) after the book's publication, violating the gentlemanly ethic requiring publishers and editors to protect a writer's identity if asked.[25] While there were rumblings about Fern's real identity before Moulton's revelation, his disclosure cleared up the mystery once and for all, and it helped make the author and her book sensations.[26]

Mason Brothers could not have scripted a better scenario if it had tried. One of the most popular columnists in America, who had made her name speaking truth to patriarchy and whose identity was already the subject of intense speculation, had written what was reported to be a tell-all autobiography barely disguised as a novel. To boot, she was none other than the put-upon sister of a renowned and influential celebrity author-editor, a man who had, ironically, helped launch the careers of some of the most prominent women writers of the era. Though Moulton tried to salvage Willis's character in his vindictive collected writings/pseudo-biography, *The Life and Beauties of Fanny Fern* (1855)—which the New York *Daily Times* called "the worst book of the season . . . the most unwholesome . . . the meanest"—trade insiders saw through Moulton's posturing, aware that neither Willis nor Moulton himself were due much sympathy.[27] William Gilmore Simms had not even read *Ruth Hall* but believed everything Fern reportedly said about her famous brother. "I have long known Willis to be a contemptible skunk, & think I once told you so," he wrote to a friend.[28] "I knew that he had lied, & I could believe all the rest of him." Willis's work was as derided as his character. For many he was a symptom of everything that was wrong with the culture of letters in America, a man whose celebrity was the result of nonstop puffing.[29] For Simms and others, Willis really was, as Fern styled him, a "heartless dog" (*RH*, 159) and a "sensuous fop" (70).

Nevertheless, many reviewers shared Chandler's outrage and condemned the book. One reviewer charged Fern with squandering the moral capital she had banked since her first appearance in print in 1852: "Oh, Fanny Fern, we grieve to learn that you possess so hard a heart, so malignant a spirit! We have gloried in your genius, and trusted in your wonderful powers to awaken the wayward, through your brief life sketches, to a sense of wrong-doing.... Oh, Fanny Fern, you have perverted the good your covert hints of reform might have accomplished!"[30] Fern's ridicule of actual figures in her life, as opposed to "caricaturing the sins and follies of humanity in a general way," earned her the scorn of polite society and its "noble-hearted women."[31] "If the book has any purpose in its anger, its heedlessness and overstraining will defeat them," said the reviewer for *Putnam's Monthly*, echoing the trade's general reaction to *Ruth Hall*. It was "full and overflowing with an unfemininely bitterness and spite."[32] With a knowing nod to those who thought women should keep to their homes, and if they did leave them to behave accordingly, the *Knickerbocker* said the book was "'out-spoken.'"[33] Even the *National Era*, the abolitionist magazine that a few years later would mock conservative editors' attitudes toward women writers—"'Women! away with your nonsensical books. Keep to your sphere. Wash my linen! Cook me good, fat dinners!'"—noted that whatever Fern's real-life "trials," *Ruth Hall* could not "be commended or justified," a reaction that mirrored that of the *Anti-Slavery Standard*.[34] The reviewer for the *Daily Times* expressed shock that a "delicate, suffering woman can hunt down even her persecutors so remorselessly." The point was that Fern lacked tact. So did her protagonist, not to mention many of her women characters. Fern has Ruth sympathize and even empathize with prostitutes, crying for them because she "knew ... how it could be" (*RH*, 91). She does not denounce a mother, Mrs. Skiddy, who leaves her husband and child. Instead, she portrays her as rational and, worse, she implies that her behavior is warranted and makes her into a happy, proficient breadwinner. And Fern has Ruth mourn for the "hopelessly crazy" (110) Mary Leon after she is abandoned by her well-to-do husband and dies in an asylum amid "the gibbering screams of ... maniacs" (111). It all added up to "a peculiarly unchristianized, not to say uncivilized, style of imagination."[35] Prominent editor Sarah J. Hale, herself a widow with four children, refused to even review the book in *Godey's*.

Unlike reviewers who attempted, often clumsily, to dilute Fern's criticism, Elizabeth Cady Stanton reinforced it, noting that what mattered in *Ruth Hall* was its abstraction of antebellum moral realities. Stanton, who reviewed the book for the *Una*, granted that it made no difference whether *Ruth Hall* was technically true. It was a political act, a history of a gendered subjectivity and its construction. "To me the tale of sorrow is beautifully and truthfully told," she wrote. "It matters not whether the selfish male monsters so graphically sketched in 'Miss Hall,' that compound of ignorance, formality, and cant, are all of her own family,—enough that plenty of just such people live." *Ruth Hall* "is *some* woman's experience," she concluded.[36] A few years later, when Elizabeth Gaskell published a biography of Charlotte Brontë to mixed reviews, Fern reiterated Stanton's belief in the importance of women's narrative experiences in her review of Gaskell's work. If critics were put off by "the sad and gloomy views of life presented by the Brontes in their tales," Fern said, they should consider the sources of the fiction in the life of the woman writer. They "should know how such words were wrung out of them by the living recollection of the long agony they suffered." The fiction was less the result of the Brontës' "imagination" than "the hard cruel facts, pressed down, by an external life upon their very senses, for long months and years together." The Brontës wrote "out what they saw, obeying the stern dictates of consciences."[37] This was exactly what Stanton said about *Ruth Hall*. "If you do not wish us to paint you as wolves, get you into lambs' clothing as quickly as possible." "It is our right, our duty, to condemn what is false and cruel wherever we find it." The emphasis on the act of representation—writing, painting—is key. What Stanton admired about Fern was, in turn, what Fern admired about Gaskell and Gaskell about Brontë: the ability to render in language women's experience not necessarily realistically, per se, but authentically.

While many critics contested Fern's rendering of her experience of her family, others contested her depiction of the business of print. *Ruth Hall* made the trade nervous. If readers were so quick to believe so "angry" a book's view of an author's family, what else might they believe about the other characters? If tradesmen privately and publicly acknowledged the fidelity of Fern's portrait of one of their own—*Tait's Magazine* noted "that the book contains one undoubted portrait [Willis], which will be recognized by every literary man"—what might people think of the trade at large?[38] Another British reviewer saw "a wholesome bitterness in her satire which cannot be lost upon its subjects."[39] The satire *did* hit home, and it made the American trade restless. *Putnam's Monthly*, complaining that the "scenes with publishers savor strongly of romance," tried to assure readers that *Ruth Hall* grossly exaggerated Fern's usage by the trade. "We are not called upon to discuss the verisimilitude of the characters in the book. Yet it cannot *all* be true," *Putnam's* assured its readers with a hint of desperation, hoping perhaps to plant enough doubt to forestall more criticism of a business that had already heard its share.[40] *Putnam's* recognized that Fern's satire extended far beyond her family. It was a rendering of what one contemporary, Virginia Penny, viewed as the de facto gendering of American business—the fact that the "mass of men have not very liberal, just, or correct views, of what women may, and can, do with propriety."[41] In the remainder of this chapter, I want to discuss what women did do and how Fern rendered it. And I want to argue that *Ruth Hall* was a particularly, though not peculiarly, moral rendering of what women, and especially women authors, could and did do in the world of antebellum work. To understand the latter, we can turn to Virginia Penny.

BLESSED BE THE SMART BUSINESSWOMAN[42]

Penny, a former schoolteacher, began researching the lives of working women in the United States in 1859. Her goal was to fill a vacuum in her culture's knowledge of these women and their experiences. "It is very easy to obtain book after book on 'The Sphere of Woman,' 'The Mission of Woman,' and 'The Influence of Woman,'" she complained. But there was "no work giving a true history of woman's condition in a business capacity. Socially, morally, mentally, and religiously, she is written about; but not as a working, every-day reality, in any other capacity than that pertaining to home life."[43] Penny set out to discover that reality. Using an inheritance, she published her research in 1863 as *The Employments of Women: A Cyclopaedia of Women's Work*.

The book is an astonishing log of the conditions, wages, and hours for jobs women either did or could do—516 in all, from street musician to milliner to lawyer. In her introduction, Penny made explicit the conclusion implied throughout the text: women are unsuited to most occupations not by nature but by custom. This was not necessarily a groundbreaking claim. Fern and many others had said as much. "God made no distinction of *sex* when he said—'The laborer is worthy of his hire.' Man's cupidity puts that interpretation on it," Fern had written a decade earlier, satirizing the same attitude she would represent in Ruth's father-in-law, Dr. Hall.[44] But where Fern relied primarily on rhetoric, Penny marshaled statistics and anecdotes of the lives of working women. She knew how much a bone-collector earned ("fifteen cents a half bushel") because she had interviewed bone-collectors; she knew the dangers of handling quinine because she spent time with women working in a laboratory that smelled "so offensive that I could not rid myself of the taste for several hours after I left the room"; and she knew that women made as good astronomers as men because a woman astronomer in Nantucket told her so.[45] The astronomer told her that she suspected that many of the calculations performed by male astronomers were the handiwork of their female assistants.

Penny illustrated in remarkable detail what labor historians have since corroborated: that women had made their way into the public world of work in surprising ways and in hitherto unimagined numbers. Despite the labor-saving inventions of the sewing machine and cotton gin, the industrialization of cheese- and butter-making (which had, before large-scale mechanization, employed many women), and the prohibitive stereotypes about what women could and could not do, there were more women in the American workforce than at any time in the nation's history.[46] Most worked in textiles, but they had also begun to work in a greater variety of occupations even before the Civil War forced them to fill jobs men had had to set aside. Inconsistencies in census job titles makes estimating who was doing what jobs difficult, but historians suggest that by mid-century women had doubled the 100 or so occupations they had performed only decades earlier—Penny's research, of course, explodes that number—and that between 1815 and 1850 women's wages almost doubled in proportion to men's.[47] Penny believed that given the same educational opportunities and freedom from prejudice, women were capable of most of the jobs men performed and had already illustrated their abilities.[48] They managed boardinghouses, millinery establishments, and dry goods concerns, of course, but they owned ironworks, ran lighthouses, and oversaw china stores and junk shops as well. By 1870, one-tenth of the working women in the Midwest alone were owners or managers of their businesses.[49] While there are no comparable studies for Eastern cities, it is likely that women there were more involved in ownership and management than we have thought.

Penny's findings are corroborated by the records of R. G. Dun and Company, the commercial credit-rating agency whose archive provides a window on contemporary attitudes toward gender and work. These records reveal a predictable double standard. Women who were meticulous and discriminating—qualities praised in businessmen—were described by the firm's agents as "'Disagreeable'" and were seen as unrealistically demanding and recalcitrant.[50] Wendy Gamber suggests that such appraisals indicate that men "found it difficult to reconcile their economic interests with their cultural beliefs regarding the nature of womanhood."[51] Lucy Eldersveld Murphy, who has also studied the R. G. Dun archive, points to another example wherein a woman grocer was described as ugly yet smart—a "money maker and yet a woman."[52] Hence Penny's frustrated conclusion in *The Employments of Women* that "Prejudice has exaggerated . . . portraitures" of working women.[53] At the same time, though, such references are much less frequent than might be expected, and some of the agency's reports actively counter popular stereotypes, including the belief that women lacked the competitive drive and practical intelligence to participate, much less succeed in trade. One report, for example, judged the manager of a Cincinnati artificial flower business a "smart & shrewd woman," if slightly too "ambitious to do more than her neighbors."[54] (An 1848 report said the same of George Palmer Putnam.)[55] As a matter of fact, in at least one case the only thing standing between women and even greater success in business was their husbands. This was not how it was supposed to be, according to the ideology of true womanhood. Women were not supposed to be capitalistic, and they certainly were not supposed to be better at business than their husbands. A Mrs. S. Tyndale was the widow of a Philadelphia merchant who, before he died, had purchased a store in the heart of the city's commercial district on Chesnut Street. Though business was good, her husband had a habit of spending the earnings on just about everything but his $35,000 mortgage. Were it not for her dead husband, the credit agent figured, Tyndale, "a driving, indus[trious], enterpris[ing] woman," would "now be rich."[56] In Cincinnati, meanwhile, a credit agent noted in his assessment that a fifty-eight-year-old dry goods merchant had earned enough from her "little 8 x 10 affair" to attract unwanted interest from suitors. The report reads: "She has managed to save a little each y[ear] has been mar[ried] sev[eral] times—her present husband is seldom seen or heard of—she has accumulated quite a little fortune owns her store & dwelling w[ith] some 8 [thousand dollars] & is believed to have money secreted about the house, she has therefore been an object for fortune seekers (having no other attractions) but they have been sadly disappointed she is too sharp to allow any one to manage her affairs but herself."[57] Were it not for the laws of coverture, which subordinated the earnings of businesswomen, however successful, to their husbands, however profligate, the dry goods merchant would not have had to hide her profits from gold-hunting suitors. From the perspective of creditors who would have access to the report, the longer she stayed in control of her business, the better. In all, it was not common for an agent of R. G. Dun and Company to recommend against extending credit based on gender alone. Nor did these agents make a point of denigrating women's ability to run successful businesses or be successful employees.

We should not exaggerate the degree to which the public world of work was accepting of women or the extent to which women had control over their professional lives. By and large, as Penny protested, the idea of work was still intrinsically masculine. Despite her considerable evidence of women's presence in and significance to labor and management, Penny admitted that "Many men would banish women from the editor's and author's table, from the store, the manufactory, the workshop, the telegraph office, the printing case, and every other place, except the school room, sewing table, and kitchen."[58] Yet the R. G. Dun and Company archive suggests that the antebellum world of work was not as bifurcated along gender lines as we tend to assume, and that women who worked outside the home did so in many more places than textile mills. The "mass of men" could believe whatever it wanted; the business community had its own standards for success, and these standards were not comprehensively gendered, or at least not comprehensively discriminatory in matters of ability or ambition.

Of course, most mid-nineteenth-century women writers did not do the kind of work about which Penny wrote. They did not set type from illegible manuscripts or spend most of their days sewing shawls. They did not staff jewelry counters or pack and then repack boxes for fourteen hours a day to make a store appear bustling to passersby on the street. They did not negotiate new markets opened by an expanded network of canals and railroads or have to search out reliable and profitable trading partners (a rare combination) in those markets. And they did not have to answer nosy credit agents using private-investigator tactics to discover whether they paid their debts on time. As Gail Hamilton half-joked, the author was popularly seen as "'an eternal child,' in all that relates to practical business matters, and a terrible child at that."[59] "Happy, Happy Bard," James T. Fields chided Henry Wadsworth Longfellow, "that knoweth not the fangs of the merchant who goeth into State St. every day to encounter Shylocks who demand '2 pr. cent a month!'"[60] As Hamilton discovered, a little knowledge of business went a long way toward protecting an author's interests. She also noted that most male authors were at least thought to be capable of understanding business if only they would set their minds to it rather than dreaming up fictions. Women were popularly seen as having no such facility, though archival evidence suggests they were as quick a study as their male counterparts in what Fern called the "field of labor."[61]

Actually, women writers could conduct their business as frankly as their male counterparts, and many understood or came to understand that they could not allow a publisher's "personal regard" to interfere with the efficient conduct of "commercial civilities," even in this era of the so-called gentleman publisher.[62] In 1848,

Greenwood wrote a two-part letter to Fields. The first part she identified as the "business letter," in which she told the publisher how she wanted her next book of poems to look and when she wanted it published.[63] The second part was the personal letter. Where the first began "Dear Sir," the second began "My dear friend": "I was delighted to hear from you again—especially in your friendly and unofficial capacity." Greenwood valued the personal element of her relationship with Fields, but she also wanted to be sure that her professional concerns were unmistakable, and for this reason she led with the "business letter." The same was true of Sarah J. Hale, who would in one letter, in suitably legalistic language, propose a contract for a work to be published by Harper and Brothers and in another sign herself "Truly yr. friend."[64]

What did their business letters say? More important, how did they say it? Established women writers dictated everything from the way they wanted their books to look to when they expected the work to be completed. Often they did so with a false modesty, as when Greenwood told Fields in an 1849 letter that she knew "nothing of business."[65] As suggested above, she knew plenty. A letter from the previous year concerned how her next book should look and when she would like it published. And even her claim in the 1849 letter was plainly disingenuous, though politely so. She said she was a novice only after telling Fields first that she wanted to retain her copyright and second that it was his job to "arrange it." New writers could also be forthright, dictating, for example, how much gilding to use, how their books should be bound, how much to charge, and what percentage of the profits they should receive from the publisher.[66]

Once a book was in production, these writers were not shy about expressing concerns about publishers' handling of the process. "I have occasionally found, after I had taken pains [to] revise, to arrange the punctuation as I thought the sense required, that the printer had thought proper to add twice as many commas of his own—making the matter into a perfect hodgepodge," Caroline Kirkland complained to George Palmer Putnam. "Does our friend let the page stand as I leave it, except where he observes an obvious mistake?" she asked pointedly, insisting, albeit respectfully, that her command of the language was not to be questioned by a tradesman.[67] It is a point made by Ruth as well, though, characteristically, she sympathizes with the pressures on printers who, like her, had cares and concerns that extended far beyond their work.

Equally forthright was Catherine Beecher. She could afford to be: her *Treatise on Domestic Economy* went through more than fifteen editions between 1841 and 1856 and made her one of the most successful writers in the country. Nevertheless, proposing terms of publication to a firm like Harper and Brothers took wherewithal, whatever one's sex. She wrote to New York in 1854: "As, in your first communication, you offered to take the *Letters to the People* [*on Health and Happiness*], I accept what I consider the spirit of your offer . . . ie, *half the profits*—of all sales—charged at current prices for paper printing & binding—all risk to be assumed by the publishers. If 'a *per centage* equaling half the profits' is the best mode of calculating I of course have no objections to this form, but I wish to wait for further counsel on this point."[68] By "counsel" Beecher did not necessarily mean friendly advice. She wanted Harper and Brothers to be more candid before she made her decision. And she reminded the firm that it was *her* decision to make. Short of actually becoming publishers themselves, these writers acquired a detailed understanding of the practical questions of production, and did so aggressively.

In the credit assessments of R. G. Dun and Company, the practical was often tinged by the moral. Successful merchants combined "moral char[acter]" with "g[oo]d capac[ity]"—that is, they understood that one's "manner of d[oin]g bus[iness]" was what "inspired confidence" not only in commercial ability, but in moral decency.[69] As businesswomen, women writers emphasized the same union of the practical and the moral. When Harriet Beecher Stowe suspected that she had been duped by John P. Jewett, the publisher of *Uncle Tom's Cabin* (1852), she wanted to publicly shame him by writing a book about his behavior.[70] Gail Hamilton, meanwhile, talked about it, then she did it. Writers like Hamilton and Stowe tried to impress upon publishers and editors that they wanted to be dealt with with "justice" and with "common propriety"—with the same regard for fairness with which these publishers and editors supposedly dealt with one another.[71] And propriety meant more than good manners. In abusing Stowe's right to a fair profit, Jewett had acted unmannerly, to be sure, but for Stowe such behavior called into question the publisher's "general character."[72] "Miss Sedgwick says, 'Manners are minor morals,'" an indignant writer once reminded George Palmer Putnam.[73] Actually, what Catharine Maria Sedgwick said was that manners were "manifestations" of moral principles.[74] There is a difference. Manners testified to the "inward principle" envisioned by Freeman Hunt; they announced the presence of the natural merchant envisioned by Ralph Waldo Emerson. Did not publishers boast of their manners in the press on an almost weekly basis? Thus when Stowe declared that her publisher's "character" made her feel "he is *not* the man I wish to be in business relations with," she was expressing a moral logic of commercial behavior that was not just legitimate but orthodox for writers and for merchants alike. It is this logic that Fern illustrated in *Ruth Hall*. And it is significant, I want to argue, that she located it expressly in the character of the woman writer.

EDITORS ARE BUT MEN, AND OTHER APOLOGIES FOR THE STATUS QUO

Ruth Hall is a book about business, from Dr. Hall's habit of "speculating on what Ruth was about" (*RH*, 23) after having "been to the market" to Mrs. Hall's wonder at the volume of Harry's enterprise ("'Company, company, company'" [38], she puns), to the panorama of women workers (milliners, seamstresses, dressmakers, boardinghouse managers, asylum matrons, actresses, prostitutes) that forms the novel's working class. Even before Ruth becomes a "business woman" and is compelled to walk the "business streets" (122) looking for a home for her writing, business affects her life. Her poverty is the direct result of her honest businessman of a husband who, like the poor but honest trimmings dealer described earlier, trusted not wisely but too well. If business torments Harry in life—on his death-bed he feverishly imagines himself back in his counting room listening to "the shrill whistle of the cars, recalling him to the city's whirl of business; he had stocks to negotiate; he had notes to pay; he had dividends due" (57)—it all but terrorizes Ruth after his death.

It is then that Ruth is forced to contend with what Freeman Hunt called the "mighty vortex" of "money-getting."[75] The vast majority of the money-getters in *Ruth Hall* are not made in Harry's image. The novel's most notorious example is Ruth's brother, Hyacinth, an editor whose conservative rag, the aptly titled *Irving Magazine*, maintains its status on the backs of ghostwriters who labor away in garrets like "pliant tool[s]" (*RH*, 159). Hyacinth's most egregious sin is certainly his failure to help Ruth, as Willis had failed to help Fern. But beyond that there is really little to differentiate Hyacinth from most of the novel's other editors. He is just another literary businessman: one of the "comfortably-fed gentlemen" (158) who spend their time gorging themselves in fine restaurants and dissembling profit motives beneath a carefully manicured public image. Another is Tom Develin, a bookseller whose foppishness nearly rivals Hyacinth's and whose lack of honor easily does. Like Hyacinth, who desperately wishes someone would inform Ruth at Harry's funeral that "'her hair is parted unevenly and needs brushing sadly'" (58), Develin is content to live in a world of assiduously serviced appearances where morality is at best cosmetic. Even his bookstore is a moral façade, its windows filled with "engravings of departed saints—who with their last breath had, with mock humility, requested somebody to write their obituaries" (75)—and paintings selected "with a peculiar eye to the greenness of the trees, the blueness of the sky, and the moral 'tone' of the picture." It is no coincidence that when John Walter pronounces sentence on Hyacinth later in the novel, he does so to Develin, because what he says applies as much to the bookseller as to the editor: "'Fashion is his God; he recognizes only the drawing-room side of human nature'" (207). Fern's readers would have understood the sentence. In the middle decades of the nineteenth century a devotion to fashion was a repudiation of any attempt at what Karen Haltunen has called "moral self-improvement."[76] As offensive as Tom Develin and Hyacinth Ellet are, however, neither is as eerily inhuman as the businessman upon whom Ruth leans at Harry's internment. Fern describes him as "a dry, flinty, ossified man of business; a man of angles—a man of forms—a man with veins of ice, who looked the Almighty in the face complacently, 'thanking God he was not as other men are;' who gazed with stony eyes upon the open grave, and the orphan babes, and the bowed form at his side, which swayed to and fro like the young tree before the tempest blast" (*RH*, 63–64). The "wooden" (64) man is an amalgam of all the businessmen in the novel. He is also a metaphor for the world of trade generally, the world in which Ruth finds herself after Harry's death: unsympathetic, inconsiderate, condescending, and sanctimonious.

The wooden man appears a third of the way into the novel. Then begins Ruth's accelerated declension. Soon she is broke. Her husband and first daughter are dead. So too is her friend Mary Leon, who dies alone in an asylum where she is confined by a husband who had "wearied" (*RH*, 112) of her. Ruth has been kicked out of her home after her landlady realizes there is more profit in running an apartment building than a boardinghouse. Unable to afford an apartment in the newly designated building, she endures another remove from the idyllic cottage she once shared with Harry. Her new lodgings amount to an objectionable tenement lorded over by a vindictive woman who spends her spare time dissecting stray cats and "fondling a pet skull" (113). The derelict building soon makes both Ruth and a daughter sick. This proves convenient for the landlady, who does a side business in expensive, homemade drugs. Denied help by her families, Ruth tries to get a job, but her former middle-class status rules out common labor—"She offered to come and sit down among those [working] girls, and work *with* them. My God, Mary! Harry Hall's wife!'" (80), exclaims a businessman when Ruth applies for a job as a milliner—and her precipitous fall from that class exiles her from the affections and charity of friends. Unable to work in textiles, she considers teaching, but after sitting for a teacher's exam that asks that nagging question "'Was Christopher Columbus standing up, or sitting down, when he discovered America?'" (102) Ruth is turned away. In the end, she has no recourse when, upon refusing to purchase her landlady's overpriced and likely toxic drugs, she is told that in addition to her rent, for which she gets a room and a tiny shelf in the flooded cellar on which to keep her bread and milk, she must scrub the stairs. In other words, she must work for nothing. It is at this point that Ruth decides to become an author and enters the "business streets."

It seems a measure of her naïveté that she actually expects anyone to help her, as though she expects the literary world to be more interested and accommodating than her barbaric personal world. She seems to think that the editors she meets will have the grace of Mr. Bond, the old man who lives above her and who "always stepped aside, and with a deferential bow waited for Ruth to pass" (*RH*, 114). When she finally meets an editor, he is a far cry from Mr. Bond and his "refined and courteous manners" (127). Actually, everyone is:

> "Is this 'The Daily Type' office?" asked Ruth of a printer's boy, who was rushing down five steps at a time, with an empty pail in his hand.
>
> "All you have to do is ask, mem. You've got a tongue in your head, haven't ye? women folks generally has," said the little ruffian.
>
> Ruth, obeying this civil invitation, knocked gently at the office door. A whir of machinery, and a bad odor of damp paper and cigar smoke, issued through the half-open crack.

"I shall have to walk in," said Ruth, "they never will hear my feeble knock amid all this racket and bustle;" and pushing the door ajar, she found herself in the midst of a group of smokers, who, in slippered feet, and with heels higher than their heads, were whiffing and laughing, amid the pauses of conversation, most uproariously. Ruth's face crimsoned as heels and cigars remained, in *status quo*, and her glance was met by a rude stare. (120)

The narrator's explanation that these men were unaware that "their manner towards Ruth" lacked "respectful courtesy" (122) is not a comment on the men themselves. This is the "status quo," after all. The narrator is commenting on Ruth, who expects manners where there are none.

Ruth's problem is not naïveté; it is character. This is the conclusion of the phrenologist who examines Ruth later in the novel. "'The fact is,'" he tells her, "'you are made of finer clay than most of us'" (*RH*, 171). Ruth already knew this, and so did we. So too did John Walter, who is responsible for her being there in the first place. Walter wants to know what makes Ruth so good, and phrenology, the reading of the skull as an objective correlative for everything from depression to heroism, is the only thing that can tell him. The diagnosis is moral character—Ruth has it, in excess. She worships, we are told, the "good'" and the "noble'" (168). She is endowed with "'feeling, sympathy, sentiment, and religious devotion'" (171). She boasts prodigious "'moral courage'" (169). She "'demand[s] goodness'" from the men around her. As Freeman Hunt would say, Ruth makes "*character* supreme."

None of this is news, necessarily, but the episode does set up an important debate between author and editor over the morality of the trade. To her surprise, Ruth agrees with the phrenologist's diagnosis, with two exceptions. First, he had said her active mind makes her "'muscular system . . . rather defective'" (*RH*, 167). Nonsense, she tells Walter. "'I can walk longer and faster than any six women in the United States'" (172). Second, she is too sensitive to criticism. More nonsense. The phrenologist misread her sensitivity to injustice as a sensitivity to criticism. She explains: "'When my sense of justice is thus wounded, I do feel keenly, and I have sometimes thought that if such persons knew the suffering that such thoughtlessness, to baptize it by the most charitable name, may cause a woman, who must either weep in silence over such injustice, or do violence to her womanly nature by a public contention of her rights, such outrages would be much less frequent. It seems to me . . . were I a man, it would be so sweet to use my powers to defend the defenseless.'" Ruth's moral sense is so highly developed that she responds physically to injustice—she feels it. She even associates the idea of redressing injustice with a sensory sweetness. Walter's response is revealing. "'Bravo, Ruth, you speak like an oracle. Your sentiments are excellent, but I hope you are not so unsophisticated as to expect ever to see them put in universal practice,'" he lectures. If Ruth wants morality from the world, she should look to another profession. "'How is it, in these days of female preachers, that you never contemplated the pulpit or the lecture-room?'" (173). The phrenologist was right. "'The world is hardly finished nice enough for you'" (169), he had concluded. "'You are too exacting in this respect.'"

If Ruth seems to expect too much of the world, according to Walter and the professor, then she certainly expects too much from the trade. "'Editors are but men,'" Walter reminds her, "'and in the editorial profession, as in all other professions, may be found very shabby specimens of humanity. A petty, mean-spirited fellow, is seldom improved by being made an editor of; on the contrary, his pettiness, and meanness, are generally intensified. It is a pity that such unscrupulous fellows should be able to bring discredit on so intelligent and honorable a class of the community'" (*RH*, 172–73). John Walter's apology would have earned Evert Duyckinck's scorn. Despite the presence of a "'better class of editors'" (173)—including, not incidentally, himself—Walter does not believe that the trade is capable of anything close to universal morality. If Ruth wants to champion "'the cause of right'" (172) she should become a "'preacher'" and look toward heaven, not the counting room. The business of literature is no forum for virtue.

By this point in the novel, readers are well acquainted with a first-rate specimen of a "'petty, mean-spirited fellow'" in the form of John Tibbetts. Tibbetts plays the rake who when confronted with the specter of an end to his relationship with his star contributor uses physical force to attempt to bend her will. Warning her that he will ruin her reputation, Tibbetts blocks Ruth's exit from his office after she informs him of her intent to leave his employ. "'Stay!' exclaimed Mr. Tibbetts, placing his hand upon the latch; 'when you see a paragraph in print that will sting your proud soul to the quick, know that John Tibbetts has more ways than one of humbling so imperious a dame'" (*RH*, 157). Ruth's response—she tells him that the editor could hardly defame her when he has already so actively praised her virtues—elicits from Tibbetts a lesson on magazinedom: quid pro quo. "'I am aware, most logical of women, that I stand committed before the public *there*,'" he explains, "'but I have many an editorial friend, scattered over the country, who would loan me *their* columns for this purpose.'" When he realizes he is losing Ruth as an author, he strikes out at her as a woman. Beyond physically barring her exit—"'*Shall* not [leave], Mr. Tibbetts?'" Ruth responds, "'I have yet to learn that I am not free to go, if I choose'" (156)—he accuses her of having a "'proud soul'" (157) and of being overbearing. Ruth, recognizing the box she has been placed into, remarks sarcastically that her editor's fear-mongering is "'a *manly* act; but your threat does not move *me*.'" As it happens, Ruth moves at will, and the last thing Tibbetts sees is her dress as it "fluttered out the door." This episode takes place only a few chapters before Walter and Ruth's debate over trade morality and thus makes Walter's rebuke of Ruth's moral idealism seem both naïve and patronizing. Ruth is quite aware by then that editors can be "'petty'" and "'mean-spirited.'" She knows more than that. She knows that they can be discourteous, ignorant, lazy, greedy, deceptive, hypocritical, misogynistic, and violent. She does not need Walter to tell her the trade is immoral. She needs him to confirm her belief that it ought to be moral—further, that it could be moral, if people like him would speak out.

At the end of their debate, Walter jokes that Ruth is incapable of checking her "'sentiments'" (*RH*, 173). He means that Ruth cannot curb her opinions. He also means that Ruth cannot smother her goodness. Of course, neither can he. Ruth immediately apprehends the irony of Walter's charge. "'As you please,' replied Ruth, 'but people who live in glass houses should not throw stones.'" Fern's introduction of Walter earlier in the novel—"In one of the thousand business offices, in one of the thousand crowded streets of a neighboring city, sat Mr. Walter" (140)—belies his goodness. He is nothing like the editors in those "thousand business offices." Nor is he like the other literary tradesmen Fern depicts in *Ruth Hall*. Horace Gates comes close, but of Gates all we really see is him railing, Invisible-Man like, against the inequities of the trade. Walter does not just rage. He acts. He writes to Ruth to express his "warm, brotherly interest in [her] welfare" (143). Ruth wavers at first but ultimately responds because he seems, like Mr. Bond, like someone she can believe in: "Then, again she seized her pen, and with a quick flush, and a warm tear, said, half pettishly, half mournfully, 'Away with these ungenerous doubts! Am I never again to put faith in human nature?'" (144). Ruth experiences "a peace to which she had long been a stranger," in part because "it was so sweet to believe in *somebody* once more." She mails her response to Walter "with more hopeful feelings than Noah probably experienced when he sent forth the dove from the ark for the third time." Like Noah's, Ruth's prayers are answered and her faith is rewarded. She rediscovers her own trusting nature in the private sympathy and public courtesy of a businessman whose dogmatic righteousness matches her own, a man whose professional manners are highly developed and advertised. This is the man telling her not to expect too much of the trade, and doing so only a few paragraphs before Fern announces that Ruth "had become a regular business woman"? Ruth's career teaches Walter that it is not the trade that is false, but its characters.

A RUTHLESSLY MORAL CAPITALISM

Not long after Harry's funeral, Dr. Hall passes judgment on Ruth's competence in trade: "'She's fit for nothing but a parlor ornament,' said the doctor, 'never was. No more business talent in Ruth Ellet, than there is in that chany ornament of yours on the mantle-tree, Mis. Hall'" (*RH*, 130). By this point, Dr. Hall's role in the novel as a spokesman for the "Victorian nonsense" of true womanhood is plain. Hence our delight in watching him get ripped off by a dressmaker as he and Ruth's mother-in-law prepare for Harry's funeral as though it were the social event of the season:

"I forgot to ask you how wide a hem I should allow on your black crepe veil," said Miss Skinlin, tying on her bonnet to go. "Half a yard width is not considered too much for the *deepest* affliction. Your daughter, the widow, will probably have that width," said the crafty dress-maker.

"In my opinion, Ruth is in no deeper affliction that we are," said the doctor, growing very red in the face; "although she makes more fuss about it; so you may just make the hem of Mis. Hall's veil half-yard deep too, and send the bill into No. 20, where it will be footed by Doctor Zekiel Hall, who is not in the habit of ordering what he can't pay for." (63)

Fern's goal here is more than to show that Dr. Hall is a buffoon. It is also to show that as a businesswoman the dressmaker is anything but. As well, the exchange sets up a masterful demonstration in the following chapter of just how misinformed Dr. Hall is about his daughter-in-law's "business talent," a talent she has the moral intelligence to use honorably.

Immediately after Dr. Hall's estimation of Ruth's abilities she arrives in Lescom's counting room, where the editor, with priggish delight, informs the struggling author that her columns have made multiple exchanges, a kind of informal syndication that could dramatically increase a newspaper's readership and thus its profits, and that also could radically undermine an author's control over her work.[77] This, Lescom explains, is a "'good sign'" (*RH*, 130) for Ruth, "'a good test of your popularity.'" In fact, it is neither a sign nor a test. It is proof that Ruth has become a commodity, however little she owns or even profits from that status. Commodification in *Ruth Hall* is a thorny issue, and it has occasioned stark disagreement among critics, who debate to what extent Ruth does or even can participate in the market economy with a deliberate agency, and to what extent she wishes to do so. While these debates over possessive individualism and unstable property claims are productive, in this final section I want to look at *Ruth Hall*'s engagement with capitalism in a different way and suggest that the novel presents a theory of moral capitalism that is both a rebuke of the status quo and a vision of what *ought* to be, however fantastical.

Back to Ruth's "'good news.'" True to character, she reacts physically, and, of course, is misread by the editor:

Ruth's eyes sparkled, and her whole face glowed.

"Ladies like to be praised," said Mr. Lescom, good-humoredly, with a mischievous smile.

"Oh, it is not that—not that, sir," said Ruth, with a sudden moistening of the eye, "it is because it will be bread for my children."

Mr. Lescom checked his mirthful mood, and said, "Well, here is something good for me, too; a letter from Missouri, in which the writer says, that if "Floy" (a pretty *nom-de-plume* that of yours, Mrs. Hall) is to be a contributor for the coming year, I may put him down as a subscriber. . . . That's good news for *me*, you see," said Mr. Lescom, with one of his pleasant, beaming smiles. (*RH*, 130)

Lescom reads Ruth's physical reactions as signals of narcissism and selfishness when in fact they signal modesty and selflessness. The body language tells the story: the editor smiles a "beaming" smile at his own good fortune; Ruth nearly cries for that of her daughters. Her spirits lifted by this news, Ruth immediately hits the next wall for nineteenth-century women workers: wages. After being told that she is the reason "Mr. Lescom's subscription list" is "swelling" (131)—a good example of the sexual innuendo woven into the novel's economic language—Ruth wonders if "*she* ought not to profit by" the swollen list as well. Fern uses the language of moral obligation ("ought") to reinforce the sense of duty presumed by the question. As for the question itself, we never hear it. We only see her take "her gloves on and off" before she finally "mustered the courage" to ask the editor for a raise.

Again Lescom misreads Ruth's motives. "'Now that's just *like* a woman'" (*RH*, 131) he says in response to the question, "'give them the least foot-hold, and they will want the whole territory.'" Lescom's humor is severely patronizing and is the consequence, most likely, of fear. He is aware that Ruth is quickly developing a shrewd commercial intelligence, deducing, as she has, the logic of supply and demand and learning the injustice of her position. Lescom wields his solution to this problem like a blunt instrument: when talking to the supplier, he will simply keep quiet about the demand. The fact that he tells her this and even boasts that he could secure her "'the offer of a handsome salary for publishing such things'" is a function of his confidence, as Virginia Penny modeled it, that as a woman Ruth will not press her moral rights much less her advantage in the masculine labor sphere. "'It won't do,'" Lescom admits, "'to talk so unprofessionally to you.'" He then pays Ruth from his purse, and she deposits "the usual sum" into her own.

What Ruth has learned is that wages are never "neutral."[78] As economic historian Alice Kessler-Harris suggests, they are better thought of as "a set of gendered instructions." In her follow-up to *The Employments of Women, Think and Act* (1869), Virginia Penny turned her attention to exactly this problem. Most men would limit a woman's "duties entirely to home, whether she has one or not," Penny argued. "They would not permit women to enter the store, the workshop, the counting-room, nor even the more exalted and refining atmosphere of the study, or the *atelier*."[79] Once a woman did gain admittance, Penny found, she only encountered the more abstract hurdle of wages. Ruth is told, for example, that the impersonal, gender-neutral force of supply and demand dictates wages. She quickly gleans its false logic. Penny later tried to unpack that logic. "The value of labor is too apt to be estimated, not by its usefulness, and the good it may bring, but by the rate at which it may be obtained—by the necessities of the laborers."[80] In other words, wage calculation was exactly the opposite of what it was supposed to be in theory: objective. Because men controlled most wages, women were on the losing side of the equation. This way of conducting business along gendered lines was, Penny wrote angrily, "a relic of barbarous ages and barbarous nations."[81] But she recognized it, much as Ruth does, as the status quo. This status quo had an effect on the psychology of women workers. "Women want moral and mental courage," Penny suggested. "They receive such wages as men offer, without considering whether it is a fair compensation. They feel that to demand higher wages is a barrier they cannot surmount."[82] Hence Ruth's moment of hesitancy, taking her gloves on and off, mustering her courage. And hence Lescom's view—"the same view that almost any other business man would have taken"—to maximize profits. Ruth reminds herself (and us) that he is a businessman and that his view is simply "a business one": "retain her at her present low rate of compensation, till he was necessitated to raise it by a higher bid from rival quarter." This does not make Lescom a villain. It makes him, Fern suggests, a businessman, albeit one who boasts only part of the character contemporaries theorized ought to belong to all successful businessmen.

Now aware of "'her value'" (*RH*, 132)—that is, aware that her wages are not the result of her social capital but of her knowledge, courage, and ability to leverage that capital—Ruth also takes a "business view" and acts accordingly: she seeks out Lescom's competitors. Fern makes a pretense of reminding us again that Ruth is "a novice in business-matters" (131) who behaves the way she does because of her "strong common sense." But this common sense is remarkably attuned to the logic of capital. When Tibbetts tries to force Ruth to write under another pseudonym, she reminds him that her pseudonym is the source of her symbolic and thus her economic capital. It would be "'foolish to throw it away,'" (132) she teaches the clueless editor. Tibbetts's "business talent" is no match for Ruth's, and she wins from him a slightly higher wage than the one she receives from Lescom. This is all she needs to force Lescom's hand.

To this point, *Ruth Hall* functions more or less as business conduct literature in its practical capacity. Now, however, Fern privileges its ethical dimension. With her bargaining position strengthened considerably by Walter's offer, Ruth returns to Lescom's office, where she is told that her articles are not long enough. The ensuing exchange is worth quoting in full, beginning with Ruth's measured response:

"If you would like more matter, Mr. Lescom, I wonder you have not offered me more pay."

"There it is," said Mr. Lescom, smiling; "women are never satisfied. The more they get, the more grasping they become. I have always paid you more than you could get anywhere else."

"Perhaps so," replied Ruth. "I believe I have never troubled you with complaints; but I *have* looked at my children sometimes, and thought that I must try somehow to get more; and I have sometimes thought that if my articles, as you have told me, were constantly bringing you new subscribers, friendship, if not justice, would induce you to raise my salary."

"*Friendship* has nothing to do with business," replied Mr. Lescom; "a bargain is a bargain. The law of supply and demand regulates prices in all cases. In literature, at present, the supply greatly exceeds the demand, consequently the prices are low. Of course, I have to regulate my arrangements to my own inter-ests, and not according to the interests of others. You, of course, must regulate your arrangements according to *your* interests; and if anybody else will give you more than I do, you are at liberty to take it. As I said before, *business* is one thing—*friendship* is another. Each is good in its way, but they are quite distinct." (*RH*, 147)

Lescom summarizes the logic of capitalism with efficient clarity. But what Fern calls attention to in this exchange is not so much its strict definition—a definition Ruth already understands intuitively; after all, she goes to Lescom knowing what he will say—but the place of morality in this system. Her implied question is not *how* busi-ness works but *why* Lescom does not act on impulses other than economic, impulses she articulates as "'friendship'" and "'justice.'" It is the same question Harriet Beecher Stowe asked of John P. Jewett in 1852 and that Gail Hamilton asked of James T. Fields in 1868, a question that presumes a moral basis in capitalism and a moral intelligence in capitalistic behavior. Lescom's response is to disqualify "'friendship'" from the debate, suggesting that in its own right it is "'good'" but that it is irrelevant to his professional life, and should, by implication, be irrelevant to Ruth's. In other words, business based on capitalism is not immoral but amoral. The narrator notes that when Lescom finishes he smiles, "as if he would say, 'Well, now, I'd like to know what you can find to say to that?'" (148). Ruth does find something to say, though it is not what most readers probably expect.

Based on her earlier statement that Lescom ought to offer her more money out of selfless motives, most readers probably expect Ruth to appeal, a la Pierre, to an absolute morality that is incompatible with the demands of capitalism. Instead, Ruth adopts Lescom's logic that both parties must pursue their self-interest. "'I am glad . . . that you think so, for I have already acted in accordance with your senti-ments,'" Ruth tells the shocked editor, deploying his own laissez-faire theory against him. Initially this response seems at odds with Ruth's character, as though she has become too calculating, perhaps too "regular" a businessperson—too "Ruth-less," as Grace Greenwood would pun.[83] Ann Douglas has argued that there are essentially two Ruths. The Ruth of the second half of the novel is "a shrewd, bitter, business-oriented and aggressive woman" who all but eclipses the gentle, sentimental Ruth of the first half of the novel.[84] I am arguing that there is just one Ruth Hall. The morality that defines her domestic existence before she becomes a writer and businesswoman is the same morality that suffuses her professional life after. Ruth does not "outwit" the "male culture experts"—Lauren Berlant's useful phrase—so much as she *betters* them.[85] Lescom represents a narrow interpretation of the social imperatives of capitalism. Ruth represents a much fuller interpreta-tion, one that accounts for the prickly balance between sympathy and self-interest that business writers in Fern's era saw as the key to the fulfillment of the American commercial character.

As economic historians suggest, this balance is also the key to understanding Smithian capitalism insofar as Smith's body of work may be seen as an attempt to "coordinate" ethics and economics. "The analysis of economic matters was not disjunct from moral philosophy in Smith's thought," Richard Teichgraeber notes, "indeed, he identified it as an integral component of his moral philosophy."[86] Smith privileged sympathy, not selfishness, as a primary idea and force, where sympathy was defined as the act of picturing another's reality: in Smith's words, "what we ourselves should feel in like situations."[87] Because one person can never know what it feels like to be someone else, imagination is pivotal to Smith's philosophy, and it was this willingness and ability to imagine another's reality that formed, said political economists, the bonds among individuals on which society was based. Lescom's reading of Smithian capitalism is in fact a prominent misreading. Sympathy and self-interest "only contradict each other," Knud Haakonssen points out, "if Smithian sympathy is misinterpreted as benevolence and self-interest is narrowed to selfishness and then taken to be the reductive basis for all human motivation."[88] What Smith required of agents is that they sympathize with another's reality by imagining what it might feel like and then not acting according to selfishness but according to enlightened and humane self-interestedness. This self-interestedness is neither disinterested benevolence nor altruism, because it is fundamentally based on what is right for the agent. But it is also based on not doing injury to another. In this way, economists and historians such as Teichgraeber and Haakonssen argue, Smith's economic theory may be read as a philosophy of humanism, much as it was read by antebellum business writers.[89]

When Ruth begins her argument by telling Lescom that she has "'looked at my children sometimes, and thought that I must try somehow to get more,'" she is imagining how they must feel. In a word, she is sympathizing. And it is sympathy she tries to elicit in her editor by trying to get him to imagine what it must feel like for her to have to raise her children in poverty. (John Walter illustrates this sympathy in spades.) Ruth argues that friendship is a fundamental part of business; or, put differently, sympathy is integral to capitalism, a capitalism Lescom is either ignorant of or that he willfully misunderstands. Hence Ruth's pun on "sentiments" in her rejoinder to Lescom: "'I have already acted in accordance with your sentiments.'" Lescom's "sentiments" are devoid of sentiment as defined by the theory of capitalism Lescom presumes to know so well. Ruth's actions, in turn, are determined by sentiment.

Ruth Hall is a statement on the sentimental ethics of capitalism as abused in theory and practice by literary tradesmen like Lescom and Tibbetts, whose very manners indicate their ignorance of its moral foundations. Ruth's dealings with the trade exhibit not "instinctual repulsion" at their "working-world manners and mores," as one commentator has argued, but at the perversion of these manners and mores.[90] The inability of these tradesmen to conduct themselves with courtesy is for Ruth and for Fern, as it would be for Sedgwick, a categorical symptom of their moral depravity—a depravity that is the result of their lack of character, not the result of the fact that they are businessmen. What offends Ruth, that is, is not tradesmen's lack of deference to Ruth's "class" but their lack of manners period, their lack of tact. The market does not "figure as a home without sentiment" so much as it does another home for sentiment.[91]

Men and brethren, we live in a commercial age. I suspect that, if we knew history well enough, we should discover that all ages have been commercial, and that all our predecessors had experiences like these.

WALTER F. PAGE, *A Publisher's Confession*[1]

Epilogue

What Lies Back of the Contract

IN THE DECADES following the Civil War, most of the men responsible for the first great era of American publishing died: Evert Duyckinck, George Palmer Putnam, William Appleton, Charles Scribner, Henry Carey, all four Harper brothers, and James T. Fields. All lived during and in varying degrees exemplified the early stages of the nation's transition into industrial capitalism and the attendant rise of the corporation, a world, the usual line of argument goes, in which money eclipsed manners altogether. And while many of the publishers who assumed the mantle of the trade were the sons of that first generation, American publishing houses largely ceased to be the family concerns they had been.[2]

There is little need to rehash the changes to American publishing in these years, and especially following the Panic of 1873, but a brief survey is in order. Even despite the disruption caused by the war, publishing grew steadily, becoming an industry proper. Between 1850 and 1880, the number of printing and publishing firms increased five times over, and the number of men, women, and children employed in the industry rose from 8,268 to 58,478.[3] The trade, broadly defined to include all of its many manufacturing components, became markedly more capitalized, from nearly $16 million in 1850 to over $39 million in 1860 and over $135 million in 1880. Census figures for 1880 valued the trade's entire output at $189 million, a 658% increase from 1850. Historians argue that many of the changes in the economy and the business sector were not necessarily a result of the war so much as they were stages in the maturation of existing trends. Postwar publishing bears out this argument: many if not most of the changes in publishing were already under way before the war.[4] Publishing and bookselling became further differentiated, with both trades

self-identifying to a greater extent, and publishers continued to become more specialized with regard to the kinds of texts they produced. The long struggle for international copyright, which had defined so much of the century's trade talk, finally
ended in 1891. Author-publisher relations became more standardized, in part because
of the increased presence of literary agents. Agents had long though irregularly been
involved in literary publishing but now began to become a fixture in the scene, a
controversial development.[5] Like the literary agent, the traveling book salesman was
also a much more influential presence, covering distances via rail that early salesmen
like Parson Weems, who traversed the Southeast hawking volumes from his trusty
cart on behalf of Mathew Carey, could only dream of.[6] Larger markets held the
promise of bigger profits, but they also exacerbated age-old problems for publishers.
The late nineteenth-century publisher wanted to be as "assured of his market" as the
late eighteenth-century printer, but gauging demand for supply was still largely
guesswork, albeit guesswork on a continental scale.[7] Thus, while the postwar publisher was no longer the "fledgling capitalist" the eighteenth-century printer was, the
challenges he faced in doing his business were in some fundamental ways analogous.
It was the scale that was unimaginably bigger.[8]

In his invaluable account of American publishing between the Civil War and
World War I, *This Was Publishing* (1952), Donald Sheehan observes "a constant
undercurrent of complaint" in and about the trade.[9] Like most businesses, publishing houses had "divested themselves of one morality and seemed not greatly interested in finding another."[10] In lieu of searching, they reminisced about the antebellum
trade, which was generally remembered as a world of special moral temperance.
However, as I have argued, that world was largely a projection. Preindustrial American business was not necessarily dominated by a "gentlemanly" ethos. Certainly such
an ethos existed, and certainly it was more dominant in the 1770s than in the 1870s.
But the dry goods dealer in 1790 did not finalize every transaction with a handshake
alone, nor did he build his business exclusively on the goodwill of his neighbors or
enlightened self-interest. The merchants of early America could be as underhanded
as their robber-baron successors. By way of epilogue, I want to talk about one final
feud in the business of print, one that is broadly representative of the moral continu-
ity of the trade and of writers' skepticism of that morality.

James T. Fields died in 1881, and the tributes came rolling in. Edwin Percy
Whipple spoke for many admirers when he said that Fields, perhaps more than
any other publisher, "understood both the business and the literary side of his
occupation."[11] But for Gail Hamilton that idealized literary tradesman had died
over a decade earlier. "He is evaporated," Hamilton wrote in a letter in 1869. "He
squirmed out of my sight one day, and in his stead I saw some one before me with a
mean face and ophidian eyes. *That* is not the man I cared for at all. The man I cared
for has departed this life. He never came into it. He was never born."[12] That same
year she began to try to convince other Ticknor and Fields authors, from James
Parton to Ralph Waldo Emerson, that Fields was and had long been right at home

FIGURE 7.1 Gail Hamilton [Mary Abigail Dodge], Courtesy General Research Division, New York Public Library, Astor, Lenox and Tilden Foundations.

in the new era of corporate capitalism. Then, in 1870, she tried to tell the entire country by publishing a book about her experiences with America's most famous gentleman publisher.

Hamilton was not the first to dare to criticize Fields. All publishers came in for their share of flak, even him. During his long career, Fields was accused of being, among other things, a hypocrite, a thief, a bore, and the worst kind of elitist—a Boston elitist. In 1852, a credit reporter for R. G. Dun and Company implied that Fields seemed more interested in "poeticizing" in Europe than in running a business.[13] What the reporter failed to understand was that knowing literature was part of being a literary businessman. Fields was establishing a list that would make his already vital firm the envy of the trade, a list that by 1868 would make Ticknor and Fields worth an estimated $500,000.[14] Compare that value to that of a more conventionally successful firm, E. P. Dutton and Company, which moved into Ticknor and Fields' vacated Old Corner Bookstore, and which was valued at a respectable $25,000.[15]

It was about this time that Hamilton, whose real name was Mary Abigail Dodge, began to believe that Ticknor and Fields' remarkable profits were stolen, in part, from its writers.[16] In December 1867 she read a newspaper article that said customary pay for a novice writer was 10 percent on the retail price of a book. Hamilton, a moderately successful writer who had published seven books with the firm, calculated that she was earning royalties as high as 10 percent but as low as 6.66 percent. How could this be, especially when she published with a firm known far and wide for its liberality toward authors? Fields had always seemed less "a business man" than "a friend" to Hamilton.[17] But now Hamilton needed Fields the businessman to explain why she was earning less than his other authors. She asked him this question in a friendly letter full of wit and deference, both characteristic of Hamilton's sparkling epistolary style. Fields sat on the letter for three weeks. When he did deign to reply he did not answer her question. Rather than give an explanation—Fields did not like to talk numbers; it was ungentlemanly—he reminded her that they had been over all this before. If they went over it again, it would need to be in person, because that was the way civilized publishers did things.

He would have had her remember that the Civil War had been bad for the book business. Publishers coped by trimming lists and deferring new titles. Some firms, like Ticknor and Fields, were especially proactive, dramatically scaling back operations before anyone knew for sure what the effect of the war would be on the trade. This may be one reason an October 1863 credit assessment of the firm noted it was "good [at] making money fast." Ticknor and Fields knew how to deal with downturns. But when the firm's preemptive maneuvering proved insufficient, it raised the prices on its books incrementally from $1.25 to $2.00 and renegotiated contracts with some authors. The house also changed the way it calculated royalties. Where once they were based on a percentage of the retail cost of a book, they now were based on a fixed rate of so many cents of the retail price. This change did and did not affect writers. So long as the retail price remained consistent, there was no significant difference between the two systems for an author earning the standard royalty. A book that sold for $1.00 earned its author 10¢ whether she was promised 10 percent or 10¢. If the book rose in price and retailed for $2.00, however, an author on the fixed system still received 10¢ while an author on the percentage system received

20¢. A fixed rate did not generally benefit authors because, as Hamilton put it, an author's profit "was fixed against a rise, but flexible toward a fall" *(BB*, 40).[18] On the other hand, the fixed rate did benefit publishers, who realized a larger share of the total profit.

Only later did Hamilton realize this. She knew almost nothing about how the business worked, nor did she care. She was a staunch believer before and after the controversy in the division of literary labor, reasoning that she could "master" the "details" of publishing if she wished, "just as I could in cooking," but why bother? "If you have a cook or a publisher for the express purpose of doing the business for you, what is the use of perplexing yourself about it?" *(BB*, 30). Fields's reputation as a fair dealer, especially among women writers, was unrivaled. Thus when he told Hamilton in the midst of the war that he needed to change the formula used to calculate her royalties, she did not so much agree with him as defer to him. "*Of course* I concurred in your views," she told him later, trying to explain the extent of her trust and its implications during the early days of the controversy. "If you had said to me, 'Owing to the state of the trade and manufactures, all the trees are now going to be bread and cheese, and all the rivers ink,' I should have said, 'Yes, that is a very wise measure'" (15). Changing her royalty rate *was* a wise move for Ticknor and Fields, but not for Hamilton. There was little chance book prices would do anything but rise over the long term, earning the firm more and its writers less. Also, Fields had not adjusted the terms of all the firm's authors, contrary to what he told Hamilton. As Warren Tryon notes, the publisher "stacked the cards to his advantage."[19]

The changes to Hamilton's contracts were executed informally in "the rather haphazard way things are done when everyone is supposed to trust each other," as Susan Coultrap-McQuin observes.[20] While written contracts were becoming more common, they were not yet the rule in the United States. Agreements were usually informal and were often spelled out in letters. The presumption was that doing so was better for writers, who did not want to be bothered by the business side of literature. "Oh! we publishers, what wretches we are—but aren't you lucky to have *one* publisher who lets you do just as you like and is willing to publish without contracts," Thomas Niles of Roberts Brothers chided Louisa May Alcott in 1870, well aware that it was the norm to publish without a contract.[21] (Niles bent the truth a number of times in his letters to Alcott; a few months earlier he had lied about how much of a percentage the publisher could afford to pay on *An Old-Fashioned Girl*.)[22] Written contracts were even less common for Ticknor and Fields, in part because Fields believed they degraded the sacred trust between author and publisher and cheapened the cultivated image of his business. Instead, writers and publishers worked, in Hamilton's words, by "mutual understanding" *(BB*, 202).

Many of the firm's writers seemed comfortable with this arrangement. Others were not. Grace Greenwood was anxious, but she was too polite to do anything but imply that there could misunderstandings or, worse, exploitation. "As yet singularly enough we have not exchanged a word on pecuniary matters, but I know that all must be well," Greenwood wrote to Fields, as much to reassure herself as him that her interests would be honored, even if she did not understand exactly how.[23] Lydia Maria Child was more explicit, though still tactful; or at least she spoke in euphemism. "In view of the uncertainty of human life," she told Fields, "I would . . . suggest the propriety of having some contract signed."[24] What kinds of uncertainty? The Old Corner Bookstore might burn to the ground with Fields in it. That was not very likely, of course. More likely was that Fields would misremember what he had said or not said in a letter. Or, however unimaginable, he might unintentionally (or intentionally) say one thing and do another. Suspicions of publishers' questionable accounting practices and motives became so pronounced that in 1896 a New York court forced firms to open their books to writers. Most publishers were fine with doing so, though they were skeptical of writers' claims that there was a vast conspiracy to screw them out of profits. Joseph Harper suggested that such a conspiracy would simply be too involved. Walter Page said that it would be too immoral.[25] Many writers thought that where publishers were involved no scheme could be too involved or too immoral.

Scrutinizing publishers' accounts did not necessarily clear up the mystery of publishing for writers, including Hamilton, who was eventually granted access to Ticknor and Fields' books. She characterized the records of the firm's dealings with her as "a most perplexing medley—a sort of contra dance between written contracts and verbal agreements" (*BB*, 229). "According to their practice, it seems we all agree, in writing, as to what we will do, for the sake of saying afterwards that we won't do it" (230).[26] She found it funny and frustrating that publishers like Ticknor and Fields held up their account books as unmitigated truth. "Any demur is met by an invitation to come and look at 'the books,'" she mocked. "The tail of the Serpent is over all the rest of the world, but 'the books' have escaped contamination or original sin and shine with the purity of Paradise. Burglars blow open safes, banks and directors and cashiers and tellers come to grief, but 'the books' always tell the truth, the whole truth, and nothing but the truth" (260). "The books," she concluded, anthropomorphizing publisher's accounts, "are not always 'reliable gentlemen'" (260–61). Not until Ticknor and Fields produced actual receipts for actual payments made to actual manufacturers would she believe what the firm claimed in person or in its books.

However, what was or was not in the books was largely irrelevant. "Don't you see," she tried to explain to Fields, that "the trouble lies back of the contract? Why did you *wish* me to be having seven or eight per cent. [*sic*] when other people are getting ten?" (*BB* 15–16). This was the crux of her complaint. The problem was not that a publisher failed to abide by a contract, written or oral. The problem was that he had changed the contract in the first place when he knew that Hamilton, trusting in his honor, would agree that whatever her publisher said must be good or right.

Fields apparently thought so, too, at least in his dealings with women writers. He could not understand why Hamilton was angry. Tryon suggests that the publisher believed so entirely in his righteousness that he became "a prisoner of his own conceits."[27] At the very least he was a prisoner of the kinds of stereotypes discussed earlier, namely, that women lacked the ability to understand business and that it was inappropriate for them to try.[28] Hamilton broke this stereotype, as Hannah Adams and Fanny Fern had before her. Like Fern, she did so with a vengeance. She learned the business of publishing with impressive speed, motivated by the suspicion that her complacence (read: faith in the inherent goodness of her publisher) was the biggest factor in her current predicament. William French, the friend and judge who initially served as an intermediary between her and Ticknor and Fields and who later helped Hamilton prosecute her case against the firm, shared this suspicion. He told Hamilton that her trust in Fields had obviated the need for "sharp bargaining" (*BB*, 29), which only confirmed the publisher's impression that she was unable to "comprehend matters of business." "But you and I know better. Your mind is logical, and your simplicity as to business a sham."

It seems that Fields thought he could tell Hamilton just about anything about the business of publishing and she would believe it. For a while, she did. But in early 1868, when he tried to tell her that her books were more expensive to produce than others, that while another firm might pay her more the quality of the books would be lower, and that she had profited more by her books than the firm had, Hamilton saw through the artifice. "I can't tell a lie, pa" (*BB*, 46), she half-joked with French. "I wish I was satisfied, but I am not." And she found it telling that her publisher evaded explanations until French, a man, asked for them. Only after Fields assured her during a face-to-face meeting in June 1868 that he had long ago written to explain what was "back of the contract" did Hamilton put away her guns and declare "peace" (71). She remained incredulous, though. She did not remember receiving such a letter; indeed, there likely was no letter. And she swore she would never again write for Ticknor and Fields. "Where I have been on terms of such intimate friendship I cannot come down to mere business relations."[29]

The peace was short-lived. During a visit to Concord, Hamilton learned that Sophia Hawthorne was also having trouble with Ticknor and Fields. Hamilton was struck by the "remarkable" correspondence between the cases. In her words: "No accounts had been rendered for years, the author trusting entirely in the friendship of his publishers; so that of course there were no papers to be produced. But there was the same change from a still higher percentage to a lower fixed sum; the same assertion on the one side, of a full explanation made and accepted, which explanation was totally denied on the other; and the same declaration of regard for the author himself" (*BB*, 75–76). Sophia Hawthorne's doubts had been raised when, three years after her husband's death in 1864, she asked about the royalties on his novels, royalties that were so modest that she was unable to afford, she said, even rudimentary living expenses.[30] As Sophia saw it, she never would have been in this position if Hawthorne's British and, by implication, American publishers had more dutifully considered their "honor."[31] Fields hemmed and hawed until she threatened

FIGURE 7.2 James T. Fields, Nathaniel Hawthorne, and William D. Ticknor, Courtesy General Research Division, New York Public Library, Astor, Lenox and Tilden Foundations.

to change publishers. This got his attention. While Ticknor and Fields' profits from Hawthorne's books were fairly modest, the prestige the house enjoyed as the publisher and once-trusted friend of one of the nation's most eminent writers was invaluable. The matter was resolved only after another threat, this one from Sophia's sister, Elizabeth Peabody, who reminded Fields that even the appearance of impropriety toward Hawthorne's widow would damage his reputation. Fields agreed to let Peabody see the firm's books, which she did. Peabody, a former publisher with mixed feelings about the ethics of the trade, confirmed that the numbers added up. But she also noticed, as Hamilton might say, something amiss "back of the contract." Ticknor and Fields had been "*legally* righteous" in its dealings with the Hawthornes, Peabody said, by which she meant that the firm had not been morally righteous.[32] There was a difference. The house could have acted more magnanimously toward the Hawthornes, but had not. Peabody and Hamilton thought they knew why.

For Hamilton, it came as an epiphany. "It came to me clear at once, as clear as light, that I was doing exactly what [Ticknor and Fields] had wisely counted on our all doing, in case we did anything," she wrote: "that is, fretting a little, perhaps, but eventually letting it all drop, silenced if not convinced" (*BB*, 76–77). Ticknor and Fields had accumulated so much moral capital that it had become untouchable. How "ridiculous" it would be "to charge this house, whose praise for liberality is in all the churches" (77) with immorality. Armed with the knowledge that her predicament "was no longer an isolated case, but part of a regular system" (76) of abuse, Hamilton renewed her campaign. She was convinced now that there really *was* something "back of the contract," something worse than negligence, something unwarranted even by the de facto compromise ethics of post–Civil War America, where it was argued that competition, in the form of "rational egoism," would yield "as high a standard of general morality as we can expect to get."[33] Hamilton believed that Fields had acted with full knowledge that a change in her contract would benefit the firm at her expense. He had defrauded her not financially, but morally.

For the remainder of 1868 and the first months of 1869, Hamilton and William French pressured Ticknor and Fields to confess its wrongs and pay what it ought. More to the point, Hamilton wanted to prove that the firm's vaunted character was a fraud, that Ticknor and Fields flouted the moral laws underwriting the conduct of business. French put the matter best: "Inasmuch as you put yourself into his hands to do what was right, he was bound to pay you as much as others receive upon whose winnings the profits are made. This is Law, Gospel, & Co. If he did more, it would be generosity; if less, meanness or worse" (*BB*, 27). Hamilton's case was that Fields was guilty of the "worse"—"where they think it is safe to screw . . . they screw unmercifully," she told James Parton—and later that year she began to write to other authors to tell them her story and ask about their own experiences with the firm.[34] Hamilton was building a case, and that worried Ticknor and Fields. Annie Fields confided to her diary that Hamilton had become "a thorn in dear Jamie's side." Her letters, which were circulating "all about the country," were hurting the firm's reputation. "This is very bad," she concluded simply but with full knowledge of the potential effect of Hamilton's crusade.[35]

In the mid-nineteenth century, as in later decades, there was in most writers' minds a clear division of labor in the literary trade. There were publishers, and there were authors. To the publisher, whose "sphere" (*BB*, 77) and "home" was the market, fell the task of superintending "the external material parts of books" (218). To the author fell the task of fashioning "the interior and intangible souls of books." Everything else was just so much "trash" (193), as Hamilton put it: the business of businessmen. Generally, the reputation of Ticknor and Fields was based on running this business both profitably and morally. More specifically, its reputation was based on four things: its successful encouragement of domestic authors; its liberality toward domestic and foreign authors alike; the material quality of its books; and its market savvy. The fourth was key. Authors needed businessmen like Fields to navigate the market. Even authors who knew something about business knew little about the ins and outs of the market; it was simply too abstract. "Suppose a writer sets out with the determination to be prudent and sagacious, where shall he begin?" (253) Hamilton asked rhetorically. Knowing what books should cost, knowing what readers would pay for them—these were occult processes, and they were becoming only more complex as the railroad opened new markets. The "author has not and cannot have the least notion of the market value of his products." Only the publisher had this experience and skill, and this made the author a ward of the business. It was for this reason that a publisher's character mattered, Hamilton warned. Honorable publishers do not take advantage of the ignorance of authors in matters of business. To do so was an abuse of what Émile Durkheim would describe as a contract's "non-contractual elements": the "common morality" underlying all formal contracts in capitalist societies.[36] Hamilton called this idea of trust in motives the "principle" (BB, 218) behind the division of literary labor, and it is this principle that was supposed to brace contracts. There was nothing new in this. Thomas Hobbes, David Hume, and Adam Smith all argued that contracts were the "legal equivalents" of promises—guarantees that dependence was not misplaced—and thus had what one ethicist calls "moral weight."[37]

Finally, in early 1869 Hamilton's dispute with Ticknor and Fields went before referees, who decided in Hamilton's favor, awarding her $1,250 and ordering Ticknor and Fields to pay her 10 percent on all future editions of books for which she had received less. For Hamilton, this was a victory, of sorts. While she had asked for royalties owed (based on 10 percent of retail sales) at 7 percent interest as well as $3,000 for expenses, the fact that she received anything substantiated her material complaint. However, the referees did not comment on her moral complaint, or what she termed the "hurts of other kinds to which money bears no relation" (BB 247). It was to redress these "hurts" and probe what lay "back of the contract" that she published an account of the controversy, A Battle of the Books, in 1870. She called it "my incendiary publication."[38] Her goal was to set fire to the reputation of the trade generally and of James T. Fields specifically.

The book begins with a declaration that puts the reader in mind of the Declaration. "When, in the course of human events, it becomes necessary for an author to dissolve the bands which have connected him with his publishers, a decent respect for the opinions of mankind requires that he should declare the causes which impel him to the separation" (BB, 7). In an editorial introduction, Hamilton claimed to have discovered the manuscript containing these words in a ship's cabin, in a manuscript she pretends—only barely—to be the real-life story of a bitter falling out of a writer, M. N., and her publisher, Brummel and Hunt. In her editorial guise, Hamilton deduced that M. N. could only have lived in the "barbarous past" (3) because in

Hamilton's own day something like this was unimaginable. "The state of society described in this narrative is surely no nearer than a hundred years," she reasoned. "It chronicles an age of barbarism, when author and publisher were natural enemies, and relieved the monotony of their lives by petty skirmishing or pitched battles with each other. This age, happily for us, has passed away, and exists only in tradition.... No longer does the wily publisher lie in wait, seeking what chance he may have to devour his author. Rather he woos him to receive his dues, wins open with gentle urgency the hand no longer grasping, but modest and reluctant, and presses into it the crisp, abundant bills." Authors, in turn, no longer toasted the execution of publishers, a la Byron, but "raise their harps and join voices to sing their benefactor's praise. Who has not seen in all the newspapers the affecting tale of the great house of Fields, Osgood, & Co.,—*nomen clarum et venerabile*—on whom has fallen the mantle of Ticknor & Fields?" (3–4). How could an author complain now, in this "golden age of love" (6) brought about by Boston's most famous publisher? This is the only place in the book where Hamilton mentions Ticknor and Fields by name.

The sarcasm of Hamilton's introduction would be almost overwrought were it not based on an October 1867 article published in the *Atlantic Monthly*, the same article discussed at the conclusion of Chapter 1.[39] The author was James Parton, the model for Fern's moral mouthpiece in *Ruth Hall* (and now her husband), who in a letter earlier that year said that Ticknor and Fields was pressuring him to write about international copyright.[40] His October article was dutifully titled "International Copyright." While it was about that debate, it was also a panegyric to the virtues of American publishers, namely Ticknor and Fields:

There are no business men more honorable or more generous than the publishers of the United States, and especially honorable and considerate are they toward authors. The relation usually existing between author and publisher in the United States is that of a warm and lasting friendship.... The relation ... is one of a singular mutual trustfulness. The author receives his semiannual account from the publisher with as absolute a faith in its correctness as though he had himself counted the volumes sold; and the publisher consigns the manuscript of the established writer to the printer almost without opening it, confident that, whether it succeeds or fails, the author has done his best.[41]

Hamilton quoted much of this passage in her introduction to *A Battle of the Books*. However, her account of the trade inverts the utopia envisioned by Parton. Apart from needling Parton, whom she knew had written "International Copyright," she likely parodied his article because it perpetuated the myths she deconstructs in her book, none more fallacious than this: "We have heard of instances in which a publisher had serious cause of complaint against an author, but never have we known an author to be intentionally wronged by a publisher."[42] Parton was wrong, Hamilton said, both in her correspondence with him and in her book. The trade was neither generous nor honorable, and not only did some respected publishers wrong their authors, but they did so intentionally to benefit themselves, defying in the process "Law, Gospel, & Co." This conduct was, she told Parton, as "unwise" as it was "dishonorable," and, at least as far as Ticknor and Fields was concerned, "the farce of folly can no further go."[43]

How successful was Hamilton's exposé? In 1884, after Fields's death, John Greenleaf Whittier assured Annie Fields that *A Battle of the Books* "fell dead from the press."[44] That was not quite true, but it was what she wanted to hear. She had long believed that Hamilton left Ticknor and Fields because she wanted more money than she was getting from the firm. "'Gail' and Mrs. Hawthorne, having conjured up a fancied wrong, they nurse it well," she wrote in her diary.[45] In 1870, 1,500 copies did not exactly make a best seller, as Coultrap-McQuin points out, but the book reached enough of its intended audience of authors and publishers to become a topic of conversation and to earn Hamilton an even greater reputation as a card-carrying member of the *genus irritabile*.[46] Indeed, the book seems to have made tradesmen wary. Many felt, as Whittier did, that Hamilton had followed a "foolish" and "unjust course" by publicly criticizing her publisher based on "misapprehensions" of his honorable intentions.[47] (In his 1893 article "The Man of Letters as a Man of Business," Fields's successor at the *Atlantic Monthly*, William Dean Howells, recommended that just as Corinthians taught adults to "put away childish things," authors "had better put away" their conspiracy theories about the trade.[48]) Whittier felt so strongly that his friend was in the wrong that he offered to help her defray the cost of pulping the book before it hit the shelves, though this did not stop him from spreading news of its charges around Boston.[49] Whittier, after all, had held up Fields as a moral exemplar in "The Tent on the Beach" (1867), and it would not do to have that image tarnished.

The reviews of *A Battle of the Books* were predictably dutiful to the reputation of James T. Fields. It is true that a surprising number did acknowledge that Ticknor and Fields was "in the wrong" in its handling of Hamilton's royalties.[50] However, they loudly reported Hamilton's own recommendation that writers ought to be more careful in their dealings with the trade. And they suggested that Hamilton had behaved like the stereotypical woman author: in short, that she understood neither business nor discretion. The whole episode smacked of "revenge," one reviewer wrote, saying that the book read "like the heated and reckless utterances of a spoiled, disappointed, and mortified woman."[51] Another reviewer suggested that the book was characterized by "a certain intense, persistent, and heated shrillness of expression, which would seem to be peculiar to the aggrieved female," as though he were cataloguing a new species of bird.[52] The comment was reminiscent of estimates of *Ruth Hall*. It was also coincidentally reminiscent of Fields's own estimate of Hamilton's gift for satire in an 1863 letter: "Gail is a queer bird with plenty of cleverness in her beak and wings. She is a not a 'pretty warbler,' but she has one good eye."[53]

What is important, if unsurprising, is that Hamilton's critique of trade morality went unremarked. One reviewer did inadvertently illustrate its validity, noting that

Hamilton did not accuse Ticknor and Fields of economic "fraud," but "merely, that they took advantage of her ignorance and confidence." "The forceful moral of the *Battle of the Books*," he continued, "is that all persons should endeavor to gain some knowledge of their own concerns, and that friendship in matters of business is often 'a sham, a delusion and a snare.'"[54] It is true that Hamilton did not accuse Ticknor and Fields of financial fraud. It is true, too, that Hamilton did lay a portion of the blame for authorial disaffection at the feet of authors themselves, though in a way that underpinned her argument. But the book's "forceful moral" lay elsewhere. There *was* something wrong when publishers "merely" played confidence games with authors while authors were encouraged and even expected to put all their trust in the character of the trade.

Most of *A Battle of the Books* is a droll portrayal of author-trade relations in the Civil War era. There is, however, a conspicuous shift in tone in the book's final pages, where Hamilton offered an assessment of publishing in the stark terms of liberal capitalism:

> Individuals and societies wheedle and flatter and threaten and torture according to the fashion, or passion, or panic of the hour, but under it all, the great, pitiless, unseen, inexorable law of the world, holds from age to age, never relaxing its grasp, never revoking its decree, deaf to the wail of weakness, dumb to the cry of despair, forever and forever teaching with unrelenting persistency, *by* unrelenting persistency, the good and wholesome lesson that will be taught no other way. Under this law there is no sex, no chivalry, no deference, no mercy. There is nothing but supply and demand; nothing but buy and sell. (*BB*, 287–88)

The quicker writers learned to accept the fact that the publisher is, as Bourdieu said, a "cultural businessman" whose job is to create and exploit symbolic capital, the better off they would be. To illustrate, Hamilton closed *A Battle of the Books* with an image of two writers. The first accepts the immorality of publishing and in turn the business of print becomes a "chariot of state bearing him on to fame and fortune." The second is disposed to believe in trade morality, and as a result the chariot changes into "a car of Juggernaut, crushing him beneath its wheels, without passion, but without pity." Authors ought to be careful what they believe. It was an uncharacteristically pessimistic view for Hamilton, who in most matters had a progressive's faith that society and its institutions became fairer and more just over time—just not publishers.[55]

Notwithstanding her skepticism about the ethics of publishing, Hamilton did not advocate doing away with the status quo altogether. Nor did she agree with the radical argument that authors would be better off becoming publishers themselves. The author could never "be so good a business manager as one who is to the manner born" (*BB*, 256). But authors tried nonetheless. In the 1870s a group of disgruntled writers founded the Authors' Publishing Company. *Publishers' Weekly*, formerly the

American Publishers' Circular, was skeptical. It warned that it was a mistake to base a company on "the superstition of a natural enmity between authors and publishers."[56] The reconstituted *Literary World* observed a "feeling, amounting to a prejudice" about the firm's name, a name that was probably chosen to chaff the trade.[57] Hamilton would have sympathized with the motive that inspired the new firm, but not with the outcome. The idea was "chimerical in the last degree" (*BB*, 256), she said. Authors were not inherently more moral than publishers. Further, they did not live with the temptations publishers did; they were not ready, as antebellum business writers might say, for the "hottest part of [the] furnace" where trade virtues were formed.[58] As "soon as authors turn publishers they fall into all the publisher's temptations without acquiring his business power" (*BB*, 257). For Hamilton, the author-cum-publisher was a freak—"an amalgam wholly and disastrously different from either of the original simples, namely, a publisher minus the common sense." Hamilton was right. In 1880, the Authors' Publishing Company ceased to be. The official explanation was that it was changing its name, but in fact the firm folded, unable to compete in the business of publishing.

NOTES

INTRODUCTION

1. Ralph Waldo Emerson, *Nature*, in *The Collected Works of Ralph Waldo Emerson*, ed. Alfred A. Ferguson, 6 vols., 7–45 (Cambridge: Belknap Press, 1971–87), 1: 26.

2. Henry James, *The American Scene* (London: Chapman and Hall, 1907), 136.

3. In *The Cost Books of Ticknor and Fields and Their Predecessors, 1832–1858* (New York: Bibliographical Society of America, 1949), Warren S. Tryon and William Charvat list four Dix imprints from the 1840s: *An American Tract for the Times* (1843), *Wreck of the Glide* (1846), *The Winter Evening Fireside* (1847), and *Pompeii and Other Poems* (1849). On James T. Fields, see James C. Austin, *Fields of* The Atlantic Monthly: *Letters to an Editor, 1861–1870* (San Marino, CA: Huntington Library, 1953); Warren S. Tryon, *Parnassus Corner: A Life of James T. Fields, Publisher to the Victorians* (Boston: Houghton Mifflin, 1963); and Michael Winship, *American Literary Publishing in the Mid-Nineteenth Century: The Business of Ticknor and Fields* (New York: Cambridge University Press, 1995).

4. Susan Coultrap-McQuin, *Doing Literary Business: American Women Writers in the Nineteenth Century* (Chapel Hill: University of North Carolina Press, 1990), 29. The critique of Harper and Brothers is in James Kirke Paulding to T.W. White, March 3, 1836, in Ralph M. Aderman, ed., *The Letters of James Kirke Paulding*, 41–42 (Madison: University of Wisconsin Press, 1962), 173. I use gender-exclusive language such as "tradesmen" in much of this study because most printers, publishers, and other people involved in the production of print—and discussed in this book—were men. There are important exceptions, from Ann Franklin to Elizabeth Peabody. On women in the trade, see Susan Albertine, ed., *A Living of Words: American Women in Print Culture* (Knoxville: University of Tennessee Press, 1995).

5. John Greenleaf Whittier, "The Tent on the Beach," in *The Tent on the Beach and Other Poems*, 9–21 (Boston: Ticknor and Fields, 1867), 12.

6. John Greenleaf Whittier to Elizabeth Stuart Phelps, May 9, 1881, in *The Letters of John Greenleaf Whittier*, ed. John B. Pickard, 3 vols., 435–36 (Cambridge: Belknap Press, 1975), 3: 435.

7. Grace Greenwood [Sara Jane Lippincott] to James T. Fields, February 3, 1849, James Thomas Fields Papers, box 40, FI 1849, Huntington Library.

8. C[yrus] A[ugustus] Bartol to James T. Fields, December 15, 1855, James Thomas Fields Papers, box 40, FI 263.

9. Quoted in J. C. Derby, *Fifty Years among Authors, Books and Publishers* (New York: G.W. Carleton, 1884), 627, 628.

10. William Giles Dix to Ticknor and Fields, May 2, 1865, as copied in Dix to Henry Wadsworth Longfellow, May 4, 1865, Letters to Henry Wadsworth Longfellow, MS Am 1340.2, folder 1609, Houghton Library, Harvard University, used by permission.

11. Ticknor and Fields to Dix, May 3, 1865, MS Am 1340.2, folder 1609, as copied in ibid.

12. Dix to Longfellow, May 4, 1865, Letters to Henry Wadsworth Longfellow.

13. Ralph Waldo Emerson to Thomas Carlyle, February 9, 1838, in Joseph Slater, ed., *The Correspondence of Emerson and Carlyle* (New York: Columbia University Press, 1964), 177. In an 1841 speech on reform Emerson referred again to the idea: "It is the love of greatness, it is the need of harmony, the contrast of the dwarfish Actual with the exorbitant Idea." Emerson, *Collected Works*, 1: 180–81.

14. "Our dear friend Longfellow has met with a sad calamity," Fields wrote to a mutual friend, "and as I sat with him today he asked me to write to you and inform you of the affliction." James T. Fields to Ferdinand Freiligrath, July 28, 1861, James Thomas Fields Papers, box 19, FI 2112.

15. William Giles Dix to Henry Wadsworth Longfellow, April 2, 1866, Letters to Henry Wadsworth Longfellow, MS Am 1340.2, folder 1609.

16. Evert Duyckinck, Duyckinck Family Papers, MssCol 873, undated notebook "Original American Anecdotes I," Manuscripts and Archives Division, New York Public Library, Astor, Lenox and Tilden Foundations, used by permission.

17. See "Literature," *Putnam's Monthly Magazine* 1 (March 1853): 2.

18. William Giles Dix to George Palmer Putnam, September 18, 1854, George Palmer Putnam Collection, C0685, box 1, folder 68, Manuscripts Division, Department of Rare Books and Special Collections, Princeton University.

19. In "Notices of New Books," *United States Magazine and Democratic Review* 16 (May 1845): 507–9, Duyckinck penned a lukewarm review of Putnam's book, *American Facts* (1845). "It is not worth while to bandy words about the *justice* of the criticism," Putnam wrote to Duyckinck, though he saw no problem in rebuking Duyckinck for the injustice of his review. "Leaving everything like courtesy or generosity out of the question, I am bound to protest against the *justice* of what you have said." In fact, Putnam's two letters to Duyckinck, written by the self-proclaimed "victim," were all about "courtesy and generosity." George Palmer Putnam to Evert Duyckinck, June 27, 1845, Duyckinck Family Papers, box 13, folder Putnam, George Palmer.

20. Evert Duyckinck, undated notebook "Original American Anecdotes I."

21. Thomas Delf to Evert Duyckinck, December 1, 1847, Duyckinck Family Papers, box 18, folder Letters, 1847.

22. Quoted in Megan Marshall, *The Peabody Sisters: Three Women Who Ignited American Romanticism* (Boston: Houghton Mifflin, 2005), 424.

23. Delf to Evert Duyckinck, December 1, 1847.

24. F[rederick] A[ugustus] Pike to Moses Phillips, June 21, 1857, Ch.J.2.40, Rare Books Department, Boston Public Library.

25. Frederick Marryat to Osmond de Beauvoir Priaulx, November 27, 1836, quoted in Frederick Marryat, *Life and Letters of Captain Marryat*, 2 vols. (London: R. Bentley and Son, 1872), 1: 251.

26. Quoted in Louisa May Alcott to Bronson and Abigail Alcott, June 1, 1870, in Martha Saxton, *Louisa May: A Modern Biography of Louisa May Alcott* (Boston: Houghton Mifflin, 1977), 305.

27. William Gilmore Simms to James Lawson, November 6, 1860, in *The Letters of William Gilmore Simms*, ed. T. C. Duncan Eaves, Alfred Taylor Odell, and Mary C. Simms Oliphant, 6 vols. (Columbia: University of South Carolina Press, 1952–82), 4: 255.

28. William Gilmore Simms to Evert Duyckinck, March 18, [1859], in ibid., 4: 137.

29. "International Copyright," *American Publishers' Circular and Literary Gazette*, January 24, 1857, 50.

30. Robert Darnton, "What Is the History of Books?" *Daedalus* 111.3 (Summer 1982): 69.

31. On "techno-determinism," see Michael Warner, *The Letters of the Republic: Publication and the Public Sphere in Eighteenth-Century America* (Cambridge: Harvard University Press, 1990), 6; D. F. McKenzie, *Bibliography and the Sociology of Texts* (London: British Library, 1986; reprint, Cambridge, UK: Cambridge University Press, 1999), 14.

32. Adrian Johns, *Piracy: The Intellectual Property Wars from Gutenberg to Gates* (Chicago: University of Chicago Press, 2009), 11.

33. Adrian Johns, *The Nature of the Book: Print and Knowledge in the Making* (Chicago: University of Chicago Press, 1998), 34.

34. Pierre Bourdieu and Loïc J. D. Wacquant, *An Invitation to Reflexive Sociology* (Chicago: University of Chicago Press, 1992), 108–9.

35. In *The Business of Letters: Authorial Economies in Antebellum America* (Stanford: Stanford University Press, 2008), Leon Jackson historicizes and theorizes both economic and noneconomic transactions in regard to authorship. See especially 31–37.

36. Pierre Bourdieu, "The Field of Cultural Production," in *The Field of Cultural Production: Essays on Art and Literature*, ed. Randal Johnson, 29–73 (New York: Columbia University Press, 1993), 34. Bourdieu divides this space into two parts, field and habitus: the former, the objective arrangement of positions within the "social space"; the latter, the sum of subjective perceptions of and value judgments about that arrangement. See also Bourdieu, *Outline of a Theory of Practice*, trans. Richard Nice (Cambridge, UK: Cambridge University Press, 1977), 72–95; Bourdieu and Wacquant, *Invitation to Reflexive Sociology*, 16; and David Swartz, *Culture and Power: The Sociology of Pierre Bourdieu* (Chicago: University of Chicago Press, 1997), 95–116. On disposition, see Bourdieu and Wacquant, *Invitation to Reflexive Sociology*, 132–37.

37. Bourdieu, "The Field of Cultural Production," 61.

38. For a concise introduction to virtue ethics, deontological ethics, and utilitarian ethics, see Rosalind Hursthouse, *On Virtue Ethics* (New York: Oxford University Press, 1999), 1–24. On virtue ethics, see also Ted Honderich, ed., *The Oxford Companion to Philosophy*, 2nd ed. (New York: Oxford University Press, 2005), 947–48; and Deidre N. McCloskey, *The Bourgeois Virtues: Ethics for an Age of Commerce* (Chicago: University of Chicago Press, 2006), 63–68. On deontological ethics, see Honderich, ed., *Oxford Companion to Philosophy*, 199–200.

39. Quoted in Derby, *Fifty Years among Authors, Books and Publishers*, 26.

40. Quoted in Eugene Exman, *The Brothers Harper: A Unique Publishing Partnership and Its Impact upon the Cultural Life of America from 1817 to 1853* (New York: Harper and Row, 1965), 46.

41. Robert C. Solomon finds the problem of theorizing in a vacuum the same for those studying and teaching ethical decision making in business schools. "How can a blow-by-blow account

of the internal debates among Kantian deontologists, libertarians, and utilitarians provide anything but oversimplification and confusion where ethical decision is required?" "Business and the Humanities: An Aristotelian Approach to Business Ethics," in *Business as a Humanity*, ed. Thomas J. Donaldson and R. Edward Freeman, 45–75 (New York: Oxford University Press, 1994), 47.

42. William Ellery Channing, "Address on Self-Culture," in *The Works of William E. Channing, D.D.*, 2nd ed., 6 vols., 349–411 (Boston: James Munroe, 1843), 2: 358.

43. Alasdair MacIntyre, *Whose Justice? Which Rationality?* (Notre Dame: University of Notre Dame Press, 1988), 9. Stuart Blumin expresses similar caution about colonial British America, where value systems were "repacked from place to place . . . with different terms and even with different understandings of similar terms, such that some of the most significant cultural divergences resided within the meanings attached to 'self-interest,' 'community,' 'common good,' and other terms that nearly everyone appeared to accept or defend in some way." Blumin, "The Social Implications of U.S. Economic Development," in *The Cambridge Economic History of the United States, Volume 2: The Long Nineteenth Century*, ed. Stanley L. Engerman and Robert E. Gallman, 813–64 (New York: Cambridge University Press, 2000), 856. Values were local. Throughout this study I want to suggest that they were also, as John E. Crowley argues about the eighteenth century, posteriori insofar as they were "responses to behavior, as efforts to understand, define, and shape it, and therefore as manifestations of the mediation of experience and consciousness." Crowley, *This Sheba, Self: The Conceptualization of Economic Life in Eighteenth-Century America* (Baltimore: Johns Hopkins University Press, 1974), 2.

44. Karen Haltunen, *Confidence Men and Painted Women: A Study of Middle-class Culture in America, 1830–1870* (New Haven: Yale University Press, 1982). For an overview of the ethical turn in literary criticism, see Lawrence Buell, "Introduction: In Pursuit of Ethics," *PMLA* 114 (January 1999): 7–19, and "What We Talk about When We Talk about Ethics," in *The Turn to Ethics*, ed. Marjorie Garber, Beatrice Hanssen, and Rebecca L. Walkowitz (New York: Routledge, 2000), 1–13. Buell's observation that "there is no unitary ethics movement, no firm consensus among MLA members who think of themselves as pursuing some form of ethically valenced inquiry" ("Introduction," 7) still applies.

45. Even as I argue that virtue ethics played a more significant role in print culture than we have imagined, I do not do so in order to propose timeless truths or to suggest, a la the much-demonized Martha Nussbaum, that literature "develops moral capacities." Nussbaum, *Poetic Justice: The Literary Imagination and Public Life* (Boston: Beacon, 1995), 12. See also Nussbaum, *Love's Knowledge: Essays on Philosophy and Literature* (New York: Oxford University Press, 1990). As Buell suggests, what unsettles literary critics about arguments that use literature as a tool of moral philosophy "is not so much the specter of rampant moralism as such as it is longstanding reluctance on the part of many if not most literary scholars to allow the central disciplinary referent to be located in anything but language" ("What We Talk about," 7). In contrast, the central claim of most of these critics is that "the ethical value of literature lies in the felt encounter with alterity that it brings to its reader," who in turn becomes aware of his responsibility to those other than himself. Dorothy J. Hale, "Aesthetics and the New Ethics: Theorizing the Novel in the Twenty-First Century," *PMLA* 124 (May 2009): 899. On the ethics of self, see Michel Foucault, *Ethics: Subjectivity and Truth*, ed. Paul Rabinow, trans. Robert Hurley, et al. (New York: New Press, 1997). For a Lacanian application of alterity, see Terry Eagleton, *Trouble with Strangers: A Study of Ethics* (Malden, Mass: Wiley-Blackwell, 2009). In a welcome move, critics have begun to close the distance between moral philosophy and literary post-structuralism. See, for example, Mark

Sanders, "Ethics and Interdisciplinarity in Philosophy and Literature," *Diacritics* 32.3–4 (Fall–Winter 2002): 3–16; and Hale, "Aesthetics and the New Ethics."

46. Richard Grant White to Messrs Little, Brown and Company, September 19, 1867, Richard Grant White Papers, box 2, folder R. G. White, 1862–67, New York Historical Society.

47. S. S. [Haldeman] to Evert Duyckinck, February 15, 1849, Duyckinck Family Papers, box 18, folder Letters, 1849.

48. Carey, Lea, and Blanchard to Harrison Gray, April 27, 1835, Lea and Febiger Records, ms. 227B, Letterbook, Carey, Lea, and Blanchard, June 17, 1834, to September 2, 1835, pp. 336–37, Historical Society of Pennsylvania, Philadelphia; Harper and Brothers to Ticknor and Fields, October 24, 1859, Misc. American Harper, MA 1950, folder Harper and Brothers, firm, publishers, New York, Morgan Library Department of Literary and Historical Manuscripts, New York. The phrase "ordinary civility" is struck out of Harpers' letter, along with other aggressive language about the "inimical course" Ticknor and Fields had "lately adopted toward" the New York house. In both letters, the phrases refer to the practice of trade courtesy discussed in Chapter 1.

49. My hope is that this book will enter into a critical dialogue called for by Susan S. Williams, who writes that "Case studies of particular authors . . . need to attend to the author's own self-understanding of his or her profession and the host of external factors—grouped together under the rubric of the 'literary market'—that influenced those self-understandings." "Authors and Literary Authorship," in *The Industrial Book, 1840–1880*, vol. 3 of *The History of the Book in America*, ed. Scott E. Casper, Jeffrey D. Groves, Stephen W. Nissenbaum, and Michael Winship, 90–116 (Chapel Hill: University of North Carolina Press and the American Antiquarian Society, 2007), 97. This call evokes William Charvat's argument for the importance of "the whole complex organism of the book and magazine trade" in understanding historical authorship. Charvat, "Literary Economics and Literary History," originally delivered in 1949 and reproduced in *The Profession of Authorship in America, 1800–1870: The Papers of William Charvat*, ed. Mathew J. Bruccoli, 283–97 (Columbus: Ohio State University Press, 1968; reprint, New York: Columbia University Press, 1992), 284. More recent superlative contributions to this conversation, all of which inform this study, include Coultrap-McQuin, *Doing Literary Business*; Warner, *Letters of the Republic*; Richard H. Brodhead, *Cultures of Letters: Scenes of Reading and Writing in Nineteenth-Century America* (Chicago: University of Chicago Press, 1993); Sheila Post-Lauria, *Correspondent Colorings: Melville in the Marketplace* (Amherst: University of Massachusetts Press, 1996); Rosalind Remer, *Printers and Men of Capital: Philadelphia Book Publishers in the New Republic* (Philadelphia: University of Pennsylvania Press, 1996); Grantland S. Rice, *The Transformation of Authorship in America* (Chicago: University of Chicago Press, 1997); Meredith L. McGill, *American Literature and the Culture of Reprinting, 1834–1853* (Philadelphia: University of Pennsylvania Press, 2003); Ronald J. Zboray and Mary Saracino Zboray, *Literary Dollars and Social Sense: A People's History of the Mass Market Book* (New York: Routledge, 2005); Melissa J. Homestead, *American Women Authors and Literary Property, 1822–1869* (New York: Cambridge University Press, 2005); and Jackson, *The Business of Letters*.

50. James J. Barnes, "Edward Lytton Bulwer and the Publishing Firm of Harper & Brothers," *American Literature* 38 (March 1966): 36. James L.W. West III provides a usefully brief summary of the transatlantic book trade during this period in "Book-Publishing 1835–1900: The Anglo-American Connection," *Papers of the Bibliographical Society of America* 84 (December 1990): 357–75. A comprehensive transatlantic treatment of piracy is Johns, *Piracy*.

51. Edgar Allan Poe to Frederick W. Thomas, August 27, 1842, in *The Letters of Edgar Allan Poe*, ed. John Ward Ostram, 2 vols. (New York: Gordian Press, 1966), 1: 209.

52. Quoted in Louis Ginsberg, *A. Hart, Philadelphia Publisher (1829–1854)* (Petersburg, VA: n.p., 1972), 31.

53. J. Pope of Rome, L. Prince de Cunnigo, D. Dawdling, A.O.F.A.F.&c. [Harper and Brothers], "Proclamation to the World," *Morning Courier and New York Evening Post*, September 4, 1836, 1. See also Raymond L. Kilgour, *Messrs. Roberts Brothers Publishers* (Ann Arbor: University of Michigan Press, 1952), 49. On reprinting, see McGill, *American Literature and the Culture of Reprinting*, which argues that reprinting had a complex logic irreducible to simple economic expediency. McGill's argument is persuasive and revealing of the ways in which we tend to look at the early American market through the eyes of its authors, using their perspective "to frame and organize [our] insights" (15). In sum, most American authors did not like the practice of reprinting and so most literary historians critics have demonized it.

54. Thomas Jefferson to Peter Carr, August 10, 1787, in Jefferson, *The Papers of Thomas Jefferson*, ed. Julian P. Boyd, 34 vols. to date (Princeton: Princeton University Press, 1950–), 12: 15.

55. Thomas Carlyle to Ralph Waldo Emerson, April 3, 1844, in *The Correspondence of Emerson and Carlyle*, 360.

56. William Gilmore Simms, "Copy-Right. No. 1," *American Monthly Review* 9, new series 3 (February 1837): 156.

57. William Gilmore Simms to James Grant Wilson, July 1868, in *Letters of William Gilmore Simms*, 5: 149.

58. Quoted in Francis Wolle, *Fitz-James O'Brien: A Literary Bohemian of the Eighteen-Fifties* (Boulder: University of Colorado Press, 1944), 55. Wolle notes that there are varying accounts of this demonstration and that O'Brien may well have been joking. Even a joke, however, would have made light of the popular conception of Harpers as inhospitable to writers. See 54–55.

59. Gail Hamilton [Mary Abigail Dodge], *A Battle of the Books* (Cambridge: H.O. Houghton, 1870), 282–83.

60. Ibid., 9.

61. "The Trade Sale," *American Publishers' Circular* 1 (April 1854): 160 (brackets in original).

62. "Topics of the Week," *New York Times*, August 25, 1906, BR522.

63. "Literary Property and International Copyright," *Morning Courier and New-York Enquirer*, January 18, 1838, 1.

64. [David Masson], "The History of Pendennis; His Fortunes and Misfortunes; His Friends and His Greatest Enemy," *North British Review* (May 1850): 349; reprint, "The Literary Profession—Authors and Publishers," *Harper's New Monthly Magazine* 1 (September 1850): 548; "Authors and Publishers," *Literary World*, September 21, 1850, 235–36; and "The Literary Profession," *Eclectic Magazine of Foreign Literature* 21 (November 1850): 368.

65. Thomas Carlyle to Ralph Waldo Emerson, April 30, 1860, in *Correspondence of Emerson and Carlyle*, 532.

66. Frederick Marryat to unnamed recipient, n.d., quoted in *Life and Letters of Captain Marryat*, 1: 253.

67. Evert Duyckinck to George Duyckinck, January 14, 1840, quoted in Ezra Greenspan, *George Palmer Putnam: Representative American Publisher* (University Park: Penn State University Press, 2000), 162.

68. Royall Tyler, "The Lucubrations of Old Simon," *American Yeoman*, October 17, 1817; reprint, *The Prose of Royall Tyler*, ed. Marius B. Péladeau (Montpelier: Vermont Historical Society, 1972), 344. On early national writers' attitude toward market capitalism, see Steven Watts,

"Masks, Morals, and the Market: American Literature and Early Capitalist Culture, 1790–1820," *Journal of the Early Republic* 6 (Summer 1986): 127–50.

69. James Kirke Paulding to Mathew Carey and Son, July 5, 1815, in *Letters of James Kirke Paulding*, 41.

70. James Kirke Paulding to William Wilson, December 17, 1848, in ibid., 491.

71. "Publishers, Good, Bad, and Indifferent," *National Quarterly Review* 6 (December 1862): 127.

72. Henry Rowe Schoolcraft to Evert Duyckinck, August 9, 1851, Duyckinck Family Papers, box 14, folder Schoolcraft, Henry Rowe.

73. William Gilmore Simms to Evert Duyckinck, March 18, [1859], in *Letters of William Gilmore Simms*, 4: 137.

74. Jotham Carhart, "Free-Stone for Authors," *Literary World*, May 22, 1852, 363.

75. Samuel Goodrich, *Recollections of a Lifetime; or, Men and Things I Have Seen*, 2 vols. (New York: Auburn, Miller, Orton and Mulligan, 1856), 2: 275.

76. Horace Greeley, *Recollections of a Busy Life* (Boston: J. B. Ford, 1868), 443.

77. George Palmer Putnam, "Rough Notes of Thirty Years in the Trade," in Ezra Greenspan, ed., *The House of Putnam, 1837–1872: A Documentary Volume*, 261–72 (Detroit: Gale, 2002), 271.

78. George Palmer Putnam, "'Free-Stone'—Authors—Publishers," *Literary World*, June 5, 1852, 396.

79. George Palmer Putnam, "Rough Notes of Thirty Years in the Trade," 272.

80. Greeley, *Recollections of a Busy Life*, 442.

81. Asa Mitchell to George Palmer Putnam, November 13, 1854, George Palmer Putnam Collection, box 2, folder 75.

82. Harriet Martineau to Moses Phillips, January 25, 1845, Ms.Eng.244.15, Boston Public Library.

83. E. Middleton to [George Palmer Putnam], February 1854, George Palmer Putnam Collection, box 2, folder 73.

84. Fitz-James O'Brien, "Literature as a Profession—Difficulties of Writers," New York *Daily Times*, November 13, 1852, 3; reprint, Wayne R. Kime, ed., *Fitz-James O'Brien: Selected Literary Journalism, 1852–1860* (Selinsgrove: Susquehanna University Press, 2003), 48–53.

85. Pierre Bourdieu, "The Production of Belief: Contribution to an Economy of Symbolic Goods," in *Field of Cultural Production*, 74–111, 75.

86. George Stillman Hillard, *The Dangers and Duties of the Mercantile Profession* (Boston: Ticknor, Reed, and Fields, 1850), 17.

87. James Russell Lowell to Charles F. Briggs, June 10, 1853, James Russell Lowell Papers, MS Am 765, folder 13, Houghton Library, Harvard University.

88. James T. Fields to Bayard Taylor, July 1, 1850, James Thomas Fields Papers, box 18, FI 1957.

89. Ralph Waldo Emerson to William Henry Furness, August 9, 1857, in *The Letters of Ralph Waldo Emerson*, ed. Eleanor M. Tilton, 10 vols. (New York: Columbia University Press, 1939–), 8: 528.

90. William Giles Dix to George Palmer Putnam, May 28, 1853, George Palmer Putnam Collection, box 1, folder 68.

91. Greeley, *Recollections of a Busy Life*, 443.

92. Carey and Lea to James Fenimore Cooper, May 1827, James Fenimore Cooper Papers, box 2, folder 13, American Antiquarian Society, used by permission.

93. Derby, *Fifty Years among Authors, Books and Publishers*, 592.

94. Samuel Drake to David Dole Plummer, August 7, 1829, Ms.Am.1598, Boston Public Library.

95. Erastus Ellsworth to George Palmer Putnam, September 1, 1854, George Palmer Putnam Collection, box 1, folder 80.

96. Entry on G. P. Putnam and Co., New York, Vol. 365, p. 178, September 13, 1854, R. G. Dun and Company Collection, Baker Library Historical Collections, Harvard Business School, Harvard University, used by permission. On the history of credit reporting in the United States, see James H. Madison, "The Evolution of Commercial Credit Reporting Agencies in Nineteenth-Century American," *Business History Review* 48 (Summer 1974): 164–86; James D. Norris, *R.G. Dun & Co., 1841–1900: The Development of Credit-Reporting in the Nineteenth Century* (Westport: Greenwood, 1978); and Scott A. Sandage, *Born Losers: A History of Failure in America* (Cambridge: Harvard University Press, 2005).

97. Entry on G. P. Putnam and Co., New York, Vol. 365, p. 200A, March 4, 1859, R. G. Dun and Company Collection.

98. Zboray and Zboray, *Literary Dollars and Social Sense*, xxii; Darnton, "What Is the History of Books?" 72. Compare Zboray's estimate to the prevailing belief that in antebellum America 95 percent of businesses failed. See Edward J. Balleisen, *Navigating Failure: Bankruptcy and Commercial Society in Antebellum America* (Chapel Hill: University of North Carolina Press, 2001), 3.

99. George Palmer Putnam, "'Free-Stone'—Authors—Publishers," 396.

100. John Sutherland, "Publishing History: A Hole at the Centre of Literary Sociology," *Critical Inquiry* 14 (Spring 1988): 579. Principle studies of American publishing include Hellmut Lehmann-Haupt, *The Book in America: A History of the Making and Selling of Books in the United States* (1939; 2nd edition, revised and expanded by Lawrence C. Wroth and Rollo G. Silver, New York: Bowker, 1951); Donald Sheehan, *This Was Publishing: A Chronicle of the Book Trade in the Gilded Age* (Bloomington: Indiana University Press, 1952); William Charvat, *Literary Publishing in America, 1790–1850* (Philadelphia: University of Pennsylvania Press, 1959; reprint, Amherst: University of Massachusetts Press, 1993); John Tebbel, *A History of Book Publishing in the United States*, 4 vols. (New York: R. R. Bowker, 1972–81); and Winship, *American Literary Publishing in the Mid-Nineteenth Century*. *A History of the Book in America*, under the general editorship of David D. Hall, is the new standard for American publishing history (vol. 1, New York: Cambridge University Press and the American Antiquarian Society, 2001; vols. 3–5, Chapel Hill: University of North Carolina Press and the American Antiquarian Society, 2007–9).

101. On the limitations of the term "print culture," see Leslie Howsam, *Old Books and New Histories: An Orientation to Studies in Book and Print Culture* (Toronto: University of Toronto Press, 2006), 3–15. My use of the term is meant to highlight the presence of human agency in the world of texts and textual production. For a discussion of field nomenclature that privileges the text rather than the social practices of production, see Thomas R. Adams and Nicolas Barker, "A New Model for the Study of the Book," in David Finkelstein and Alistair McCleery, eds., *The Book History Reader*, 2nd ed., 46–65 (London: Routledge, 2006).

102. Bourdieu, "The Production of Belief," 78, 79.

103. See Jytte Klausen, *The Cartoons that Shook the World* (New Haven: Yale University Press, 2009).

104. Randy Cohen, "The Ethicist," *New York Times*, March 29, 2010, http://www.nytimes.com/2010/04/04/magazine/04FOB-ethicist-t.html?emc=eta1.

105. See Ted Solotaroff, "The Literary-Industrial Complex," *New Republic*, June 8, 1987, 28–45.

106. Hamilton, *Battle of the Books*, 3.

107. Timothy Pitkin, *A Statistical View of the Commerce of the United States of America*, 2nd ed. (New York: James Eastburn, 1817), 1, 2.

108. Quoted in Saul Engelbourg, *Power and Morality: American Business Ethics 1840–1914* (Westport: Greenwood Press, 1980), 8.

109. Thorstein Veblen, *The Theory of Business Enterprise* (New York: Augustus M. Kelley, 1965), 53.

110. Charles F. Dole, *The Golden Rule in Business* (New York: Thomas Y. Crowell, 1896), 35; George Haven Putnam, *Authors and Publishers*, 4. The view that an "almost rustic simplicity" prevailed in early American business has been around at least as long as Matthew Josephson's classic study *The Robber Barons: The Great American Capitalists, 1861–1901* (New York: Harcourt Brace, 1934). Engelbourg, *Power and Morality*, 12. Josephson provided a historical synthesis in which antebellum America (or, when refined, pre-1840 America) was a pre-lapsarian golden age "in which man and his life were 'the measure of all things' and, to a greater extent than ever afterward, of his business" (10), while postbellum America was a post-lapsarian hell, at least in terms of commerce. On the development of business history as a field and the dissolution of the kind of synthesis history practiced by Josephson, see Louis Galambos, "What Makes Us Think We Can Put Business Back into American History?" *Business and Economic History*, 2nd series 20 (1991): 1–11. In *Manufacturing the Employee: Management Knowledge from the 19th to 21st Centuries* (London: Sage, 1996), Roy Jacques suggests that part of the reason for this romanticization is that modern management theory looks back at the nineteenth-century's "discourse of character" (27) uncritically. For more nuanced readings of preindustrial American business life, see Richard Hofstadter, *Anti-intellectualism in American Life* (New York: Knopf, 1966); Thomas Augst, *The Clerk's Tale: Young Men and Moral Life in Nineteenth-Century America* (Chicago: University of Chicago Press, 2005); Stephen Mihm, *A Nation of Counterfeiters: Capitalists, Con Men, and the Making of the United States* (Cambridge: Harvard University Press, 2007); and Jane Kamensky, *The Exchange Artist: A Tale of High-Flying Speculation and America's First Banking Collapse* (New York: Viking, 2008).

111. Thomas Paine, *Complete Writings of Thomas Paine*, 2 vols., ed. Philip Foner (New York: Citadel, 1945), 2: 213.

112. George Haven Putnam, *Authors and Publishers: A Manual of Suggestions for Beginners in Literature* (New York: G. P. Putnam's Sons, 1883), 2.

113. Geoffrey Turnovsky, "The Enlightenment Literary Market: Rousseau, Authorship, and the Book Trade," *Eighteenth-Century Studies* 36 (Spring 2003): 388.

114. I would add as well that everything from *Common Sense* to Dickens's letters on copyright are, as we teach our students, only slightly less slanted than their explicitly fictional counterparts. While "the *first* task of any literary analysis is not to interpret . . . [texts'] meaning, but to reconstruct their predicament," as Peter D. McDonald argues, that does not mean, I want to suggest, that the second task cannot be the interpretation of a text as a representation—or, in the case of this book, a critique of—that predicament. McDonald, *British Literary Culture and Publishing Practice, 1880–1914* (New York: Cambridge University Press, 1997), 13. Much as Paul K. Saint-Amour has demonstrated that some texts "are not occupied by copyright so much as *preoccupied* with it"—that "copyright's presence within literary texts is far more pervasive than has previously been recognized"—I argue that some texts share a similar preoccupation with ethical issues connected to their production. Saint-Amour, *The Copywrights: Intellectual Property and the Literary Imagination* (Ithaca: Cornell University Press, 2003), 12. An impressive and imposing counterexample, meanwhile, is Jackson, *Business of Letters*.

115. George Haven Putnam, *Authors and Publishers*, 1.

116. Fanny Fern [Sara Payson Willis], *Ruth Hall and Other Writings*, ed. Joyce W. Warren (New Brunswick: Rutgers University Press, 1986), 173.

117. Hamilton, *Battle of the Books*, 3.

118. Gail Hamilton to [George] Wood, November 14, 1868, in Hamilton, *Gail Hamilton's Life in Letters*, ed. H. Augusta Dodge, 2 vols. (Boston: Lea and Shepard, 1901), 2: 622.

119. "Destructive Fire," New York *Daily Times*, December 12, 1853, 1.

120. Exman, *Brothers Harper*, 56.

121. Erastus Ellsworth to George Palmer Putnam, December 20, 1853, George Palmer Putnam Collection, box 1, folder 80.

122. George Palmer Putnam to Harper and Brothers, December 14, 1853, in Greenspan, ed., *House of Putnam, 1837–1872*, 70.

CHAPTER 1

1. Stylus [Eugene Didier], *American Publishers and English Authors* (Baltimore: [E. L. Didier], 1879), 19; James Jackson Jarves to Harper and Brothers, September 23, 1855, Misc American Harpers, folder Jarves, James Jackson, 1818–1888. "Harpies" was a fairly common tag for Harper and Brothers. See, for example, "Harpers or Harpies?" *Scotts Weekly*, October 11, 1890, 527. It was especially popular in the South during the Civil War, when the firm made no secret of its scorn for the Confederacy. See "Editor's Cable," *Southern Literary Messenger*, November 1, 1862, 689.

2. John Esten Cooke to Evert Duyckinck, July 15, 1865, Duyckinck Family Papers, box 4, folder Cooke, John Esten; D. A. Gallagher to Evert Duyckinck, July 9, 1860, Duyckinck Family Papers, box 19, folder Evert A. Duyckinck, General Correspondence, 1860.

3. William Gilmore Simms to James Lawson, November 6, 1860, in *Letters of William Gilmore Simms*, 4: 255.

4. Evert Duyckinck to Frederick Saunders, October 8, 1845, Duyckinck Family Papers, vol. 13, E. A. Duyckinck Letterbook, 1844.

5. Evert Duyckinck to James Russell Lowell, December 17, 1841, James Russell Lowell Papers, folder 299. On Duyckinck, see Perry Miller, *The Raven and the Whale: The War of Words and Wits in the Era of Poe and Melville* (New York: Harcourt Brace, 1956; reprint, Baltimore: Johns Hopkins University Press, 1997); Kermit Vanderbilt, *American Literature and the Academy: The Roots, Growth, and Maturity of a Profession* (Philadelphia: University of Pennsylvania Press, 1986), 61–79; Edward Widmer, *Young America: The Flowering of Democracy in New York City* (New York: Oxford University Press, 1999), 93–111; and Greenspan, *George Palmer Putnam*, 158–82.

6. [Evert Duyckinck], "The Morality of Publishers," *Literary World*, February 13, 1847, 29.

7. Samuel Osgood, "Evert Augustus Duyckinck," *New-England Historical and Genealogical Register* 33 (April 1879): 144.

8. Sandage, *Born Losers*, 42–43. On challenges to the theory of the market revolution and especially its impact, see Daniel Walker Howe, *What Hath God Wrought: The Transformation of America, 1815–1848* (New York: Oxford University Press, 2007). The conventional thesis is articulated by Charles Sellers, *The Market Revolution: Jacksonian America, 1815–1846* (New York: Oxford University Press, 1991). On commercial morality, see Thomas L. Haskell, "Capitalism and the Origins of the Humanitarian Sensibility, Part 1," *American Historical Review* 90 (April 1985): 339–61; and Haskell, "Capitalism and the Origins of the Humanitarian Sensibility, Part 2," *American Historical Review* 90 (June 1985): 547–66; Thomas Augst, "The Commerce of Thought: Professional Authority and Business Ethics in Nineteenth-Century America," *Prospects* 27 (2002): 49–76; Augst, *Clerk's Tale*; and Stewart Davenport, *Friends of the Unrighteous Mammon: Northern Christians and Market Capitalism, 1815–1860* (Chicago: University of Chicago Press, 2008).

9. Sandage, *Born Losers*, 41; John Esten Cooke to Evert Duyckinck, July 15, 1865.

10. Not everyone trusted Duyckinck or his judgment of the character of other tradesmen, of course. Bostonians, who tended to look down on all New Yorkers as unregenerate capitalists, had their suspicions. According to Edwin Whipple, Boston's "general impression" of Duyckinck and other New York literati was one of "hostility." Whipple to Evert Duyckinck, October 12, 1848, Duyckinck Family Papers, box 17, folder Whipple, Edwin Percy. But not everyone trusted Bostonians, either. "What a *nasty*, good for-nothing set *many* of those Bostonians are," publisher Charles Dennet complained to Duyckinck; "they have neither brains enough in their head or beef in their breeches, to keep their equilibrium." Charles F. Dennet to Evert Duyckinck, March 13, 1851, Duyckinck Family Papers, box 4, folder Dennet, Charles F. On the regional politics of mid-nineteenth-century literary culture, see Miller, *Raven and the Whale*.

11. Freeman Hunt, *Worth and Wealth: A Collection of Maxims, Morals and Miscellanies for Merchants and Men of Business* (1856; reprint, New York: Stringer and Townsend, 1857), 446.

12. Francis Wayland, *Elements of Moral Science* (New York: Cooke, 1835), 4.

13. On the evolution of moral philosophy into political economy, see Gladys Bryson, "The Emergence of the Social Sciences from Moral Philosophy," *International Journal of Ethics* 42 (April 1932): 304–23; and Davenport, *Friends of the Unrighteous Mammon*, 23–33. For my understanding of political economy in the period I am indebted as well to Wilson Smith, *Professors and Public Ethics: Studies of Northern Moral Philosophers before the Civil War* (Ithaca: Cornell University Press, 1956); Henry F. May, *Protestant Churches and Industrial America* (New York: Octagon Books, 1963); D. H. Meyer, *The Instructed Conscience: The Shaping of the American National Ethic* (Philadelphia: University of Pennsylvania Press, 1972); and Paul K. Conkin, *Prophets of Prosperity: America's First Political Economists* (Bloomington: Indiana University Press, 1980).

14. Adam Smith, *An Inquiry in the Nature and Causes of the Wealth of Nations*, ed. R. H. Campbell and A. S. Skinner, 2 vols. (Indianapolis: Liberty Fund, 1981), 1: 26–27.

15. Adam Smith, *The Theory of Moral Sentiments*, ed. D. D. Raphael and A. L. MacFie (Indianapolis: Liberty Fund, 1982), 25. On the "Adam Smith problem," see Richard F. Teichgraeber III, "Preface: The Problem of Adam Smith," in Teichgraber, *"Free Trade" and Moral Philosophy: Rethinking the Sources of Adam Smith's* Wealth of Nations, xi–xviii (Durham: Duke University Press, 1986); and Davenport, *Friends of the Unrighteous Mammon*, 23–33 and 203–11.

16. Alexis de Tocqueville, *Democracy in America*, 2 vols. (New York: Knopf, 1994), 2: 83.

17. Herman Melville, *Moby-Dick; or, The Whale*, vol. 6 of *The Writings of Herman Melville*, ed. Harrison Hayford, Hershel Parker, and G. Thomas Tanselle, 14 vols. to date (Evanston and Chicago: Northwestern University Press and the Newberry Library, 1968–), 6.

18. Charles Dickens to various recipients, July 7, 1842, in *The Letters of Charles Dickens*, ed. Madeline House and Graham Storey, 12 vols. (Oxford: Clarendon Press, 1965–2002), 3: 259; Dickens, *American Notes*, ed. Patricia Ingham (New York: Penguin, 2004), 267–68.

19. Cotton Mather, *A Man of His Word* (Boston: John Allen, 1713), 2.

20. Ibid., 3.

21. "The Scribbler, No. IV—For the Port Folio," *Port-Folio* 1 (May 1809): 421.

22. Quoted in Hunt, *Worth and Wealth*, 382.

23. Solomon, "Business Ethics," 354.

24. Harriet Martineau, *Society in America*, vol. 2 (London: Saunders and Otley, 1837), 142. On Martineau's views on political economy, see Eleanor Courtemanch, "'Naked Truth Is the Best Eloquence': Martineau, Dickens, and the Moral Science of Realism," *ELH* 73 (Summer 2006): 383–407.

25. "The Scribbler, No. IV—For the Port Folio," 424.

26. Peter Baida, *Poor Richard's Legacy: American Business Values from Benjamin Franklin to Donald Trump* (New York: William Morrow, 1990), 21.

27. Henry W. Bellows, *The Ledger and the Lexicon* (Cambridge: John Bartlett, 1853), 20.

28. Ibid., 20–21.

29. Henry W. Bellows, *The Christian Merchant* (New York: C. S. Francis, 1848), 7.

30. Davenport, *Friends of the Unrighteous Mammon*, 55.

31. Ibid., 8, 55. On the "clerical economists," see 9–105. The historiography on the evangelical Protestant encounter with capitalism in nineteenth-century America is extensive. For an overview, see Mark A. Noll, "Introduction," in *God and Mammon: Protestants, Money, and the Market, 1790–1860*, ed. Noll (New York: Oxford University Press, 2002), 3–20.

32. Daniel D. Barnard, "Commerce, as Connected with the Progress of Civilization," *Merchant's Magazine* 1 (July 1839): 20.

33. William M. Allen, "Stephen Allen," in Freeman Hunt, ed., *Lives of American Merchants*, 2 vols. (New York: Office of Hunt's Merchants' Magazine, 1856–58; reprint, New York: Derby and Jackson, 1858), 2: 191. These proverbs were published originally as "Maxims for Young Merchants," *Hunt's Merchants' Magazine* 26 (January 1852): 135.

34. Hunt, *Worth and Wealth*, 186. For an alternate reading of Hunt's moral philosophy, see Jerome Thomases, "Freeman Hunt's America," *Mississippi Valley Historical Review* 30 (December 1943): 399–400.

35. Jonathan Dymond, *Essays on the Principles of Morality, and on the Private and Political Rights and Obligations of Mankind* (1829; reprint, New York: Harper and Brothers, 1834). Dymond's influence on early American business ethics has gone largely unremarked. He is better known for his *Inquiry into the Accordancy of War with the Principles of Christianity* (1823), one of the definitive position statements of Quaker pacifism in both England and the United States, which has been studied for its influence on writers like Henry David Thoreau. See James Duban, "Thoreau, Garrison, Dymond: Unbending Firmness of Mind," *American Literature* 57 (May 1985): 309–17.

36. John Greenleaf Whittier to Thomas Case, October 18, 1883, in *Letters of John Greenleaf Whittier*, 3: 480; Hunt, *Worth and Wealth*, 38.

37. Edwin T. Freedley, *A Practical Treatise on Business*, 5th ed. (Philadelphia: Lippincott, Grambo, 1852), 31.

38. Ibid., 67. In his chapter "On Business," Freedley suggested that business is nothing less than a safeguard of the virtues. See 32–33.

39. Hunt, *Worth and Wealth*, 405.

40. Freedley, *Practical Treatise on Business*, 31; Hunt, *Worth and Wealth*, 183.

41. Joanne Freeman, *Affairs of Honor: National Politics in the New Republic* (New Haven: Yale University Press, 2001), xvii.

42. Wayland, *Elements of Moral Philosophy*, 279.

43. Dymond, *Essays on the Principles of Morality*, 168; Hunt, *Worth and Wealth*, 446; Freedley, *A Practical Treatise on Business*, 27.

44. Emerson, *Collected Works*, 3: 54–55. David M. Robinson suggests that Emerson's conception of character was an evolution of his thinking on self-culture. See *Emerson and the Conduct of Life: Pragmatism and Ethical Purpose in the Later Work* (New York: Cambridge University Press, 1993), 76. In *Character Is Capital: Success Manuals and Manhood in Gilded Age America* (Chapel

Hill: University of North Carolina Press, 1997), 127, Judy Hilkey notes that the principle of character was instrumental through the turn of the twentieth century.

45. Contemporary business ethicists continue to debate the place of virtue ethics, the theory that, in Solomon's words, one "begins with the idea that it is individual virtue that counts: good corporate and social policy will follow." Solomon, "Business and the Humanities," 51.

46. Evert Duyckinck to George Duyckinck, February 26, 1847, Duyckinck Family Papers, box 23, folder 1847, January–June.

47. Richard Grant White to Evert Duyckinck, February 5, 1847, Duyckinck Family Papers, box 17, folder White, Richard Grant.

48. On the mammoth weeklies, see Barnes, *Authors, Publishers and Politicians*, 8; and Johns, *Piracy*, 302–4.

49. Ralph Waldo Emerson to Thomas Carlyle, April 29, 1843, in *Correspondence of Emerson and Carlyle*, 342.

50. Carey, Lea, and Blanchard to Harper and Brothers, November 17, 1834, Lea and Febiger Records, Letterbook, Carey, Lea, and Blanchard, June 17, 1834, to September 2, 1835, p. 172.

51. William Beckford, *Italy: With Sketches of Spain and Portugal* (Philadelphia: Key and Biddle, 1834).

52. Quoted in Derby, *Fifty Years among Authors, Books and Publishers*, 551. This was old hat for Carey. In 1823, when Carey and Lea received advance sheets of cantos of Byron's *Don Juan*, the firm had them on bookstore shelves in thirty-six hours after farming them out to "thirty or forty compositors" (141). On Carey's tactics, and especially on his battles with Harper and Brothers, see David Kaser, *Messrs. Carey & Lea of Philadelphia: A Story in the History of the Book Trade* (Philadelphia: University of Pennsylvania Press, 1957), 148–55.

53. Carey, Lea, and Blanchard to Harper and Brothers, June 20, 1835, Lea and Febiger Records, Letterbook, Carey, Lea, and Blanchard, June 17, 1834, to September 2, 1835, pp. 381–82.

54. Johns, *Piracy*, 299. For a brief account of some of the more salacious episodes in this trade war, see 295–99.

55. Evert Duyckinck to George Duyckinck, November 15, 1847, Duyckinck Family Papers, box 23, folder 1847, July–December.

56. Benjamin Larkin to John Mycall, January 15, 1785, Benjamin Larkin Correspondence, 1780–1796, box 1, folder 5, American Antiquarian Society, used by permission.

57. Edward L. Ayers, *Vengeance and Justice: Crime and Punishment in the 19th Century American South* (New York: Oxford University Press, 1984), 25.

58. Bertram Wyatt-Brown, *Southern Honor: Ethics and Behavior in the Old South* (1982; reprint, New York: Oxford University Press, 2007), 14.

59. Warner, *Letters of the Republic*, 42. As suggested earlier, publishers generally used the word "honor" in reference to a kind of commercial caste system, where a firm's reputation for moral conduct dictated its position, as publisher Walter F. Page implied when he wrote in his memoir that honorable publishers "have the respect of all the book world. Authors and readers, who do not know definitely why they should hold them in esteem, discern a high a sense of honor and conduct in them." Page, *A Publisher's Confession* (New York: Doubleday, Page, 1923), 65–66.

60. Henry C. Carey to Cummings and Hilliard, September 24, 1821, Lea and Febiger Records, Letterbook, Henry Carey, September 15, 1821, to March 1, 1822, letter 55.

61. See Henry C. Carey to Cummings and Hilliard, October 5, 1821, ibid., letter 207.

62. EAD [Evert Duyckinck], "Literary Prospects of 1845," *American Whig Review* 1 (February 1845): 148.

63. Cornelius Mathews, untitled manuscript draft of article published in London *Athenaeum*, May 27, 1843, 510–11, Duyckinck Family Papers, box 11, folder Literary Correspondence, Mathews, Cornelius, Lit. Mss.

64. Cornelius Mathews to Evert Duyckinck, [1843], Duyckinck Family Papers, box 11, folder Mathews, Cornelius, Lit. Mss. This letter seems to be notes for the article draft cited in n. 63. Interestingly, the phrase "morality of the system" does not appear in that draft.

65. "Festus," *American Review* 5 (January 1847): 43–61; "Festus. Part 1," *American Review* 6 (February 1847): 123–35; and "Festus. Part 2," *American Review* 6 (February 1847): 136–48. Duyckinck was responding only to the first installment.

66. [Cornelius Mathews], "The International Copyright Law, and Mr. Dickens," *Arcturus* 3 (March 1842): 248.

67. Ibid., 247.

68. "Festus," *American Review* 5 (January 1847): 44.

69. Ibid., 48.

70. [Evert Duyckinck], "The Morality of Publishers," 29. The *American Review* quotation comes from "Festus." The source of the final quotation is unknown.

71. D [Evert Duyckinck], "Authorship," *Arcturus* 1 (December 1840): 21.

72. EAD [Evert Duyckinck], "Literary Prospects of 1845," *American Whig Review* 1 (February 1845): 146.

73. Ibid., 148.

74. Evert Duyckinck to William Jones, May 12, 1839, Duyckinck Family Papers, box 9, folder Jones, William A.

75. Evert Duyckinck to William Jones, March 14, 1839, ibid.

76. Francis Lieber, "The Character of the Gentleman" (Cincinnati: J. A. James, 1846).

77. Evert Duyckinck to Francis Lieber, June 26, 1863, Papers of Francis Lieber, LI 1384, Huntington Library.

78. Davenport, *Friends of the Unrighteous Mammon*, 155.

79. Ibid., 172.

80. Ibid., 180.

81. Ibid., 192–93.

82. Evert Duyckinck to George Duyckinck, January 1, 1848, Duyckinck Family Papers, box 23, folder 1848, January–March.

83. Thomas Delf to Evert Duyckinck, December 1, 1847, Duyckinck Family Papers, box 18, folder Letters, 1847.

84. Evert Duyckinck to George Duyckinck, November 15, 1847.

85. Hamilton, *Battle of the Books*, 5.

86. "Publishers and Publishing in New York," *Norton's Literary Gazette*, April 15, 1854, 191.

87. Ibid., 166.

88. "Sketches of the Publishers," *Round Table*, January 6, 1866, 11.

89. "Roberts Brothers, Boston," *American Publishers' Circular*, July 1, 1871, 119.

90. [James Parton], "International Copyright," *Atlantic Monthly* 20 (October 1867): 442.

91. "Public Dinner to Louis A. Godey," *Godey's Lady's Book and Magazine* 52 (March 1856): 275; "The Book Trade," 173.

92. "Public Dinner to Louis A. Godey," 295.

93. John W. Francis, "Reminiscences of Printers, Authors, and Booksellers in New-York," *International Monthly Magazine*, February 1, 1852, 258–59; Noah Webster, *The Prompter* (Hartford: B. Hudson and Goodwin, 1791), iv.

94. Francis, "Reminiscences of Printers, Authors, and Booksellers in New-York," 259.

95. Ibid., 254.

96. Exman, *Brothers Harper*, 1.

97. Hunt, "Mathew Carey," in *Lives of American Merchants*, 1: 318, 1: 319. Hunt's text is based on Carey's memoir, "Autobiography of Mathew Carey," *New-England Magazine* (December 1833): 489–97. On Mathew Carey, see James N. Green, *Mathew Carey: Publisher and Patriot* (Philadelphia: Library Company of Philadelphia, 1985).

98. See Johns, *Piracy*, 208–10.

99. George Stillman Hillard, "James Brown," in *Lives of American Merchants*, 2: 519–20. This was a reprint of George Stillman Hillard, *A Memoir of James Brown* (Boston: privately printed, 1856).

100. Ibid., 2: 522.

101. Ibid., 2: 570.

102. Carter, "Some Recollections of the Book Trade," 354.

103. Hillard, "James Brown," 2: 528.

104. Ibid., 2: 523.

105. Ibid., 2: 528.

106. Ibid., 2: 569.

107. Sheehan, *This Was Publishing*, 7. As Winship points out, citing the tale of Fields's discovery of the story that would become *The Scarlet Letter* (1850), accounts of publishing too often romanticize the trade and especially publishers' relationship to authors. Winship, *Literary Publishing in the Mid-Nineteenth Century*, 188–89.

108. Theodore Bliss, *Theodore Bliss, Publisher and Bookseller: A Study of the Character and Life in the Middle Period of the XIX Century* (Norwalk: American Publishers, 1911), 38–39.

109. James Rivington to [Thomas] Bradford, March 5, 1796, Bradford Family Papers, ms. 1676, box 2, folder 12, Historical Society of Pennsylvania.

110. James Rivington to [Thomas] Bradford, March 14, 1796, ibid.

111. Carey, Lea, and Blanchard to J. Robinson, August 22, 1834, Lea and Febiger Records, Letterbook, Carey, Lea, and Blanchard, June 17, 1834, to September 2, 1835, p. 73.

112. Carey and Lea to James Fenimore Cooper, February 6, 1826, James Fenimore Cooper Papers, box 2, folder 11.

113. Hugh Gaine to Isaiah Thomas, January 14, 1789, Isaiah Thomas Papers, American Antiquarian Society, used by permission.

114. Howard B. Rock, *Artisans of the New Republic: The Tradesmen of New York City in the Age of Jefferson* (New York: New York University Press, 1979), 243. On the unrest in Washington, D.C., see William S. Pretzer, "'The British, Duff Green, the Rats and the Devil': Custom, Capitalism, and Conflict in the Washington Printing Trade, 1834–36," *Labor History* 27 (Winter 1985–86): 5–30. Remer provides a careful overview of the causes and effects of trade organization in *Printers and Men of Capital*. See also Adolph Growoll, *Book-Trade Bibliography in the United States in the XIXth Century* (New York: n.p., 1898), iii–x; Ethelbert Stewart, *Early Organizations of Printers*, Vol. 61, *Bulletin of the Bureau of Labor* (n.p.: Department of Commerce and Labor, 1905); and Bruce Laurie, "Labor and Labor Organization," in *Industrial Book*, 70–89.

115. Obadiah Bowe to Rufus Griswold, August 2, 1838, Merrill Griswold Collection, Ms. Gris., folder 70, Boston Public Library.

116. On the Philadelphia Typographical Society, see Remer, *Printers and Men of Capital*, 39–68. For a broader history of regulation in the American trade, see Sheehan, *This Was Publishing*, 199–237.

117. Boston Association of Booksellers Record Book, 1801–1820, Boston Booksellers Records, n.p., American Antiquarian Society, used by permission.

118. Boston Association of Booksellers Record Book, 1801–1814, Boston Booksellers Records, p. 1, used by permission.

119. Ibid., 108.

120. Boston Association of Booksellers Record Book, 1801–1820, Boston Booksellers Records, p. 23.

121. Ibid., 34.

122. Ibid., n.p.

123. [Cummings and Hilliard], *Cheap List. Catalogue of Books* (Boston: Cummings and Hilliard, 1822).

124. D. H. Reins to the Philadelphia Typographical Society, September 9, 1809, in George A. Tracy, *History of the Typographical Union* (Indianapolis: International Typographical Union, 1913), 30.

125. John Childs to the New York Typographical Union, October 28, 1809, in *History of the Typographical Union*, 31.

126. Price list of the Philadelphia Typographical Society, February 22, 1802, in *History of the Typographical Union*, 21. For an introduction to trade sales see Tebbel, *A History of Book Publishing in the United States*, 1: 230–38.

127. William Elder, *A Memoir of Henry C. Carey* (Philadelphia: Henry Carey Baird and Company, 1880), 31–32.

128. Ronald J. Zboray, *A Fictive People: Antebellum Economic Development and the American Reading Public* (New York: Oxford University Press, 1993), 24.

129. Hugh Gaine, "An Oration before the Booksellers Convened in New-York, at Their First Literary Fair, June 4th, 1802," Edward Carey Gardiner Collection, ms. 227a, Historical Society of Pennsylvania.

130. "An Hour at the Book Trade Sales," *Norton's Literary Gazette* 3 (April 1853): 61.

131. "Harpers' View on Trade Sales," *American Publishers' Circular*, September 8, 1855, 17–18.

132. Bliss, *Theodore Bliss*, 68.

133. [Parton], "International Copyright," 430.

134. Ibid., 443.

135. Harper and Brothers to E. D. Morgan, February 24, 1868, Misc American Harper, folder, Harper and Brothers, firm, publishers, New York.

136. Harper and Brothers to E. D. Morgan, February 28, 1868, ibid.

137. See, for example, Carey, Lea, and Blanchard to Harper and Brothers, November 17, 1834.

138. Harper and Brothers to E. D. Morgan, February 27, 1868, Misc American Harper, folder Harper and Brothers, firm, publishers, New York.

139. James Parton, Minute Book of International Copyright Committee, 1868, James Parton Additional Papers, MS Am 2198, fMS 8, p. 8, Houghton Library, Harvard University.

140. Ibid., 11.

141. [Mathews], "The International Copyright Law, and Mr. Dickens," 243.

142. Max Weber, *The Protestant Ethic and the Spirit of Capitalism*, translated by Talcott Parsons (London: Routledge, 2004), 19. Both R. H. Tawney's *Religion and the Rise of Capitalism* (1926)

and Weber's *The Protestant Ethic and the Spirit of Capitalism* explore the history and legitimacy of the claim that, in Tawney's words, "the good Christian was not wholly dissimilar from the economic man." Tawney, *Religion and the Rise of Capitalism* (New York: Mentor Books, 1954), 210. Weber finds them not in the least dissimilar, positing that Protestantism was instrumental in the development of an "ascetic tendency" (33) in the businessman that came to govern the pursuit and acquisition of wealth.

143. James Parton, "The Pilgrim Fathers as Men of Business," 1871, James Parton Additional Papers, MS 8, p. 42. Historians have long debated capitalism's beginnings in the United States. The moral economy view argues that colonial America was not capitalist—that colonials had other interests than profit—while market historians suggest that a capitalist mentality is quantifiable in colonials' motivations. On the latter position, see Winifred Barr Rothenberg, *From Market-Places to a Market Economy: The Transformation of Rural Massachusetts, 1750–1850* (Chicago: University of Chicago Press, 1992), which argues that American capitalism may be sourced to the years following the Revolution. A representative of the former view, with which James Parton and other contemporary business commentators would have sympathized, is Stephen Innes, *Creating the Commonwealth: The Economic Culture of Puritan New England* (New York: Norton, 1995). Allan Kulikoff negotiates the competing views in *The Agrarian Origins of American Capitalism* (Charlottesville: University Press of Virginia, 1992). Naomi R. Lamoreaux productively deemphasizes the capitalist–anti-capitalist binary by calling attention to the ways in which such a binary elides the complex motives of merchants, motives that could be based both on profit and on noncapitalist factors such as family obligations. See "Rethinking the Transition to Capitalism in the Early American Northeast," *Journal of American History* 90 (September 2003): 437–61.

144. [Parton], "International Copyright," 442–43.

145. On courtesy of the trade, see Barnes, "Edward Lytton Bulwer and the Publishing Firm of Harper & Brothers"; Jeffrey D. Groves, "Courtesy of the Trade," in *Industrial Book,* 139–48; and Johns, *Piracy,* 300–2.

146. Booksellers Company of Philadelphia, Minutes, 1802–1803, (Phi)Am 31175, May 8, 1802, Historical Society of Pennsylvania.

147. [Parton], "International Copyright," 441. Parton lists the first three but not the last dealing with retribution.

148. Carey, Lea, and Blanchard to Key and Biddle, January 29, 1835, Lea and Febiger Records, Letterbook, Carey, Lea, and Blanchard, June 17, 1834, to September 2, 1835, p. 254.

149. [Parton], "International Copyright," 440–41.

150. Carey, Lea, and Blanchard to Harper and Brothers, November 17, 1834.

151. Thomas Wentworth Higginson, *Merchants: A Sunday Evening Lecture* (Newburyport: A. A. Call, 1851), 4.

152. "Walks among the Publishers," *Southern and Western Monthly Magazine and Review* 2 (November 1845): 353.

CHAPTER 2

1. Paine, *Complete Writings*, 1: 4.

2. Benjamin Franklin, *Writings*, ed. J. A. Leo Lemay (New York: Library of America, 1987), 159.

3. Daniel Vickers, "Competency and Competition: Economic Culture in Early America," *William and Mary Quarterly* 3rd series, 47 (January 1990): 4. See also Crowley, *This Sheba, Self;*

and Johns, *Piracy*, 159–64. My approach in this chapter to the ethics underwriting professional relations between writers and printers differs from Vernon Dibble's notion of "occupational ideology" as employed by scholars such as Stephen Botein. Dibble's term considers the ideological opinions held by professionals and the ways in which these opinions are transformed by their passage into the public realm. By contrast, in this chapter I am interested in the values influencing occupational behavior. See Dibble, "Occupations and Ideologies," *Journal of American Sociology* 68 (September 1962): 229–41; and Botein, "'Meer Mechanics' and an Open Press: The Business and Political Strategies of Colonial American Printers," *Perspectives in American History* 9 (1975): 129.

4. David Saunders and Ian Hunter, "Lessons from the 'Literatory': How to Historicize Authorship," *Critical Inquiry* 17 (Spring 1991): 485.

5. Bourdieu, "The Production of Belief," 76. Bourdieu's term is arguably applicable primarily to post-Romantic constructions of authorship. But what is interesting is that the authorial model proposed by Paine is less republican than expressive in its vision of authorial identity and economics.

6. Warner, *Letters of the Republic*, 65. For an overview of the debate over the meaning and historical legitimacy of republicanism, particularly as delineated by Gordon S. Wood and J. G.A. Pocock, see Daniel T. Rodgers, "Republicanism: The Career of a Concept," *Journal of American History* 79 (June 1992): 11–38.

7. I am not suggesting that the relatively newfound legitimacy of the individual as a concept did not occur in the eighteenth century as a result of Enlightenment philosophies, the evolution of Western legal systems, and the articulation of laissez-faire economics. However, the idea of the community as a moral entity was still very real to colonials. In *Peaceable Kingdoms: New England Towns in the Eighteenth Century* (New York: Knopf, 1970), Michael Zuckerman argues that the historical record shows a tendency toward community throughout much of the late colonial period. Other historians, such as William Nelson, note the effect of this communal emphasis on the law and social structures of the period. See Nelson, *Americanization of the Common Law: The Impact of Legal Change on Massachusetts Society, 1760–1830* (Athens: University of Georgia Press, 1993), 1–64. Jack P. Greene provides an alternate reading of the role of virtue in the colonial society in "The Concept of Virtue in Late Colonial British America," in Greene, ed., *Imperatives, Behaviors, and Identities: Essays in Early American Cultural History*, 208–35 (Charlottesville: University Press of Virginia, 1992).

8. Nelson, *Americanization of the Common Law*, 6.

9. Ibid., 40.

10. Crowley, *This Sheba, Self*, 4–5.

11. Gordon S. Wood, *The Radicalism of the American Revolution* (New York: Knopf, 1992), 217.

12. *The Religious Trader* (New York: Hodge and Shober, 1773), 47.

13. William Dover, *Useful Miscellanies; or, Serious Reflections* (Philadelphia: James Chattin, 1753), 39. According to Crowley, the colonial "moral disposition toward social harmony was reinforced by the prevailing paradigm of economic change," a model in which wealth was ideally equally distributed among individuals (*This Sheba, Self*, 4). Economic success came at the expense of one's fellow citizens. Though colonials subscribed in large part to the belief in the inherent if unseen presence of the "invisible hand" of market regulation and direction articulated by economists such as Adam Smith, they also believed that there were discernible limits to commercial self-interest. In many ways, selfishness was a central evil for colonials' ethics.

14. Quoted in Wood, *Radicalism of the American Revolution*, 218.

15. William Christian, "The Moral Economics of Tom Paine," *Journal of the History of Ideas* 34 (July 1973): 371.

16. Paine, *Complete Writings*, 1: 359.

17. The evolution of Paine's sometimes paradoxical economic beliefs is treated in a number of studies. For an overview, see Joseph Dorfman, "The Economic Philosophy of Thomas Paine," *Political Science Quarterly* 53 (September 1938): 372–86. See also Eric Foner's treatment of Paine's role in the Silas Deane affair in *Tom Paine and Revolutionary America* (New York: Oxford University Press, 1976), 145–82; and John Keane, *Tom Paine: A Political Life* (Boston: Little, Brown, 1995), 168–80. Jack Fruchtman considers Paine's economic thought in the context of eighteenth-century moral philosophy in *Thomas Paine and the Religion of Nature* (Baltimore: Johns Hopkins University Press, 1993). On the revolutionary economy and issues of regulation, see E. James Ferguson, *The Power of the Purse: A History of American Public Finance, 1776–1790* (Chapel Hill: University of North Carolina Press, 1961), 70–105.

18. Among the thirty-eight master printers working in British North America prior to 1740, almost half were European trained, mostly in England. Of the twenty-one printers trained in the colonies, over half were connected to the Green family, the printing dynasty that began with Samuel Green, Jr., in the seventeenth century. See William S. Reese, "The First Hundred Years of Printing in British North America: Printers and Collectors," *Proceedings of the American Antiquarian Society* 99 (October 1989): 337–73, especially 340–44. As a result, the customs of colonial printing, although different in certain key respects due to drastic differences in resources and markets, often mirrored those of Europe.

19. J. R. T. Hughes, *Social Control in the Colonial Economy* (Charlottesville: University Press of Virginia, 1976), 18.

20. I am aware of using the word "custom" in what E. P. Thompson calls a "clumpish" sense, "which by gathering up so many activities and attributes into one common bundle may actually confuse or disguise discriminations that should be made between them." Thompson, *Customs in Common* (New York: New Press, 1993), 13. Nonetheless, I am using it in accord with Thompson's own broad definition of custom as "a usage so long exercised that it had taken on the colour of a privilege or a right" (4).

21. Benjamin Franklin, *Benjamin Franklin's* Autobiography: *An Authoritative Text, Backgrounds, Criticism*, ed. J. A. Leo Lemay and P. M. Zall (New York: Norton, 1986), 45.

22. Ibid., 46.

23. John Holt to William Goddard, February 2, 1778, Book Trades Collection, box 1, folder 6, ts, p. 1, American Antiquarian Society, used by permission.

24. John Holt, "James Rivington" (New York: John Holt, 1774).

25. Quoted in Robert Kany, "David Hall: Printing Partner of Benjamin Franklin," Ph.D. thesis, Pennsylvania State University, 1963, 137–38.

26. Freeman, *Affairs of Honor*, xvii.

27. Stewart identifies these societies as early as 1776; see *Early Organizations of Printers*, 860. Johns identifies them as operating by 1724; see *Piracy*, 197.

28. Quoted in ibid., 865.

29. "William McCulloch's Additions to Thomas's *History of Printing*," *Proceedings of the American Antiquarian Society* 31 (April 1921): 136–37.

30. Ibid., 99.

31. Benjamin Towne, "To the Public" (Philadelphia: Benjamin Towne, 1770).

32. John Witherspoon, "The Humble Confession, Declaration, Recantation, and Apology of BENJAMIN TOWNE, Printer in Philadelphia" (Philadelphia: R[obert] Bell, 1778), 2.

33. Ibid., 5.

34. In "'Meer Mechanics' and an Open Press," Botein argues that where a "politics of neutrality" made good business sense before hostilities began, after the war printers found more profit in partisanship (160). Although Towne's actions and the suspect business conduct of other printers make more sense in this context, printers were nevertheless popular targets for just about everyone. "Only during the prolonged crisis of the Revolutionary period did printers as a group begin to act in ways that promoted a politics directly expressive of tension and dissent" (199). See also Stephen Botein, "The Anglo-American Book Trade before 1776: Personnel and Strategies," in *Printing and Society in Early America*, ed. William B. Joyce, et al. (Worcester: American Antiquarian Society, 1983), 48–82.

35. Benjamin Franklin, "Apology for Printers," *Pennsylvania Gazette*, June 17, 1731; reprint, in *The Papers of Benjamin Franklin*, ed. Leonard Labaree, 39 vols. (New Haven: Yale University Press, 1959–), 1: 195.

36. Ian Gadd, "The Mechanicks of Difference: A Study in the Stationers' Company Discourse in the Seventeenth Century," in *The Stationers' Company and the Book Trade, 1550–1990*, ed. Robin Myers and Michael Harris, 93–112 (New Castle, Del.: Oak Knoll, 1997), 96.

37. Henry Parker, "The Humble Remonstrance of the Company of Stationers, LONDON" (1643); reprint, *A Transcript of the Registers of the Company of Stationers of London 1554–1640 A.D.*, ed. Edward Arber (London: n.p., 1875), 584.

38. Gadd, "The Mechanicks of Difference," 96.

39. Parker, "The Humble Remonstrance of the Company of Stationers," 584.

40. David Saunders, *Authorship and Copyright* (London: Routledge, 1992), 2.

41. William Zachs, *The First John Murray and the Late-Eighteenth-Century London Book Trade* (New York: Oxford University Press, 1998), 3. Botein notes that by the eighteenth century the reputation of English printers suffered as printers became less educated and more aggressively ridiculed for their ignorance. Despite notable exceptions, such as John Murray, English printers' social importance paled in comparison to that of their colonial counterparts. See "Meer Mechanics," 139–40.

42. [Patrick] Smyth to Mathew Carey, March 17, 1788, Edward Carey Gardiner Collection.

43. Isaiah Thomas, *The History of Printing in America* (Worcester: Isaiah Thomas, 1810; reprint, ed. Marcus A. McCorison, New York: Weathervane, 1970), 3.

44. Lawrence C. Wroth, *The Colonial Printer* (New York: The Grolier Club, 1931; reprint, Charlottesville: University Press of Virginia, 1964), 187–88.

45. Ibid., 187.

46. On the abstraction of print into an unlocalized discourse, see Warner, *Letters of the Republic*, 68. Despite his argument, Warner nevertheless acknowledges the importance of the physical space of the print shop.

47. Lawrence C. Wroth, *The First Press in Providence: A Study in Social Development* (Worcester: American Antiquarian Society, 1941), 31.

48. Richard Gimbel, *Thomas Paine: A Bibliographical Check List of Common Sense with an Account of Its Publication* (Port Washington, N.Y.: Kennikat, 1973), 57; Robert A. Ferguson, "The Commonalities of *Common Sense*," *William and Mary Quarterly*, 3rd series, 57 (July 2000): 466. Ferguson draws his statistics from Keane, *Tom Paine*, 108–11.

49. Trish Loughran, *Republic in Print: Print Culture in the Age of U.S. Nation Building, 1770–1870* (New York: Columbia University Press, 2007), 50. Gimbel's publication history is in *Thomas Paine*, 15–57. Loughran argues that "*Common Sense's* circulation numbers, often posed in the language of accounting, carry with them the objective force of the mathematical, but like accounting itself, they stand instead as relics of the cultures of production that made them" (43). "Nobody will ever know," she concludes, "how many copies were printed or sold, how many were purchased and how many given away, for whom most copies were printed, by whom they were read, or how many readers came into contact with any single copy" (56). See 37–58.

50. Thomas, *History of Printing in America*, 395. Thomas asserts that Robert Bell had to salvage paper for the first edition, although textual evidence compiled by Gimbel suggests that Bell used inferior paper only in subsequent editions. See Gimbel, *Thomas Paine*, 43; and Thomas, *The History of Printing in America*, 395.

51. In *Printing and Bookselling in Dublin, 1670–1800: A Bibliographical Inquiry* (Dublin: Irish Academic Press, 1998), James W. Phillips suggests that print historians often aggrandize the term "pirate" in relation to the practice of reprinting in Ireland. Noting the lack of a "complete justification" for applying these terms to tradespeople and texts in Ireland, Phillips argues that "in its application to books printed for and sold to the Irish reader" the term "piracy" is "misapplied. There was nothing illegal about this practice, although the ethics were questionable" (107). See 107–9. Phillips is overly idealistic, however, about printers' intentions for their stocks. There was more money to be made in exporting titles than in selling them to their own constituents. On the Dublin trade, see Johns, *Piracy*, 145–77. On the ostensible misuse of the term in American publishing history, see Chapter 4.

52. James N. Green, "English Books and Printing in the Age of Franklin," in *The Colonial Book in the Atlantic World*, vol. 1 of *A History of the Book in America*, ed. Hugh Amory and David D. Hall, 248–98 (Cambridge, UK: Cambridge University Press and the American Antiquarian Society, 2001), 287.

53. On Robert Bell, see Thomas, *History of Printing in America*, 394–96; "William McCulloch's Additions to Thomas's History," 97, 176, 219, 288, 232; D. B. Landis, "Robert Bell, Printer," *Papers Read before the Lancaster County Historical Society* 12 (1908): 195–202; Robert F. Metzdorf, "The First American 'Rasselas' and Its Imprint," *Papers of the Bibliographical Society of America* 47 (1953): 374–76; Carl and Jessica Bridenbaugh, *Rebels and Gentlemen: Philadelphia in the Age of Franklin* (New York: Hesperides, 1962), 84–86; Mary Pollard, *A Dictionary of Members of the Dublin Book Trade, 1550–1800* (London: Bibliographical Society, 2000), 29; Richard B. Sher, *The Enlightenment and the Book: Scottish Authors and Their Publishers in Eighteenth-Century Britain* (Chicago: University of Chicago Press, 2006), 511–31; and Johns, *Piracy*, 183–85.

54. "William McCulloch's Additions to Thomas's *History of Printing*," 232.

55. Green, "English Books and Printing in the Age of Franklin," 287.

56. Robert Bell, "Proposals, Addressed to Those Who Possess a Public Spirit," in *History of the Reign of Charles the Fifth*, by William Robertson, vol. 3, 3 vols. (Philadelphia: Robert Bell, 1771).

57. Green, "English Books and Printing in the Age of Franklin," 287. See also Johns, *Piracy*, 51–56.

58. "William McCulloch's Additions to Thomas's *History of Printing*," 176. Later Paine would speak of Benjamin Rush's role in this debacle deferentially. Paine admitted "he knew nothing of Robert Bell, who was engaged to print [*Common Sense*] by gentlemen of the city, and who can but be concerned for the unpleasant situation in which he hath, though from a well-meaning motive,

involved his friend." Paine, "To the Public," *Philadelphia Evening Post*, January 30, 1776, 54. However unwittingly, Paine implies, the esteemed Rush threw him to the dogs.

59. Robert Bell, "To the Public," *Philadelphia Evening Post*, February 22, 1776, 93.

60. "William McCulloch's Additions to Thomas's *History of Printing*," 232.

61. Robert Bell, "To the Public," *Philadelphia Evening Post*, January 27, 1776, 49.

62. See Johns, *Piracy*, 164, 195. I am adopting Johns's use of the terms "civilities" and "courtesies" to indicate the ethical, customary behavior of printers. See Johns, *Piracy*, especially 11–12, 164–65. As Johns notes, while trade civilities "had little, if any legal weight, there is ample evidence that they were respected by printers and booksellers and seen as a basis for harmony in their community" (12).

63. Sam[uel] Hall to Rev. Dr. Whitaker, April 1, 1774, Book Trades Collection.

64. "The wretch who will write on any subject for bread, or in any service for pay, and he who will plead in any case for a fee, stands equally in rank with the prostitute who lets out her person." Thomas Paine, "Serious Address to the People of Pennsylvania on the Present State of Their Affairs," *Complete Writings*, 2: 283. Paine does not deny the right of authors to payment but rather criticizes the notion of writing exclusively for profit and not for some greater good.

65. James N. Green, "Author-Publisher Relations to 1825," unpublished essay, n.d. Green argues that this was a landmark agreement in colonial and early America as it was the first time an author was to have been paid in money by the printer. Such an agreement would suggest that Paine exerted some power over the negotiation of the contract but that Bell was intensely interested in printing *Common Sense*. I would like to thank James N. Green for sharing with me a draft of this essay.

66. Thomas Paine to Henry Laurens, January 14, 1779, *Complete Writings*, 2: 1162.

67. On copyright regulation in the colonies, see Bruce Bugbee, *Genesis of American Patent and Copyright Law* (Washington, D.C.: Public Affairs Press, 1967), 65–67.

68. Johns, *Piracy*, 196. As Johns notes, even after the creation of federal copyright, the law was unevenly invoked. See 196–97. On trade courtesy in Europe, see Cyprian Blagden, *The Stationer's Company: A History, 1403–1959* (Cambridge: Harvard University Press, 1960), 31–33; Mary Pollard, *Dublin's Trade in Books, 1550–1800* (New York: Oxford University Press, 1989), 166–81; and Phillips, *Printing and Bookselling in Dublin*, 128–29.

69. Paine to Laurens, January 14, 1779.

70. Thomas Paine, "To the Public," *Philadelphia Evening Post*, January 25, 1776, 43.

71. Robert Bell, "To the Public," *Philadelphia Evening Post*, January 27, 1776, 49.

72. Ibid., 50.

73. Paine may have been sincere about his intentions for the profits as he donated his income from subsequent publications to charity. Foner notes Paine's history of charity work beginning in England in *Tom Paine*, 14.

74. Robert Bell, "To the Public," *Philadelphia Evening Post*, February 1, 1776, 58.

75. Green, "English Books and Printing in the Age of Franklin," 288.

76. Robert Bell, "To the Public," *Philadelphia Evening Post*, February 22, 1776, 93.

77. Loughran, *Republic in Print*, 80. On republican discourse as a "negation" of "personhood" see Warner, *Letters of the Republic*, 42–43; on republicanism as a metadiscourse, see 63–67.

78. Bell, "To the Public," *Philadelphia Evening Post*, February 1, 1776, 58.

79. Bell, "To the Public," *Philadelphia Evening Post*, February 22, 1776, 93.

80. Loughran also reads Bell's attack as a rhetorical critique, writing that he "effectively labeled Paine an antirepublican pretender, aspiring to a brand of honor, disinterestedness, and anonymity

that his own licentious desires—for fame, profit, and control—had already made impossible" (*Republic in Print*, 87). She cites the debate, however, as an illustration not of the relative agency of the early American publisher or of the moral politics of the print trade but of the limitations of the Habermasean public sphere. "Paine himself habitually resisted the idea that he could (as an author) be reduced to his particular person," Loughran observes. "But the phrase 'Common Sense' proved in the end to be an unstable double entendre, one that neatly encapsulates the untenable material basis of the disembodied (or representative) authorship he aspired to" (92). The practical failure of this authorial and textual disembodiment, according to Loughran, suggests the problem posed by the Revolution to the theory of the public sphere as a space existing outside of legitimat-ing institutions and persons—as a space in which public discourse can exist without either individual or corporate referents. "Paine's troubled history as an author does more . . . than simply describe the failure of the public sphere as a liberatory model for one individual," she suggests. "It also challenges the larger idea that the institutions of the public sphere (including print culture) helped to produce a functionally disembodied and disinterested revolutionary col-lectivity, or national 'public.'" Ultimately, in Loughran's view the debate between Paine and Bell indicates that the public sphere was but a "theoretical cover for the Revolutionary generation's own need to abstract the Revolution into a unanimous, nonparticular, and populist event" despite the very real personalities and personal agendas driving it (93).

81. While it would be usefully ironic if Bell had printed the copy of *Revolution of America* used by Paine to formulate his preface about the immorality of printers, as biographer John Keane asserts, it is probably not the case. Keane suggests that Paine read a version of Raynal's text printed by Bell "in Philadelphia in the autumn of 1781" (*Tom Paine*, 230). While Bell did eventually reprint the book twice in 1782, he did so only after Paine had already published his response in the form of *Letter to the Abbe Raynal*. The edition used by Paine must have been that printed by James Rivington, perhaps an even more notorious printer than Bell himself, in New York City in 1781.

82. Paine, *Complete Writings*, 2: 217.

83. Quoted in ibid., 2: 213.

84. Ibid., 2: 212.

85. Ibid., 2: 213.

86. Ibid., 2: 141.

87. Ibid., 2: 149.

88. Ibid., 2: 213.

89. Ibid., 1: 3.

90. Ibid., 1: 30.

91. Ibid., 1: 40.

92. Ibid., 1: 58.

93. Ibid., 1: 214.

94. Edward Larkin, *Thomas Paine and the Literature of Revolution* (New York: Cambridge Uni-versity Press, 2005), 50.

95. Ibid., 51.

96. Paine, *Complete Writings*, 1: 43.

97. In the late eighteenth century this affective approach to human conduct owed much to the Stoic moralism of the Third Earl of Shaftesbury, Anthony Ashley Cooper, as well as to Hutcheson and Smith. Charles Taylor provides an enlightening discussion of the range, sources, and connec-tions between ancient and modern moralists in *Sources of the Self: The Making of the Modern*

Identity (Cambridge: Harvard University Press, 1989), 249–65. See also John Dwyer, *Virtuous Discourse: Sensibility and Community in Late-Eighteenth-Century Scotland* (Edinburgh: J. Donald Publishers, 1987); Lawrence Klein, *Shaftesbury and the Culture of Politeness: Moral Discourse and Cultural Politics in Early Eighteenth-Century England* (Cambridge, UK: Cambridge University Press, 1994); and Eagleton, *Trouble with Strangers*, 12–82; On the application of moral thought to the Revolutionary period, see Wood, *Radicalism of the American Revolution*, 213–15; Greene, "The Concept of Virtue in Late Colonial British America"; and Fruchtman, *Tom Paine and the Religion of Nature.*

98. Paine, *Complete Writings*, 2: 213n70.

99. Thorvald Solberg, ed., *Copyright Enactments of the United States 1783–1906* (Washington, D.C.: Government Printing Office, 1906), 11.

CHAPTER 3

1. See Leon Jackson, "Jedidiah Morse and the Transformation of Print Culture in New England, 1784–1826," *Early American Literature* 34 (January 1999): 8.

2. John Lowell, *Review of Dr. Morse's "Appeal to the Publick"* (Boston: n.p., 1814), 28.

3. On Hannah Adams as a writer, see Michael Vella, "Theology, Genre, and Gender: The Precarious Place of Hannah Adams in American Literary History," *Early American Literature* 28 (January 1993): 21–41; and Gary D. Schmidt, *A Passionate Usefulness: The Life and Literary Labors of Hannah Adams* (Charlottesville: University Press of Virginia, 2004). Outside of Vella's and Schmidt's work, most studies treat Adams's authorship only in passing. See, for example, Frances Murphy Zauhar, "Creative Voices: Women Reading and Women's Writing," in *The Intimate Critique: Autobiographical Literary Criticism*, ed. Diane P. Freedman, Olivia Frey, and Frances Murphy Zauhar (Durham: Duke University Press, 1993), 103–16; and Mary Kelley, *Learning to Stand and Speak: Women, Education, and Public Life in America's Republic* (Chapel Hill: University of North Carolina Press, 2006), 114–16, 138–39, 191–93, 213–15. On gender and vocation in the period, see Elizabeth Anthony Dexter, *Career Women of America, 1776–1840* (Francestown, N.H.: Marshall Jones, 1950), especially 90–115; and Mary Kelley, ed., *Woman's Being, Woman's Place: Female Identity and Vocation in American History* (Boston: Hall, 1977). While she treats Adams only tangentially, Angela Vietto's *Women and Authorship in Revolutionary America* (Burlington, Vt.: Ashgate, 2005) is a cogent introduction to and useful recontextualization of women's authorship in the era.

4. Charles Brockden Brown, "*A Summary History of New England*," *Monthly Magazine, and American Review* 1 (September–December 1799): 446.

5. "Literary Notices," *Ladies Magazine* 5 (May 1832): 238.

6. Hannah Adams and Hannah F. S. Lee, *Memoir of Miss Hannah Adams, Written by Herself, with Additional Notices by a Friend* (Boston: Gray and Bowen, 1832), 33.

7. Fern, *Ruth Hall*, 173; Emily Dickinson, *The Poems of Emily Dickinson, Variorum Edition*, vol. 2., ed. R.W. Franklin (Cambridge: Belknap Press, 1998), 742.

8. "Literary Notices," 239.

9. "An Authoress," *Ladies Magazine* 2 (January 1829): 30.

10. "On the Female Character," *The Gleaner, or, The Monthly Magazine* 1 (January 1809): 210. On women's education in the era, see Kelley, *Learning to Stand and Speak*, 34–111.

11. "Thoughts on Women, by a Celebrated Writer," *Lady's Magazine and Repository of Entertaining Knowledge* 1 (August 1792): 111.

12. Maria Edgeworth, *Letters for Literary Ladies* (London: J. Johnson, 1795; reprint, New York: Garland, 1974), 7.

13. "An Authoress," 30–31.

14. "On the Female Character," 210.

15. Janet Wilson James, *Changing Ideas about Women in the United States, 1776–1825* (New York: Garland, 1981), 238.

16. Van Wyck Brooks, *The Flowering of New England, 1815–1865* (New York: E. P. Dutton, 1936), 121.

17. Ronald Story, "Class and Culture in Boston: The Athenaeum, 1807–1860," *American Quarterly* 27 (June 1975): 195.

18. "Miss Hannah Adams," *Ladies Magazine* 1 (July 1828): 312.

19. Nina Baym, "Between Enlightenment and Victorian: Toward a Narrative of American Women Writers Writing History," *Critical Inquiry* 18 (Autumn 1991): 26. On women historians, see Baym, *American Women Writers and the Work of History, 1790–1860* (New Brunswick: Rutgers University Press, 1995); and Kelley, *Learning to Stand and Speak,* 191–244.

20. "Miss Hannah Adams," 313. For a treatment of Adams's scholarship, particularly her religious historiography, see Thomas A. Tweed, "An American Pioneer in the Study of Religion: Hannah Adams (1755–1831) and Her 'Dictionary of All Religions,'" *Journal of the American Academy of Religion* 60 (September 1992): 437–64; and Tweed, "Introduction," *A Dictionary of All Religions and Religious Denominations* (Atlanta: Scholar's Press, 1992), vii–xxxiv. It is unfortunate, especially given her apparent influence, that little substantial work has been done on Adams's colonial history outside of her contexts as a religious historian because, as Baym notes, her "interpretation of the United States as the outgrowth of New England was to dominate school-room history for generations" (*American Women Writers,* 215). In fact, despite contrary moves, its approach still governs some of our constructions of colonial British North American and American history.

21. Brown, "*A Summary History of New England*," 446.

22. Ibid., 447.

23. Mary Kelley, *Private Woman, Public Stage: Literary Domesticity in Nineteenth-Century America* (New York: Oxford University Press, 1984), xi.

24. Adams and Lee, *Memoir of Miss Hannah Adams,* 13.

25. John Bidwell, "Printers' Supplies and Capitalization," in *Colonial Book in the Atlantic World,* 172.

26. Ibid., 169–71.

27. Adams and Lee, *Memoir of Miss Hannah Adams,* 15.

28. Benjamin Rush to [John Coakly Lettsom], April 16, 1790, in Rush, *Letters of Benjamin Rush,* 2 vols., ed. L. H. Butterfield (Princeton: Princeton University Press, 1951), 1: 549–50.

29. Quoted in Rollo G. Silver, *The American Printer, 1787–1825* (Charlottesville: University Press of Virginia, 1967), 100.

30. On subscription practices, see Remer, *Printers and Men of Capital,* 17–18, 46–48.

31. Rollo G. Silver, *The American Printer,* 103.

32. Adams and Lee, *Memoir of Miss Hannah Adams,* 20.

33. Benjamin Edes is best known as a staunchly partisan—that is, patriot—printer during the Revolution. See Rollo G. Silver, "Benjamin Edes, Trumpeter of Sedition," *Papers of the Bibliographical Society of America* 47 (1953): 248–68.

34. Hugh Gaine, "An Oration before the Booksellers Convened in New-York."

35. Adams and Lee, *Memoir of Miss Hannah Adams*, 16. Leon Jackson rightly suggests that we tend to overemphasize monetary payment for literary production and thus overstate both the importance of economic capital and the notion of authorial professionalization. For a thorough corrective, see *The Business of Letters*, especially 9–52. I stress the economic argument here because it was of principal concern to Adams.

36. Ibid., 34.

37. Ibid., 33–34.

38. Ibid., 15.

39. Tebbel, *History of Book Publishing in the United States*, 1: 135.

40. Adams and Lee, *Memoir of Miss Hannah Adams*, 13.

41. Ibid., 20.

42. Baym, "Between Enlightenment and Victorian," 37.

43. Mathew Carey, "Address to the Printers and Booksellers throughout the United States" (Philadelphia: Mathew Carey, 1801), n.p.

44. Michael T. Gilmore, "The Literature of the Revolutionary and Early National Periods," in *The Cambridge History of American Literature, Vol. 1: 1590–1820*, ed. Sacvan Bercovitch, 539–694 (New York: Cambridge University Press, 1994), 546.

45. Linda K. Kerber and others have argued that the transmission of republican values relied on an accommodation of women's domestic roles. Republicanism, in these terms, could be taught by what Kerber calls the "republican mother," who "guaranteed the steady infusion of virtue into the Republic." Kerber, *Women of the Republic: Intellect and Ideology in Revolutionary America* (Chapel Hill: University of North Carolina Press, 1980), 11. See also Mary Beth Norton, *Liberty's Daughters: The Revolutionary Experience of American Women, 1750–1800* (Boston: Little, Brown, 1980); Baym, "Women and the Republic: Emma Willard's Rhetoric of History," in *Feminism and American Literary History: Essays* (New Brunswick: Rutgers University Press, 1992), 121–35; Baym, "Between Enlightenment and Victorian," 23–41; and Mary Kelley, "Designing a Past for the Present: Women Writing Women's History in Nineteenth-Century America," *Proceedings of the American Antiquarian Society* 105 (October 1995): 315–46.

46. Baym, "Between Enlightenment and Victorian," 24.

47. Kelley, "Designing a Past for the Present," 323.

48. Mercy Otis Warren, *History of the Rise, Progress and Termination of the American Revolution, Vol. 1* (Boston: Manning and Loring, 1805), iv.

49. "An Authoress.—No. II," *Ladies Magazine* 2 (March 1829): 131.

50. Norton, *Liberty's Daughters*, 298.

51. Adams and Lee, *Memoir of Miss Hannah Adams*, 22.

52. Hannah Adams, *An Abridgement of the History of New-England for the Use of Young Persons* (Boston: A. Newell, 1805), iv.

53. Kelley, "Designing a Past for the Present," 319.

54. Baym, *American Women Writers and the Work of History*, 215.

55. Adams and Lee, *Memoir of Miss Hannah Adams*, 34.

56. Kelley, "Designing a Past for the Present," 319.

57. On the "impersonality" of republican discourse, see Warner, *Letters of the Republic*, 36–39.

58. Thomas Prentiss (1747–1814) was a Congregationalist minister and physician in Adams's hometown of Medfield. Although not liberal by Unitarian standards, Prentiss evidently respected

various doctrines of faith, thereby making him a fitting champion of Adams's study of religious diversity. More to the point, Prentiss began and maintained one of the best libraries in Massachusetts, the Medfield library. His respect for scholarship and the scholarly endeavor would make Adams attractive to him, and he suggests in his note to her book that scholarship should not be gendered. See Clifford K. Shipton, *Sibley's Harvard Graduates*, vol. 16 (Boston: Massachusetts Historical Society, 1972), 415–18.

59. Thomas Prentiss, "To the Readers," in *An Alphabetical Compendium of the Various Sects* by Hannah Adams, i–ii (Boston: B. Edes and Sons, 1784). i.

60. Ibid., ii.

61. James, *Changing Ideas about Women in the United States*, 238.

62. Prentiss, "To the Readers," i.

63. Baym, "Women and the Republic," 2.

64. Hannah Adams, *A History of the Jews from the Destruction of Jerusalem to the Nineteenth Century* (Boston: John Eliot, 1812), iii.

65. Stephen Higginson (1743–1828), grandfather of Thomas Wentworth Higginson, was a merchant member of the Continental Congress and a Federalist advisor (unofficially) both to government and to his party. See James T. Adams, "Higginson, Stephen," in *Dictionary of American Biography*, 22 vols. (New York: Scribners, 1928–58), 5: 15–16. William Smith Shaw (1778–1826) was a lawyer and was best known as President John Adams's private secretary and as the librarian of the Boston Athenaeum from 1807 to 1822. He also helped oversee *The Monthly Anthology*. He was an ardent supporter of Adams in more respects than just this controversy, helping raise an annuity for her in her later life, giving her access to the Athenaeum and other libraries, and introducing her to learned friends. Charles K. Bolton, "Shaw, William Smith," in *Dictionary of American Biography*, 9: 49.

66. The breadth of religious, legal, institutional, literary, and personal implications complicated this dispute. As Lawrence Buell suggests, at stake were competing visions of New England religion and religious history—the liberal Unitarian factions versus Morse's conservative Congregationalists—which were then implicated in the Unitarian assumption of power at Harvard in the first decades of the nineteenth century. See Buell, *New England Literary Culture: From Revolution through Renaissance* (New York: Cambridge University Press, 1986), 214–38; and Richard J. Moss, *The Life of Jedidiah Morse: A Station of Peculiar Exposure* (Knoxville: University of Tennessee Press, 1995), 84–86, 103–4, 106–12. See also James, *Changing Ideas about Women in the United States*, 250–54; and Schmidt, *A Passionate Usefulness*, 154–64, 188–95, 207–22, 255–75.

67. Jedidiah Morse, *An Appeal to the Publick, on the Controversy Respecting the Revolution in Harvard College and the Events Which Followed It* (Charlestown: Morse, 1814), 14.

68. Hannah Adams, *A Narrative of the Controversy between the Rev. Jedidiah Morse, D.D. and the Author* (Boston: John Eliot, 1814), 93.

69. Morse, *Appeal to the Publick*, 14.

70. Vella, "Theology, Genre, and Gender," 88–89.

71. Morse, *Appeal to the Publick*, 93.

72. Ibid., 6.

73. James, *Changing Ideas about Women in the United States*, 251.

74. See also Vella's discussion of the "fundamental ambiguity . . . between a self-determined woman capable of shrewd adaptive behavior, and one whose self-expression is solicited and shaped by male patronage" (33).

75. Morse, *Appeal to the Publick*, 30.

76. Vella, "Theology, Genre, and Gender," 32.

77. Moss, *The Life of Jedidiah Morse*, 104.

78. Adams, *Narrative of the Controversy*, 8–9.

79. Ibid., 9.

80. Adams and Lee, *Memoir of Miss Hannah Adams*, 13, 14–15.

81. This relegation of gender to a rhetorical construct does not undermine contemporary critical readings, such as this one, that see Adams as a pioneer for her sex. Rather, this reading speaks even more confidently to her pursuit of an authorial self at once gendered but hopeful of existing outside of gender as well.

82. Morse, *Appeal to the Publick*, 85.

83. Quoted in ibid., 104.

84. Meredith L. McGill, "The Matter of the Text: Commerce, Print Culture, and the Authority of the State in American Copyright Law," *American Literary History* 9 (Spring 1997): 42. See also McGill, *American Literature and the Culture of Reprinting*, 45–75.

85. James, *Changing Ideas about Women in the United States*, 250.

86. See John D. Gordan III, "*Morse v. Reid*: The First Reported Federal Copyright Case," *Law and History Review* 11 (Spring 1993): 21–41.

87. Ibid., 33.

CHAPTER 4

1. "North-American Book-Men," *Punch* 12.306 (1847): 209.

2. B. Zorina Khan, *The Democratization of Invention: Patents and Copyrights in American Economic Development, 1790–1920* (New York: Cambridge University Press, 2005), 260.

3. "English Authors—American Booksellers," *Punch* 12.308 (1847): 235.

4. Steven Mintz, *Moralists and Modernizers: America's Pre-Civil War Reformers* (Baltimore: Johns Hopkins University Press, 1995), xiii.

5. Cornelius Mathews, "An Appeal to American Authors and the American Press in Behalf of International Copyright," *Graham's Magazine* 21 (September 1842): 121.

6. Greenspan, *George Palmer Putnam*, 89.

7. Quoted in Louis Ginsberg, *A. Hart, Philadelphia Publisher*, 25.

8. Andrew J. Eaton, "The American Movement for International Copyright, 1837–1860," *Library Quarterly* 15 (April 1945): 104; Rice, *Transformation of Authorship in America*, 91.

9. On the normalizing function of modern copyright discourse, see Laura J. Murray, "Copyright Talk: Patterns and Pitfalls in Canadian Policy Discourse," in *In the Public Interest: The Future of Canadian Copyright Law*, ed. Michael Geist, 15–40 (Toronto: Irwin Law, 2005).

10. On moral economy, see Thompson, *Customs in Common*, 185–351.

11. Dickens, *American Notes*, 270.

12. "Literary Property," *American Jurist and Law Magazine* 1 (January 1829): 157. Because this chapter makes use of a number of identical titles, including "International Copyright," "International Copy-Right," "International Copyright Law," "International Copy-Right Law," and "Literary Property," nonconsecutive notes for these titles give full bibliographical detail.

13. Quoted in Rose, *Authors and Owners*, 45.

14. Saunders, *Authorship and Copyright*, 10.

15. The literature on English copyright is extensive. In addition to sources cited elsewhere in this chapter, see Benjamin Kaplan, *An Unhurried View of Copyright* (New York: Columbia University

Press, 1967); John Feather, *Publishing, Piracy, and Politics: An Historical Study of Copyright in Britain* (London: Mansell, 1994); Saint-Amour, *Copywrights*; and Catherine Seville, *The Internationalisation of Copyright Law: Books, Buccaneers, and the Black Flag in the Nineteenth Century* (New York: Cambridge University Press, 2006). For a wide-ranging history of intellectual property, see Carla Hesse, "The Rise of Intellectual Property, 700 BC to AD 2000," in David Vaver, ed., *Intellectual Property Rights: Critical Concepts in Law*, vol. 1, 3 vols. (London: Routledge, 2006), 51–71.

16. Richard Rogers Bowker, *Copyright: Its History and Its Law* (Boston: Houghton Mifflin, 1912), 7. Bowker's use of "privilege" suggests the way in which *Donaldson v. Beckett* negatively affected what he deemed an indisputable, perpetual right; it is not a reference to the system of royal privileges—which legally embodied such a right—eliminated by French and German copyright law in the late eighteenth and early nineteenth centuries. On the privilege system in France, see Carla Hesse, *Publishing and Cultural Politics in Revolutionary Paris, 1789–1810* (Berkeley: University of California Press, 1991), 83–124. *Donaldson v. Beckett* has been the subject of a great deal of commentary. See Mark Rose, "The Author as Proprietor: Donaldson v. Beckett and the Genealogy of Modern Authorship," *Representations* 23 (Summer 1988): 51–85; Trevor Ross, "Copyright and the Invention of Tradition," *Eighteenth-Century Studies* 26 (Fall 1992): 1–27; William St. Clair, *The Reading Nation in the Romantic Period* (Cambridge: Cambridge University Press, 2004), especially 103–21; and Johns, *Piracy*, 109–43. Counter to Rose and St. Clair, Sher cautions against reading *Donaldson v. Beckett* as "the chief turning point in the history of eighteenth-century copyright." *The Enlightenment and the Book*, 27. See especially 27–30.

17. FB, "Copyright," *Maine Monthly Magazine* 1 (February 1837): 360.

18. Connecticut's constitution (1783) was the first to make use of such language, finding it "perfectly agreeable to the principles of natural equity and justice" that profits "should be secured" for writers. Solberg, *Copyright Enactments of the United States 1783–1906*, 11. Other states were equally explicit. Massachusetts declared that "such security is one of the natural rights of all men, there being no property more peculiarly a man's own than that which is produced by the labour of his mind" (14). This pronouncement, and especially its attendant redefinition of property along Lockean lines, was heady, but not so much that New Hampshire and Rhode Island felt uncomfortable following suit. North Carolina and Georgia went even further, actually opening their copyright clauses with this assertion of an author's natural right to intellectual property.

19. Solberg, *Copyright Enactments of the United States 1783–1906*, 31.

20. *Report on the Copy-Right Case of Wheaton v. Peters* (New York: James Van Norden, 1834), 103.

21. On the development of and reactions to American copyright law in the mid-nineteenth century, see Eaton, "The American Movement for International Copyright, 1837–1860"; Frank Friedel, "Lieber's Contribution to the International Copyright Movement," *Huntington Library Quarterly* 8 (December 1945): 200–206; Barnes, *Authors, Publishers and Politicians*; Siva Vaidhyanathan, *Copyrights and Copywrongs: The Rise of Intellectual Property and How It Threatens Creativity* (New York: New York University Press, 2003), 35–55; McGill, *American Literature and the Culture of Reprinting*; Martin Buinicki, *Negotiating Copyright: Authorship and the Discourse of Literary Property Rights in Nineteenth-Century America* (New York: Routledge, 2006); Homestead, *American Women Authors and Literary Property*; and Seville, *Internationalisation of Copyright Law*, 146–252. Claudia Stokes's "Copyrighting American History: International Copyright and the Periodization of the Nineteenth Century," *American Literature* 77 (June 2005): 291–317 is a nuanced appraisal of the rhetoric and motives of late nineteenth-century copyright reformers.

22. [Willard Phillips], "Art. VI—Remarks on Literary Property," *North American Review* 48 (January 1839): 260.

23. Ibid., 259.

24. "International Copyright," *Southern Quarterly Review* 4 (July 1843): 22.

25. [William Scott], "Rights of Authors," *Southern Literary Messenger* 3 (January 1837): 39. Perhaps opponents were on to something when they accused reformers of doing the bidding of the English: this modernization of the Declaration was an Englishman's handiwork. My thanks to Leon Jackson for identifying the author.

26. Khan, *Democratization of Invention*, 17.

27. Ibid., 234. Jane C. Ginsburg contends that evidence from debates in the drafting of the Constitutional provision for copyright suggest that framers weighed moral rights as much as the public interest. See Ginsburg, "A Tale of Two Copyrights: Literary Property in Revolutionary France and America," in *Of Authors and Origins: Essays on Copyright Law*, ed. Brad Sherman and Alain Strowel, 131–58 (Oxford: Clarendon Press, 1991).

28. "Literary Property," *American Jurist and Law Magazine* 1 (January 1829): 157.

29. Folsom v. Marsh, 9 F.Cas. 342 (C.C.D. Mass. 1841).

30. On Joseph Story's inconsistent statements on patent law, see Frank D. Prager, "The Changing Views of Justice Story on the Legal Construction of Patents," *Journal of American Legal History* 4 (January 1960): 1–21.

31. Edmund Burke, *Reflections on the Revolution in France* (New Haven: Yale University Press, 2003), 51.

32. David Hume, *An Enquiry Concerning the Principles of Morals* (Indianapolis: Hackett, 1983), 20.

33. Jeremy Bentham, *A Comment on the Commentaries and a Fragment on Government*, ed. J. H. Burns and H. A. L. Bart (London: Athlone Press, 1977), 17.

34. Ibid., 28.

35. On the use of natural law discourse, see Benjamin Fletcher Wright, *American Interpretations of Natural Law: A Study in the History of Political Thought* (New York: Russell and Russell, 1962). Invariably nineteenth-century definitions of natural law were redactions of William Blackstone's *Commentaries on the Laws of England* (1765–69): the "eternal, immutable laws of good and evil" extant "in the nature of things antecedent to" civilization or written its written law. These "ethics," as Blackstone called natural law, rely on the god-given right of the individual to seek "true and substantial happiness" in life, a right respected and enforced "immemorially" by common law, the "ancient collection of unwritten maxims and customs" so fundamental to English and, some would argue, American law. Blackstone, *Commentaries on the Laws of England*, vol. 1, 16th ed. (London: A. Strahan, 1825), 39.

36. [John L. O'Sullivan], "The International Copyright Question," 121.

37. Harper and Brothers to E. D. Morgan, February 27, 1868, Misc American Harper, folder Harper and Brothers, firm, publishers, New York.

38. See, for instance, Robert E. Goodin, *Protecting the Vulnerable: A Reanalysis of Our Social Responsibilities* (Chicago: University of Chicago Press, 1985), 52.

39. "International Law of Copy-Right," *Southern Literary Messenger* 5 (October 1839): 663.

40. Henry David Thoreau, "Civil Disobedience," in *Walden and Civil Disobedience*, ed. Owen Thomas, 224–43 (New York: Norton, 1966), 225.

41. George Ticknor Curtis, *A Treatise on the Law of Copyright* (Boston: Charles C. Little and James Brown, 1847), 2.

42. "International Copyright," *Southern Quarterly Review* 4 (July 1843): 29–30. On natural law as remedy for statutory law, see Wright, *American Interpretations of Natural Law,* 331; and Leo Strauss, *Natural Right and History* (Chicago: University of Chicago Press, 1953), 2. Literary historians are right to note that, in Susan Eilenberg's words, the "argument from common law … was based upon a falsehood, or, at least, upon a confusion." Eilenberg, *Strange Power of Speech: Wordsworth, Coleridge, and Literary Possession* (New York: Oxford University Press, 1992), 202. Such a "fabulous" (203) idea—the supposed legal golden age of author's rights that was in fact a fabrication of booksellers—does not mean, however, that the natural law argument in either domestic or international copyright reform was not compelling. Nor does it mean that it was irrelevant.

43. Cornelius Mathews, "A Survey of the International Copyright Question," *Literary World,* May 8, 1852, 328.

44. Cornelius Mathews, "The Loiterer. Mr. Mathews's Speech on International Copyright," *Arcturus* 3 (March 1842): 312.

45. William Glyde Wilkins, ed., *Charles Dickens in America* (New York: Haskell House, 1970), 241–42.

46. Mathews, "The Loiterer," 314.

47. For a contemporary example of this discourse, see Peter Drahos, "Intellectual Property and Human Rights," *Intellectual Property Quarterly* 3 (1999): 349–71.

48. Mathews, "Appeal," 121.

49. American Copyright Club, *An Address to the People of the United States in Behalf of the American Copyright Club* (New York: The Club, 1843), 17–18, 18.

50. J[oseph] R[eed] Ingersoll to Francis Lieber, December 27, 1843, Papers of Francis Lieber, LI 2433.

51. James Russell Lowell to Charles Briggs, March 6, 1844, James Russell Lowell Papers, folder 6. It is difficult to tell whether Lowell knew that Briggs *was* the author of the pamphlet he was praising. Given his penchant for inside jokes, he likely did.

52. Thomas Adamson [Charles Briggs], *A Reply to "Considerations and Arguments, Proving the Inexpediency of an International Copyright Law, by John Campbell"* (New York: Bartlett and Welford, 1844), 4. Briggs's admission of his authorship is in his August 6, 1848 letter to Rufus Griswold in Griswold, *Passages from the Correspondence and Other Papers of Rufus W. Griswold,* ed. William Griswold, 240–42 (Cambridge: W. M. Griswold, 1898), 241.

53. As Melissa Homestead and George Goodspeed note, most commentators assume that Bryant was the primary author based on his top billing on the title page. Given how uncharacteristic the prose style of the *Address* would be for Bryant, however, Mathews is a more likely candidate. See Goodspeed, "The Home Library," *Papers of the Bibliographical Society of America* (1948): 112; Bryant, *The Letters of William Cullen Bryant, Vol. II: 1836–1849,* ed. William Cullen Bryant II and Thomas G. Voss (New York: Fordham University Press, 1977), 247; and Homestead, *American Women Authors and Literary Property,* 76n28.

54. Dickens to various recipients, July 7, 1842; Charles Briggs to Rufus Griswold, August 6, 1848, in Griswold, *Passages,* 242.

55. Miller, *Raven and the Whale,* 80. Miller's account of mid-nineteenth-century New York literary culture is indispensable, though it reads too many of Mathews's critics uncritically. As George E. Mize observes, Mathews had "distinguished enemies." Mize, "The Contributions of Evert A. Duyckinck to the Cultural Development of Nineteenth Century America," PhD thesis, New York University, 1954, 22. For a more even-handed evaluation of Mathews's relations with

his fellow literati, see Eaton, "The American Movement for International Copyright"; and Barnes, *Authors, Publishers and Politicians.*

56. James Russell Lowell to Charles Briggs, August 8, 1845, James Russell Lowell Papers, folder 7.

57. "International Copyright," *Southern Quarterly Review* 4 (July 1843): 42, 39.

58. Ibid., 38, 39.

59. Cornelius Mathews, "The Loiterer. Mr. Mathews's Speech on International Copyright," *Arcturus* 3 (March 1842): 315.

60. "Mr. C. Mathews on International Copyright," *New World*, February 26, 1842, 142.

61. Washington Irving to George Palmer Putnam, December 27, 1852, George Palmer Putnam Collection, box 2, folder 42.

62. "International Copyright," *Southern Quarterly Review* 4 (July 1843): 1, 2.

63. Thomas Gray, "The Progress of Poesy," in H. W. Starr and J. R. Hendrickson, eds., *The Complete Poems of Thomas Gray: English, Latin and Greek*, 12–17 (Oxford: Clarendon Press, 1966), 16.

64. "Ladies' Anti-slavery Convention," *Philanthropist*, June 15, 1837, 1.

65. See, for example, "J. G. Whittier," *Liberator*, December 24, 1836, 207; and "Meeting in Marlboro Chapel," *Liberator*, March 15, 1839, 43.

66. Louis S. Gerteis, *Morality and Utility in American Slavery Reform* (Chapel Hill: University of North Carolina Press, 1987), 18–19.

67. Cornelius Mathews to Robert Carter, July 16, 1842, Ch.B.6.13, Boston Public Library; "let our motto" quoted in Susan M. Ryan, *The Grammar of Good Intentions: Race and the Antebellum Culture of Benevolence* (Ithaca: Cornell University Press, 2003), 167.

68. George Palmer Putnam to Charles Sumner, May 22, 1856, Papers of Charles Sumner, Ms Am 1, microfilm reel 13, Houghton Library, Harvard University.

69. George Palmer Putnam to Charles Sumner, August 31, 1855, ibid., reel 12; George Palmer Putnam to Charles Sumner, September 20, 1855, ibid., reel 12 (brackets in original). Sumner did not attend the dinner, but his regrets would have delighted Putnam: "the whole scene, where differing Authors commingle under auspices of differing Publishers, will be an augury of that permanent cooperation and harmony which will secure to the pen its mightiest triumphs." Charles Sumner to George Palmer Putnam, September 26, 1855, ibid., reel 71.

70. Cornelius Mathews, "A Survey of the International Copyright Question," *Literary World*, May 8, 1852, 328.

71. [John L. O'Sullivan], "The International Copyright Question," *United States Magazine and Democratic Review* 12 (February 1843): 115.

72. Ibid., 116.

73. Ibid., 115.

74. Cornelius Mathews, "A Survey of the International Copyright Question," *Literary World*, April 24, 1852, 294.

75. "Literary Property," *American Jurist* 1 (January 1829): 157–58.

76. Folsom v. Marsh.

77. Horace Greeley, *Recollections of a Busy Life*, 436.

78. Ibid., 295.

79. "International Copyright," *Southern Quarterly Review* 4 (July 1843): 37, 39.

80. Lewis Gaylord Clark, "Editor's Table," *Knickerbocker* 22 (October 1843): 388. Clark quoted the passage from *Dublin University Magazine*, claiming it "embodies the opinion generally entertained of [Mathews's] efforts on this side of the Atlantic."

81. Hugh Blair, *Lectures on Rhetoric and Belles Lettres*, 13th American ed. (New York: James and John Harper, 1824), 145.

82. "International Copyright," *American Publishers' Circular*, January 24, 1857, 49; William Gilmore Simms to Edwin DeLeon, July 8, 1844, in Simms, *Letters*, 1: 423. Simms's views on copyright are summarized by Michael O'Brien in *Conjectures of Order: Intellectual Life and the American South, 1810–1860*, vol. 1 (Chapel Hill: University of North Carolina Press, 2004), 564–71. For an account of the function of metaphor in current copyright debates, see William Patry, *Moral Panics and the Copyright Wars* (New York: Oxford University Press, 2009).

83. Francis Lieber, "The Character of a Gentleman," 46.

84. John Smith [Cornelius Mathews], "John Smith, a Convicted Felon, upon the Copyright," *Arcturus* 3 (April 1842): 370.

85. Fulgura Frango [Charles Briggs], "International Copy-Right," *Knickerbocker* 22 (October 1843): 361.

86. HC, "Copyright Law. No. 3. To the Readers of the United States," *American Monthly Review* 10 (October 1837): 374.

87. "International Copyright," *New-York Mirror*, December 30, 1837, 215.

88. [Phillips], "Art. VI—Remarks on Literary Property," 266.

89. An American Writer, "A Letter to the Proprietors of Harpers Magazine," *American Whig Review* 16 (July 1852): 16, 15. On the media hysteria over Algerian pirates, see Lawrence A. Peskin, "The Lessons of Independence: How the Algerian Crisis Shaped Early American Identity," *Diplomatic History* 28 (June 2004): 298–301.

90. For observations on the technical uses of "piracy" and "pirate" see Raymond H. Shove, *Cheap Book Production in the United States, 1870 to 1891* (Urbana: University of Illinois Press, 1937), viin7; John Feather, "The English Book Trade and the Law, 1695–1799," *Publishing History* 12 (1982): 64; John Feather, ed., *A Dictionary of Book History* (New York: Oxford University Press, 1987), 207; and Sheila McVey, "Nineteenth Century America: Publishing in a Developing Country," in *Perspectives on Publishing*, ed. Philip G. Altbach and Sheila McVey, 187–229 (Lexington, Mass.: D.C. Heath, 1976), 191.

91. G. M. Warton, "On International Copyright," *North American Review* 52 (April 1841): 385.

92. On framing and stereotyping as creative acts, see Walter Lippman, *Public Opinion* (New York: Free Press, 1949), 73.

93. Johns, *Nature of the Book*, 32. Johns notes that piracy "capture[s] something of the sheer sense of outrage displayed by the aggrieved," who designated reprinting piracy regardless of strict legal inaccuracies (xx). The term was used originally "to describe the rapacious practices of London printers and booksellers. . . . But it soon came to stand for a wide range of perceived transgressions of civility emanating from print's practitioners" (32). See also Johns, *Piracy*, 1–15.

94. [Evert Duyckinck], "The Morality of Publishers," 29.

95. "International Copyright," *American Publishers' Circular*, January 24, 1857, 49.

96. Henry Holt, "The Recoil of Piracy," *Forum* 5 (March 1888): 27.

97. Simms to DeLeon, July 8, 1844.

98. Philip Nicklin, *Remarks on Literary Property* (Philadelphia: P. H. Nicklin and T. Johnson, 1838), 19.

99. "International Law of Copy-Right," *Southern Literary Messenger* 10 (October 1839): 663.

100. Mathews, "An Appeal," 122.

101. "International Copyright," *New-York Mirror*, December 30, 1837, 215.

102. "Copyright Law. No. II," *American Monthly Review* 9 (March 1837): 284.

103. "Mr. Midshipman Easy, by the Author of 'Peter Simple,' &c. Boston. Marsh, Capen & Lyon," *American Monthly Magazine* 9 (January 1837): 81.

104. William Ellery Channing, "Slavery," in *Works of William E. Channing*, 2: 7. On the moral countenance of American abolitionism, see Gerteis, *Morality and Utility in American Antislavery Reform*, 3–85. Homestead observes that the author-slave analogy was more prevalent after the Civil War; see *American Women Authors and Literary Property*, 49–52 and 144–49.

105. William Gilmore Simms, *The Morals of Slavery*, in *The Pro-Slavery Argument*, 175–285 (Charleston: Walker, Richards, 1852; reprint, New York: Negro University Press, 1968), 251, 253, 259–61.

106. Incongruities like these may have mattered little in the long run. Natural law arguments proved increasingly ineffective as the nineteenth century wore on, in part because of the kinds of contradictions inherent in and illustrated by the advocacy of people like Simms. The courts struggled to accommodate an unwritten natural law ostensibly endorsing the fundamental human rights of racial others with statute, a problem that ultimately contributed to the eventual diminution of natural law as a valid category in nineteenth-century American jurisprudence. When such cases pitted the unwritten rights of blacks or other racial minorities against custom or positive law, the once-vaunted, seemingly impervious natural law argument was conveniently found less compelling. On the diminished influence of natural law arguments in the period, see G. Edward White, *The Marshall Court and Cultural Change, 1815–35*, vol. 3–4, *History of the Supreme Court of the United States* (New York: Macmillan, 1988), 674–740.

107. S[amuel] E[lliott] Morse, "American Authors and English Publishers," *New York Observer and Chronicle*, July 17, 1847, 114. Morse notes that his letter to the London *Times*, reproduced here, had yet to be printed in England.

108. Nicklin, *Remarks on Literary Property*, 16.

109. Ibid., 13–14.

110. See, for example, "Crosby & Nichols. Reminiscences of an Old Bookselling Firm," *Boston Daily Advertiser*, June 21, 1894, 4.

111. See Craig Calhoun's description of Hegel's idea of public opinion as "dispersed among people in the form of prejudices, not true knowledge." Calhoun, "Introduction: Habermas and the Public Sphere," in Calhoun, ed., *Habermas and the Public Sphere*, 1–50 (Cambridge: MIT Press, 1993), 19.

112. "International Copyright," *Southern Quarterly Review* 4 (July 1843): 1.

113. Evert Duyckinck to George Palmer Putnam, December 1, 1843, Duyckinck Family Papers, box 18, folder Letters, 1843.

114. "The International Copy-Right Law," *Brother Jonathan*, May 14, 1842, 74.

115. George Palmer Putnam, *American Facts* (London: Wiley and Putnam, 1845), 84n.

116. Augustin-Charles Renouard, *Traité des Droits d'Auteurs, dans la Litterature, les Sciences, et les Beaux-Arts* (Paris: J. Renouard, 1838–39); partial translation and reprint, "Theory of the Rights of Authors," *American Jurist and Law Magazine* 22 (October 1839): 39–93. The *American Jurist* translation was subsequently issued as a stand-alone volume: *Theory of the Rights of Authors in Literature, Sciences, and in Fine Arts* (Boston: Charles C. Little and James Brown, 1839).

117. Carey's theory of literary property seemed to differ in practice. He was adamantly opposed to international copyright throughout his life. Yet in an 1835 dispute with a fellow publisher whom Carey charged with stealing sheets destined for him, Carey implied the existence of moral rights belonging to authors and publishers: "*until published it* [the packet of sheets] *was sacred as a letter under seal*, being the exclusive property of the authoress or ourselves & its appropriation by any

other person no more defensible than the appropriation of any other species of property—[.]" Carey, Lea, and Blanchard to L. M. Walter, January 14, 1835, Lea and Febiger Records, Letterbook, Carey, Lea, and Blanchard, June 17, 1834, to September 2, 1835, pp. 230–31.

118. Renouard, "Theory of the Rights of Authors," 46.

119. Ibid., 80.

120. Ibid., 46.

121. Ibid., 63.

122. Francis Lieber, *On International Copyright: In a Letter to the Hon. William C. Preston* (New York: Wiley and Putnam, 1840).

123. William Campbell Preston to Francis Lieber, April 30, [18]40, Papers of Francis Lieber.

124. [O'Sullivan], "International Copyright Question," 115.

125. "Editorial Remarks," *Southern Literary Messenger* 10 (1844): 388.

126. A sharp application of Lockean labor theory to the debate is Rice, *Transformation of Authorship*, 70–96. For a redaction of both Lockean and Hegelian property theory, see Justin Hughes, "The Philosophy of Intellectual Property," *Georgetown Law Journal* 77 (December 1988): 288–366, especially 297–300 and 330–39.

127. Orville Dewey to Cornelius Mathews, September 25, 1843, Autograph File, D, Houghton Library, Harvard University.

128. William Giles Dix to Henry Wadsworth Longfellow, Letters to Henry Wadsworth Longfellow, MS Am 1340.2, folder 1609, Houghton Library, Harvard University.

129. John Esten Cooke to Rufus Griswold, April 24, 1851, Merrill Griswold Collection, Ms.Gris., folder 206, Boston Public Library. Cooke was referring to "A Kingdom Mortgaged," which appeared in 1855 in the *Southern Literary Messenger*.

130. John Esten Cooke to George Palmer Putnam, January 27, 1853, George Palmer Putnam Collection, box 4, folder 55, discussing *Leather Stocking and Silk* (New York: Harper and Brothers, 1854). The nonrequest for a puff is in John Esten Cooke to Evert Duyckinck, December 10, 1853, Duyckinck Family Papers, box 4, folder Cooke, John Esten.

131. John Esten Cooke to Evert Duyckinck, October 2, 1854, Duyckinck Family Papers, box 4, folder Cooke, John Esten.

132. Grace Greenwood to James T. Fields, April 10, 1849, James Thomas Fields Papers, box 40, FI 1770. On Greenwood's copyright parodies, see Homestead, *American Women Authors and Literary Property*, 1–11. See also Lesley Ginsberg, "The Making of Grace Greenwood: James T. Fields, Antebellum Authorship, and the Woman Writer," in Mary de Jong and Earl Yarington, eds., *Popular Nineteenth-Century American Writers and the Literary Marketplace*, 189–214 (Newcastle upon Thames: Cambridge Scholars Press, 2007).

133. Ticknor and Fields to Charles Eliot Norton, July 6, 1865, Charles Eliot Norton Papers, Ms Am 1088, folder 7373, Houghton Library, Harvard University.

134. Sampson Low, Son and Marston to Louisa May Alcott, May 21, 1870, Louisa May Alcott Papers, Ms Am 800.23, folder 167, Houghton Library, Harvard University, regarding Alcott, *An Old-Fashioned Girl* (Boston: Roberts Brothers, 1870; London: Sampson Low, 1870), used by permission.

135. Low's threat is noted in William J. Niles to Louisa May Alcott, July 6, 1871, ibid., folder 126.

136. Niles's reminders to Alcott about the need to publish her work first in a British territory are in William J. Niles to Louisa May Alcott, September 30, 1870, ibid., and July 17, 1871, ibid.

137. Carey and Hart to Henry Wadsworth Longfellow, February 10, 1846, Henry Wadsworth Longfellow Papers, folder 968, used by permission.

138. Richard Grant White to Alfred Pell, May 7, 1868, Richard Grant White Papers, New York Historical Society.

139. James Kirke Paulding to James Grant Wilson, September 1855, in *Letters of James Kirke Paulding*, 584.

140. Ibid., 585.

141. *"American Notes for General Circulation," Edinburgh Quarterly Review*, reprint in *Campbell's Foreign Monthly Magazine* 2 (January–April 1843): 319.

142. McGill, *American Literature and the Culture of Reprinting*, 82.

143. Khan, *Democratization of Invention*, 224–25.

144. John Lauritz Larson, *Internal Improvement: National Public Works and the Promise of Popular Government in the Early United States* (Chapel Hill: University of North Carolina Press, 2001), 6, 150.

145. "International Copyright," *Cincinnati Weekly Herald and Philanthropist*, January 20, 1844, 2.

146. Franck Taylor to McCarty and Davis, December 20, 1837, McCarty and Davis Business Records, box 3, folder 455, ts, American Antiquarian Society, used by permission.

147. Harper and Brothers to Morgan, February 27, 1868. Such claims are given further credence when we recall that the majority of publishing was geared toward lawyers, doctors, and educators. See Jack Larkin, "The Merriams of Brookfield: Printing in the Economy and Culture of Rural Massachusetts in the Early Nineteenth Century," *Proceedings of the American Antiquarian Society* 96 (April 1986): 39–73.

148. "International Copyright," *Putnam's Monthly Magazine* 9 (January 1857): 85.

149. "Copyright, Tariff, &c.," *Brother Jonathan*, February 19, 1842, 212.

150. American Writer, "A Letter to the Proprietors of Harpers Magazine," 13.

151. McGill, *American Literature and the Culture of Reprinting*, 92.

152. H[enry] C. Carey, *Letters on International Copyright* (Philadelphia: A. Hart, 1853), 44.

153. Rice, *Transformation of Authorship in America*, 77.

154. Arnold Plant, "The Economic Aspects of Copyright in Books," *Economica*, new series 1 (May 1934): 168.

155. McGill, *American Literature and the Culture of Reprinting*, 78.

156. I am more comfortable with Homestead's reading of the author-advocate: "[They] found themselves contending with conflicting and contradictory discourses of authorship: their arguments in favor of the expansion of copyright demonstrate that they knew the limits of their position under the American law, but they also gestured toward the more expansive symbolic powers and the legal proprietary rights for authors potentially underwritten by the Romantic ideology of authorship." Homestead, *American Women Authors and Literary Property*, 114.

157. "[At a meeting of the Book-Publishers' Association]," *American Publishers' Circular*, January 17, 1857, 33.

158. "International Copyright," *American Publishers' Circular*, January 24, 1857, 49.

159. Ibid., 50.

160. McGill, *American Literature and the Culture of Reprinting*, 202.

161. Nathan Hale to Evert Duyckinck, August 29, 1842, Duyckinck Family Papers, box 7, folder Hale, Nathan.

162. George Henry Moore to Evert Duyckinck, December 18, 1843, Duyckinck Family Papers, box 7, folder Moore, George Henry.

163. Edgar Allan Poe, "Marginalia," in *The Complete Works of Edgar Allan Poe*, ed. James A. Harrison, 17 vols. (New York: T. Y. Crowell, 1902; reprint, New York: AMS Press, 1965), 16: 78. On

Poe's vexed relationship to literary property, see McGill, *American Literature and the Culture of Reprinting*, 141–214.

164. Ibid., 14: 161.

165. Ibid., 14: 161–62.

166. Ibid., 14: 162.

167. Ibid., 16: 78.

168. Roger Bradburn, *Understanding Business Ethics* (New York: Continuum, 2001), 7.

169. Poe, *Complete Works*, 16: 34.

170. Ibid., 16: 79.

171. "International Copyright," *Southern Quarterly Review* 4 (July 1843): 35, 46.

172. James Russell Lowell, *A Fable for Critics*, in *Poems of James Russell Lowell*, 157–99 (London: Oxford University Press, 1912), 166.

CHAPTER 5

1. Herman Melville, *Writings of Herman Melville*, 9: 20, 7: 244, 14: 191. Subsequent references to *The Writings of Herman Melville* are abbreviated *WHM* parenthetically in the text.

2. [Cornelius Mathews], "The International Copyright Law, and Mr. Dickens," 243.

3. Sellers, *Market Revolution*, 152.

4. Richard Henry Dana, Sr., to Richard Henry Dana, Jr., December 2, 1849, quoted in *The Melville Log: A Documentary Life of Herman Melville, 1819–1891*, ed. Jay Leyda, revised edition (New York: Harcourt Brace, 1951; reprint, with additional material, New York: Gordian Press, 1969), 1: 342.

5. "Mr. Melville and Copyright in England," *Literary World*, March 2, 1850, 205. The accusation appeared in "International Copyright," *London Times*, January 22, 1850; the response of his second British publisher, Richard Bentley, was published in the *Times* on January 25 before being reprinted in the *Literary World*, which also printed the anonymous defense of Melville by "K" (quoted here) in the same article. For more on the episode, see Hershel Parker, *Herman Melville: A Biography*, 2 vols. (Baltimore: Johns Hopkins University Press, 1996 and 2002), 1: 710.

6. James Russell Lowell to Charles Briggs, June 10, 1853, James Russell Lowell Papers, folder 13.

7. See, for example, Michael T. Gilmore, *American Romanticism and the Marketplace* (Chicago: University of Chicago Press, 1985), 132–45; David Kuebrich, "Melville's Doctrine of Assumptions: The Hidden Ideology of Capitalist Production in 'Bartleby,'" *New England Quarterly* 69 (September 1996): 381–405; and Naomi C. Reed, "The Specter of Wall Street: 'Bartleby, the Scrivener' and the Language of Commodities," *American Literature* 76 (June 2004): 247–73. A brief commentary on the business ethics of Melville's story in their contemporary context is provided by John H. Randall III, "Bartleby vs. Wall Street: New York in the 1850's," *Bulletin of the New York Public Library* 78 (Winter 1975): 138–44.

8. Parker's *Herman Melville: A Biography* is invaluable to critics of Melville's authorial career in the context of the transatlantic publishing scene of the mid-nineteenth century. I am also indebted to Sheila Post-Lauria's treatment of Melville's engagement with editorial ideologies of the literary periodicals in which he published in *Correspondent Colorings*. See also Jeanne Barker-Nunn and Gary Alan Fine, "The Vortex of Creation: Literary Politics and the Demise of Herman Melville's Reputation," *Poetics* 26 (November 1998): 81–98.

9. Widmer, *Young America*, 119.

10. [George Ripley], review of *White-Jacket*, *New York Daily Tribune*, [9] April 1850; reprint, in Leyda, *Melville Log*, 1: 372.

11. "Complimentary Fruit Festival of the New York Book Publishers' Association to Authors and Booksellers, at the Crystal Palace, September 27, 1855," *American Publishers' Circular,* September 29, 1855, 66. See also Warren French, "'Honor to Genius': The Complimentary Fruit and Flower Festival to Authors, 1855," *New York Historical Society Quarterly* 39 (1955): 357–67; Madeleine Stern, *Books and Book People in 19th-Century America* (New York: Bowker, 1978), 146–53; and Ronald J. Zboray, *Fictive People,* 358–66.

12. "Publishers: Their Past, Present, and Future in the U.S.—The Present," *American Publishers' Circular,* November 17, 1855, 165.

13. See Ronald J. Zboray, "Literary Enterprise and the Mass Market: Publishers and Business Innovation in Antebellum America," *Essays in Economic and Business History* 10 (1992): 168–82. Zboray notes the tendency to highlight the cultural importance of antebellum publishers at the expense of their considerable economic impact.

14. "Complimentary Fruit Festival," 69.

15. Ibid., 78.

16. Melville habitually equated reviews with sales figures, thus mistakenly assuming that the relative success of *Typee* in the United States indicated success abroad. His earnings are available in G. Thomas Tanselle, "The Sales of Melville's Books," *Harvard Library Bulletin* 17 (1969): 195–215.

17. Lynn Horth, "Richard Bentley's Place in Melville's Literary Career," *Studies in the American Renaissance* (1992): 240.

18. Hershel Parker, "Contract: *Pierre,* by Herman Melville" *Proof: The Yearbook of American Bibliographical and Textual Studies* 5 (1977): 32.

19. "The Literary Profession—Authors and Publishers," *Harper's New Monthly Magazine* 1 (September 1850): 549.

20. On the debate over the composition of *Pierre* and, specifically, the claim that Melville later added the sections detailing Pierre's authorial career, see Brian Higgins and Hershel Parker, introduction to *Critical Essays on Herman Melville's "Pierre; or, the Ambiguities"* (Boston: G. K. Hall, 1983), 1–30. See also "Historical Note VII" in the *Writings of Herman Melville,* 6: 689–700; Parker, *Herman Melville,* especially 2: 70–110; and Higgins and Parker, *Reading Melville's* Pierre; or, The Ambiguities (Baton Rouge: Louisiana State University Press, 2006), 144–74.

21. "In fine, I look upon business as one vast scene of moral action." Orville Dewey, *Moral Views of Commerce, Society and Politics, in Twelve Discourses* (New York: A. M. Kelley, 1969), 52.

22. "The Merchant: Literature and Statistics of Commerce," *American Review* 4 (November 1846): 460.

23. Henry W. Bellows, "Influence of the Trading Spirit upon the Social and Moral Life of America," *American Review* 1 (January 1845): 97.

24. Dewey, *Moral Views,* vi, vii. As discussed in Chapter 1, segments of the clergy were making similar points. See, for example, Edwin Hubbell Chapin, *Moral Aspects of City Life: A Series of Lectures* (New York: H. Lyon, 1853), 33. On the social role of the evangelical clergy during this period, see Donald M. Scott, *From Office to Profession: The New England Ministry, 1750–1850* (Philadelphia: University of Pennsylvania Press, 1978).

25. Horace Greeley, *Hints toward Reforms, in Lectures, Addresses, and Other Writings* (New York: Harper and Brothers, 1850), 369. Though the golden rule predates the Bible, it is perhaps best known as it appears in Matthew 7: 12 and Luke 6: 31.

26. Chapin, *Moral Aspects,* 187. See also Scott, *From Office to Profession,* 138.

27. See, for example, Joshua Bates, *A Discourse, on Honesty in Dealing* (Middlebury: J. W. Copeland, 1813); Charles Grandison Finney, *Lectures on Revivals of Religion* (n.p., Leavitt, Lord and Company, 1835); and Channing, "Self-Culture."

28. [John H. Amory], *Alnomuc: or The Golden Rule: A Tale of the Sea* (Boston: Weeks, Jordan, 1837), 43. See also, for example, Emily C. Judson, *Charles Linn; or How to Observe the Golden Rule* (New York: Dayton and Saxton, 1841).

29. For a discussion of commercial ethics, see Chapter 1. These writers participated in a tacit Christian-capitalist discourse, a legacy of such Enlightenment figures as Adam Smith, who translated the golden rule into modern economic terms by correlating, however paradoxically, sympathy and self-interest, and Immanuel Kant, one of Melville's favorite whipping posts in *Pierre*, who in *The Groundwork for the Metaphysics of Morals* (1785) dressed up the golden rule in the form of the categorical imperative. Dewey's adaptation of the golden rule—"We are indeed to do to others as we would have them do to us; but we ought not to wish them to do anything to us, which is inconsistent with the general welfare of the community"—looks strikingly like Kant's categorical imperative (*Moral Views*, 21). Daniel Walker Howe also notes the relationship between Dewey's theology and Kantian ethics; see Howe, "The Cambridge Platonists of Old England and the Cambridge Platonists of New England," *Church History* 57 (December 1988): 482.

30. Dewey, *Moral Views*, 15, 23.

31. Paul E. Johnson, *A Shopkeeper's Millennium: Society and Revivals in Rochester, New York, 1815–1837* (New York: Hill and Wang, 1978), 8.

32. Scott, *From Office to Profession*, 101.

33. Parker, *Herman Melville*, 2: 177. Melville scorned Dewey's sermons on poverty, which argued that the sufferings of the poor were a matter less of physical suffering than of envy. While Parker notes only Melville's acquaintance with Dewey's work after the 1830s, given Dewey's reputation among circles the Melvilles moved in and his close friendship with Lemuel Shaw, Melville's father-in-law, Melville was probably familiar with Dewey's earlier work on trade morality as well, and it is likely that he would have seen in it the same Christian charade he saw in Dewey's later sermons. See Parker, *Herman Melville*, 2: 65–69, 80, and 176–77 for these discussions.

34. Dewey, *Moral Views*, 21. Parker suggests that Plinlimmon is Melville's "intellectual embodiment of nominal Christianity," through whom we learn that "what passed for Christianity in midcentury America . . . was very far from Christlike" (*Herman Melville*, 2: 67, 69).

35. [Evert Duyckinck], "The Morality of Publishers," *Literary World*, February 13, 1847, 29. For examples of relevant conduct literature, see Joseph Hopkinson, *Lecture upon the Principles of Commercial Integrity, and the Duties Subsisting between a Debtor and His Creditors* (Philadelphia: Carey and Lea, 1832); and James Alexander et al., *The Man of Business, Considered in His Various Relations* (New York: Anson D. F. Randolph, 1857).

36. Derby, *Fifty Years among Authors, Books and Publishers*, 106.

37. John P[endleton] Kennedy to George Palmer Putnam, December 23, 1858, George Palmer Putnam Collection, box 2, folder 48.

38. Edward Morris to George Palmer Putnam, March 6, 1857, George Palmer Putnam Collection, box 2, folder 77.

39. Quoted in Tebbel, *History of Book Publishing*, 1: 310. See also Greenspan, *George Palmer Putnam*, 381–86.

40. Evert Duyckinck to George Duyckinck, March 9, 1848, Duyckinck Family Papers, box 23, folder 1848, January–March.

41. For an account of Putnam's reputation abroad, see Horatio Southgate to George Palmer Putnam, March 30, 1844, George Palmer Putnam Collection, box 3, folder 53.

42. Henry William Herbert to [George Palmer Putnam], April 29, 1848, George Palmer Putnam Collection, box 2, folder 25.

43. John Prágay to George Palmer Putnam, September 30, 1850, George Palmer Putnam Collection, box 3, folder 20.

44. S[amuel] Austin Allibone to George Palmer Putnam, July 9, 1855, George Palmer Putnam Collection, box 1, folder 1. The proviso about Putnam's exclusive right to Allibone's work is in Allibone to George Palmer Putnam, June 15, 1857, ibid., box 1, folder 2.

45. "Publishing Business," 11. Putnam's comments on the Harpers and on his own gentility are quoted in Greenspan, *George Palmer Putnam*, 162, 120.

46. Bayard Taylor to George Palmer Putnam, September 30, 1849, in John Richie Schultz, ed., *The Unpublished Letters of Bayard Taylor in the Huntington Library* (San Marino: Huntington Library Publications, 1937), 23.

47. Henry C. Carey, *Principles of Political Economy* (Philadelphia: Carey, Lea, and Blanchard, 1840), 3: 259, 255. This is not to say that Carey was proselytizing. He was skeptical of the Christian Church, writing approvingly to Joseph Hopkinson of his skepticism of the practical uses of religion that his sentiment "is one for which you deserve the thanks of the whole of that portion of the community that has nothing to gain—no private end to be answered by the continuance of the present system, and who are desirous that common sense should be applied to religion as well as to other matters." Henry C. Carey to Joseph Hopkinson, January 16, 1830, quoted in *Joseph Hopkinson, 1770–1842, Jurist-Scholar-Inspirer of the Arts: Author of* Hail Columbia (Philadelphia: University of Pennsylvania Press, 1931), 279. On Carey's economic theories, see Paul Conkin, *Prophets of Prosperity: America's First Political Economists*, Chapters 10 and 11; Andrew Dawson, "Reassessing Henry Carey (1793-1879): The Problems of Writing Political Economy in Nineteenth-Century America," *Journal of American Studies* 34 (December 2000): 465–85; and especially Johns, *Piracy*, 309–25.

48. Joshua Bates, *A Discourse, on Honesty in Dealing* (Middlebury, Vt.: J. W. Copeland, 1813), 4; Bellows, *Christian Merchant*, 17–18. The golden rule also went back further; see Cotton Mather, *Lex Mercatoria. Or, The Just Rules of Commerce Declared* (1704; reprint, Boston: Timothy Green, 1705), 10; and *The Religious Trader* (New York: Hodge and Shober, 1773), 63.

49. Algernon Tassin, "American Authors and Their Publishers," *The Bookman* 39 (April 1914): 182.

50. EAD [Evert Duyckinck], "Literary Prospects of 1845."

51. [James Parton], "International Copyright," 441.

52. See George Borrow, *Lavengro: The Scholar—The Gypsy—The Priest; In Three Volumes* (London: John Murray, 1851); and Exman, *Brothers Harper*, 56. For accounts of this feud see George Haven Putnam, *George Palmer Putnam: A Memoir* (New York: G. P. Putnam's Sons, 1912), 144–47; Exman, *Brothers Harper*, 349–51; and Greenspan, *George Palmer Putnam*, 259–61.

53. George Palmer Putnam, "Borrow's Lavengro," *Literary World*, February 22, 1851, 158.

54. George Haven Putnam, *George Palmer Putnam*, 145; Greenspan, *George Palmer Putnam*, 260. See also Candy Gunther Brown, *The Word in the World: Evangelical Writing, Publishing, and Reading in America, 1789–1880* (Chapel Hill: University of North Carolina Press, 2004), 74–78.

55. See Exman, *Brothers*, 121; and "Publishers: Their Past, Present, and Future," 165.

56. "Printers' Enterprise," *Knickerbocker* 2 (1833): 152.

57. See Eugene Exman, *The House of Harper: One Hundred and Fifty Years of Publishing* (New York: Harper and Row, 1967), 40.

58. J. Henry Harper, *I Remember* (New York: Harper and Brothers, 1934), 26.

59. See Joel Myerson and Chris L. Nesmith, introduction to *The Harper Establishment: How Books Are Made,* by Jacob Abbott (New York: Harper and Brothers, 1855; reprint, New Castle, DE: Oak Knoll Press, 2001), xviii.

60. James Kirke Paulding to Edward L. Carey and Abraham Hart, May 4, 1846, in *Letters of James Kirke Paulding,* 433.

61. "Publishing Business," 12. See "Harpers' Views on Trade Sales," *American Publishers' Circular,* September 8, 1855, 17–18.

62. [Evert Duyckinck], "The Morality of Publishers," 29.

63. Nicklin, *Remarks on Literary Property,* 23; Henry C. Carey, *Letters on International Copyright,* 55.

64. On Melville's use of the cityscape in *Pierre,* see Wyn Kelley, *Melville's City: Literary and Urban Form in Nineteenth-Century New York* (New York: Cambridge University Press, 1996), especially 145–61. See also Barbara Foley, "From Wall Street to Astor Place: Historicizing Melville's 'Bartleby,'" *American Literature* 72 (March 2000): 87–116.

65. Sean Wilentz, *Chants Democratic: New York City and the Rise of the American Working Class, 1788–1850* (New York: Oxford University Press, 1984), 377, 379.

66. See Charlene Avallone, "Calculations for Popularity: Melville's *Pierre* and *Holden's Dollar Magazine,*" *Nineteenth-Century Literature* 43 (June 1988): 82–110; and Donald Yanella, "Writing the 'Other Way': Melville, the Duyckinck Crowd, and Literature for the Masses," in *A Companion to Melville Studies,* ed. John Bryant (New York: Greenwood, 1986), 63–81.

67. D [Evert Duyckinck], "Authorship," 23.

68. Thomas Hove, "Ethical Ideals, Non-Rational Forces: Melville's Critique of Morality," PhD thesis, University of Illinois, 1998, 36.

69. Brian Higgins, "Plinlimmon and the Pamphlet Again," *Studies in the Novel* 4 (1972): 34.

70. [Evert Duyckinck], "The Morality of Publishers," 29.

71. Cf. Nicola Nixon, "Compromising Politics and Herman Melville's Pierre," *American Literature* 69 (December 1997): 719–41, especially 733.

72. Review of *Pierre, Boston Post,* August 4, 1852; reprint, in Brian Higgins and Hershel Parker, *Contemporary Reviews* (New York: Cambridge University Press, 1995), 420; Evert Duyckinck, review of *Pierre, Literary World,* August 21, 1852; reprint, in Higgins and Parker, *Contemporary Reviews,* 431, 430.

73. Henry A. Murray, "Bartleby and I," in *Melville Annual 1965; A Symposium: Bartleby the Scrivener,* ed. Howard P. Vincent (Kent: Kent State University Press, 1966), 7, 5, 5–6.

74. Allan Silver, "The Lawyer and the Scrivener," *Partisan Review* 48 (1981): 422.

75. Review of *Pierre, New York Day Book,* September 7, 1852; reprint, in Higgins and Parker, *Contemporary Reviews,* 436.

76. Parker, *Herman Melville,* 2: 288. Exactly which manuscript this was remains uncertain. Parker believes it to be "The Isle of the Cross," which Melville allegedly delivered to Harper and Brothers in June 1853. See Parker, *Herman Melville,* 2: 136–61.

77. Brook Thomas, *Cross-examinations of Law and Literature: Cooper, Hawthorne, Stowe, and Melville* (New York: Cambridge University Press, 1987), 173.

78. See, for example, Michael Murphy, "'Bartleby, the Scrivener': A Simple Reading," *Arizona Quarterly* 41 (Spring 1985): 143–51; and Thomas Dilworth, "Narrator of 'Bartleby': The Christian-Humanist Acquaintance of John Jacob Astor," *Papers on Language and Literature* 38 (Winter 2002): 49–75.

79. Gilmore, *American Romanticism and the Marketplace,* 134.

80. Allan Silver, "The Lawyer and the Scrivener," 422.

81. Kelley, *Melville's City,* 201.

82. For an account of Colt-Adams affair and especially its bizarre afterlife, see Andie Tucher, *Froth and Scum: Truth, Beauty, Goodness, and the Ax Murder in America's First Mass Medium* (Chapel Hill: University of North Carolina Press, 1994), 99–107.

83. Quoted in T.H. Giddings, "Melville, the Colt-Adams Murder, and 'Bartleby,'" *Studies in American Fiction* 2 (1974): 127.

84. Ibid., 130, 129.

85. Steven Doloff, "The Prudent Samaritan: Melville's 'Bartleby, the Scrivener' as Parody of Christ's Parable to the Lawyer," *Studies in Short Fiction* 34 (Summer 1997): 359.

86. Higginson, *Merchants: A Sunday Evening Lecture,* 19.

87. Murray, "Bartleby and I," 7. Allan Silver establishes the story's contemporary ethical resonance, especially in terms of the "routinized moralities" of the post-Enlightenment West ("Lawyer," 416–23). Doloff argues for a broader allusive context for "Bartleby" but arrives at familiar conclusions regarding the role of Christianity in the narrator's actions: the story "would seem to be a parody of the parable, as we see a self-professed 'saved' Christian attempt the good deeds of the Biblical Samaritan but, ironically, still fall short of Christ's 'divine' injunction, spiritually hampered by his self-justifying, earthbound prudence" ("Prudent Samaritan," 360). Other studies are noteworthy for their readings of Bartleby and Christian symbolism: H. Bruce Franklin, *The Wake of the Gods: Melville's Mythology* (Stanford: Stanford University Press, 1963), 126–36; William Stein, "Bartleby: The Christian Conscience," in Vincent, *Bartleby the Scrivener,* 104–12; Donald Fiene, "Bartleby the Christ," *ATQ,* 2nd series, 7 (Summer 1970): 18–23; and Richard Kopley, "The Circle and Its Center in 'Bartleby the Scrivener,'" *ATQ* 2 (1988): 191–206. See as well Augst's revealing contextualization of "Bartleby" in the moral world of antebellum middle-class labor in *Clerk's Tale,* 207–55.

88. See Greenspan, *George Palmer Putnam,* 309. Greenspan notes that *Putnam's* editors most likely read "Bartleby" not as an attack on "the literary and social status quo" (310) but rather as acquiescence to it.

89. Gilmore, *American Romanticism,* 145.

90. D [Evert Duyckinck], "Authorship," 22–23.

91. "Literary Profession," *Harper's New Monthly Magazine,* 54.

92. For a counterargument to my reading of the narrator as a moral analogy, as well as to similar readings, see Richard R. John, "The Lost World of Bartleby, the Ex-Officeholder: Variations on a Venerable Literary Form," *New England Quarterly* 70 (December 1997): 631–41.

CHAPTER 6

1. Emily Dickinson to T[homas] W[entworth] Higginson, April 15, 1862, in Dickinson, *The Letters of Emily Dickinson,* ed. Thomas H. Johnson (Cambridge: Belknap Press, 1986), 403.

2. Thomas Wentworth Higginson, "Letter to a Young Contributor," *Atlantic Monthly* 9 (April 1862): 403. See Brenda Wineapple, *White Heat: The Friendship of Emily Dickinson and Thomas Wentworth Higginson* (New York: Knopf, 2008), 7.

3. *Haney's Guide to Authorship Intended as an Aid to All Who Desire to Engage in Literary Pursuits for Pleasure or Profit* (New York: Jesse Haney and Company, 1867), 6. On nineteenth-century conduct literature, see John Kasson, *Rudeness and Civility: Manners in Nineteenth-Century Urban America* (New York: Hill and Wang, 1990); and C. Dallet Hemphill, *Bowing to Necessities: A History of Manners in America, 1620–1860* (New York: Oxford University Press, 1999).

4. *Haney's Guide to Authorship*, 12.

5. Fanny Fern, "A Bit of Injustice," in Fern, *Ruth Hall and Other Writings*, 318; first published in the New York *Ledger*, June 8, 1861.

6. Warren S. Tryon, *Parnassus Corner: A Life of James T. Fields, Publisher to the Victorians* (Boston: Houghton Mifflin, 1963), 336.

7. E.D.E.N. Southworth to Robert Bonner, December 26, 1869, quoted in Coultrap-McQuin, *Doing Literary Business*, 50. On Southworth's relationship to the trade, see 50–78. On Bonner's opportunistic timing, see 68–69 and Joyce W. Warren, *Fanny Fern: An Independent Woman* (New Brunswick: Rutgers University Press, 1992), 144–49. Southworth, who had been publishing her work for eight years by the time she began to write for Bonner, may have overstated her dependence on his expertise. As I discuss later in this chapter, such overstatement was not uncommon for women writers, among them Grace Greenwood, who carefully managed her relationship with James T. Fields and the production and marketing of her works. See Lesley Ginsberg, "The Making of Grace Greenwood."

8. Ella Rodman, "An Author's Vicissitudes," *Graham's Magazine* 39 (August 1851): 105–12; J. T. Trowbridge, *Martin Merrivale: His X-Mark* (Boston: Phillips, Sampson, 1854). On *Martin Merrivale* as trade critique, see Ronald J. Zboray and Mary Saracino Zboray, *Literary Dollars and Social Sense*, 73–83.

9. Wendy Gamber, *The Female Economy: The Millinery and Dressmaking Trades, 1860–1930* (Urbana: University of Illinois Press, 1997), 14.

10. Susan S. Williams, *Reclaiming Authorship: Literary Women in America, 1850–1900* (Philadelphia: University of Pennsylvania Press, 2006), 17, 20. The benchmark reading of *Ruth Hall* as a parable of feminist authorial agency that posits the woman writer as a confident, capable professional is articulated most famously by Kelley in *Private Woman, Public Stage*. Early work on authorship in *Ruth Hall* and women's authorship generally is a variation on this theme, from Ann Douglas's thesis that the novel was "a cry from the rooftops that other women writers hardly wished to whisper in the basement" ("The 'Scribbling Women' and Fanny Fern: Why Women Wrote," *American Quarterly* 23 [1971]: 13) to Warren's 1992 biography, *Fanny Fern: An Independent Woman*, which pictures the professional world Ruth enters as a patriarchal society in which the "rules of publishing . . . excluded women" (140). For Warren, as for Douglas and Kelley, the novel is a "triumphant portrayal of female success" that recounts Fern's own experience. Lauren Berlant complicates these readings of Ruth's oppositional and representational status in her theorization of the female complaint. Berlant sees the print trade as a "site of gender discipline" where male managers define authorship as abnormal and Ruth's writing as "vulgar." Berlant, "The Female Woman: Fanny Fern and the Form of Sentiment," in Shirley Samuels, ed., *The Culture of Sentiment: Race, Gender, and Sentimentality in Nineteenth-Century America*, 265–82 (New York: Oxford University Press, 1992), 430, 431.

11. Fern, *Ruth Hall*, 173. Subsequent references to *Ruth Hall* are abbreviated *RH* parenthetically in the text.

12. Joan W. Scott, "The Evidence of Experience," *Critical Inquiry* 17 (Summer 1991): 797.

13. Karen A. Weyler, "Literary Labors and Intellectual Prostitution: Fanny Fern's Defense of Working Women," *South Atlantic Review* 70 (Spring 2005): 116, 115.

14. See Weyler, "Literary Labors and Intellectual Prostitution"; Kristie Hamilton, "The Politics of Survival: Sara Parton's *Ruth Hall* and the Literature of Labor," in *Redefining the Political Novel: American Women Writers, 1797–1901*, ed. Sharon M. Harris, 86–108 (Knoxville: University of Tennessee Press, 1995); and Homestead, *American Women Authors and Literary Property*, 150–91.

15. See Gillian Brown, *Domestic Individualism: Imagining Self in Nineteenth-Century America* (Berkeley: University of California Press, 1990), which argues that "the real scandal of *Ruth Hall* lies in its unabashed commitment to market individualism" (140)—the idea that Ruth has, as C. B. Macpherson might say, property in herself. A more measured reading of the ways in which women authors were "unintentionally afforded" capacities by the market is offered by Lara Langer Cohen, "Mediums of Exchange: Fanny Fern's Unoriginality," *ESQ* 55 (2009): 59–95. For representative counterarguments, see Hamilton, "The Politics of Survival"; and Weyler, "Literary Labors and Intellectual Prostitution."

16. Fanny Fern, "Sewing Machines," in Fern, *Ruth Hall and Other Writings*, 248; first published in the *True Flag*, January 29, 1853.

17. Maria C. Sanchez, "Re-Possessing Individualism in Fanny Fern's *Ruth Hall*," *Arizona Quarterly* 56 (Winter 2000): 26. In *Capital Letters: Authorship in the Antebellum Literary Market* (Iowa City: University of Iowa Press, 2009), David Dowling also discusses *Ruth Hall* as a commentary on antebellum publishing ethics, arguing that the book endorses a kind of moral capitalism predicated on "sympathy" for and "altruism" toward women writers rather than on free trade, a principle that is, according to Dowling, upset by Walter's "breach" of trade courtesy (71). This argument relies, however, on a mischaracterization of mid-nineteenth-century trade courtesy as an ethic governing domestic author-publisher relations. While by the 1880s trade courtesy was being applied in limited ways to domestic authors, there is no evidence that it was so employed prior to the Civil War, when the principle was used, as it had been for decades, to structure commercial traffic in foreign titles in the absence of international copyright. See Ellen B. Ballou, *The Building of the House: Houghton Mifflin's Formative Years* (Boston: Houghton Mifflin, 1970), 345; and Richard Ohmann, "Diverging Paths: Books and Magazines in the Transition to Corporate Capitalism," in *Print in Motion: The Expansion of Publishing and Reading in the United States, 1880–1940*, vol. 4 of *A History of the Book in America*, ed. Carl F. Kaestle and Janice A. Radway, 102–15 (Chapel Hill: University of North Carolina Press and the American Antiquarian Society, 2009), 113–14. Between the Copyright Act of 1790 and the 1880s, any application of trade courtesy to American authors would have to be by analogy.

18. Quoted in Susan Geary, "The Domestic Novel as a Commercial Commodity: Making a Best Seller in the 1850s," *Papers of the Bibliographical Society of America* 70 (1976): 383–84.

19. Ibid., 384.

20. "Art. VI.—Ruth Hall; A Domestic Tale of the Present Time," *Southern Quarterly Review* 10 (April 1855): 449–50. Warren suggests that this campaign was "one of the first examples of modern advertising methods in America. [Mason Brothers] not only advertised heavily in newspapers and magazines across the country, they also attempted to create a need, and to create a public image of the book." Warren, *Fanny Fern*, 122. In the first few weeks after publication, Mason Brothers maintained the public relations blitz, remarking publicly how many copies had been sold and how their presses were unable to meet the public outcry for the book. See Patricia McGinnis, "Fanny Fern, American Novelist," *Biblion* 2 (Spring 1969): 13–19; and Geary, "The

Domestic Novel as a Commercial Commodity," 383–91. See also Janice A. Radway, *Reading the Romance: Women, Patriarchy, and Popular Literature* (Chapel Hill: University of North Carolina Press, 1984), 19–25, which provides a nuanced introduction to the highly commodified world of antebellum domestic-fiction production.

21. Nina Baym, *Novels, Readers, and Reviewers: Responses to Fiction in Antebellum America* (Ithaca: Cornell University Press, 1984), 255.

22. Ellen Louise Chandler Moulton to Phillips, Sampson, and Company, July 27, 1856, Ch.D.10.54, Boston Public Library.

23. Ellen Louise Chandler Moulton to Phillips, Sampson, and Company, September 3, 1854, Ch.B.11.29, Boston Public Library. A few months before, she spoke jealously to her publisher of Fern's sales and of the advertising campaign behind her books. Chandler would later marry William Moulton, parodied in *Ruth Hall* as John Tibbetts.

24. Moulton to Phillips, Sampson, and Company, July 27, 1856. Chandler may have also been jealous that she too had published work in Moulton's *True Flag* but had not realized the same success.

25. Fern's "Apollo Hyacinth" was published in the *Musical World and Times*, June 18, 1853.

26. Thomas N. Baker has shown that Fern's identity was public at the time of *Ruth Hall's* publication. In 1854, the *Boston Transcript* published a reference to Fern and her family, including her father, a reference reprinted in Willis's *Home Journal.* Baker, *Sentiment and Celebrity: Nathaniel Parker Willis and the Trials of Literary Fame* (New York: Oxford University Press, 1999), 173.

27. "Review," *New York Daily Times*, February 28, 1855, 2.

28. William Gilmore Simms to William Elliott, January 8, [1855], in *Letters of William Gilmore Simms*, 3: 358.

29. See, for example, "Puny Poets and Piratical Publishers," *American Whig Review* 7 (January 1851): 70.

30. A New Contributor, "A California Lady's Opinion of Fanny Fern," 364.

31. Ibid., 368.

32. "Literature," *Putnam's Monthly Magazine* 4 (July 1854): 216.

33. "Ruth Hall: A Domestic Tale of the Present Time," *Knickerbocker* 45 (January 1855): 84.

34. Thrace Talmon [Ellen Tryphosa Harrington], "The Latest Crusade. Lady Authors and Their Critics," *National Era*, June 25, 1857, 101; "Review 2," *National Era*, April 5, 1855, 55. On Harrington, see Williams, *Reclaiming Authorship*, 20.

35. "Ruth Hall; a Domestic Tale of the Present Time," *Plough, the Loom and the Anvil* 7 (January 1855): 444–45.

36. Elizabeth Cady Stanton, "Ruth Hall," *Una* (February 1855): 29 (emphasis added). On the literary representation of historical subjects, see Gayatri Spivak, "Literary Representations of the Subaltern: A Woman's Text from the Third World," in *In Other Worlds: Essays in Cultural Politics*, 241–68 (New York: Routledge, 2006) and especially Scott's application of Spivak to history writing in "The Evidence of Experience."

37. Fanny Fern, "Facts for Unjust Critics," *Fresh Leaves*, 297–302 (New York: Mason Brothers, 1857), 297, 299 (emphasis removed).

38. "Ruth Hall," *Eclectic Magazine of Foreign Literature* 35 (June 1855): 199. The article was a reprint of a review that appeared in London's *Tait's Magazine.*

39. "Notices of New Books," *New York Daily Times*, December 20, 1854, 2.

40. "Literature," *Putnam's Monthly Magazine*, 216 (emphasis added).

41. Virginia Penny, *Think and Act: A Series of Articles Pertaining to Men and Women, Work and Wages* (Philadelphia: Claxton, Remsen, and Haffelfinger, 1869), 310–11 (emphasis removed).

42. "Blessed be the 'smart business woman,'" Fern wrote in an 1861 column, who "is able to look back on the weary track and see the sweet flower of faith and trust in her kind still growing." Fern, "A Bit of Injustice," 318.

43. Virginia Penny, *The Employments of Women: A Cyclopaedia of Women's Work* (Boston: Walker, Wise, 1863), v–vi. Susan Albertine cites this opening in "Breaking the Silent Partnership: Businesswomen in Popular Fiction," *American Literature* 62 (June 1990): 238–61. On Penny, see Susan H. Gensemer, "Virginia Penny," in Robert W. Dimand, Mary Ann Dimand, and Evelyn L. Forget, eds., *A Biographical Dictionary of Women Economists*, 330–34 (Cheltham, UK, and Northampton, Mass.: Edward Elgar, 2000), 331. In *All-American Girl: The Ideal of Real Womanhood in Mid-Nineteenth-Century America* (Athens: University of Georgia Press, 1989), Frances B. Cogan suggests that there was "a cultural embarrassment concerning the subject" (218) of women's employment among writers of advice manuals.

44. Fern, "Sewing Machines," 248.

45. Penny, *Employments of Women*, 435, 397, 1–2. The astronomer was likely the celebrated Maria Mitchell. See Renée Berglund, *Maria Mitchell and the Sexing of Science: An Astronomer among the American Romantics* (Boston: Beacon, 2008).

46. See Claudia Goldin, "The Economic Status of Women in the Early Republic: Quantitative Evidence," *Journal of Interdisciplinary History* 16 (Winter 1986): 375–404. The accepted wisdom is that women's employment declined in the Jacksonian period. Goldin argues that it increased steadily.

47. Barbara Mayer Wertheimer, *We Were There: The Story of Working Women in America* (New York: Pantheon, 1977), 60; Angel Kwolek-Folland, *Incorporating Women: A History of Women and Business in the United States* (New York: Twayne, 1998), 58.

48. Penny, *Employments of Women*, xiii.

49. Kwolek-Folland, *Incorporating Women*, 57.

50. Wendy Gamber, "Gendered Concerns: Thoughts on the History of Business and the History of Women," *Business and Economic History* 23 (1994): 137. See also David A. Gerber, "Cutting Out the Shylock: Elite Anti-Semitism and the Quest for Moral Order in the Mid-Nineteenth-Century American Market Place," *Journal of American History* 69 (December 1982): 615–37. On the language of credit reporting, see Sandage, *Born Losers*.

51. In a study of gender attitudes among printers, Ava Baron reaches an almost identical conclusion. "Male printers became caught," she writes, "in their own cultural contradictions." Baron, "Women and the Making of the American Working Class: A Study of the Proletarianization of Printers," *Review of Radical Political Economics* 14 (1982): 26. See also Wertheimer, *We Were There*, 92–94.

52. Quoted in Lucy Eldersveld Murphy, "Business Ladies: Midwestern Women and Enterprise, 1850–1880," *Journal of Women's History* 3 (Spring 1991): 78.

53. Penny, *Employments of Women*, 38.

54. Entry on John Jamieson, Ohio, Vol. 78, p. 210, November 2, 1850, R. G. Dun and Company Collection. The quoted section of the report regards Jamieson's wife, who is unnamed by the reporter.

55. Entry on Geo[rge]. P. Putnam, New York, Vol. 364, p. 82, December 5, 1848, R. G. Dun and Company Collection.

56. Entry on Mrs. S. Tyndale, Pennsylvania, Vol. 131, p. 91, September 16, 1845, R. G. Dun and Company Collection.

57. Entry on Mrs. Mary A. Downard, Ohio, Vol. 79, p. 102, April 4, 1856, R. G. Dun and Company Collection.

58. Penny, *Employments of Women*, vii.

59. Hamilton, *Battle of the Books*, 7.

60. James T. Fields to Henry Wadsworth Longfellow, November 10, 1853, James Thomas Fields Papers, box 19, FI 1854.

61. Fern "To Literary Aspirants," in *Fresh Leaves*, 55; Hamilton, *Battle of the Books*, 7. As Weyler notes, in *Ruth Hall* Fern equates Ruth's work as a writer to the work of milliners and especially prostitutes, all wage-laborers of one kind or another, though by the end of the novel, after Ruth has successfully negotiated more control over her earnings, she is represented as more of an entrepreneur, creating opportunities and wielding control over her decisions. I would suggest that by analogy Ruth moves from being a milliner working for a wage to the owner of a millinery shop dictating earnings. She is both a laborer and a manager, representing the broad spectrum of women's labor in the mid-nineteenth century.

62. Hamilton, *Battle of the Books*, 79.

63. Grace Greenwood to James T. Fields, October 19, 1848, James Thomas Fields Papers, box 40, FI 1750.

64. Sarah J. Hale to Harper and Brothers, December 29, 1489, and February 24, 1852, Misc American Harper, folder Hale, Sarah Josepha (Buell).

65. Grace Greenwood to James T. Fields, 1849, James Thomas Fields Papers, FI 1733.

66. [Emma Berents] to George Palmer Putnam, February 1855, George Palmer Putnam Collection, Box 4, folder 14.

67. Caroline Kirkland to George Palmer Putnam, August 5, 1852, George Palmer Putnam Collection, box 2, folder 53.

68. Catherine Beecher to Harper and Brothers, November 17, 1854, Misc American Harper, folder Beecher, Catherine, 1800–78.

69. Entry on Wiley and Halstead, New York, Vol. 364, p. 82, December 8, 1852, ibid.; entry on Sophia Hart, Pennsylvania, Vol. 131, p. 75, February 13, 1861, R. G. Dun and Company Collection.

70. Joan D. Hendrick, *Harriet Beecher Stowe: A Life* (New York: Oxford University Press, 1994), 224.

71. William Dowe to [Charles Briggs], 1853, George Palmer Putnam Collection, box 4, folder 72.

72. Quoted in Michael Winship, "'The Greatest Book of Its Kind': A Publishing History of *Uncle Tom's Cabin*," *Proceedings of the American Antiquarian Society* 109 (2002): 322. On the debate between Stowe and Jewett, see Susan Geary, "Harriet Beecher Stowe, John P. Jewett, and Author-Publisher Relations in 1853," *Studies in the American Renaissance*, ed. Joel Myerson (Boston: Twayne, 1977), 345–67; and Claire Parfait, *The Publishing History of* Uncle Tom's Cabin, *1852–2002* (Burlington, VT: Ashgate, 2007), 35–46.

73. Julia R. McMasters to George Palmer Putnam, August 17, 1854, George Palmer Putnam Collection, box 8, folder 49.

74. Catharine Maria Sedgwick, *Morals of Manners; or, Hints for Our Young People* (New York: G.P. Putnam, 1854), vi.

75. Hunt, *Worth and Wealth*, 183.

76. Haltunen, *Confidence Men and Painted Women*, 63.

77. Homestead, *American Women Authors and Literary Property*, 154–70.

78. Alice Kessler-Harris, "Ideologies and Innovation: Gender Dimensions of Business History," *Business and Economic History,* 2nd series, 20 (1991): 50.

79. Penny, *Think and Act,* 310.

80. Ibid., 82.

81. Ibid., 83.

82. Ibid., 86.

83. "In 1854 'Ruth Hall' (I had almost said Ruth-less Hall) was published." Grace Greenwood, "Fanny Fern—Mrs. Parton," in James Parton, ed., *Eminent Women of the Age* (Hartford: S. M. Betts, 1868), 73. This was Greenwood's only substantive comment on the novel, though it appeared in a work that commented at length on Fern's other work, suggesting that even Greenwood was less than pleased with its tone.

84. Wood [Douglas], "The 'Scribbling Women' and Fanny Fern," 23.

85. Berlant, "The Female Woman," 266.

86. Teichgraeber, *"Free Trade" and Moral Philosophy,* 4.

87. Smith, *Theory of Moral Sentiments,* 25, 9.

88. Knud Haakonssen, "Introduction," in Adam Smith, *The Theory of Moral Sentiments,* ed. Haakonssen, vii–xxiv (Cambridge, UK: Cambridge University Press, 2002), xxiv.

89. Ibid., viii.

90. Sanchez, "Re-Possessing Individualism in Fanny Fern's *Ruth Hall*," 44.

91. Ibid., 46.

EPILOGUE

1. Page, *A Publisher's Confession,* 168.

2. On post–Civil War publishing, see Sheehan, *This Was Publishing;* Tebbel, *A History of Book Publishing in the United States, Vol. 2;* Laura J. Miller, *Reluctant Capitalists: Bookselling and the Culture of Consumption* (Chicago: University of Chicago Press, 2006), 1–54; Scott E. Casper, ed., et al., *Industrial Book;* Michael Winship, "The Rise of a National Book Trade System in the United States," in *Print in Motion,* 56–77; and Ohmann, "Diverging Paths."

3. Casper, "Introduction," in *Industrial Book,* 7. Census figures in the following sentences are drawn from 10–11, 14–17.

4. James Oliver Robertson, *America's Business* (New York: Hill and Wang, 1985), 132.

5. Henry Holt, *Garrulities of an Octogenarian Editor* (Boston: Houghton Mifflin, 1923), 211. Holt originally made the observation in the February 12, 1910 issue of *Publishers' Weekly.* On the figure of the literary agent, see James L. W. West III, *American Authors and the Literary Marketplace since 1900* (Philadelphia: University of Pennsylvania Press, 1988), 77–88; and West, "The Expansion of the National Book Trade System," in *Print in Motion,* 87–88.

6. On Mason Locke ("Parson") Weems, see Lewis Leary, *The Book-Peddling Parson* (Chapel Hill: Algonquin Books, 1984).

7. Peter J. Parker, "The Philadelphia Printer: A Study of an Eighteenth-Century Businessman," *Business History Review* 40 (Spring 1966): 35.

8. Ibid., 46.

9. Sheehan, *This Was Publishing,* 3.

10. Ibid., 10.

11. Edwin P. Whipple, "Recollections of James T. Fields," *Atlantic Monthly* 48 (August 1881): 256. The title is a quote from Hamilton, *Battle of the Books,* 45.

12. Hamilton to Mr. G., May 11, 1869, in *Gail Hamilton's Life in Letters*, 2: 630.

13. Entry on Ticknor, Reed, and Fields, Massachusetts, Vol. 67, p. 146, August 4, 1852, R. G. Dun and Company Collection. In 1868, Ticknor and Fields was renamed Fields, Osgood, and Company. For consistency and because authors in the 1860s did so, I refer to the firm as Ticknor and Fields throughout.

14. Entry on Ticknor and Fields/Fields, Osgood, and Company, Massachusetts, Vol. 67, p. 147, November 6, 1868, R. G. Dun and Company Collection.

15. Entry on E. P. Dutton and Company, Massachusetts, Vol. 67, p. 216a/17, April 1, 1867, R. G. Dun and Company Collection.

16. Ticknor and Fields' profits were in fact based on considerably more factors than how much the firm paid its authors. See Winship, *American Literary Publishing in the Mid-Nineteenth Century*, 170–87.

17. Hamilton, *Battle of the Books*, 18. All subsequent references are abbreviated *BB* and appear parenthetically in the text. As James C. Austin notes, with the exception of dates and names (e.g., M.N. for Hamilton, Brummel and Hunt for Ticknor and Fields), the letters in *A Battle of the Books* are accurate reproductions of the ones exchanged by the various parties. See Austin, *Fields of the Atlantic Monthly*, 312.

18. This change affected many writers. Maria Cummins, for example, "went from receiving a 10 percent royalty on her first two novels to 15 percent on her third and then 30¢ per copy for her 1864 novel *Haunted Hearts*. This flat payment did not keep pace with the rising retail price of the novel, as a percentage royalty would have." Ballou, *The Building of the House*, 92–93.

19. Tryon, *Parnassus Corner*, 338.

20. Coultrap-McQuin, *Doing Literary Business*, 122.

21. Thomas Niles to Louisa May Alcott, June 21, 1870, quoted in Martha Saxton, *Louisa May: A Modern Biography of Louisa May Alcott* (Boston: Houghton Mifflin, 1977), 305.

22. Niles to Alcott, February 14, 1870, in ibid., 302.

23. Lippincott to James T. Fields, January 4, 1850, James Thomas Fields Papers, box 40, FI 1765.

24. Lydia Maria Child to James T. Fields, November 20, 1863, James Thomas Fields Papers, FI 673.

25. Sheehan, *This Was Publishing*, 52–54. See also Khan, *Democratization of Invention*, 265n15.

26. On Ticknor and Fields' payments to authors, see Tryon, *Parnassus Corner*, 168–75; and Winship, *American Literary Publishing in the Mid-Nineteenth Century*, 132–35, 139–40. Winship suggests, with good reason, that given Ticknor and Fields' "relaxed attitude, the firm must be credited for managing to avoid more frequent misunderstandings and for maintaining good relationships with its authors while pursuing the business of literary publishing" (140). Ballou provides a usefully concise explanation of the three most common kinds of contracts in *Building of the House*, 141–42.

27. Tryon, *Parnassus Corner*, 338.

28. Ibid., 336.

29. Hamilton to Mr. Wood, March 23, 1868, in *Gail Hamilton's Life in Letters*, 2: 611.

30. "My dear friend," Sophia Hawthorne wrote, "I am on the curb of bankruptcy and actually have no money to buy some coal." She was due money from the firm that July, "but what will be the use of money in July if we all freeze and starve in April, May and June?" Sophia Hawthorne to James T. Fields, March 28, 1868, Ms.C.1.11(119), Boston Public Library.

31. Sophia Hawthorne to James T. Fields, August 2, 1868, Ms.C.1.11(119), Boston Public Library.

32. Quoted in Tryon, *Parnassus Corner*, 346 (emphasis added).

33. Arthur Twining Hadley, *Standards of Public Morality* (New York: Macmillan, 1908), 44. Hadley would later become president of Yale.

34. Gail Hamilton to James Parton, September 15, 1869, James Parton Correspondence and Other Papers, Ms Am 1248.1, folder 95, Houghton Library, Harvard University.

35. Quoted in Tryon, *Parnassus Corner*, 341.

36. Émile Durkheim, *The Division of Labor in Society*, trans. W. D. Halls (New York: Free Press, 1997), 320. On Durkheim's contract theory and the moral assumptions on which it is based, see also ibid., 154–65; and Steven Lukes, *Émile Durkheim, His Life and Work: A Historical and Critical Study* (Stanford: Stanford University Press, 1985), 137–78.

37. Goodin, *Protecting the Vulnerable*, 42, 50.

38. Gail Hamilton to Wood, February 16, 1870, in *Gail Hamilton's Life in Letters*, 2: 643.

39. For an account of Fields's tenure as editor of the *Atlantic Monthly*, see Ellery Sedgwick, *The Atlantic Monthly, 1857–1909: Yankee Humanism at High Tide and Ebb* (Amherst: University of Massachusetts Press, 1994), 69–113.

40. James Parton to [E. P.] Clark, May 16, 1867, Rogers Memorial Collection, Ms Thr 470, Series 1: Papers of James R. Osgood and A. V. S. Anthony, folder Parton, James (47), Harvard Theater Collection, Houghton Library, Harvard University.

41. [James Parton], "International Copyright," *Atlantic Monthly* 20 (October 1867): 442–43.

42. Gail Hamilton to James Parton, September 21, 1869, James Parton Correspondence and Other Papers, Ms Am 1248.1, folder 95. In her letter, Hamilton warned Parton not to try to "creep out" of acknowledging his authorship. "I know all about that," she wrote: "Since you branched off into other matters I will branch off also—Heaven forbid that I should ever permit a man to have the last word!—And say that the firm have treated me with a meanness and with an outrage compared to which are the meanness and outrage I ever experienced or heard or dreamed of in all my life besides is but as the small dust of the balance . . .! Your regard for them can be no greater than was mine for six years. . . ." As Milton E. Flower notes, both Parton and Fanny Fern, while sympathetic to Hamilton, tried to dissuade her from writing *A Battle of the Books*. Flower, *James Parton: The Father of Modern Biography* (New York: Greenwood Press, 1968), 101.

43. Gail Hamilton to James Parton, September 27, 1869, James Parton Correspondence and Other Papers, Ms Am 1248.1, folder 95.

44. John Greenleaf Whittier to Annie Fields, December 1, 1884, in *Letters of John Greenleaf Whittier*, 3: 491–92.

45. Quoted in Rita K. Gollin, *Annie Adams Fields: Woman of Letters* (Amherst: University of Massachusetts Press, 2002), 104. The accusation that Hamilton was simply out for more money is on page 90.

46. Coultrap-McQuin, *Doing Literary Business*, 130.

47. John Greenleaf Whittier to Annie Fields, December 1, 1884, in *Letters of John Greenleaf Whittier*, 3: 492.

48. William Dean Howells, "The Man of Letters as a Man of Business," *Scribners' Magazine* 13 (May 1893): 436.

49. John Greenleaf Whittier to Annie Fields, December 1, 1884, in *Letters of John Greenleaf Whittier*, 3: 491.

50. "Literature of the Day," *Lippincott's Magazine* 5 (June 1870): 685.

51. "General Literature," *American Presbyterian Review* 2 (July 1870): 579.

52. "The Battle of the Books," *Overland Monthly and Out West Magazine* 4 (June 1870): 581.

53. James T. Fields to Henry Wadsworth Longfellow, March 5, 1863, Henry Wadsworth Longfellow Papers, folder 1972.

54. "Literature of the Day," *Hours at Home* 11 (May 1870): 100.

55. On Hamilton's progressivism, see Maurine Beasley, "Mary Abigail Dodge: 'Gail Hamilton' and the Process of Social Change," *Essex Institute Historical Collections* 116 (April 1980): 82–100; and Erika M. Kreger, "The Nineteenth-Century Female Humorist as 'Iconoclast in the Temple,'" *Studies in American Humor* 3.11 (2004): 5–38. The best introduction to Hamilton's thought in general is Susan Coultrap-McQuin, "Introduction," in Coultrap-McQuin, ed., *Gail Hamilton: Selected Writings* (New Brunswick: Rutgers University Press, 1992), xi–xxxvii.

56. "Literary and Trade News," *Publishers' Weekly*, September 5, 1874, 247.

57. "[A Feeling]," *Literary World*, December 18, 1880, 464.

58. Bellows, *The Christian Merchant*, 7.

INDEX

119–22, 129–34, 217n29, 217n34; relationships
    with publishers of, 117–21, 215n8, 216n16,
    219n76
Memoir of Miss Hannah Adams, The (Adams),
    68, 74, 84
mercantile societies, 142
Merchants' Magazine and Commercial Review, 28
Millar v. Taylor, 93–94
Miller, Perry, 99, 209n55
Milton, John, 57
Mitchell, Asa, 15
Mitchell, Maria, 224n45
Mize, George E., 209n55
Moby-Dick (Melville), 16, 22, 115, 117, 119
Mohammed, 17–18
moral capitalism, 21, 45
"Morality of Publishers, The," 23–25, 30–38, 47
Morals of Slavery, The (Simms), 105
moral structure of publishing. *See* character of
    publishing
moral values of trade, 3, 8–10, 50–55, 62–66,
    181n41
Morris, Robert, 63
Morse, Jedidiah, 19, 67–69, 78–87, 205n66
Morse v. Reid, 86–87
Moss, Richard J., 82
Moulton, William, 146, 223nn23–24
Mr. Lescom (character), 159–63
Mrs. Skiddy (character), 147
Murphy, Lucy Eldersveld, 150
Murray, Henry A., 133, 138
Murray, John, 55, 118, 124, 198n41
Mycall, John, 32

*Narrative of the Controversy Between the Rev.
    Jedidiah Morse, D. D. and the Author,
    A* (Adams), 80, 82–83
National Era, 147
natural law, 212n106; authors' rights under,
    92–97, 108–9, 112, 208n35, 209n42; of money
    and morality, 26–30, 45; of slavery, 104–6,
    212n106
Nature (Emerson), 3
Nelson, William, 196n7
Newman, Mark H., 38
New York Book-Publishers' Association, 7, 44,
    101, 112, 117–18
New York Typographical Society, 43
Nicklin, Philip, 104, 105–6, 107, 128

Niles, Thomas, 169
Niles, William J., 213nn135–36
"North-American Book-Men" *(Punch),* 89–91
Norton, Mary Beth, 76

O'Brien, Fitz-James, 15, 184n58
occupational ideology, 195n3
Old Corner Bookstore (Boston), 4, 168
Old Fashioned Girl, An (Alcott), 109, 169
Omoo (Melville), 118
O'Sullivan, John L., 101–2, 108

Page, Walter F., 170, 191n59
Paine, Thomas, 19, 47, 49–50; on authorship,
    64–65, 84, 196n5, 200n64; challenge to liter-
    ary trade custom by, 60–62, 201n81; conflicts
    with printers of, 55–62, 199n50, 199n58,
    200n65, 200n73, 200n80; on courtesy, 65–66,
    201n97; economic theories of, 51–52, 197n17;
    on reprinting, 62–63; on the righteousness
    of the Revolution, 62–63; on trade morality,
    62–66
Panic of 1837, 97, 123–24
Panic of 1873, 165
paper production, 43, 72
Paradise Lost (Milton), 57
"Paradise of Bachelors and the Tartarus of
    Maids, The" (Melville), 130
Parish, Elijah, 79, 85
Parker, Hershel, 119, 215n8
Parton, James: Hamilton's communication with,
    166, 173, 175–76, 228n42; romantic portrayal
    of publishing of, 25, 44–47, 195n143; on trade
    courtesy, 126
pastoral moralists, 37
Paulding, James K., 14, 109–10, 128
Peabody, Elizabeth Palmer, 6, 41, 172–73
Pendennis (Thackeray), 13
Pennsylvania Gazette, 50
Penny, Virginia, 148–51, 160–61, 224n43,
    224n45
Philadelphia Typographical Society, 53
Phillips, James W., 199n51
Phillips, Sampson, 6, 144–45
Pierre; or, The Ambiguities (Melville), 20, 116,
    119–21, 134; on authors and publishers,
    129–33; on commercial morality, 122, 217n29
"Pilgrim Fathers as Men of Business, The"
    (Parton), 45